REA's Books Are The Best...
They have rescued lots of grades and more!

(a sample of the <u>hundreds of letters</u> REA receives each year)

"Your books are great! They are very helpful, and have upped my grade in every class. Thank you for such a great product."

Student, Seattle, WA

"Your book has really helped me sharpen my skills and improve my weak areas. Definitely will buy more."

Student, Buffalo, NY

"Compared to the other books that my fellow students had, your book was the most useful in helping me get a great score."

Student, North Hollywood, CA

"I really appreciate the help from your excellent book. Please keep up your great work."

Student, Albuquerque, NM

"Your book was such a better value and was so much more complete than anything your competition has produced (and I have them all)!"

Teacher, Virginia Beach, VA

(more on next page)

(continued from previous page)

"Your books have saved my GPA, and quite possibly my sanity. My course grade is now an 'A', and I couldn't be happier."

Student, Winchester, IN

"These books are the best review books on the market. They are fantastic!"

Student, New Orleans, LA

"Your book was responsible for my success on the exam. . . I will look for REA the next time I need help."

Student, Chesterfield, MO

"I think it is the greatest study guide I have ever used!"

Student, Anchorage, AK

"I encourage others to buy REA because of their superiority. Please continue to produce the best quality books on the market."

Student, San Jose, CA

"Just a short note to say thanks for the great support your book gave me in helping me pass the test . . . I'm on my way to a B.S. degree because of you !"

Student, Orlando, FL

LATIN

Benjamin L. D'Ooge, Ph.D.
and the Staff of
Research & Education Association

Research & Education Association
Visit our website at
www.rea.com

Research & Education Association
61 Ethel Road West
Piscataway, New Jersey 08854
E-mail: info@rea.com

SUPER REVIEW®
OF LATIN

Published 2009

Printed in the United States of America

Library of Congress Control Number 2001086394

ISBN-13: 978-0-87891-381-7
ISBN-10: 0-87891-381-5

Bibliographical Note

This REA edition, first published in 2001, is a republication of
Elements of Latin by Benjamin L. D'Ooge, originally published by
Ginn and Company, Boston, 1921.

BACULUS IUBET LOCUM MŪRŌ ALTŌ MŪNĪRĪ

(See page 291)

WHAT THIS Super Review
WILL DO FOR YOU

"Tradition!"
    –Tevye, in "Fiddler on the Roof" (1971)

Latin Super Review is cast in the mold created by 19th century German grammarians, who established the pedagogical tradition used for teaching Latin in America for much of the 20th century. For me, personally, the no-nonsense style of Benjamin D'Ooge's book brings back welcome memories of Crosby and Shaeffer's *An Introduction to Greek*, the text used in my baby Greek class some 40 years ago.

D'Ooge has provided here a book that is useful as a text for reviewing the basics of Latin, with a view toward reading Caesar. The content provides a convenient summary that will be helpful to students who have learned Latin by using either the grammar/translation approach or the so-called reading method. *Latin Super Review* is organized in the manner of the reference grammar produced by Allen and Greenough—that is, with sequentially-numbered items of grammar and syntax, as well as end-tables of forms, word lists, and Latin-to-English and English-to-Latin vocabularies. Included in each Lesson are clear and simple explanations of points of grammar and syntax. Also in each Lesson, there are opportunities for both translation and composition, as well as opportunities for sight reading practice at the end.

Research & Education Association is to be congratulated for re-introducing a worthwhile addition to the growing number of resources designed to assist students in reviewing Latin. *Latin Super Review* will help to meet the increasing need of Latin students to prepare not only for tests within their school programs, but also for national or standardized examinations, such as the National Latin Exam, the SAT Latin Subject Test, the International Baccalaureate Latin Exam, and the Advanced Placement Latin Exam.

Ronald B. Palma
Holland Hall School
Tulsa, Oklahoma
October 2005

Ronald Palma built the Latin program at Holland Hall School into a full-time position, added Honors and AP Latin programs to the curriculum, co-authored the Latin textbook series currently used by the school, and has received awards and recognition at both the state and national levels for his excellence in teaching. He has taught more than 4,000 students.

CONTENTS

CONTENTS   ix

CONTENTS

CONTENTS

LIST OF ILLUSTRATIONS

ELEMENTS OF LATIN

TO THE STUDENT — BY WAY OF INTRODUCTION

LATIN, THE LANGUAGE OF THE ROMANS

Rome was the whole world, and all the world was Rome. — SPENSER

Latium,[1] a small district on the western coast of ancient Italy, was the home of the Latins. The chief city of the Latins was Rome, which, according to tradition, was founded 753 years before Christ. Beginning as a small settlement on the banks of the Tiber and the surrounding hills, and controlling at first a territory of not more than twenty-five square miles, the city remained weak and insignificant for many centuries, and its very existence was frequently threatened by warlike neighbors. But the Romans, inspired by a spirit that never owned defeat, gradually extended their boundaries. Before the middle of the third century before Christ they had conquered all Italy. Then they reached out for the lands across the sea and beyond the Alps, and finally Rome became the head of a mighty empire, which ruled over the whole ancient world for more than four hundred years.

The Latin language, meaning the language of Latium, was spoken by the Romans and other inhabitants of Latium, and Latin was the name applied to it after the armies of Rome had carried the knowledge of her language throughout the

---

[1] Pronounced *Lā'shĭ-ŭm*.

world. Rome impressed not only her language but also her laws, customs, beliefs, and ideals upon the subject nations; and the world has remained largely Roman ever since.

LATIN AND THE MODERN WORLD

Even after the fall of the Roman Empire Latin lived on, and lives today as Italian, Spanish, French, and other so-called Romance, or Roman, languages. Many millions of people are therefore still speaking a modernized form of Latin which differs from ancient Latin little more than modern English differs from the English of bygone centuries. Latin is not a dead language, but has only changed its name. During the Dark Ages the knowledge of Latin was the only light of learning that kept burning, and in the succeeding years Latin continued to be the common language of the schools and universities, and is even yet, more nearly than any other tongue, the universal language of the learned. It survives, too, in the services of the Roman Catholic Church and in much sacred poetry and song. The life of today is much nearer the life of ancient Rome than the lapse of centuries would lead one to suppose. You and I are Romans still in many ways, and if Cæsar and Cicero should appear among us, we should not find them, except for dress and language, unlike men of today.

LATIN AND ENGLISH

Do you know that more than half the words in the English dictionary are Latin and that you are speaking more or less Latin every day? How did this come about?

In the first place Latin and English, along with most of the other languages of Europe, are descended from a very ancient mother speech, which has long since disappeared. They are, therefore, sister languages and have many words in common.

Furthermore, in the year 1066 William the Conqueror invaded England with an army of Normans and established a Norman civilization among the Anglo-Saxons. The Normans spoke a kind of French, which, as has been said, is a modern form of Latin, and from this source hundreds of so-called Latin derivatives were added to our vocabulary. Some of these derivatives are pure Latin and others differ only in their endings. Note the following examples:

LATIN WORDS	ENGLISH WORDS
horror	horror
census	census
animal	animal
labor	labor
superior	superior
inferior	inferior
calamitas	calamity
barbarus	barbarous
virtus	virtue

Besides, in later years many Latin words have been brought into English through the writings of scholars, and many of the technical terms used in the sciences and the professions of law, medicine, engineering, etc., are of Latin derivation, and many new inventions are given Latin names.

WHY STUDY LATIN?

Latin, as we have seen, touches the life of the modern world in many ways and the study of it adds greatly to our intelligence and efficiency. Indeed, few studies are more practical. You may be asked why you are studying Latin. The following summary of reasons will help you to make a forceful and convincing reply:

1. Latin was the language of the Romans, on whose civilization our own civilization is largely based. In their writings we find the origin and the reason for many of our institutions.

2. In Roman literature we find the models which modern writers have imitated. Our literature is full of allusions and quotations which only the student of Latin can fully understand.

3. A knowledge of French, Spanish, Portuguese, or Italian is best obtained by studying Latin first. The value of these languages to an American is greater today than ever before.

4. Latin grammar makes English grammar easy, and a knowledge of Latin words makes clear the meaning of English words. A mastery of English is gained by the study of Latin, and the ability to use good English promotes success in every calling. Even a year or two of Latin will be a great help in grammar, spelling, and composition.

A knowledge of Latin is of great service in the pursuit of the sciences and professions. That is why Latin is beneficial for entrance to schools of medicine, law, engineering, and other higher institutions of learning.

QUESTIONS

What is Latin? Where is Latium? Where is Rome? What river flows through Rome? What date is given for the founding of Rome? How long did the Roman Empire endure? How wide was its power? What was the language of the Roman Empire? What besides their language did the Romans impress upon the world? What is meant by the Romance languages? If you wish to master French or Spanish, what language should you study first? Why? Is Latin a dead language? What great service did Latin render during the Dark Ages? Why do some scholars still write their books in Latin? What proportion of English words is of Latin origin? How did this come about? What five reasons can you give for the study of Latin? Which one of these reasons do you consider the most important?

FIRST HALF YEAR

THE ALPHABET AND SOUNDS OF THE LETTERS

Errāre hūmānum est — To err is human[1]

THE ALPHABET

1. The Latin alphabet is the same as the English except that it has no *j* or *w*.

2. The vowels, as in English, are **a, e, i, o, u, y.** The other letters are consonants.

3. The letter **i** is used both as a vowel and as a consonant. When standing first with a vowel following it, or between vowels within a word, it has the value of a consonant, and is called *i consonant.*

Thus, in **iam** and **maior**, i is a consonant; in **iānitor** the first **i** is a consonant, the second is a vowel.

SOUNDS OF THE LETTERS

4. The sounds of the letters are best learned by hearing them correctly pronounced. The matter in sections 5–7 is, therefore, intended for reference rather than for assignment as a lesson. As a first step it is suggested that the teacher pronounce the examples in class, the pupils following.

[1] From Seneca, a Roman philosopher.

5

5. Vowels. Vowels are either long or short. In this book long vowels are marked (ā), short ones are unmarked (a). The vowels have the following sounds:

LONG	SHORT
ā as in *artist* : **hāc, stās**	a as in *artistic* : **amat, canās**
ē as *a* in *fate* : **tēla, mēta**	e as in *net* : **tenet, pedēs**
ī as in *machine* : **sertī, prātī**	i as in *bit* : **sītis, bibī**
ō as in *bone* : **Rōma, ōrīs**	o as in *obey* : **modō, bonōs**
ū as in *rude* : **ūmor, tūber**	u as in *full* : **ut, tūtus**

6. Diphthongs. A diphthong is a combination of two vowels in a single syllable. The Latin diphthongs and their sounds are as follows:

ae as *ai* in *aisle* : **taedae**	**eu** almost like *ew* in *new* : **seu**
au as *ou* in *out* : **gaudet**	**oe** as *oi* in *boil* : **foedus**
ei as in *eight* : **hei**	**ui** almost like *we* : **cui, huic**

ROMAN CHILDREN AT PLAY

7. Consonants. Consonants are pronounced as in English, with the following exceptions :

---

c always has the sound of *k* : **cadō, cibus, cēna**
g is always like *g* in *get* : **gemō, gignō**
i, when a consonant, is sounded like *y* in *yes* : **iam, iocus, cuius**
qu, gu, and sometimes su before a vowel, have the sound of *qw*,
    gw, and *sw*, respectively : **inquit, lingua, suādeō**
s is always like *s* in *sea* : **rosa, is**
t is always like *t* in *native* (never as in *nation*) : **ratiō, nātiō**
v has the sound of *w* : **vīnum, vir**
x always has the sound of *ks* : **extrā, exāctus**
bs, bt, are like *ps, pt* : **urbs, obtineō**
ch, ph, th, are like *c, p, t* : **pulcher, Phoebē, theātrum**

---

8. Learn the following Latin mottoes :

Ē plūribus ūnum, *one out of many* (motto of the United States).
_{out of many one}

Ad astra per aspera, *to the stars through difficulties* (motto of Kansas).
_{to stars through difficulties}

Labor omnia vincit, *toil conquers all things* (quotation from the
_{toil all things conquers}
Latin poet Vergil).

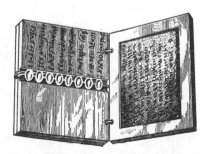

ROMAN WRITING TABLETS

SYLLABLES, QUANTITY, AND ACCENT

Fēstīnā lentē— Make haste slowly [1]

SYLLABLES

9. A Latin word has as many syllables as it has vowels and diphthongs.

Thus, **lī-ber'-tās** has three syllables, **au-di-en'-dae** has four.

10. Words are divided into syllables as follows:

a. A single consonant between two vowels is pronounced with the following vowel: as, **a-mā'-bi-lis, a'-best, pe-rē'-git**; also **bl, br, tr,** and similar combinations with **l** or **r** that can be pronounced in one syllable are pronounced with a following vowel:[2] as, **pū'-bli-cus, ē'-bri-us, mā'-tris, a'-grī.**

b. In all other combinations of consonants the last of the group is pronounced with the following vowel: as, **mag'-nus, e-ges'-tās, hos'-pes, an'-nus, su-bāc'-tus, sānc'-tus, il'-le.**

c. The last syllable of a word is called the *ul'ti-ma* ; the next to the last, the *pe-nult'*; that before the penult, the *an'te-pe-nult'.*

Thus, **amantur** consists of **a-** (antepenult), **-man-** (penult), **-tur** (ultima).

QUANTITY OF SYLLABLES

11. The quantity of a syllable is the time occupied in pronouncing it. About twice as much time should be given to long (that is, slow) syllables as to short (that is, quick) ones.

12. A syllable is long if it contains a long vowel or a diphthong : as, **cū'-rō, poe'-nae, aes-tā'-te**; or if it ends in a consonant which is followed by another consonant : as, the first

---

[1] A favorite saying of Augustus, the first emperor of Rome.
[2] But prepositional compounds follow rule *b* : as, **ab'-luō, ab-rum'pō,** etc.

8

syllables of cor'-pus and mag'-nus. All other syllables are short: as, a'-ni-mal, me-mo'-ri-am, nu'-me-rus, pa'-tri-a.

NOTE. The *vowel* in a long syllable may be either long or short, and should be pronounced accordingly. Thus, in ter-ra, in-ter, the first syllable is long, but the vowel in each case is short and should be given the short sound. In words like saxum the first syllable is long because x has the value of two consonants (cs or gs).

ACCENT

13. Words of two syllables are accented on the first: as, mēn'-sa, Cae'-sar.

14. Words of more than two syllables are accented on the penult if the penult is long. If the penult is short, the antepenult is accented. Thus, mo-nē'-mus, re'-gi-tur, a-gri'-co-la, a-man'-dus, a-man'-tur.

15. Sing the following translation of the first two stanzas of "America":[1]

Tē canō, Patria,
candīda, lībera;
tē referet
portus et exulum
et tumulus senum;
lībera montium
vōx resonet.

Tē canō, Patria,
semper et ātria
ingenuum;
laudō virentia
culmina, flūmina;
sentiō gaudia
caelicolum.

THE PARTS OF SPEECH

16. Words, according to their use, are divided into eight classes called parts of speech: nouns, pronouns, adjectives, verbs, adverbs, prepositions, conjunctions, and interjections. The parts of speech in English and in Latin are the same.

[1] Translated by Professor George D. Kellogg, Union College, and published in the *Classical Weekly*, VIII, 7.

17. Nouns. A noun is the name of a person or thing: as, Caesar, *Cæsar*; Rōma, *Rome*; domus, *house*; virtūs, *virtue*.

18. Pronouns. A pronoun (*pro*, 'instead of,' and *noun*) is a word used instead of a noun.

Thus, in *I am studying Latin*, *I* is used instead of the speaker's name. Pronouns are often used to avoid repeating the same noun: as, *The soldiers are weary;* **they** *have marched many hours.*

a. Nouns and pronouns are called *substantives.*

19. Adjectives. An adjective is a word that describes a noun or pronoun, and is said to belong to the word which it describes: as, *The* **great** *forest was* **full** *of* **beautiful** *flowers.*

20. Verbs. A verb is a word which asserts something (usually an act) about a person or thing: as, *The girl* **is carrying** *water. She* **has** *a rose in her hair.*

INTERIOR VIEW OF A ROMAN HOUSE

LESSON I

FIRST PRINCIPLES OF SYNTAX

21. Subject and Predicate. A sentence is a group of words expressing a thought. A sentence consists of two parts, a *subject* and a *predicate*.

22. The *subject* is the person or thing spoken of.

23. The *predicate* says something about the subject.

SUBJECT	PREDICATE
Puel'la *The girl*	rēgī'nam vo'cat *calls the queen*
Les'bia *Lesbia*	bo'nam memo'riam ha'bet *has a good memory*

24. Transitive and Intransitive Verbs. Some verbs are followed by nouns or pronouns which receive their action and complete the sense. Such verbs are called *transitive* verbs, and the nouns or pronouns are called the *direct objects*.

Thus, in the sentences above, **vocat** (*calls*) and **habet** (*has*) are transitive verbs, and **rēgīnam** (*queen*) and **memoriam** (*memory*) are their direct objects.

25. Verbs that have no direct object are called *intransitive* verbs : as,

Puel'la pro'perat, *the girl hastens*
Agri'cola labō'rat, *the farmer toils*

---

[1] From Horace, a Roman poet. Literally, *Seize the day.*

26. A form of the verb *to be* (*is, are, was,* etc.), connecting the subject with a noun or adjective in the predicate, is called the *copula* ('joiner' or 'link') : as,

Iū'lia *est* pul'chra puel'la, *Julia is a pretty girl*

EXERCISE

27. Pronounce the Latin of the following sentences and name the nouns, pronouns, adjectives, verbs, copulas, subjects, objects, and predicates, and state whether the verbs are transitive or intransitive :

1. E'go   pa'triam   a'mō.
   I   (my) country   love.

2. Puel'lae   in   mag'nam   sil'vam   pro'.perant.
   (The) girls   into   (the) great   forest   are-hastening.

3. Les'bia,   pul'chra   fi'lia   agri'colae,   nūl'lam
   Lesbia,   (the) beautiful   daughter   of (the) farmer,   no
   pecū'niam ha'bet.
   money   has.

4. Agri'cola   fi'liam   ex   par'vā   ca'sā   vo'cat.
   (The) farmer   (his) daughter   from   (the) little   cottage   calls.

5. Is   pul'chram   puel'lam   a'mat.
   He   (the) pretty   girl   loves.

6. Lin'gua   Latī'na   est   pul'chra.
   The language   Latin   is   beautiful.

NOTE. Latin has no article *the* or *a* ; thus **puella** may mean *the girl, a girl,* or simply *girl.* Further, the possessive adjectives *my, your, his, her,* etc. are not expressed if the meaning of the sentence is clear without them. Note, too, in 6 that in Latin the adjective may follow the noun.

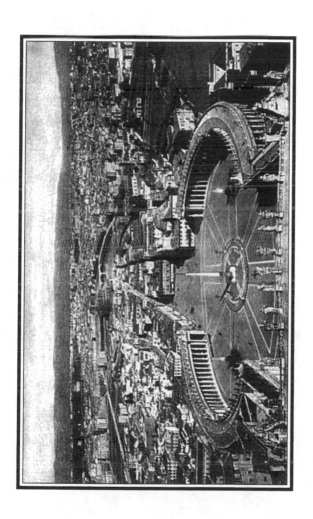

VIEW OF ROME FROM THE DOME OF ST. PETER'S CATHEDRAL

From the dome of St. Peter's, over four hundred feet high, the work of Michelangelo, one obtains a wonderful view of the city. Immediately below is the Piazza of St. Peter's, an imposing ellipse inclosed by huge colonnades. In the middle distance are the Tiber and the circular tomb of Hadrian. The flat expanse beyond the river, now densely peopled, was the Campus Martius of ancient Rome and almost without buildings

LESSON II

INFLECTION AND CASES

28. Inflection. Words may change their forms to indicate some change in their meaning, or their use in a sentence: as, *is, are* ; *know, knew* ; *we, us* ; *woman, woman's, women*. This change is called *inflection*.

29. The inflection of a verb is called its *conjugation* ; that of a noun, adjective, or pronoun, its *declension*.

30. Declension. To decline a word means to give in order all its different forms : as, *who, whose, whom*. Each one of the forms is called a *case*.

31. Cases in English. Observe the following sentences :

> *Who* is this man ?
> *Whose* son is he ?
> *Whom* do I see ?

We use the form *who* as the subject, *whose* to denote possession, and *whom* as the object. The three forms illustrate the three cases found in English.

The subject case is called the *Nominative* case.

The case of the possessor is called the *Possessive* case.

The object case is called the *Objective* case.

32. Cases in Latin. In Latin the subject case is called the *Nom'inative* ; the possessive, or case of the possessor, is called the *Gen'itive* ; and the object case is called the *Accu'sative*,

---

[1] From Vergil, Rome's greatest epic poet.

13

Gal'ba (NOMINATIVE) est agri'cola, *Galba* (SUBJECT) *is a farmer*
Gal'bae (GENITIVE) fi'lia est Les'bia, *Galba's* (POSSESSOR) *daughter is Lesbia*
Gal'bam (ACCUSATIVE) fi'lia a'mat, (*his*) *daughter loves Galba* (OBJECT)

33. Rule for Nominative Subject. *The subject of a finite verb is in the Nominative and answers the question* **Who?** *or* **What?**

34. Rule for Genitive of the Possessor. *The word denoting the owner or possessor of something is in the Genitive and answers the question* **Whose?**

35. Rule for Accusative Object. *The direct object of a transitive verb is in the Accusative and answers the question* **Whom?** *or* **What?**

36. When the nominative singular ends in -a (as, **Galba**), the genitive singular ends in -ae and the accusative singular in -am.

EXERCISES

37. In the following sentences add the proper Latin endings :

1. *Lesbia* (SUBJECT) *loves the farmer* (OBJECT), **Lesbi-ⱥamat agricol-ⱥM**
2. *The farmer's* (POSSESSOR) *daughter* (SUBJECT) *loves Galba* (OBJECT) **agricol-ⱥfili-ⱥ amat Galb-ⱥM**
3. *The farmer* (SUBJECT) *calls Galba's* (POSSESSOR) *daughter* (OBJECT), **agricol-ⱥ vocat Galba-ⱥfili- ⱥM**

38. State what nouns in the following sentences would be nominative, genitive, and accusative if translated into Latin :

1. A lion was terrifying the villagers. 2. A hunter found the lion's den. 3. The hunter shot the lion and captured the lion's cubs. 4. The lion's cubs bit the hunter's hand.

LESSON III

FORMS AND POSITION

39. English and Latin Compared. Observe the following sentences :

> *Galba loves his daughter*
> *His daughter loves Galba*

The nouns *Galba* and *daughter* have the same form in both these sentences, although the noun that is the subject in the one becomes the object in the other. In other words, the nominative and the objective case are alike in English, and the only way to distinguish them is by the order of the words.

In the Latin of this sentence no doubt can arise, for the subject ends in -a and the object in -am, and this remains true no matter in what order the words are written.

> Gal'ba a'mat fi'liam ⎫
> Fi'liam a'mat Gal'ba ⎪
> A'mat Gal'ba fi'liam ⎬ *Galba loves his daughter*
> Gal'ba fi'liam a'mat ⎭

As you see, all these arrangements mean the same thing. The *form* of the Latin noun, therefore, and *not its position* in the sentence, shows its use.

40. Position of Subject and Verb. The *subject* of a short, disconnected sentence generally stands *first*; the *verb, last*. But **est,** *is,* and other forms of the verb *to be* usually stand, as in English, between the subject and a noun or adjective in the predicate : as,

> **Gal'ba est agri'cola,** *Galba is a farmer*

[1] From the Latin translation of the Bible.

41. Position of Genitive. The genitive may stand either before or after the noun to which it belongs : as, **Gal'bae fi'lia** or **fi'lia Gal'bae,** *Galba's daughter.*

VOCABULARY

42. Learn the following words so that you can give the English for the Latin or the Latin for the English :

agri'cola, *farmer*   a'mat, *loves, is-loving*
fi'lia, *daughter*   pro'perat, *hastens, is-hastening*
puel'la, *girl*   vo'cat, *calls, is-calling*
        rēgī'na, *queen*

EXERCISES

NOTE. In translating a Latin genitive into English we may use either the preposition *of* and the noun, or its possessive case : as, **filia rēgīnae,** *the daughter of the queen,* or *the queen's daughter.*

43. 1. Rēgīna puellam amat.   2. Puella rēgīnam amat. 3. Fīlia agricolae properat.   4. Puella fīliam agricolae vocat. 5. Fīlia agricolae puellam amat.   6. Rēgīna agricolam vocat, agricola properat.

44. 1. The farmer is-calling (his) daughter.   2. The daughter is-calling the farmer.   3. The girl loves the queen's daughter. 4. The queen's daughter calls the girl.   5. The queen is-hastening.

SINGING THE WEDDING SONG

LESSON IV

Omne initium est difficile — Every beginning is hard [1]

NUMBER · AGREEMENT OF VERBS

45. Number. Latin, like English, has two numbers, *singular* and *plural*.

46. Plural of Nouns. In English the plural of nouns is usually formed by adding *-s* or *-es* to the singular. So Latin changes the singular to the plural by changing the ending.

SINGULAR

Nom. (subject)   puell-a, *girl*
Gen. (possessor)   puell-ae, *girl's, of the girl*
Acc. (object)   puell-am, *girl*

PLURAL

Nom. (subject)   puell-ae, *girls*
Gen. (possessor)   puell-ārum, *girls', of the girls*
Acc. (object)   puell-ās, *girls*

Note that the genitive singular and the nominative plural are alike.

a. Some Latin words ending in -a have passed into English without change and form the plural in -ae: as, *alumna, alumnae*; *formula, formulae*; *minutia, minutiae*; *nebula, nebulae*; *vertebra, vertebrae*. Consult the dictionary for the meaning of these words.

47. Plural of Verbs. Verbs, as well as nouns, form the plural with different endings. In the singular the third person ends in -t, in the plural in -nt. Thus,

porta-t, *he (she, it) carries*   **porta-nt**, *they carry*
puella portat, *the girl carries*   **puellae portant**, *the girls carry*

---

[1] A Latin proverb.

17

The endings -t and -nt, which show the person and number of the verb, are called *personal endings*, and take the place of the English personal pronouns.

48. **Rule for Agreement of Verbs.** *The verb agrees with its subject in person and number.*

EXERCISES

49. Write and give orally the nominative, genitive, and accusative, singular and plural, of the Latin nouns meaning *farmer, daughter, queen, girl*.

50. Write and give orally the third person singular and plural of the Latin verbs meaning *love, call, hasten*.

51. **Derivation.** Define the following English words : *vocal, vocation, filial, amiable, agriculture*. To what Latin words are they related ?

PLAYING JACKSTONES

LESSON V

Bis dat quī cito dat— He gives twice who gives quickly[1]

THE DATIVE CASE · INDIRECT OBJECT · PREDICATE NOUN

52. Dative Case. In English many relationships between words are expressed by *to, for, from, with, in, at,* and the like. These are called prepositions. Latin, too, often makes a similar use of prepositions, but frequently expresses such relationships by means of case forms that English does not possess. One of these cases is called the *Da'tive.*

53. The dative case is used after verbs and adjectives to express the relation conveyed in English by the prepositions *to* or *for* somebody or something.

He gave the money *to John*   They are ready *for war*
She was kind *to him*   He is no match *for you*

NOTE. *To* or *for* in expressions of motion, like *He went to New York, He sailed for Europe,* are not denoted by the dative.

54. What dative relations do you discover in the following ?

To Captain Smith was given the cross of war, an honor great enough for any man. He was always ready for action and was equal to all demands. To him nothing seemed impossible. No wonder the general said to him, " France gives to you an honor well deserved."

55. Case Endings of Dative. When the nominative singular ends in **-a,** the dative singular ends in **-ae** and the dative plural in **-īs.**

NOTE. The genitive singular, the dative singular, and the nominative plural have the same ending, **-ae** ; but the uses of the three cases are different.

[1] From Andrea Alciati, an Italian author of maxims.

56. Indirect Object. In English the person to whom something is *given*, *told*, *refused*, etc. is called the *indirect object*.

The queen gives money **to the girl** (or *gives* **the girl** *money*)

57. The indirect object is clearly a dative relation (§ 53) and is expressed in Latin by the dative case.

Rēgīna *puellae* pecūniam dat

58. Rule for Dative of Indirect Object. *The indirect object of a verb is in the dative.*

59. The indirect object may either precede or follow the direct object.

60. Predicate Noun. A noun standing in the predicate, describing or defining the subject and connected with it by some form of the verb *to be*, is called a *predicate noun*.

Galba est *agricola*, *Galba is a farmer*

61. Rule for Predicate Noun. *A predicate noun agrees with the subject in case.*

EXERCISES

62. Write the nominative, genitive, dative, and accusative, singular and plural, of the nouns **agricola, rēgīna, puella.**

First learn the special vocabulary, page 361

63. 1. Puella est rēgīna. 2. Puellae sunt rēgīnae. 3. Agricola properat. 4. Agricolae properant. 5. Fīliae agricolārum rēgīnam vocant. 6. Fīlia agricolae rēgīnam vocat. 7. Rēgīna puellīs agricolae pecūniam dat. 8. Fīliae rēgīnae fābulās puellīs agricolārum nārrant.

64. 1. The queen is a farmer's daughter. 2. The girls give the farmers' money to-the-queen. 3. The girl is-telling the queen's daughter a story. 4. The girl loves the queen's daughter. 5. The girls are daughters of-farmers.

LESSON VI

Ars longa, vīta brevis — Art is long, time is fleeting[1]

THE ABLATIVE CASE · THE FIRST DECLENSION

65. Ablative Case. Another case lacking in English, but found in Latin, is the *Ab'lative*. This case is used to express the relations conveyed in English by the prepositions *from, by, with, at, in,* or *on.* Sometimes, as will be shown later (§ 79), Latin uses similar prepositions with the ablative.

66. Ablative Relations. What ablative relations do you discover in the following sentences?

> At two o'clock the troops began to march by, the general with his staff leading the van. Many thousands were in line and the ground shook with their martial tread. From sidewalks, windows, and housetops the spectators viewed the wonderful sight. On every side flags were waving in the breeze and everyone was wild with joy. Our boys were back from France.

67. Case Endings of Ablative. When the nominative singular ends in -a, the ablative singular ends in -ā, and the ablative plural in -īs.

a. Note that the final -a is long in the ablative and short in the nominative: **aqua**, nominative; **aquā**, ablative.

b. Note that the ablative plural is like the dative plural.

68. Declensions. Latin has five declensions.

---

[1] Latin form of a saying attributed to the Greek writer Hippocrates. Literally, *Art long, life short.* The verb *to be* is often omitted when it can readily be supplied.

69. The declension to which a noun belongs is shown by the ending of the genitive singular.

70. First Declension. Nouns having the ending -ae in the genitive singular belong to the First Declension. They are declined as follows :

NOUN	TRANSLATION	USE OF EACH CASE
	SINGULAR	
NOM. aqua	*the water*	The subject
GEN. aquae	*of the water,* or *the water's*	The possessor
DAT. aquae	*to* or *for the water*	The indirect object
ACC. aquam	*the water*	The direct object
ABL. aquā	*from, by, with, at, in,* or *on the water*	Relation denoted by the prepositions *from, by, with, at, in,* or *on*
	PLURAL	
NOM. aquae	*the waters*	The subject
GEN. aquā'rum	*of the waters,* or *the waters'*	The possessor
DAT. aquīs	*to* or *for the waters*	The indirect object
ACC. aquās	*the waters*	The direct object
ABL. aquīs	*from, by, with, at, in,* or *on the waters*	Relation denoted by the prepositions *from, by, with, at, in,* or *on*

a. The nouns **fīlia**, *daughter*, and **dea**, *goddess*, have **fīliābus** and **deābus** in the dative and ablative plural.

71. Base. That part of the word which remains unchanged throughout the declension, and to which the terminations are added, is called the *base*. Thus, **aqu-** is the base of **aqua**.

72. How to learn a Declension. First pronounce each form carefully, with due regard for the sounds of the letters and the accent, giving the corresponding English meaning. Repeat again and again until you have the declension memorized. Then close your book and write the Latin forms, marking the quantity of the long vowels in the case endings, and write also the meaning of each form. Then open your book and correct any errors in your work. For further drill make a blank scheme of the declension as shown below, and, pointing rapidly with your pencil to the different spaces, give quickly the Latin forms that would appear there, using a variety of words. Persist in drilling yourself until you can give the ten Latin forms complete in ten seconds.

	SINGULAR	PLURAL
Nom.	----------	----------
Gen.	----------	----------
Dat.	----------	----------
Acc.	------	------
Abl.	----------	----------

EXERCISES

73. Write the declension of **puella, dea,** and **agricola,** with the meaning of each form.

74. Give orally the declension of **fābula, rēgīna, fīlia, pecūnia.**

75. Give the case or the cases, and the meaning or the meanings, of the following : **puellārum, fīliābus, pecūniae, fābulā, rēgīnam, deās, agricolīs.**

76. Derivation. The noun **aqua** appears in the English words *aquarium, aqueous, aquatic, aqueduct.* What do they mean ? Consult the English dictionary if you do not know.

LESSON VII

PREPOSITIONS

77. While many relations expressed in English by prepositions are in Latin expressed by case forms, still prepositions are of frequent occurrence, but only with the accusative or ablative.

78. Prepositions with Accusative. The relations *to*, *into*, and *through* in expressions of motion are expressed in Latin by the prepositions **ad**, **in**, and **per**, with the accusative.

> **Nauta *ad* aquam properat,** *the sailor hastens to the water*
> **Nauta *in* aquam properat,** *the sailor hastens into the water*
> **Nauta *per* aquam properat,** *the sailor hastens through the water*

79. Prepositions with Ablative. The relations *from the side of*, *in company with*, and *in* or *on* are expressed in Latin by the prepositions **ā** or **ab**, **cum**, and **in**, with the ablative.

> **Nauta *ab* aquā properat,** *the sailor hastens from the water*
> **Nauta *cum* Galbā properat,** *the sailor hastens with Galba*
> **Nauta *in* aquā est,** *the sailor is in* (or *on*) *the water*

NOTE. The preposition **ā** is used only before words beginning with a consonant, **ab** before either vowels or consonants.

[1] From Juvenal, a Roman poet.

AGRICOLA

24

80. The meanings of ā (or ab), ad, in, and per are illustrated by the following diagram, the square representing the place in question:

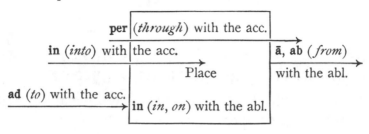

EXERCISES

First learn the special vocabulary, page 361

81. 1. Nautae aquam amant; agricolae terram amant. 2. Nauta cum filiābus rēgīnae ab terrā ad aquam properat. 3. Filiae rēgīnae in (*on*) aquā sunt. 4. Nautae per aquās properant. 5. Agricola filiābus rēgīnae aquam dat. 6. Puellae agricolārum in terrā sunt.

82. 1. Lesbia hastens from the land to the water. 2. The sailors are in the water. 3. Galba is with the farmers' daughters. 4. The queens' daughters hasten through the land.

~~~~~~~~~

First Review of Vocabulary and Grammar, §§ 732-736

LESSON VIII

GENDER · DECLENSION, AGREEMENT, AND POSITION OF ADJECTIVES · THE PREDICATE ADJECTIVE

83. Gender. Latin, like English, has three genders : masculine, feminine, and neuter.

84. Gender in English is distinction according to sex. Names of males are masculine; of females, feminine; and of things without animal life, neuter. This is called *natural* gender.

85. The rules for natural gender are applied also in Latin to beings having life : words denoting males are masculine, and words denoting females are feminine. But the gender of words denoting things is generally determined by the termination of the nominative singular. This is called *grammatical* gender. Hence nouns which in English would be neuter may in Latin be masculine, feminine, or neuter.

Thus, in Latin, **sōl**, *sun*, is masculine; **lūna**, *moon*, feminine; **caelum**, *sky*, neuter.

86. Gender of Nouns of First Declension. Nouns of the first declension are *feminine* unless they denote males.

Thus, **aqua**, *water*, is feminine, but **nauta**, *sailor*, is masculine.

87. Adjectives. Examine the following sentence :

Puella parva bonam rēgīnam amat, *the little girl likes the good queen*

In this sentence **parva**, *little*, and **bonam**, *good*, are not nouns, but descriptive words expressing quality. Such words are called *adjectives* and are said to belong to the noun which they describe.

---

[1] A Latin slogan. Literally, *Never backward.*

88. Declension of Adjectives. In English the adjective remains unchanged even when the noun changes its form : as, *the good man, the good man's, the good men.* In other words, in English, adjectives are not declined. In Latin, adjectives have declensions like those of nouns.

89. Feminine adjectives in -a have the same case forms as nouns in -a. Decline nouns and their adjectives together, as follows :

aqua (base **aqu-**), F., *water*; **bona** (base **bon-**), F., *good*

	NOUN	ADJECTIVE		TERMINATIONS
NOM.	aqua	bona	*good water*	-a
GEN.	aquae	bonae	*of good water*	-ae
DAT.	aquae	bonae	*to or for good water*	-ae
ACC.	aquam	bonam	*good water*	-am
ABL.	aquā	bonā	*from, with, by, in good water*	-ā
NOM.	aquae	bonae	*good waters*	-ae
GEN.	aquā'rum	bonā'rum	*of good waters*	-ārum
DAT.	aquīs	bonīs	*to or for good waters*	-īs
ACC.	aquās	bonās	*good waters*	-ās
ABL.	aquīs	bonīs	*from, with, by, in good waters*	-īs

90. Agreement of Adjectives. In the phrase **aqua bona**, we have a feminine noun **aqua** combined with a feminine adjective **bona**. When the phrase is declined, a change in the number or the case of the noun is accompanied by a corresponding change in the adjective. This is called *agreement.*

91. Rule for Agreement of Adjectives. *Adjectives agree with their nouns in gender, number, and case.*

92. An adjective may either precede or follow its noun.

93. Predicate Adjective. An adjective standing in the predicate, but describing the subject, is called a *predicate adjective*.

Puellae sunt pulchrae, *the girls are pretty*

NOTE. In English the predicate adjective is often called the attribute complement or subjective complement.

GALBA ET LESBIA

First learn the special vocabulary, page 361

94. Galba est agricola. Lesbia est filia Galbae. Lesbia est pulchra. Galba filiam pulchram amat. Agricola parvae puellae bonās fābulās nārrat. Galba cum Lesbiā in casā parvā habitat. Galba et Lesbia casam parvam amant. Lesbia Galbam vocat et agricola ad parvam casam properat (*see picture*).

95. 1. The little cottage is beautiful. 2. Galba hastens through the land to the pretty cottage. 3. Galba is with the sailor. 4. The girls hasten into the cottage. 5. Farmers live in small cottages.

LESSON IX

Fit via vī — Energy wins the way [1]

THE SECOND DECLENSION · THE VOCATIVE CASE

96. Second Declension. Nouns ending in -ī in the genitive singular belong to the Second Declension.

97. Gender and Declension. Nominatives of the second declension ending in -us or -er are masculine; those ending in -um are neuter.

Thus, **servus**, *slave*, and **ager**, *field*, are masculine; but **oppidum**, *town*, is neuter.

Masculine nouns in -us are declined as follows:

servus (base serv-), M., *slave*

		TERMINATIONS		TERMINATIONS
NOM.	servus	-us	servī	-ī
GEN.	servī	-ī	servōrum	-ōrum
DAT.	servō	-ō	servīs	-īs
ACC.	servum	-um	servōs	-ōs
ABL.	servō	-ō	servīs	-īs

NOTE. In learning all declensions, follow the suggestions given in § 72.

a. Some Latin words ending in -us have passed into English without change and form the plural in -i: as, *alumnus, alumni*; *syllabus, syllabi*; *focus, foci*; *radius, radii*; *stimulus, stimuli*; *narcissus, narcissi*. Consult the dictionary for the meaning of these words.

98. Vocative Case. A noun used to address or call a person is in the vocative case (from Latin **vocō**, *I call*). The form of the vocative is regularly the same as the nominative, but the vocative singular of nouns in -us of the second declension ends in -e: as, **serve**, *O slave*; **Mārce**, *O Marcus*.

[1] From Vergil, a Roman poet. Literally, *A way is made by force.*

99. In English the name of the person addressed often stands first. The Latin vocative rarely stands first.

Lesbia, the cottage is small, casa, Lesbia, est parva

EXERCISES

First learn the special vocabulary, page 362

100. 1. Quō nauta properat? 2. Nauta ad parvam casam Galbae properat. 3. Ubi est Galba? 4. Galba cum Lesbiā et cum amīcīs Lesbiae in casā parvā est. 5. Agricola parvīs

puellīs bonās fābulās nārrat. 6. Ubi, Mārce, est servus agricolae? 7. Servus agricolae equīs aquam dat. 8. Aqua est bona et equī bonam aquam amant.

101. 1. Marcus, Galba is-calling the slaves. 2. Slaves, where are the horses? 3. The horses, Galba, are-hastening to the cottage. 4. The water of-the-cottage is good. 5. The slaves are the friends of-the-horses.

LESSON X

Sīc semper tyrannīs — Thus ever to tyrants[1]

THE SECOND DECLENSION (CONTINUED) · APPOSITION

102. Declension of Nouns in -er. Masculine nouns in -er of the second declension are declined as follows :

puer (base **puer-**), M., *boy* ; **ager** (base **agr-**), M., *field*

			TERMINATIONS			TERMINATIONS
NOM.	puer	ager	—	puerī	agrī	-ī
GEN.	puerī	agrī	-ī	puerōrum	agrōrum	-ōrum
DAT.	puerō	agrō	-ō	puerīs	agrīs	-īs
ACC.	puerum	agrum	-um	puerōs	agrōs	-ōs
ABL.	puerō	agrō	-ō	puerīs	agrīs	-īs

a. Nouns in -er are declined just like **servus**, except that they have no termination -us in the nominative singular.

b. In **puer** the e appears in each case ; in **ager** it appears only in the nominative singular. Most nouns in -er are declined like **ager**. The genitive singular shows whether the noun follows **puer** or **ager**.

c. The noun **vir**, *man*, is declined like **puer**: vir, virī, virō, etc.

103. Apposition. Observe the following sentences :

Mārcus nauta ad casam properat, *Marcus, the sailor, hastens to the cottage*

Galba Mārcum nautam amat, *Galba loves Marcus, the sailor*

In each sentence the word *sailor* is added to *Marcus* to explain who he is. A noun explaining another noun, and signifying the same person or thing, is called an *appositive*, and is said to be *in apposition*. A noun and its appositive agree in case.

104. Rule for Apposition. *An appositive agrees in case with the noun which it explains.*

---

[1] Motto of the state of Virginia.

EXERCISES

First learn the special vocabulary, page 362

DIALOGUE. PUERĪ, SEXTUS ET QUĪNTUS

105. SEXTUS. Ubi, Quīnte, servī Galbae agricolae labōrant?
QUĪNTUS. In agrīs, Sexte, servī Galbae agricolae labōrant.

LESBIA PER AGRŌS PROPERAT ET AQUAM AD SERVŌS PORTAT

S. Quis per agrōs ad servōs properat?
Q. Lesbia, fīlia Galbae agricolae, per agrōs ad servōs properat.
S. Quid Lesbia, pulchra fīlia Galbae agricolae, portat?
Q. Aquam, Sexte, Lesbia portat. Aquam servīs Lesbia dat et servī Lesbiam, bonam fīliam Galbae agricolae, amant.

106. 1. Who lives with the friends of-Marcus the sailor?
2. What are the boys' horses carrying, Sextus? 3. Who is-telling stories to-Lesbia, Galba's little daughter? 4. Whither are the men carrying water?

LESSON XI

THE SECOND DECLENSION (CONTINUED) · GENERAL RULES OF DECLENSION · QUESTIONS

107. Declension of Nouns in -*um*. Neuter nouns in -**um** belong to the Second Declension, and are declined as follows :

oppidum (base oppid-), N., *town*

	TERMINATIONS			. TERMINATIONS
Nom.	oppid**um**	-**um**	oppid**a**	-**a**
Gen.	oppid**ī**	-**ī**	oppid**ōrum**	-**ōrum**
Dat.	oppid**ō**	-**ō**	oppid**īs**	-**īs**
Acc.	oppid**um**	-**um**	oppid**a**	-**a**
Abl.	oppid**ō**	-**ō**	oppid**īs**	-**īs**

a. Some Latin words ending in -**um** have passed into English without change and form the plural in -**a**: as, **stratum, strata**; **datum, data; curriculum, curricula; memorandum, memoranda.**

108. General Rules of Declension. Write side by side the declension of **servus, aqua,** and **oppidum.** A comparison of the forms gives us the following rules, which apply not only to the first and second declensions but to all five (§ 68):

a. The nominative and accusative of neuter nouns are alike, and in the plural end in -**a**.

b. The accusative of masculines and feminines ends in -**m** in the singular, and in -**s** in the plural.

c. The dative and ablative plural are alike.

d. Final -**i** and -**o** are long ; final -**a** is short except in the ablative singular of the first declension.

---

[1] From Cicero, who wrote a famous essay on friendship.

QUESTIONS

109. Questions may be introduced, as in English, by such words as **quis**? *who?* **quid**? *what?* **ubi**? *where?* and **quō**? *whither?* But questions that can be answered by *yes* or *no* have, in Latin, a special question sign **-ne** attached to the emphatic word, which stands first and is usually the verb.

> **Est'ne puella pulchra?**   *Is the girl pretty?*
> **Properant'ne puerī?**   *Are the boys hastening?*

110. There are no single Latin words meaning simply *yes* and *no*. Questions are usually answered in the affirmative by repeating the verb; in the negative, by repeating the verb with **nōn**, *not*.

> **Properant'ne puerī? Properant.**   *Are the boys hastening? Yes.*
> **Properant'ne puerī? Nōn properant.**   *Are the boys hastening? No.*

EXERCISES

111. Derivation. Using the prefixes **ex-** (*out*), **im-** (*in*), **re-** (*back*), **sup-** (*under*), **trāns-** (*across*), with **-port**, from the Latin verb **portō**, *to carry*, make five English words and define them.

112. What English words in the following paragraph do you know to be of Latin derivation? Define the words, using the dictionary if necessary, and give the Latin sources.

> Below the terrace was an aquarium fed by an aqueduct, a gift of Mr. B——, concerning whose bounty and fabulous wealth the inhabitants of the town love to tell. But these data are not essential to my narrative, and I will speak only of his love for the sea, aquatic sports, and nautical affairs.

DIALOGUE. PUELLA ET SERVUS

First learn the special vocabulary, page 362

113. PUELLA. Quō, serve, virī properant?

SERVUS. In oppidum, puella, virī properant.

P. Quis virōs et puerōs con'vocat?

S. Rēgīna bona virōs et puerōs con'vocat.

P. Cūr rēgīna bona virōs et puerōs con'vocat?

S. Ad arma, puella, rēgīna populum vocat.

P. Estne puer Sextus cum virīs?

S. Est, et arma bonae rēgīnae portat. Sextus bonam rēgīnam amat.

P. Ubi, serve, est Quīntus, amīcus puerī Sextī? Estne Quīntus in oppidō?

S. In oppidō Quīntus nōn est. Quīntus est cum Mārcō nautā.

P. Labōrant'ne Quīntus et Mārcus?

S. Labō'rant.

114. 1. Are the men of-the-town hastening, Marcus? No (*Latin*, they are not hastening). 2. What are the farmers' boys carrying? They-are-carrying arms. 3. Whither are the queens calling the peoples? 4. The queens are-calling the peoples from the fields into the towns. 5. Why do the good queens call the people together? 6. Are the slaves toiling in the fields? Yes (*Latin*, they-are-toiling).

IN NO OTHER COUNTRY IS IT SO NECESSARY AS IN OURS TO PROVIDE FULLY, FOR THOSE WHO HAVE THE CHANCE AND DESIRE TO TAKE IT, BROAD AND HIGH LIBERAL EDUCATION, IN WHICH ONE ESSENTIAL ELEMENT SHALL BE CLASSICAL TRAINING. — THEODORE ROOSEVELT

LESSON XII

Semper fidēlis — Always faithful[1]

ADJECTIVES OF THE FIRST AND SECOND DECLENSIONS
GENITIVE OF NOUNS IN -IUS AND -IUM

115. Adjectives of First and Second Declensions. We have seen that feminine adjectives in -a, like **bona**, are declined like **aqua** (§ 89). So masculine adjectives in -us, such as **bonus**, are declined like **servus**; and neuter adjectives in -um, such as **bonum**, are declined like **oppidum**. For this reason such adjectives are called Adjectives of the First and Second Declensions.

116. The adjective and noun, masculine and neuter, are declined as follows:

servus bonus (bases **serv- bon-**), M., *the good slave*

		TERMINATIONS			TERMINATIONS
Nom.	servus	bonus	-us	servī	bonī	-ī
Gen.	servī	bonī	-ī	servōrum	bonōrum	-ōrum
Dat.	servō	bonō	-ō	servīs	bonīs	-īs
Acc.	servum	bonum	-um	servōs	bonōs	-ōs
Abl.	servō	bonō	-ō	servīs	bonīs	-īs

oppidum bonum (bases **oppid- bon-**), N., *the good town*

		TERMINATIONS			TERMINATIONS
Nom.	oppidum	bonum	-um	oppida	bona	-a
Gen.	oppidī	bonī	-ī	oppidōrum	bonōrum	-ōrum
Dat.	oppidō	bonō	-ō	oppidīs	bonīs	-īs
Acc.	oppidum	bonum	-um	oppida	bona	-a
Abl.	oppidō	bonō	-ō	oppidīs	bonīs	-īs

[1] Motto of the United States marines.

36

Decline together **equus parvus,** *the small horse*; **bellum magnum,** *the great war.*

117. Genitive of Nouns in -ius and -ium. Nouns in -ius and -ium end in -ī in the genitive, not in -iī, and the accent remains on the same syllable as in the nominative : nominative **fī'lius** (*son*), genitive **fī'lī,** dative **fīliō,** etc.; nominative **auxi'lium** (*aid*), genitive **auxi'lī,** dative **auxiliō,** etc.

EXERCISES

First learn the special vocabulary, page 362

DIALOGUE. MĀRCUS ET FĪLIUS

118. MĀRCUS. Quid, fīlī,[1] servī Galbae agricolae in magnum oppidum portant?

FĪLIUS. Frūmentum, Mārce, servī Galbae agricolae in magnum oppidum portant. Rēgīna magnī oppidī populum ad arma vocat. Rēgīna novum et magnum bellum parat.[2] Arma et frūmentum et pecūniam, auxilia[3] bellī, parat.[2]

M. Ubi sunt bonī fīliī pulchrae rēgīnae?

F. Cum sociīs, Mārce, fīliī rēgīnae sunt.

M. Dantne sociī bonae rēgīnae auxilium?

F. Dant. Sociī arma nova et pecūniam magnam rēgīnae dant.

M. Estne, fīlī,[1] terra rēgīnae pulchra?

F. Pulchra et magna est terra rēgīnae. Populus oppidī bonam rēgīnam et pulchram terram amat.

1. **fīlī** is the vocative of **fīlius.** 2. Note that **parat** means *prepare for* as well as *prepare.* 3. In apposition with the preceding nouns.

119. 1. The arms of-the-new ally are good. 2. The sons of-the-allies do-give great assistance to-the-people of-the-small towns. 3. The farmers are-toiling in the new fields. 4. Why, (my) son, is the good queen calling the people together? 5. Are the new allies preparing grain? Yes.

LESSON XIII

Parvum parva decent — Small things become the small [1]

ADJECTIVES OF THE FIRST AND SECOND DECLENSIONS (CONTINUED) · ADVERBS

120. Adjectives of First and Second Declensions. The complete declension of **bonus, -a, -um,** is given below:

	MASC.	FEM.	NEUT.
NOM.	bonus	bona	bonum
GEN.	bonī	bonae	bonī
DAT.	bonō	bonae	bonō
ACC.	bonum	bonam	bonum
ABL.	bonō	bonā	bonō
NOM.	bonī	bonae	bona
GEN.	bonō'rum	bonā'rum	bonō'rum
DAT.	bonīs	bonīs	bonīs
ACC.	bonōs	bonās	bona
ABL.	bonīs	bonīs	bonīs

NOTE. Learn to recite and to write the forms of adjectives *across the page*, thus giving the three genders for each case. Make a blank scheme (cf. § 72) of the declension above and use it for drill on a variety of adjectives.

a. Decline **magnus, -a, -um ; parvus, -a, -um ; novus, -a, -um.**

121. The agreement between an adjective and its noun does *not* mean that they must have the same termination. Often the adjective and the noun belong to different declensions and hence have different terminations ; for example, **nauta,** *sailor,* being a masculine noun, requires the masculine form

[1] From Horace, Rome's greatest lyric poet.

38

of the adjective in agreement. But the masculine adjective **bonus** belongs to the second declension, while **nauta** belongs to the first ; hence, *a good sailor* is **nauta bonus.** Learn to decline nouns and adjectives together as follows :

nauta bonus (bases **naut- bon-**), M., *the good sailor*

Nom.	nauta	bonus	nautae	bonī
Gen.	nautae	bonī	nautārum	bonōrum
Dat.	nautae	bonō	nautīs	bonīs
Acc.	nautam	bonum	nautās	bonōs
Abl.	nautā	bonō	nautīs	bonīs

122. Adverbs. An adverb is a word which modifies a verb, an adjective, or another adverb.

Most adverbs answer the questions *How? Where? When? To what degree?*

123. Position of Adverbs. Adverbs, unless emphatic, stand directly before the words which they modify: as,

> **Rēgīna Galbae pecūniam saepe dat,** *the queen often gives money to Galba*

Interrogative adverbs (*where? when? why?* etc.) regularly stand first, as in English. Other adverbs, when emphatic, stand in some unusual position.

EXERCISES

First learn the special vocabulary, page 362

124. 1. Agricola bonus est in magnō agrō. 2. Mārcus nauta est amīcus agricolae bonī. 3. Mārcus agricolae bonō auxilium saepe dat. 4. Amat'ne Mārcus agricolam bonum? Amat. 5. Quō Mārcus cum Galbā, agricolā bonō, properat? In nōtum oppidum. 6. Agricolae bonī multum frūmentum per longās viās portant. 7. Suntne agrī agricolārum bonōrum magnī?

Sunt. 8. Virī oppidī nōtī agricolīs bonīs pecūniam saepe dant. 9. Cūr populī oppidōrum nōtōrum agricolās bonōs convocant? Oppida nōta longum bellum parant. 10. Socii nōtae rēgīnae cum agricolīs bonīs labōrant.

125. 1. Are the new spears long? No. 2. In the new lands are many famous towns. 3. The reputation of-the-new town is good. 4. The road through the good farmer's fields is new.

LESSON XIV

Nōn scholae, sed vītae discimus — We learn not for school, but for life [1]

ADJECTIVES OF THE FIRST AND SECOND DECLENSIONS (CONCLUDED) · THE DATIVE WITH ADJECTIVES

126. Masculine Adjectives in -*er*. Not all masculine adjectives of the second declension end in -us, like **bonus,** but some end in -er and are declined like **ager** or **puer** (§ 102). The feminine and neuter nominatives show which model to follow.

127. Declension of **līber, lībera, līberum,** *free* :

	MASC.	FEM.	NEUT.
NOM.	liber	libera	liberum
GEN.	liberī	liberae	liberī
DAT.	liberō	liberae	liberō
ACC.	liberum	liberam	liberum
ABL.	liberō	liberā	liberō
NOM.	liberī	liberae	libera
GEN.	liberōrum	liberārum	liberōrum
DAT.	liberīs	liberīs	liberīs
ACC.	liberōs	liberās	libera
ABL.	liberīs	liberīs	liberīs

[1] From Seneca, a Roman philosopher.

128. Declension of **pulcher, pulchra, pulchrum,** *pretty* :

	MASC.	FEM.	NEUT.
NOM.	pulcher	pulchra	pulchrum
GEN.	pulchrī	pulchrae	pulchrī
DAT.	pulchrō	pulchrae	pulchrō
ACC.	pulchrum	pulchram	pulchrum
ABL.	pulchrō	pulchrā	pulchrō
NOM.	pulchrī	pulchrae	pulchra
GEN.	pulchrōrum	pulchrārum	pulchrōrum
DAT.	pulchrīs	pulchrīs	pulchrīs
ACC.	pulchrōs	pulchrās	pulchra
ABL.	pulchrīs	pulchrīs	pulchrīs

129. Dative with Adjectives. We learned in § 53 for what sort of expressions we may expect the dative, and in § 57 that one of its commonest uses is with *verbs* to express the indirect object. It is also very common with *adjectives* to express the object toward which the quality denoted by the adjective is directed. In English this dative would be in the objective case after the preposition *to* or *for*: as, *near to* **town,** *fit for* **service.**

130. Rule for Dative with Adjectives. *The dative is used with adjectives to denote the object toward which the given quality is directed. Such are those meaning near, also fit, friendly, pleasing, like, and their opposites.*

> **Fābula est grāta Lesbiae,** *the story is pleasing to Lesbia*
> **Ager est proximus oppidō,** *the field is nearest to the town*

a. Among such adjectives are

> **amīcus, -a, -um,** *friendly (to)*
> **inimīcus, -a, -um,** *hostile (to)*
> **grātus, -a, -um,** *pleasing (to)*
> **proximus, -a, -um,** *nearest (to)*

ĪNSULA MĀRCĪ NAUTAE

First learn the special vocabulary, page 363

131. Galba agricola in agrīs pulchrīs habitat, Quīntus in oppidō magnō et nōtō habitat; sed Mārcus nauta in īnsulā parvā habitat. Parva īnsula est pulchra et grāta Mārcō nautae. Terra est grāta Galbae et Quīntō, sed Mārcus altās aquās amat. Īnsula parva Mārcī nautae est proxima 5

MĀRCUS FRŪMENTUM Ā TERRĀ AD ĪNSULAM PORTAT

agrīs pulchrīs Galbae agricolae. Mārcus ab īnsulā parvā ad terram saepe nāvigat et per agrōs pulchrōs ad parvam casam Galbae agricolae properat. Lesbia, fīlia Galbae, Mārcō nautae frūmentum saepe dat et Mārcus frūmentum ā terrā ad parvam īnsulam portat. Lesbia est Mārcō nautae amīca 10 sed inimīca Quīntō. Agrī nōn grātī Quīntō sunt. Quīntus arma et tēla et bella amat. Estne Mārcus servus? Nōn est. Mārcus est līber.

LESSON XV

POSSESSIVE ADJECTIVES AND PRONOUNS

132. Observe the following sentences :

Marcus is my son   *Marcus is mine*

In the first sentence *my* is a possessive adjective; in the second *mine* is a possessive pronoun. Similarly in Latin the possessives are sometimes *adjectives* and sometimes *pronouns*.

133. The Latin possessives are declined like adjectives of the first and second declensions, and are as follows :

Referring to one
- **meus, mea, meum,** *my, mine*
- **tuus, tua, tuum,** *your, yours*
- **suus, sua, suum,** *his (own), her (own), its (own)*

Referring to more than one
- **noster, nostra, nostrum,** *our, ours*
- **vester, vestra, vestrum,** *your, yours*
- **suus, sua, suum,** *their (own), theirs*

NOTE. The vocative singular masculine of **meus** is **mī**: as, **mī fīlī,** (*O*) *my son* ; **mī serve,** (*O*) *my slave.*

134. Rule for Agreement of the Possessive Adjective. *The possessive adjective agrees with the noun which it modifies in gender, number, and case.*

a. Compare the English and Latin in

Galba is calling his friends, **Galba**
Lesbia is calling her friends, **Lesbia** } **suōs amīcōs vocat**

The girls are calling their friends, **puellae suōs amīcōs vocant**

Observe that **suōs** agrees with **amīcōs** and is unaffected by the gender, number, and case of **Galba, Lesbia,** or **puellae.**

[1] A Latin slogan.

43

135. *Suus*, the Reflexive Possessive. The possessive **suus** is reflexive ; that is, it stands in the predicate and refers to the subject, indicating that the subject is the possessor. In English the meaning of the sentence *Galba is calling his daughter* is doubtful, for we cannot tell whether Galba is calling his own daughter or the daughter of someone else. But in Latin **Galba fīliam suam vocat** can mean only the former, for **suam** must refer to **Galba**.

136. Omission of Possessives. The Latin possessives are omitted whenever the meaning is clear without them.

137. Position of Possessive Adjectives. Possessive adjectives, when not emphatic, follow their nouns ; when emphatic, they precede : as,

> **Lesbia est fīlia mea,** *Lesbia is my daughter*
> **Lesbia est mea fīlia,** *Lesbia is my daughter*

EXERCISES

138. 1. Rēgīna suīs sociīs auxilium dat. 2. Servī frūmentum vestrum portant. 3. Sociī nostrī nova bella parant. 4. Tēla sunt mea, arma sunt tua. 5. Agrī pulchrī sunt grātī filiābūs meīs. 6. Populus est inimīcus suīs sociīs. 7. Īnsula nostra est proxima tuae terrae. 8. Meae viae nōn sunt tuae viae.

139. Answer the following questions in Latin, basing your replies on § 131 :

1. Quis in īnsulā habitat ?
2. Ubi Galba habitat ?
3. Ubi Quīntus habitat ?
4. Quid est grātum Mārcō ?
5. Estne īnsula nautae proxima terrae ?
6. Suntne servī līberī ?
7. Quō Mārcus saepe nāvigat ?
8. Quid Lesbia Mārcō dat ?
9. Cūr est Lesbia Quīntō inimīca ?

Second Review, Lessons VIII–XV, §§ 737–742

ON THE SACRED WAY IN THE ROMAN FORUM

This picture of the Roman Forum shows the Sacred Way with its ancient pavement. At the left rise the three remaining columns of the temple of Castor. At the right are the ruins of the temple of Saturn, and in the right background towers the Capitoline Hill

LESSON XVI

Experientia docet stultōs — Experience teaches fools

CONJUGATION · PRESENT INDICATIVE OF *SUM* · PREDICATE GENITIVE OF POSSESSOR

140. Conjugation. The inflection of the verb is called its *conjugation*. Through its conjugation the verb expresses voice, mood, tense, number, and person.

141. Voice. There are two voices, active and passive. A verb in the active voice represents the subject as *performing* the action : as,

The boy ——→ *hit* ——→ the ball

A verb in the passive voice represents the subject as *receiving* the action : as,

The girl ◄—— *was hit* ◄—— by the ball

Note the direction of the arrows.

ACTIVE VOICE

PASSIVE VOICE

142. Mood. In Latin there are three moods : indicative, subjunctive, and imperative.

143. Tense. The tense of a verb indicates its time.

144. In English there are six tenses :

1. Present, referring to present time, *I call.·*
2. Past, referring to past time, *I called.*
3. Future, referring to future time, *I shall call.*

46

4. Present perfect, denoting action completed in present time, *I have called.*

5. Past perfect,[1] denoting action completed in past time, *I had called.*

6. Future perfect, denoting action completed in future time, *I shall have called.*

There are also six tenses in Latin, with practically the same names and meanings.

145. Number. In Latin, as in English, there are two numbers, singular and plural.

146. Person. Latin, like English, has three persons. The first person is the person speaking (*I call*); the second person, the person spoken to (*you call*) ; the third person, the person or thing spoken of (*he calls*). In English, person and number are indicated by personal pronouns. In Latin, on the other hand, person and number are indicated by *personal endings* (§ 47). We have already learned that -t and -nt are endings of the third person, singular and plural. The complete list of personal endings of the active voice is as follows :

	SINGULAR		PLURAL	
1ST PERSON	-m or -ō	*I*	-mus	*we*
2D PERSON	-s	*thou or you*	-tis	*you*
3D PERSON	-t	*he, she, it*	-nt	*they*

147. Indicative Mood. The indicative mood is used to make a statement or to ask a question concerning a real or assumed fact.

148. Regular and Irregular Verbs. Most verbs form their moods and tenses after a regular plan, and are called *regular* verbs. Verbs that depart from this plan are called *irregular.*

---

[1] Also called the *pluperfect.*

149. Present Indicative of *sum.* The verb **sum,** *I am,* irregular in Latin as in English, is conjugated in the present indicative as follows :

	SINGULAR	PLURAL
1ST PERSON	sum, *I-am*	sumus, *we-are*
2D PERSON	es, *you-are*	estis, *you-are*
3D PERSON	est, *he-, she-,* or *it-is*	sunt, *they-are*

a. **Est** meaning *there is,* or **sunt** meaning *there are,* precedes its subject. In this use *there* is called an *expletive.*

Distinguish, therefore, between **īnsula est magna,** *the island is large,* and **est īnsula magna,** *there is a large island.*

150. Rule for Predicate Genitive of Possessor. *The possessive genitive often stands in the predicate, and is connected with its noun by a form of the verb* **sum.**

> **Pecūnia est servī,** *the money is the slave's,* or, freely, *belongs to the slave* (literally, *is of the slave*)

GALLIA

First learn the special vocabulary, page 363

151. Gallia est terra Gallōrum. Terra Gallōrum est pulchra, et Gallī, populus Galliae, patriam (*country*) suam amant. Sunt in Galliā multa oppida magna. In agrīs multī agricolae habitant, et equī agricolārum multum frūmentum per viās longās in oppida portant. Bella Gallīs grāta nōn sunt. 5
Sed proximī Gallīs habitant Germānī. Germānī bellum amant et semper sunt in armīs. Saepe Germānī cum sociīs suīs in Galliam properant et agrōs occupant. Tum Gallī populum ad arma vocant et cum Germānīs pugnant. Magna est fāma bellōrum et nōtae sunt victōriae. Sed victōria nōn 10 semper est Gallōrum. Saepe Germānī superant.

GAUL AND PARTS OF GERMANY, SPAIN, ITALY, AND BRITAIN

152. 1. Are you friendly to my allies? Yes. 2. Your well-known victories, my son, are pleasing to our land. 3. Are the men of your towns free? No. 4. The new spears belong to (are of) my son. 5. Are we very near to the high island? 6. No, the island is not very near.

LESSON XVII

Vōx populī vōx Deī — The voice of the people is the voice of God

THE FOUR REGULAR CONJUGATIONS · PRESENT INDICATIVE ACTIVE OF THE FIRST CONJUGATION

153. Four Regular Conjugations. There are four regular conjugations of verbs. These conjugations are distinguished from one another by the *distinguishing*, or *characteristic*, vowel appearing at the end of the present stem.

154. The present stem of each conjugation is found by dropping **-re**, the ending of the present infinitive active, which is given in the vocabularies.

155. Below are given the present indicative and the present infinitive active of a verb of each conjugation, the infinitive showing the present stem with its distinguishing vowel. These are the first two of the principal parts of the verb.

CONJUGA-TION	PRES. INDIC.	PRES. INF.	PRES. STEM	DISTINGUISH-ING VOWEL
I	vo'cō, *call*	vocā're	vocā-	ā
II	mo'neō, *advise*	monē're	monē-	ē
III	re'gō, *rule*	re'gere	rege-	e
IV	au'diō, *hear*	audī're	audī-	ī

156. From the present stem are formed the *present, past* (also called *imperfect*), and *future* tenses.

157. Present Indicative Active of First Conjugation. Verbs having the infinitive termination -āre, such as vocā're, belong to the First Conjugation.

158. The present indicative is inflected by adding the personal endings to the present stem. The distinguishing vowel -ā disappears in the first person singular, and is shortened before the endings -t and -nt in the third person singular and plural.

159. The inflection of vocō, vocāre (pres. stem vocā-), *call*, in the present indicative active is as follows :

		PERSONAL ENDINGS		PERSONAL ENDINGS
1.	vo'cō, *I-call*	-ō	vocā'mus, *we-call*	-mus
2.	vo'cās, *you-call*	-s	vocā'tis, *you-call*	-tis
3.	vo'cat, *he-, she-,* or *it-calls*	-t	vo'cant, *they-call*	-nt

160. Translation of Present. English has three forms for the present tense : *I call, I am calling, I do call.* Latin has but one form, vocō; this is used for any one of the three English forms.

THE ISLAND IN THE TIBER
On the right is the Fabrician bridge, which was built 62 B.C., in the days of Cæsar and Cicero

EXERCISES

161. Inflect the present indicative of the following verbs, all of which you have had before:

Indicative Present	Infinitive Present
a'mō, *I love*	amā're, *to love*
con'vocō, *I call together*	convocā're, *to call together*
dō, *I give*	da're, *to give*
ha'bitō, *I live, I dwell*	habitā're, *to live, to dwell*
labō'rō, *I toil*	labōrā're, *to toil*
nār'rō, *I tell*	nārrā're, *to tell*
nā'vigō, *I sail*	nāvigā're, *to sail*
oc'cupō, *I seize*	occupā're, *to seize*
pa'rō, *I prepare*	parā're, *to prepare*
por'tō, *I carry*	portā're, *to carry*
pro'perō, *I hasten*	properā're, *to hasten*
pug'nō, *I fight*	pugnā're, *to fight*

Note. In **dō, dare**, the **a** of the present stem is short. The only indicative form of **dō** having the stem vowel long is **dās,** *you give*, second person singular of the present.

162. Translate each of the following forms and give its voice, mood, tense, person, and number. When translating a verb, note first the personal ending.

1. Occupā'mus, properā'tis, con'vocant. 2. Datis, labō'rās, pugnā'tis. 3. Parās, portat, amā'mus. 4. Nārrat, dant, pro'-perat. 5. Occupā'tis, nā'vigās, portant. 6. Habitā'tis, labō'-rant, dās.

163. 1. We-dwell, we-are-dwelling, we-do-dwell. 2. You-seize (*singular*), you-are-seizing, you-do-seize. 3. We-do-carry, they-are-laboring, we-hasten. 4. He-is-giving, he-calls-together, you-are-sailing. 5. They-do-fight, he-carries, we-are-living.

LESSON XVIII

Labōrāre est ōrāre — To labor is to pray[1]

THE ABLATIVE DENOTING *WITH*

164. One of the relations denoted by the Latin ablative is expressed in English by the preposition *with* (§ 65). But *with* varies in meaning, and cannot always be translated by the Latin preposition **cum.** This becomes clear from the following sentences :

    1. The fields are thick *with* grain
    2. Marcus fights *with* his spear
    3. Julia is living *with* Lesbia
    4. Galba toils *with* great industry

With denotes *cause* in 1, *with grain* meaning *because of grain.*

With denotes *means* in 2, *with his spear* meaning *by means of his spear.*

With denotes *accompaniment* in 3, the meaning being that Julia is not living alone but *in company with* Lesbia.

With denotes *manner* in 4, *with great industry* telling how Galba works.

These four meanings of *with* are expressed in Latin by four different constructions of the ablative, known as the Ablative of Cause, the Ablative of Means, the Ablative of Accompaniment, and the Ablative of Manner.

165. Rule for Ablative of Cause. *Cause is denoted by the ablative, usually without a preposition, and answers the question* **Because of what ?**

    Agrī sunt crēbrī frūmentō, *the fields are thick with grain*

[1] Motto of the monks of the order of Saint Benedict.

53

166. Rule for Ablative of Means. *Means is denoted by the ablative without a preposition. This ablative answers the question* **By means of what?** **With what?**

Mārcus tēlō pugnat, *Marcus fights with his spear*

167. Rule for Ablative of Accompaniment. *Accompaniment is denoted by the ablative with* **cum.** *This ablative answers the question* **In company with whom?**

Iūlia cum Lesbiā habitat, *Julia is living with Lesbia*

168. Rule for Ablative of Manner. *Manner is denoted by the ablative with* **cum.** *Cum may be omitted if an adjective is used with the ablative. This ablative answers the question* **How?** **In what manner?**

Galba (cum) magnā dīligentiā labōrat, *Galba works with great industry*

EXERCISE

169. What uses of the ablative do you discover in the following passage and what question does each answer?

The day after the battle we retreated with all our forces. The roads were deep with mud and the men were weary with fighting. To make matters worse, aviators attacked our crowded ranks with bombs. The machines flew low, but with such speed that we could not hit them. At last with a sigh of relief we entered a forest so thick with trees that we were well protected by the branches. Many wretched refugees with their wives and children sought shelter there.

A ROMAN SPOON

LESSON XIX

Multum in parvō — Much in little

PAST AND FUTURE INDICATIVE OF *SUM* · THE PREPOSITION *Ē* OR *EX*

Imperfect

170. Past and Future Indicative of *sum*. The past[1] and the future indicative of the irregular verb **sum** are conjugated as follows :

PAST INDICATIVE

1. e′ram, *I-was*   erā′mus, *we-were*
2. e′rās, *you-were*   erā′tis, *you-were*
3. e′rat, *he-, she-,* or *it-was*   e′rant, *they-were*

FUTURE INDICATIVE

1. e′rō, *I-shall-be*   e′rimus, *we-shall-be*
2. e′ris, *you-will-be*   e′ritis, *you-will-be*
3. e′rit, *he-, she-,* or *it-will-be*   e′runt, *they-will-be*

171. Preposition *ē* or *ex*. Latin has two prepositions meaning *from*, with the ablative : ā or ab and ē or ex.

Vir ab castrīs properat
Vir ex castrīs properat   } *the man hastens from the camp*

But **ā** or **ab** means *from the outside of,* and **ē** or **ex** *from the inside of.* Note the diagram :

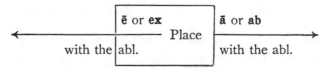

	ē or ex	ā or ab	
←	— Place —		→
	with the abl.	with the abl.	

NOTE. Write **ē** before consonants only, **ex** before either vowels or consonants.

---
[1] Also called the *imperfect.*

55

Imperfect

PUERĪ SEXTUS ET QUĪNTUS

First learn the special vocabulary, page 363

I **172.** SEXTUS. Quō, Quīnte, properās? Cūr arma nova et
L tēlum longum portās?

¾ QUĪNTUS. Ad castra proxima properō, Sexte, cum virīs et
↑puerīs oppidī nostrī. Cūr in armīs nōn es? Cūr terrae nostrae

QUŌ, QUĪNTE PROPERĀS?

⌐ tuum auxilium nōn dās?
6 S. Rōmānu· sum. Po-
⁊pulō Rōmānō bellum sem-
8 per grātum est. Sed in
9 nostrō oppidō nŏn erat
10fāma bellī. Quis, Quīnte,
11bellum parat? Eritne no-
12vum bellum cum Gallīs?
13 Q. Nōn cum Gallīs.
14Germānī, semper inimīcī
15Rōmānīs, bellum magnā
16diligentiā parant. Ex silvīs
17Germāniae cōpiās suās con-
18vocant. Mox viae, Sexte,
19erunt crēbrae equīs et virīs,
20et agrī Rōmānī proximī Ger-
21māniae in perīculō erunt.
22Sed nostra victōria erit.

173. 1. The Germans fight with long spears. 2. Soon we-
shall-be outside-of the Roman camp. 3. Shall-you-be with
Sextus? We-shall. 4. The perils of-our forces were many.

174. Derivation. Give the meaning of the following English
words and tell to what Latin words they are related:

insulate	conservation	longevity	agriculture	elaborate
sinecure	navigable	servile	virile	depopulate

LESSON XX

Nīl dēspērandum — There's no such word as fail [1]

PAST INDICATIVE ACTIVE OF THE FIRST CONJUGATION

175. Formation of Tenses. Instead of using auxiliary verbs, like *was, shall, will,* etc., to express differences in tense, Latin adds to the verb stem certain elements that have the force of auxiliary verbs. These are called *tense signs.*

176. The tense sign of the past is **-bā-**, which is added to the present stem. The past consists, therefore, of three parts :

PRESENT STEM	TENSE SIGN	PERSONAL ENDING
vocā-	**ba-**	**m**
calling-	*was-*	*I*

a. Note that the Latin verb is translated from right to left, so that English *I was calling* is in Latin **vocā'bam,** *calling-was-I.*

177. Inflection of Past Indicative Active. The personal endings of the past are the same as those of the present, except that **-m** is used instead of **-ō** in the first person singular.

SINGULAR

1. **vocā'bam,** *I-was-calling* or *I-called*
2. **vocā'bās,** *you-were-calling* or *you-called*
3. **vocā'bat,** *he-, she-, it-was-calling* or *he-, she-, it-called*

PLURAL

1. **vocābā'mus,** *we-were-calling* or *we-called*
2. **vocābā'tis,** *you-were-calling* or *you-called*
3. **vocā'bant,** *they-were-calling* or *they-called*

---

[1] From Horace, a Roman poet. Literally, *In nothing must it be despaired.*

57

lmperfect

58   PAST INDICATIVE ACTIVE, FIRST CONJUGATION

a. Note that the inflection above is somewhat like that of **eram** (§ 170), the past tense of **sum**, and that the long ā of the tense sign -bā- is shortened before final -m, -t, and -nt. A long vowel is regularly shortened before **nt** and final -m or -t. Learn this rule now.

178. Meaning of Past Tense. The Latin past tense has two uses.

a. It may represent an action as going on in past time and not yet completed, and is then translated by the English past progressive : as, **vocābam**, *I was calling.* For this reason this tense is often called the *imperfect.*

b. It usually describes a past situation, and is then translated by the English past : as, **vocābam**, *I called.* For this reason this tense is often called the *past descriptive.*

EXERCISES

179. Inflect in the past indicative active the verbs given in § 161.

180. 1. Nārrās, nārrābās, parāmus, parābāmus. 2. Pugnātis, portābat, occupant, dabam. 3. Occupābātis, nāvigātis, labōrābās, habitant. 4. Datis, pugnābam, properātis, occupābāmus.

BRITANNIA

First learn the special vocabulary, page 364, and locate on the map, page 49, the countries mentioned in the story.

181. Britannia, terra Britannōrum, est īnsula magna. Britannī erant barbarī et in silvīs magnīs et oppidīs parvīs habitābant. Britannia est proxima Galliae et Britannī erant amīcī Gallōrum. In longīs bellīs Gallōrum et Rōmānōrum Britannī sociīs suīs auxilium saepe dabant. Iam nōta populō 5 Rōmānō erat Britannia. Sed amīcitia Britannōrum et Gallōrum populō Rōmānō grāta nōn erat. Itaque Rōmānī cōpiās convocābant et arma sua et magnam cōpiam frūmentī parābant. Magnā cum dīligentiā labōrābant. Tum cum multīs virīs ad īnsulam Britanniam nāvigābant. Īnsula erat crēbra 10 silvīs et viae nōn bonae erant. Itaque Rōmānī in perīculō saepe erant. Britannī ex castrīs suīs properābant et cum Rōmānīs pugnābant. Sed victōria Rōmānōrum erat, et Rōmānī cōpiīs suīs multa oppida Britannōrum occupābant.

BRITANNĪ ERANT BARBARĪ

182. 1. The Romans were-fighting in the forest with the savage Britons. 2. The Britons carried grain to the camp with-their horses. 3. Your friendship will-be known to-the-Romans. 4. Because-of-the-rumor [1] of-war the Britons were already calling-together their forces. 5. The Romans sailed through the deep waters with great danger.

1. Ablative of cause, § 165.

LESSON XXI

Montānī semper līberī — Mountaineers are always free[1]

FUTURE INDICATIVE ACTIVE OF THE FIRST CONJUGATION

183. Formation of Future Indicative Active. The tense sign of the future in the first conjugation is -bi-. This is added to the present stem and followed by the personal endings.

PRESENT STEM	TENSE SIGN	PERSONAL ENDING
vocā-	bi-	t
call-	*will-*	*he*

184. Inflection of Future Indicative Active. The first person singular ends in -bō, the i of the tense sign disappearing. In the third person plural -bi- becomes -bu-.

1. vocā'bō, *I-shall-call*   vocā'bimus, *we-shall-call*
2. vocā'bis, *you-will-call*   vocā'bitis, *you-will-call*
3. vocā'bit, *he-, she-, it-will-call*   vocā'bunt, *they-will-call*

a. Note that the inflection is somewhat like that of erō (§ 170), the future of **sum**.

EXERCISES

First learn the special vocabulary, page 364

185. 1. Quis fābulam īnsulae[1] Britanniae nārrābit? 2. Cūr, mī fīlī, Britannī erant miserī? 3. Bellīs crēbrīs Britannī erant miserī. 4. Erantne ōrae īnsulae[1] altae[2]? Altae erant. 5. Britannī Gallīs, sociīs suīs, auxilium saepe dant. 6. Itaque Rōmānī magnīs cum cōpiīs ad ōrās altās īnsulae nāvigābunt.

---

[1] Motto of the state of West Virginia. The verb *to be* is omitted in this motto, as in many others.

7. Iam Rōmānī barbarōs multīs proeliīs [3] superābunt. 8. Magna erunt praemia victōriae. 9. Tum īnsula erit Rōmānōrum.

1. Genitive. 2. Predicate adjective, nominative plural. 3. Ablative of means.

186. 1. The shore of-the-island, nearest to-Gaul, is high. 2. We-shall-fight with the hostile savages [1] in the great forests. 3. Our friends will-be wretched because-of-the-dangers [2] of-the-battle. 4. You-will-conquer the Britons, O Romans, with-your long spears.[3] 5. Soon (**iam**) the Romans will give great rewards to their allies.

1. Ablative of accompaniment. 2. Ablative of cause. 3. Ablative of means.

187. Inflect in the future indicative active the verbs given in § 161.

ŌRAE BRITANNIAE ERANT ALTAE

LESSON XXII

Virtūs praemium est optimum — Virtue is the best prize [1]

PRESENT, PAST, AND FUTURE INDICATIVE ACTIVE OF THE SECOND CONJUGATION

188. Formation of Present, Past, and Future Indicative Active. Verbs having the infinitive termination -ēre, such as monē're, belong to the Second Conjugation.

189. The present, past, and future of the second conjugation, as of the first, are formed on the present stem.

190. The present stem of the second conjugation ends in -ē (§ 155). This characteristic vowel appears in every form of the present, past, and future.

191. The same personal endings and the same tense signs are used as in the first conjugation.

192. Inflection of Present, Past, and Future Indicative Active. The inflection below shows the present, past, and future indicative active of **vo'cō** (*I call*) of the first conjugation and of **mo'neō** (*I advise* or *warn*) of the second. Review the forms of **vo'cō** and learn the corresponding tenses of **mo'neō**.

vo'cō, vocā're (pres. stem vocā-), *call*

PRESENT

1. vo'cō, *I-call*   vocā'mus, *we-call*
2. vo'cās, *you-call*   vocā'tis, *you-call*
3. vo'cat, *he-, she-, it-calls*   vo'cant, *they-call*

---

[1] From Plautus, a writer of Latin plays.

PAST (Imperfect)

1. vocā'bam, *I-was-calling* or *I-called*
2. vocā'bās, *you-were-calling* or *you-called*
3. vocā'bat, *he-, she-, it-was-calling* or *he-, she-, it-called*

1. vocābā'mus, *we-were-calling* or *we-called*
2. vocābā'tis, *you-were-calling* or *you-called*
3. vocā'bant, *they-were-calling* or *they-called*

FUTURE

1. vocā'bō, *I-shall-call*   vocā'bimus, *we-shall-call*
2. vocā'bis, *you-will-call*   vocā'bitis, *you-will-call*
3. vocā'bit, *he-, she-, it-will-call*   vocā'bunt, *they-will-call*

mo'neō, monē're (pres. stem monē-), *advise*

PRESENT

1. mo'neō, *I-advise*   monē'mus, *we-advise*
2. mo'nēs, *you-advise*   monē'tis, *you-advise*
3. mo'net, *he-, she-, it-advises*   mo'nent, *they-advise*

PAST (Imperfect)

1. monē'bam, *I-was-advising* or *I-advised*
2. monē'bās, *you-were-advising* or *you-advised*
3. monē'bat, *he-, she-, it-was-advising* or *he-, she-, it-advised*

1. monēbā'mus, *we-were-advising* or *we-advised*
2. monēbā'tis, *you-were-advising* or *you-advised*
3. monē'bant, *they-were-advising* or *they-advised*

FUTURE

1. monē'bō, *I-shall-advise*   monē'bimus, *we-shall-advise*
2. monē'bis, *you-will-advise*   monē'bitis, *you-will-advise*
3. monē'bit, *he-will-advise*   monē'bunt, *they-will-advise*

193. Nearly all regular verbs ending in -eō belong to the Second Conjugation.

194. Shortening of Vowels. Attention has been called to the shortening of long vowels in certain forms. The following rules are of general application :

1. A long vowel is shortened before another vowel.

Thus, monē-ō becomes mone-ō.

2. A long vowel is shortened before nt and nd, before final -m or -t, and, except in words of one syllable, before final -l or -r.

Thus, vocănt, vocăndus, vocābăm, vocābăt, monĕt.

EXERCISES

First learn the special vocabulary, page 364

195. Like **moneō**, inflect the present, past, and future indicative of

DERIVATIVES

habeō, habē're, *have*   habit
teneō, tenē're, *hold, keep*   tenacious
timeō, timē're, *fear*   timid
videō, vidē're, *see*   vision, evident

196. 1. Tenētis, vocābitis, habēbant.   2. Vidēbunt, monē-bāmus, nārrābat.   3. Habēbō, timēs, vocātis.   4. Vidēsne altās ōrās īnsulae?   5. Numquam, Rōmānī, sine auxiliō sociōrum nostrōrum praemia victōriae tenēbimus.

LESSON XXIII

Lupus in fābulā — The wolf in the story[1]

LATIN ORDER OF WORDS

197. Order of Words in English and Latin Compared. In English, words are arranged in a fairly fixed order, and this order cannot be changed, as a rule, without changing or destroying the meaning of the sentence.

198. In Latin the office of the words in a sentence is shown by their forms (§ 39), and their position is much more free. Still there are general rules of order, which should be carefully observed. The rules already given in the preceding lessons are here summarized for review.

a. The subject generally stands first, the verb last. But, to avoid obscurity, **est**, *is*, and other forms of the verb *to be* usually stand, as in English, between the subject and a noun or adjective in the predicate.

NOTE. In connected narrative each succeeding sentence begins with the word or words that link it most closely to the sentence preceding. For example, in "The Rhine was the frontier of Germany. Cæsar built a bridge across this river," the order of words in Latin would be "The Rhine was the frontier of Germany. *Across this river* Cæsar a bridge built." Observe that the first words of the second sentence, "Across this river," link it to the sentence preceding and are therefore placed before the subject, "Cæsar."

b. The indirect object may either precede or follow the direct object.
c. The vocative case rarely stands first.
d. An adjective may either precede or follow its noun (cf. § 199).
e. The possessive adjective regularly follows its noun.
f. Adverbs normally stand directly before the words they modify.

[1] From Terence, a writer of Latin comedies. The expression applies to an unexpected and unwelcome appearance; cf. "Speak of the devil."

199. Words are made emphatic by placing them in unusual positions. Thus we have seen that possessive adjectives, which regularly follow their nouns, are made emphatic by placing them before their nouns (§ 137); and any adjective or other modifier is made emphatic by separating it from the word to which it belongs. Observe the following sentences:

> Caesar agrōs pulchrōs Gallōrum occupat
> Caesar *pulchrōs* Gallōrum agrōs occupat

In the first sentence **pulchrōs** is not emphatic. In the second it has been made so by separating it from its noun **agrōs**. The order of words, therefore, in a Latin sentence tells the eyes of the reader as much about the emphasis as his ears tell him when he hears a man speak. If you do not note the order, you will often fail to get the sense.

EXERCISES

200. Derivation. What Latin derivatives can you find in the following paragraph? Give the meaning of each derivative and the Latin word from which it is derived.

> Britain, because of its insular character, was not occupied by the Romans for many years. Its inhabitants were a great multitude, barbarous in their habits of life, very belligerent, and not slow to fight for their liberties. Then, too, the visible and the invisible perils of navigation in the open sea, though not insuperable, made the Romans timid.

Third Review, Lessons XVI-XXIII, §§ 743-748

THE ROMAN FORUM AS IT NOW APPEARS

No spot has greater historic interest than the Roman Forum, the center of the political and commercial life of the Roman Empire. Its magnificent buildings were restored for the last time in the sixth century. Then for more than a thousand years they were systematically destroyed and buried in rubbish, so that now the ancient pavement is at places forty feet below the present level of the ground. At the left of the picture is the Palatine Hill, and at the farther end of the Forum is the Capitoline

LESSON XXIV

Quandōque bonus dormītat Homērus — Even good Homer
sometimes nods[1]

THE DEMONSTRATIVE *IS, EA, ID*

201. Definition of a Demonstrative. A demonstrative is a
word that points out an object, as, *this, that, these, those.*
Sometimes these words are pronouns : as, *Do you hear these?*
Sometimes they are adjectives : as, *Do you hear these men?*
In the former case they are called *demonstrative pronouns,* in
the latter *demonstrative adjectives.*

202. Agreement of Latin Demonstratives. Demonstrative
pronouns agree in gender and number with the nouns to
which they refer, but their case is determined by the way they
are used.

Demonstrative adjectives, like other adjectives, agree with
their nouns in gender, number, and case.

203. Demonstrative *is, ea, id.* The demonstrative most used
is **is** (masculine), **ea** (feminine), **id** (neuter), meaning *this* or
that in the singular and *these* or *those* in the plural. It is
declined as follows :

	MASC.	FEM.	NEUT.	MASC.	FEM.	NEUT.
NOM.	is	ea	id	eī (iī)	eae	ea
GEN.	eius	eius	eius	eōrum	eārum	eōrum
DAT.	eī	eī	eī	eīs (iīs)	eīs (iīs)	eīs (iīs)
ACC.	eum	eam	id	eōs	eās	ea
ABL.	eō	eā	eō	eīs (iīs)	eīs (iīs)	eīs (iīs)

[1] From Horace. The meaning is that even the best make mistakes. Of
similar sentiment are his words "Vitiīs nēmō sine nāscitur," *no one is born
without faults.*

67

The genitive singular **eius** is pronounced *eh'yus*. The plural forms with two **i**'s are pronounced as one syllable. Hence, pronounce **iī** as **ī** and **iīs** as **īs**.

204. Position of Demonstrative Adjectives. Demonstrative adjectives, being emphatic, normally precede their nouns : as,

Ad eam īnsulam nāvigat, *he is sailing to this* (or *that*) *island*

205. Demonstratives used as Personal Pronouns. Latin demonstratives are frequently used for the personal pronouns of the third person, *he, she, it,* or (plural) *they*. **Is**, as a personal pronoun, has the following meanings :

NOM.   is, *he* ; ea, *she* ; id, *it*
GEN.   eius, *of him, his* ; eius, *of her, her, hers* ; eius, *of it, its*
DAT.   eī, *to* or *for him* ; eī, *to* or *for her* ; eī, *to* or *for it*
ACC.   eum, *him* ; eam, *her*; id, *it*
ABL.   eō, *with, from,* etc., *him* ; eā, *with, from,* etc., *her* ; eō, *with, from,* etc., *it*

NOM.   eī or iī, eae, ea, *they*
GEN.   eōrum, eārum, eōrum, *of them, their*
DAT.   eīs or iīs, eīs or iīs, eīs or iīs, *to* or *for them*
ACC.   eōs, eās, ea, *them*
ABL.   eīs or iīs, eīs or iīs, eīs or iīs, *with, from,* etc., *them*

EXERCISES

First learn the special vocabulary, page 364

206. 1. Quis ea cōnsilia Rōmānōrum iam nūntiābat? Bonus amīcus Britannōrum. 2. Quō eī Rōmānī nāvigābunt? Ad īnsulam eī Rōmānī nāvigābunt. 3. Quid in eam īnsulam portābunt? Multōs virōs et equōs et magnam cōpiam frūmentī in eam īnsulam portābunt. 4. Pugnābuntne Britannī cum Rōmānīs? Mox pugnābunt, sed eōs nōn superābunt. 5. Amantne

Britannī īnsulam suam? Amant. 6. Habentne Britannī sociōs? Nunc Gallī sunt sociī eōrum, sed auxilium Gallōrum eōs numquam servābit. 7. Iam (*soon*) magnam victōriam Rōmānī nūntiābunt. 8. Iniūriae Britannōrum erunt magnae et vīta[1] eōrum erit semper misera.

1. Observe that **vīta** is translated *lives*. The plural of **vīta** is not used except in the sense of biographies, as, **vītae magnōrum virōrum**, *lives of great men.*

207. 1. He-sees him, her, it, them. 2. This plan, that life, these boys. 3. For-those rewards, with that friend, the rumor of-that battle. 4. The story of-those wrongs, for-that life, those girls.

LESSON XXV

Aurea mediocritās—The golden mean[1]

THE POSSESSIVE OF THE THIRD PERSON

208. We learned in § 135 that the possessive of the third person, **suus, -a, -um,** *his, her, its, their,* is reflexive and is used when the subject is the possessor: as,

    Britannī īnsulam suam amant, *the Britons love their island*

209. When *his, her, its, their* do not refer to the subject, but to other persons or things, we translate *his, her, its* by **eius** (*of him, of her, of it*), and *their* by **eōrum** (*of them*) for masculine or neuter possessors and **eārum** for feminine possessors.

    Galba sees his (own) *danger,* **Galba perīculum suum videt**
    Galba sees his danger (not his own), **Galba perīculum eius videt**
    The men see their (own) *danger,* **virī perīculum suum vident**
    The men see their danger (not their own), **virī perīculum eōrum (eārum) vident**

1 From Horace, the noted lyric poet.

EXERCISES

First learn the special vocabulary, page 365

210. 1. Rēgīna amīcōs suōs servābat. 2. Rēgīna amīcōs eius [1] servābat. 3. Rōmānī fīnitimōs suōs servābunt. 4. Rōmānī fīnitimōs eōrum servābunt. 5. Eī barbarī cōpiīs suīs mūrōs altōs et lātōs eōrum tenēbant. 6. Is Gallus Rōmānōs nōn timēbat, sed eīs iniūriās suās nārrābat. 7. Amātisne patriam vestram? Clāra oppida et lātōs agrōs eius amāmus. 8. Germānī victōriās eōrum nūntiābunt. 9. Nōn sine praemiō auxilium rēgīnae dabis.

1. Do not forget that **eius**, being masculine, feminine, or neuter, may mean *his*, *her*, or *its*. Usually the context will show which meaning to use.

211. 1. That slave will-save his (*his own*) life. 2. That slave will-save his (*not his own*) life. 3. Those girls were-holding their (*their own*) prizes. 4. Those savages will-fear their (*their own*) neighbors. 5. They love their queen and see her danger.

THE ROMAN FORUM AT ITS WESTERN END

On the left are three columns of the temple of Vespasian and the arch of Septimius Severus. On the right are the ruins of the temple of Saturn. The canvas near the foot of the arch covers an excavation where were found the alleged tomb of Romulus and the oldest Latin inscription

LESSON XXVI

Fōrmōsa faciēs mūta commendātiō est—A pleasing countenance is
a silent recommendation [1]

THE PRESENT INDICATIVE ACTIVE OF THE THIRD CONJUGATION

212. Verbs having the infinitive termination -ĕre belong to
the Third Conjugation : as, regō, re'gĕre (*rule*), present stem
regĕ- (cf. § 155).

213. The present indicative active of regō is inflected as
follows :

PERSONAL ENDINGS		PERSONAL ENDINGS	
1. re'gō, *I-rule*	-ō	re'gimus, *we-rule*	-mus
2. re'gis, *you-rule*	-s	re'gitis, *you-rule*	-tis
3. re'git, *he-, she-, it-rules*	-t	re'gunt, *they-rule*	-nt

a. Note that the final -e of the present stem disappears in the first
person singular, becomes -u- in the third person plural and -i- elsewhere. The inflection is much like that of erō, the future of sum.

EXERCISES

214. Like regō, re'gere, inflect the present indicative active
of dīcō, dī'cere, *speak*, *say*; and dūcō, dū'cere, *lead*.

215. **Derivation.** From the verb dūcō many English words
are derived. Define the following :

ductile	induce	produce	adduce
duke	introduce	reduce	deduce

[1] From Publilius Syrus, a writer whose short and witty sayings were memorized in the Roman schools.

71

MAGISTER ET DISCIPULĪ[1]

First learn the special vocabulary, page 365

216. MAGISTER. Saepe, discipulī meī, dē Rōmā dīcimus, sed ubi est Rōma?

DISCIPULĪ. Rōma, magister, est in Italiā, clārā patriā Rōmānōrum.

M. Habētisne tabulam (*a map*) Italiae?

D. Tabulam bonam Italiae in librīs nostrīs habēmus.

M. Estne Italia lāta?

D. Lāta Italia nōn est. Longa est.

M. Quid librī vestrī de viīs Rōmānīs nārrant?

D. Rōmānī multās et longās viās habēbant. Eae viae per Italiam, Galliam, Germāniam patēbant. Nōta erat Appia via.[2] Dē eā librī saepe dīcunt.

M. Eratne Rōma semper magna?

D. Nōn semper. Per multōs annōs Rōma erat parva et fīnitimī eius erant inimīcī. Sed populus Rōmānus eōs multīs proeliīs superābat. Tum in (*against*) barbarōs Rōmānī cōpiās suās dūcunt et dēnique multās terrās regunt.

M. Optimē (*well done*), discipulī. Aliquandō (*some day*) ā patriā nostrā ad Italiam nāvigābitis et ōrās pulchrās et īnsulās eius et mūrōs altōs Rōmae vidēbitis.

1. *Teacher and Pupils.* 2. See page 86.

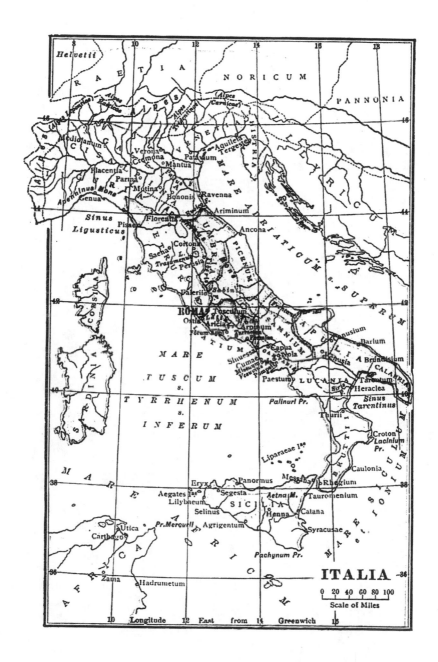

ITALIA

0 20 40 60 80 100
Scale of Miles

LESSON XXVII

Cum grāno salis — With a grain of salt[1]

THE PRESENT INDICATIVE ACTIVE OF THE FOURTH CONJUGATION

217. Verbs having the infinitive termination -īre belong to the Fourth Conjugation : as, audiō, audī're (*hear*), present stem audī- (cf. § 155).

218. The present indicative active of audiō, audī're, is inflected as follows :

	PERSONAL ENDINGS			PERSONAL ENDINGS
1. au'diō, *I-hear*	-ō	audī'mus, *we-hear*	-mus
2. au'dīs, *you-hear*	-s	audī'tis, *you-hear*	-tis
3. au'dit, *he-, she-, it-hears*	-t	au'diunt, *they-hear*	-nt

a. Note that ī, the characteristic vowel, is always long except where long vowels are regularly shortened (cf. § 194). In the third person plural u is inserted between the stem and the personal ending : as, audi-u-nt.

EXERCISES

219. Like audiō, audīre, inflect the present indicative active of veniō, venīre, *come*, and mūniō, mūnīre, *fortify*.

220. 1. Nūntiābunt, venītis, habēbat, mūnīs. 2. Vidēbātis, audīmus, timēbit, veniunt. 3. Dabit, tenēbunt, mūnītis, nāvigābās. 4. Audit, timēbātis, nārrant, habēbimus. 5. Properābunt, venīmus, parābās, mūniunt.

[1] From Pliny. An expression used to indicate that the real facts have been exaggerated : as, " That story must be taken *cum grāno salis*."

73

DĒ CASTRĪS RŌMĀNĪS

First learn the special vocabulary, page 365

221. Vidētisne castra Rōmāna? Castra sunt magna, et quattuor (*four*) portās (*gates*) habent. Per eās portās Rōmānī in castra veniunt et ex eīs portīs cōpiās suās dūcunt. In castrīs multōs virōs et equōs vidēmus. Vidēmus virōs quī in armīs sunt et virōs quī magnā dīligentiā labōrant. Eī 5

CASTRA RŌMĀNA

quī labōrant castra mūniunt. Rōmānī castra sua altō vāllō et altā fossā semper mūniunt. Vidētisne eōs quī terram ex fossā portant? Barbarī castra sua nōn mūniunt, itaque vīta[1] eōrum multīs perīculīs patet. Sed Rōmānī sine perīculō castra sua tenent nec (*nor*) barbarōs timent. In mediīs castrīs 10 est praetōrium (*general's tent*). Idne[2] vidētis? Is quī cōpiās Rōmānās dūcit est clārus vir. Saepe suōs[3] convocat. Nunc eīs[4] dīcit (*is talking*) et eī eum audiunt.

1. Translate, *lives.* 2. Made up of **id** and **-ne**, the question sign. 3. *His men.* The possessives are often pronouns (cf. § 132). 4. Indirect object.

LESSON XXVIII

Palma nōn sine pulvere — No prize without a struggle [1]

THE DATIVE WITH SPECIAL INTRANSITIVE VERBS

222. Intransitive verbs do not admit of a direct object (§ 25). Many such verbs, however, are of such meaning that they can govern a dative as indirect object (§ 58). This dative, in Latin, represents the person or thing to which a benefit, injury, or feeling is directed; but it appears in English as a direct object.

223. Learn the following list of common verbs whose meanings call for a dative as indirect object:

	DERIVATIVES
crē'dō, crē'dere, *believe* (give belief to), *trust*	creed, credit, creditor
fa'veō, favē're, *favor* (show favor to)	favorite, favorable
no'ceō, nocē're, *injure* (do harm to)	noxious, innocent
pā'reō, pārē're, *obey* (give obedience to)	
persuā'deō, persuādē're, *persuade* (make a thing agreeable to)	dissuade, suasion
resis'tō, resis'tere, *resist* (offer resistance to)	persist, insist, desist
stu'deō, studē're, *be eager* (give attention to)	study, student, studious

a. The verbs **crēdō** and **persuādeō** are transitive in some senses and take an accusative (direct object) along with the dative (indirect object): as, **Rōmānīs sua crēdunt,** *they intrust their possessions to the Romans.*

224. Rule for Dative with Intransitive Verbs. *The dative of the indirect object is used with the intransitive verbs* crēdō, faveō, noceō, pāreō, persuādeō, resistō, studeō, *and others of like meaning.*

---

[1] Literally, *No palm without dust,* referring to the palm branch, the prize of the victor in the chariot race, and the dust raised by the struggle. Compare Mrs. Browning's " No cross, no crown."

75

EXERCISES

225. Inflect the present indicative active of **servō, faveō, crēdō,** and **mūniō.**

226. Derivation. The verb **resistō,** *resist,* is composed of the verb **sistō,** *stand,* and the prefix **re-,** *back* or *again,* so that *resist* means to *stand back* in the line or *stand again* after running away.

Look up the words *consist, desist, exist, insist,* and *persist,* and note the force of each of the prefixes.

227. 1. Crēdisne sociīs eōrum? Eīs nōn crēdō. 2. Meī fīnitimī cōnsiliīs novīs tuīs nōn favent. 3. Servī bellō student. 4. Bonae puellae librīs suīs numquam nocent. 5. Equī Galbae Mārcō nautae nōn pārent.

228. 1. We-persuade our friends. 2. We-resist our neighbors. 3. That boy does not obey Lesbia. 4. You-believe them, my friends, because-of-your friendship.[1]

1. Ablative of cause, § 165.

A COCKFIGHT

A wall painting from a house in Pompeii

LESSON XXIX

Dīrigō — I point the way[1]

THE PAST INDICATIVE ACTIVE OF *REGŌ* AND *AUDIŌ*

229. Formation and Inflection. The tense sign is -bā-, as in the first two conjugations. The past indicative of **regō** is formed and inflected just like that of **moneō**. The past indicative of **audiō** has **iē** before the tense sign : as, **audiē'bam.**

THIRD CONJUGATION

1. regē'bam, *I-was-ruling* or *I-ruled*
2. regē'bās, *you-were-ruling* or *you-ruled*
3. regē'bat, *he-was-ruling* or *he-ruled*

1. regēbā'mus, *we-were-ruling* or *we-ruled*
2. regēbā'tis, *you-were-ruling* or *you-ruled*
3. regē'bant, *they-were-ruling* or *they-ruled*

FOURTH CONJUGATION

1. audiē'bam, *I-was-hearing* or *I-heard*
2. audiē'bās, *you-were-hearing* or *you-heard*
3. audiē'bat, *he-was-hearing* or *he-heard*

1. audiēbā'mus, *we-were-hearing* or *we-heard*
2. audiēbā'tis, *you-were-hearing* or *you-heard*
3. audiē'bant, *they-were-hearing* or *they-heard*

230. The Conjunction -que. The conjunction *and* is often expressed in Latin by -que added to the second of two associated words : as,

senātus populus'que Rōmānus, *the senate and the Roman people*

[1] Motto of the state of Maine.

77

a. Words which do not stand alone, but are attached to other words, are called *enclit'ics.* We have already had -ne, the question sign.

EXERCISES

231. Inflect the present and past indicative of nūntiō, studeō, crēdō, and veniō.

232. 1. Dīcēbant, audiēbātis, superābit, dūcunt. 2. Tenēbis, regitis, mūniēbāmus, habēbunt. 3. Dīcimus, timēbātis, patent, veniēbat. 4. Dūcēbam, mūniunt, vidēbitis, patēbis. 5. Servābō, audiēbās, tenēs, dīcēbāmus.

DĒ DEĪS RŌMĀNĪS

First learn the special vocabulary, page 365. The names of the gods mentioned below, being the same in English and Latin, are not included.

233. 1. Rōmānī multōs deōs et multās deās habēbant. 2. Poētae Rōmānī multās fābulās dē deīs et deābus [1] nārrābant.

3. Eīs fābulīs nōn crēdimus. 4. Populus Rōmānus deōs deāsque timēbat et eīs pārēbat. 5. In numerō deōrum erant Iuppiter et Neptūnus et Mārs. 6. Iuppiter deōs deāsque regēbat, Neptūnus in aquīs altīs habitābat. 7. Mārs erat deus bellī, et proeliīs semper studēbat. 8. In numerō deārum erant Iūnō et Minerva et Diāna. 9. Iūnō erat rēgīna deārum. 10. Minerva erat dea sapientiae. 11. Diāna erat rēgīna silvārum.

ATHĒNA DEA SAPIENTIAE   1. **dea** is declined like fīlia (§ 70. *a*), having **deābus** in the dative and ablative plural.

234. 1. Good men obey the gods. 2. Evil men resist the gods. 3. The gods never do-harm to-good boys and girls. 4. Minerva favors men who (quī) are-eager for wisdom.

LESSON XXX

In hōc signō vincēs — In this sign thou shalt conquer[1]

THE FUTURE INDICATIVE ACTIVE OF THE THIRD AND FOURTH CONJUGATIONS

235. Tense Sign and Inflection. The tense sign of the future in the third and fourth conjugations is not -bi-, as in the first and second conjugations, but -a- in the first person singular and -ē- in the rest of the tense. This tense sign takes the place of the final vowel of the present stem in verbs conjugated like **regō**, and is preceded by the stem vowel -i in verbs conjugated like **audiō**. The usual shortening of long vowels takes place (cf. § 194).

236. The inflection of the future indicative active of **regō** (third conjugation) and **audiō** (fourth conjugation) is as follows:

1. rc'gam, *I-shall-rule*   au'diam, *I-shall-hear*
2. re'gēs, *you-will-rule*   au'diēs, *you-will-hear*
3. re'get, *he-will-rule*   au'diet, *he-will-hear*

1. regē'mus, *we-shall-rule*   audiē'mus, *we-shall-hear*
2. regē'tis, *you-will-rule*   audiē'tis, *you-will-hear*
3. re'gent, *they-will-rule*   au'dient, *they-will-hear*

a. Observe that the future of the third conjugation is like the present of the second, except in the first person singular.

EXERCISES

237. Inflect the present, past, and future indicative active of **con'vocō, te'neō, dīcō,** and **mū'niō**.

[1] Translation of the Greek motto which Constantine, the first Christian emperor, is said to have seen on a flaming cross in the sky. This vision, we are told, led to his conversion, and his banners afterwards bore a cross with its motto. It is now the motto of the order of Knights Templar.

238. Derivation. Latin prepositions are often used as prefixes and added to simple verbs to make compound verbs. These same prefixes appear in English and generally have the same meanings as in Latin.

Form English derivatives from each of the following Latin compounds, and note the force of the prefix :

ab, *from* + dūcō, *lead* = abdūcō, *lead away*
ad, *to* + dūcō, *lead* = addūcō, *lead to*
dē, *down* or *from* + dūcō, *lead* = dēdūcō, *lead down* or *from*
ē, *out of* + dūcō, *lead* = ēdūcō, *lead out of*
in, *into* + dūcō, *lead* = indūcō, *lead into*

THĒ′SEUS ET MĪNŌTAU′RUS[1]

First learn the special vocabulary, page 366. Consult the general vocabulary for new words or words you have forgotten.

239. Ōlim (*once upon a time*) Mīnōs, quī īnsulam Crētam regēbat, bellum cum Graecīs gerēbat. Graecī magnō animō pugnant, sed Mīnōs eōs crēbrīs proeliīs superat. Tum Mīnōs dīcit : " Nunc, Graecī, victōria est mea et servī meī estis. Nunc iniūriīs[2] vestrīs poenam dabitis magnam. 5 Quotannīs (*every year*) ad patriam meam septem (*seven*) puerōs et septem puellās mittētis. Cum eīs ad ōrās altae Crētae nāvigābitis. Eōs in labyrinthum[1] indūcēmus. Tum barbarus Mīnōtaurus veniet. Eum vidēbunt et audient et timēbunt. Amīcōs suōs vocābunt, sed quis ad eōs auxilia 10 portābit ? Sine cōnsiliō,[3] sine armīs vītam suam Mīnōtaurō barbarō dabunt. Ea, Graecī, erit poena vestra. Quid dīcitis?''

1. *Theseus* (thē′sūs) *and the Min′o-taur.* The Minotaur was a fabulous monster, which lived on the island of Crete in the labyrinth, a structure containing so many rooms and winding passages that nobody could get out of it. The Minotaur fed on human flesh. 2. Ablative of cause. The Greeks had caused the death of a son of Minos, and this led to the war. 3. *Resource.*

THE TRIBUTE TO THE MINOTAUR

240. 1. The wretched men will-suffer punishment. 2. Whither will Minos lead the boys and girls? 3. He-will-lead them [1] to his island. 4. The forces will-wage war with great spirit.

1. Use the masculine form.

GLASS VASES FROM POMPEII

LESSON XXXI

Nōn est ad astra mollis ē terrīs via — Not easy is the way
from the earth to the stars [1]

VERBS IN -*IŌ* OF THE THIRD CONJUGATION

241. Some verbs of the third conjugation do not end in -*ō* like **regō**, but in -*iō*, like **audiō** of the fourth conjugation. The fact that they belong to the third conjugation and not to the fourth is shown by the ending of the infinitive (§ 155). Compare

    audiō, audī're (*hear*), fourth conjugation
    capiō, ca'pere (*take*), third conjugation

242. Observe that **capiō** is inflected like **audiō** throughout the past and future; but that in the present only the forms **capiō** and **capiunt** are like **audiō** and **audiunt**, all the other forms being like corresponding forms of **regō** (cf. **capis, regis**; **capit, regit**; etc.).

1 From Seneca, a Roman philosopher.

capiō, capere (pres. stem cape-), *take*

PRESENT	PAST	FUTURE
1. ca'piō	capiē'bam	ca'piam
2. ca'pis	capiē'bās	ca'piēs
3. ca'pit	capiē'bat	ca'piet
1. ca'pimus	capiēbā'mus	capiē'mus
2. ca'pitis	capiēbā'tis	capiē'tis
3. ca'piunt	capiē'bant	ca'pient

EXERCISES

243. Like capiō, inflect the present, past, and future of faciō, facere, *make, do*.

THĒSEUS ET MĪNŌTAURUS (CONTINUED)

First learn the special vocabulary, page 366

244. Miserī Graecī timent et pārent. Itaque quotannīs (*yearly*) ad Crētam septem pulchrōs puerōs et septem pulchrās puellās mittunt. Numquam posteā fīliōs fīliāsque vident.

Tum Thēseus, clārus hērōs (*hero*) Graecōrum, in patriā nōn erat. Sed mox fāmam miseram audit et in patriam 5 celeriter properat. Populum convocat et dīcit : " Semper, O Graecī, erimus servī? Semper fīliōs fīliāsque ad Crētam mittēmus? Bonum cōnsilium capiam. Minerva, dea sapientiae, auxilium dabit. Mīnōtaurum malum nōn timeō. Cum eō pugnābō et eum vincam." 10

245. 1. We-were-making, they-will-wage, you-are-sending. 2. We-shall-conquer, you-will-take, they-will-make. 3. He-was-waging, we-shall-come, you-hear. 4. They-will-say, he-will-announce, we-shall-make.

LESSON XXXII

Nē cēde malīs — Do not yield to misfortunes [1]

THE IMPERATIVE MOOD · QUESTIONS AND ANSWERS

246. The imperative mood expresses a command: as, *come!* *go! speak!*

247. The Latin imperative has two tenses, the present and future. The present is used more than the future, which is not included in this book.

248. The present imperative is used only in the second person, singular and plural. In the active voice the singular is the same in form as the present stem. The plural is formed by adding -te to the singular.

249.
FIRST CONJUGATION

2. vocā, *call-thou* vocā'te, *call-ye*

SECOND CONJUGATION

2. monē, *advise-thou* monē'te, *advise-ye*

THIRD CONJUGATION

2. rege, *rule-thou* re'gite,[2] *rule-ye*

FOURTH CONJUGATION

2. audī, *hear-thou* audī'te, *hear-ye*

250. The irregular verb **sum** has **es**, *be thou*, and **este**, *be ye*, as present imperatives.

---

[1] From Vergil, author of the Ænē'id, the greatest Latin epic poem.
[2] Note that in the third conjugation e of the stem becomes i before -te.

84

QUESTIONS AND ANSWERS

251. We learned in § 109 that questions might be introduced, as in English, by interrogative pronouns or adverbs : as, **quis ?** *who ?* **ubi ?** *where ?* **quō ?** *whither ?* **cūr ?** *why ?* and that questions expecting the answer *yes* or *no* were often introduced by -ne, the question sign, combined with the first word. But questions expecting the answer *yes* or *no* may take one of three forms :

1. **Venitne ?** *Is he coming ?* (Asking for information.)
2. **Nōnne venit ?** *Is he not coming ?* (Expecting the answer *yes*.)
3. **Num venit ?** *He isn't coming, is he ?* (Expecting the answer *no*.)

252. We learned in § 110 that *yes*-or-*no* questions are usually answered by repeating the verb, with or without a negative. Instead of this, **ita, vērō, certē,** etc. (*so, truly, certainly,* etc.) may be used for *yes* ; and **nōn, minimē,** etc. for *no* if the denial is an emphatic *by no means, not at all,* or the like.

Num via longa est ? Minimē. *The road isn't long, is it ? Not at all.*

EXERCISES

253. Give the present imperative of the following verbs : **faciō, veniō, gerō, pateō, servō.**

THĒSEUS ET MĪNŌTAURUS (CONTINUED)

First learn the special vocabulary, page 366

254. Tum Thēseus nāvigium celeriter parat et ad īnsulam Crētam nāvigat. Cum[1] ad ōram altam venit, ex nāvigiō properat et terram petit. Eum Ariadnē,[2] fīlia rēgīnae, videt. Tum eum vocat et dīcit : " Quis es, bone vir[3] ? Quid in patriā meā petis ? Nōnne Graecus es ? Crēta est inimīca 5 Graecīs et vīta tua est in perīculō." Thēseus respondet :

"Thēseus sum, Graecōrum hērōs (*hero*), nōtus fāmā [4] meā per multās terrās. Mīnōtaurum petō. Cum [1] eō pugnābō. Eum vincam. Nōnne Thēseō auxilium dabis?" Tum Ariadnē, clārā fāmā et magnō animō Thēseī commōta (*moved*), 10 eum amat et respondet: "Num barbara sum? Vītam tuam servābō. Cape arma et venī."

1. The conjunction **cum**, *when*, and the preposition **cum**, *with*, though alike, are easily distinguished, as **cum**, *with*, is followed by the ablative case. 2. Pronounce in English *A-ri-ad'ne*. 3. *Good sir.* 4. Ablative of cause.

255. 1. Nūntiā, mūnīte, mitte. 2. Pete, venī, nāvigāte. 3. Servāte, mūnī, tenē. 4. Vidēte, portā, mittite.

<hr>

Fourth Review, Lessons XXIV–XXXII, §§ 749–754

THE APPIAN WAY AND THE CLAUDIAN AQUEDUCT

The Romans excelled as engineers and builders. A system of splendid roads connected the capital with the different parts of the Empire. "All roads lead to Rome" was literally true. The Appian Way extended southeast to Brundisium, the great commercial port for the East. Equally famous were the aqueducts, bringing the city an abundant water supply

LESSON XXXIII

Accipere quam facere iniūriam praestat — It is better to suffer a wrong than to do one [1]

PRESENT INDICATIVE PASSIVE OF THE FIRST CONJUGATION

256. Passive Voice. The passive voice (§ 141) uses a different set of personal endings from those of the active. The present indicative passive of **vocō** is inflected as follows:

vo'cō, vocā're (pres. stem vocā-), *call*

	PERSONAL ENDINGS
1. vo'cor, *I-am-called*	-r or -or
2. vocā'ris or -re, *you-are-called*	-ris or -re
3. vocā'tur, *he-, she-, it-is-called*	-tur
1. vocā'mur, *we-are-called*	-mur
2. vocā'minī, *you-are-called*	-minī
3. vocā'ntur, *they-are-called*	-ntur

a. The letter **r**, which appears in all but one of the personal endings, is sometimes called the passive sign.

b. A long vowel is shortened before final -r or -ntur.

c. The forms **vocor** etc. may be translated either *I am called* etc. or *I am being called* etc.

EXERCISES

257. Like **vocor**, inflect **amor, servor, nūntior, portor, superor.**

258. Derivation. The prefix **con-** (**com-, co-**), identical with the preposition **cum** (*with*), added to simple verbs makes many compounds both in Latin and English. This prefix sometimes

---

[1] From Cicero, Rome's greatest orator and man of letters.

87

means *with* or *together*, and sometimes strengthens the simple verb with the meaning *completely, forcibly*. What is the force of this prefix in the following words?

contain (teneō)	*compete* (petō)	*conserve* (servō)
convoke (convocō)	*convince* (vincō)	*conduct* (dūcō)
collaborate[1] (labōrō)	*convene* (veniō)	*commit* (mittō)

1. The final letter of the prefix is often assimilated (*made like*) to the first letter of the simple verb.

THĒSEUS ET MĪNŌTAURUS (Concluded)

First learn the special vocabulary, page 366. Read the story as a whole

259. Tum Ariadnē Thēseum in nōtum labyrinthum indūcit et eī longum fīlum (*string*) dat et dīcit: "Tenē id fīlum.

Fīlum vēstīgia (*steps*) tua reget[1] et ex labyrinthō tē (*you*) ēdūcet. Nunc pro- 5 perā. Mīnōtaurum audiō. Num timēs? Eī fortiter resiste et clāra erit victōria tua. Vince et servā vītam puerōrum puellārumque 10 Graeciae." Mox Thēseus Mīnōtaurum videt et petit.[2] Diū pugnātur[3] nec sine magnō perīculō. Dēnique Mīnōtaurus su- 15 perātur, et posteā puerī puellaeque servantur.

PUERĪ PUELLAEQUE THĒSEUM AMANT
From a Pompeian wall painting

1. *Guide.* 2. *Attack.* 3. The form **pugnātur** means *it is fought*; translate freely, *the battle is fought* or *the contest rages*. The verb **pugnō** in Latin is intransitive, and so has no personal subject in the passive. A verb with an indeterminate subject is called impersonal, as in English *it rains*.

LESSON XXXIV

Terrās irradient — Let them illumine the earth [1]

PRESENT INDICATIVE PASSIVE OF *MONEŌ* · ABLATIVE OF THE PERSONAL AGENT

260. The present indicative passive of the second conjugation is inflected as follows:

mo'neō, monē're (pres. stem monē-), *advise*

	PERSONAL ENDINGS
1. mo'neor, *I-am-advised*	-r or -or
2. monē'ris or -re, *you-are-advised*	-ris or -re
3. monē'tur, *he-, she-, it-is-advised*	-tur
1. monē'mur, *we-are-advised*	-mur
2. monē'minī, *you-are-advised*	-minī
3. monen'tur, *they-are-advised*	-ntur

261. **Rule for Ablative of Personal Agent.** *The ablative with the preposition ā or ab is used with passive verbs to indicate the person by whom the act is performed.*

Puerī ā Rōmānīs servantur, *the boys are saved by the Romans*

NOTE. The literal meaning of ā Rōmānīs is *from the Romans*, but in our idiom *by the Romans* is a better translation.

262. **Ablative of Means and Ablative of Agent Compared.** Compare the two sentences:

Puerī ā Rōmānīs servantur, *the boys are saved by the Romans*
Puerī nāvigiō servantur, *the boys are saved by* (or *with*) *a boat*

In the first sentence ā Rōmānīs is the ablative of personal agent; in the second nāvigiō is the ablative of means. To

---

[1] Motto of Amherst College.

aid in distinguishing these two constructions, which are often confused, observe the following facts :

a. The agent is a *person* ; the means is a *thing*.

b. The ablative of personal agent has the preposition **ā** or **ab** ; the ablative of means has no preposition.

c. The ablative of personal agent is used only with a passive verb; with the ablative of means the verb may be either active or passive.

EXERCISES

263. Like **moneor**, inflect **habeor, teneor, timeor, videor.**

264. 1. Superāris, habēmur, videntur. 2. Tenētur, occupāminī, timēmur. 3. Vidēris, parantur, tenēminī. 4. Servātur, habētur, tenēmur. 5. Portāminī, habēris, teneor.

265. 1. Gallī crēbra proelia faciunt et fortiter pugnant, sed ā fīnitimīs superantur. 2. Mīnōtaurus ā fīliābus eōrum timētur. 3. Num Thēseus Mīnōtaurum barbarum timet ? Nōn timet. 4. Capite arma, Rōmānī ; ā barbarīs inimīcīs vidēminī. 5. Nec frūmentum nec aquam in castrīs habēmus. Quid faciēmus ? 6. Tenē castra, Mārce, bonīs tēlīs. Iam (*soon*) sociī nostrī auxilium mittent.

266. 1. The Gauls are quickly conquered by-the-arms of-the-Romans. 2. Are not pleasing stories told by many poets ? Yes. 3. Theseus is-advised by Minerva, the goddess of-wisdom. 4. By-the-wisdom of-Minerva we-are-saved. 5. Give that money to-the-good queen, my son. 6. The camp of-the-savages has neither wall nor ditch. 7. When we-are-seen by your men, we-shall-suffer punishment.

LESSON XXXV

Salvē! — Hail[1]

THE PAST AND FUTURE INDICATIVE PASSIVE OF THE FIRST AND SECOND CONJUGATIONS

267. The tense signs of the past and future passive are the same as in the active. The inflection of **vocō** and **moneō** in these two tenses is as follows:

vo'cō, vocā're (pres. stem vocā-), *call*

PAST INDICATIVE PASSIVE (TENSE SIGN -bā-)

	PERSONAL ENDINGS
1. vocā'bar, *I-was-called*[2]	-r
2. vocābā'ris or -re, *you-were-called*	-ris or -re
3. vocābā'tur, *he-, she-, it-was-called*	-tur
1. vocābā'mur, *we-were-called*	-mur
2. vocābā'minī, *you-were-called*	-minī
3. vocāban'tur, *they-were-called*	-ntur

FUTURE INDICATIVE PASSIVE (TENSE SIGN -bi-)

1. vocā'bor, *I-shall-be-called*	-r
2. vocā'beris or -re, *you-will-be-called*	-ris or -re
3. vocā'bitur, *he-, she-, it-will-be-called*	-tur
1. vocā'bimur, *we-shall-be-called*	-mur
2. vocābi'minī, *you-will-be-called*	-minī
3. vocābun'tur, *they-will-be-called*	-ntur

[1] Motto of the state of Idaho.
[2] Or *I-was-being-called*, etc. Thus for all verbs in the past indicative passive.

91

mo'neō, monē're (pres. stem monē-), *advise*

PAST INDICATIVE PASSIVE (TENSE SIGN -bā-)

		PERSONAL ENDINGS
1.	monē'bar, *I-was-advised*	-r
2.	monēbā'ris or -re, *you-were-advised*	-ris or -re
3.	monēbā'tur, *he-, she-, it-was-advised*	-tur
1.	monēbā'mur, *we-were-advised*	-mur
2.	monēbā'minī, *you-were-advised*	-minī
3.	monēban'tur, *they-were-advised*	-ntur

FUTURE INDICATIVE PASSIVE (TENSE SIGN -bi-)

1.	monē'bor, *I-shall-be-advised*	-r
2.	monē'beris or -re, *you-will-be-advised*	-ris or -re
3.	monē'bitur, *he-, she-, it-will-be-advised*	-tur
1.	monē'bimur, *we-shall-be-advised*	-mur
2.	monēbi'minī, *you-will-be-advised*	-minī
3.	monēbun'tur, *they-will-be-advised*	-ntur

a. In the future passive the tense sign -bi- appears as -bo- in the first and as -be- in the second person singular, and as -bu- in the third person plural.

EXERCISES

268. Inflect the following verbs in the present, past, and future, active and passive: amō, nūntiō, portō, teneō, videō, timeō.

269. 1. Amābās, amābāris, timēbis, timēberis. 2. Servat, servātur, dabit, dabitur. 3. Portāmus, portābāmus, portābimus. 4. Dabiminī, vidēbuntur, tenēmur. 5. Amantur, dabātur, timentur. 6. Vidēris, nūntiāmus, timēbat. 7. Tenent, timēbunt, monēris. 8. Vidēbant, amābiminī, portāmur. 9. Venīte, timē.

270. 1. They-will-be-feared, I-am-loved, we-were-seen. 2. We-are-carried, you-will-be-advised (*plur.*), they-have. 3. He-will-hasten, you-were-announcing (*sing.*), he-persuades. 4. I-shall-injure, you-favor (*sing.*), you-will-be-overcome (*plur.*). 5. We-shall-be-carried, I-was-eager-for, you-will-favor (*sing.*). 6. He-will-obey, we-are-held, they-were-seen.

ROMAN SWORDS

LESSON XXXVI

In mediās rēs — Into the midst of things [1]

THE PRESENT INDICATIVE PASSIVE OF THE THIRD AND FOURTH CONJUGATIONS

271. The present indicative passive of **re′gō** (third conjugation) and **au′diō** (fourth conjugation) are inflected as follows:

re′gō, re′gere (pres. stem **rege-**), *rule*

1. re′gor, *I-am-ruled*   re′gimur, *we-are-ruled*
2. re′geris or -re, *you-are-ruled* regi′minī, *you-are-ruled*
3. re′gitur, *he-, she-, it-is-ruled* regun′tur, *they-are-ruled*

au′diō, audī′re (pres. stem **audī-**), *hear*

1. au′dior, *I-am-heard*   audī′mur, *we-are-heard*
2. audī′ris or -re, *you-are-heard* audī′minī, *you-are-heard*
3. audī′tur, *he-, she-, it-is-heard* audiun′tur, *they-are-heard*

a. Observe the changes of the final stem vowel -e in the third conjugation. It appears unchanged only in the second person singular: as, re′ge-ris or re′ge-re.

[1] From Horace, Rome's greatest lyric poet.

EXERCISES

272. Like **regō**, inflect the present active and passive of **dūcō**, **vincō**, and **gerō**.

273. Like **audiō**, inflect the present active and passive of **mūniō**.

274. 1. Tenēberis, dīcitur, habēbāminī. 2. Superābitur, mūniuntur, geritur. 3. Mūnītur, parābit, vincite.

RŌMĀNĪ MAGNUM NUMERUM CAPTĪVŌRUM CAPIUNT

DĒ BELLĪS RŌMĀNŌRUM ET GALLŌRUM

First learn the special vocabulary, page 366

275. Cum bella in Galliā ā Rōmānīs geruntur, castra eōrum lātīs fossīs vāllīsque altīs celeriter mūniuntur. Tum cōpiae ex portīs (*gates*) castrōrum ēdūcuntur, sed castra fīrmō praesidiō tenentur. Saepe Rōmānī proelia in mediīs silvīs faciunt, saepe diū pugnātur[1]; sed dēnique barbarī bonīs 5 armīs Rōmānōrum vincuntur. Rōmānī magnum numerum captīvōrum capiunt. In numerō captīvōrum multī puerī puellaeque videntur. Captīvī ā Rōmānīs in Italiam indūcuntur. Ibi erunt scrvī miserī nec posteā patriam vidēbunt.

1. See § 259, note 3.

I AM A FIRM BELIEVER IN THE VALUE OF STUDYING GREEK AND LATIN. ALTHOUGH IN AFTER LIFE ONE MAY FORGET MUCH THAT HE HAS LEARNED, HE CAN NEVER LOSE THE INFLUENCE UPON HIS CHARACTER. — ELIHU ROOT, FORMER SECRETARY OF STATE

LESSON XXXVII

Repetītiŏ est māter studiōrum — Repetition is the mother of learning

THE PAST AND FUTURE INDICATIVE PASSIVE OF *REGŌ* AND *AUDĪŌ*

276. The past and future indicative passive of **regō** (third conjugation) and **audiō** (fourth conjugation) are inflected as follows :

re'gō, re'gere (pres. stem **rege-**), *rule*

PAST INDICATIVE PASSIVE (TENSE SIGN -bā-)

1. regē'bar, *I-was-ruled*   regēbā'mur, *we-were-ruled*
2. regēbā'ris or -re, *you-were-ruled* regēbā'minī, *you-were-ruled*
3. regēbā'tur, *he-, she-, it-was-ruled* regēban'tur, *they-were-ruled*

FUTURE INDICATIVE PASSIVE (TENSE SIGNS -a- and -ē-)

1. re'gar, *I-shall-be-ruled*   regē'mur, *we-shall-be-ruled*
2. regē'ris or -re, *you-will-be-ruled* regē'minī, *you-will-be-ruled*
3. regē'tur, *he-, she-, it-will-be-ruled* regen'tur, *they-will-be-ruled*

au'diō, audī're (pres. stem audī-), *hear*

PAST INDICATIVE PASSIVE (Tense Sign -bā-)

1. audiē'bar, *I-was-heard*
2. audiēbā'ris or -re, *you-were-heard*
3. audiēbā'tur, *he-, she-, it-was-heard*

1. audiēbā'mur, *we-were-heard*
2. audiēbā'minī, *you-were-heard*
3. audiēban'tur, *they-were-heard*

FUTURE INDICATIVE PASSIVE (Tense Signs -a- and -ē-)

1. au'diar, *I-shall-be-heard*
2. audiē'ris or -re, *you-will-be-heard*
3. audiē'tur, *he-, she-, it-will-be-heard*

1. audiē'mur, *we-shall-be-heard*
2. audiē'minī, *you-will-be-heard*
3. audien'tur, *they-will-be-heard*

EXERCISES

277. Like **regō**, inflect the present, past, and future, active and passive, of **dūcō**, **vincō**, and **gerō**.[1]

278. Like **audiō**, inflect the present, past, and future, active and passive, of **mūniō**.

279. 1. Dūcēbās, dūcēbāris, mūniēs, mūniēris.   2. Vincit, vincet, veniet, mūniētur.   3. Gerēbāmus, gerēbāmur, gerimus, gerēmus.   4. Dūcēminī, regiminī, audiēbantur.   5. Amābunt, nocēbunt, venient, mūnientur.   6. Timēris, mūnīmus, veniēmus,

---

[1] Extend the blank scheme (§748) of verb inflection to include the first three tenses of the passive voice, and use it for self-drill with a variety of verbs. *You cannot know verbs too well.*

capiunt. 7. Persuādent, tenēbunt, vidēberis, audientur. 8. Geruntur, gerēbātur, geritur. 9. Pārēmus, parāmur, nocēbunt, mūniēminī.

280. 1. They-are-sent, they-will-be-conquered, I-am heard, we-were-led. 2. We-are-sent, you-will-be-fortified (*sing.*), they-come. 3. He-will-resist, you-seek (*sing.*), you-will-be-conquered (*plur.*). 4. You-were-believing (*sing.*), he-carried-on, I shall-come. 5. We-shall-be-heard, I-was-leading, you-will-seek (*plur.*). 6. He-will-carry-on, we-are-fortified, they-were-carried-on.

LESSON XXXVIII

Deō, amīcīs, patriae — For God, for friends, for country

I mpYrfect

THE PRESENT, ~~PAST~~, AND FUTURE INDICATIVE PASSIVE OF *CAPIŌ*

281. The present indicative passive of **capiō** (cf. § 242) is inflected like **regor**, except the two forms **capior** and **capiuntur**, which are like **audior** and **audiuntur**. The past and future throughout are inflected like **audiēbar** and **audiar**.

PRESENT PASSIVE	PAST PASSIVE	FUTURE PASSIVE
1. ca'pior	capiē'bar	ca'piar
2. ca'peris or -re	capiēbā'ris or -re	capiē'ris or -re
3. ca'pitur	capiēbā'tur	capiē'tur
1. ca'pimur	capiēbā'mur	capiē'mur
2. capi'minī	capiēbā'minī	capiē'minī
3. capiun'tur	capiēban'tur	capien'tur

EXERCISES

282. Like **capiō**, inflect **rapiō**, *seize*, in the present, past, and future, active and passive.

DĒ LŪDŌ¹ RŌMĀNŌ

First learn the special vocabulary, page 367

283. Spectāte, amīcī meī, pictūram (*picture*) lūdī Rōmānī.
Vidētisne discipulōs (*pupils*)? Sunt ūnus,² duo, trēs, quattuor, quīnque, sex discipulī. Duo puerī stant (*are standing*)
et quattuor sedent. Quid puerī faciunt? Labōrant magnā
dīligentiā. Duo tenent tabellās.³ Trēs tenent librōs. Librī 5

Rōmānōrum erant volūmina (*rolls*). In subselliō (*bench*)
sunt duo librī et trēs tabellae³ et ātrāmentum (*ink*). Spectāte
magistrum (*teacher*). Quid facit? Magister discipulīs fābulam
nārrat. Magister multās et grātās fābulās in memoriā habet.
Cum puerī sunt tardī, tum poenam dant. Sed bonīs puerīs prae- 10
mia pulchra ā magistrō dantur. Amātisne praemia? Certē.

1. Latin has two words for school, **lūdus**, an elementary school, and
schola, an advanced school or college for adults. 2. *One.* The next five
numerals follow. Learn to count six in Latin. 3. *Writing tablets.* These
were thin boards smeared with wax (cf. picture, p. 7). The writing was done
with a **stilus**, a pointed instrument, like a pencil, made of bone or metal.

LESSON XXXIX

Dum spīrō, spērō — While I breathe, I hope[1]

THE PRESENT INFINITIVE AND THE PRESENT IMPERATIVE, ACTIVE AND PASSIVE

284. Infinitive Defined. The infinitive is a verbal noun, giving the general meaning of the verb without person or number : as, **amāre**, *to love.*

285. Present Infinitive. The present infinitive active is formed by adding -re to the present stem (§ 154). The present infinitive passive may be formed from the active by changing final -e to -ī, except in the third conjugation, which changes final -ere to -ī.

Conj.	Pres. Stem	Pres. Inf. Active	Pres. Inf. Passive
I	vocā-	vocā're, *to-call*	vocā'rī, *to-be-called*
II	monē-	monē're, *to-advise*	monē'rī, *to-be-advised*
III	rege-	re'gere, *to-rule*	re'gī, *to-be-ruled*
IV	audī-	audī're, *to-hear*	audī'rī, *to-be-heard*

a. The present infinitive of **sum** is **esse**. There is no passive.

286. Present Imperative. The active forms of the present imperative, already given in § 249, are repeated below for comparison with the passive forms. The present imperative passive ends in -re in the singular and in -minī in the plural. Thus the singular of the passive imperative is like the present active infinitive, and the plural is like the second person plural of the present indicative passive.

[1] Closing words of the motto of the state of South Carolina. Free translation, " While there 's life, there 's hope."

99

ACTIVE IMPERATIVE

CONJ.   I   vo'cā, *call-thou*   vocā'te, *call-ye*
        II   mo'nē, *advise-thou*   monē'te, *advise-ye*
        III re'ge, *rule-thou*   re'gite, *rule-ye*
        IV   au'dī, *hear-thou*   audī'te, *hear-ye*

PASSIVE IMPERATIVE

CONJ.   I   vocā're, *be-thou-called*   vocā'minī, *be-ye-called*
        II   monē're, *be-thou-advised*   monē'minī, *be-ye-advised*
        III re'gere, *be-thou-ruled*   regi'minī, *be-ye-ruled*
        IV   audī're, *be-thou-heard*   audī'minī, *be-ye-heard*

EXERCISES

287. Give the active and passive present infinitives of nārrō, rapiō, mūniō, respondeō, parō, gerō, videō, spectō, dūcō, vincō.

288. Give the imperative active of dīcō,[1] dūcō, faciō, nūntiō, veniō, crēdō, noceō, faveō, resistō, sedeō.

289. Give the imperative passive of nārrō, rapiō, portō, petō, occupō, vincō, servō, timeō, mūniō, videō.

290. 1. Hasten-thou, to-be-prepared, be-ye-sent, lead-thou. 2. To-lead, to-be-led, be-ye-seized, come-thou. 3. To-be-sent, to-save, lead-ye, speak-thou. 4. To-be-sought, be-ye-led, to-seize, to-be-held. 5. Fear-thou, come-ye, be-ye-prepared, to-be-fortified.

[1] The verbs dīcō, dūcō, and faciō have dīc, dūc, and fac in the singular of the present imperative active. The plural is formed regularly: dīcite, etc.

LESSON XL

Melius esse quam vidērī — Better to be than to seem [1]

SYNOPSES IN THE FOUR CONJUGATIONS

291. Learn to give rapidly the synopses of the verbs you have had, in any person or number, following the model given below:

FIRST CONJUGATION   SECOND CONJUGATION

INDICATIVE

	ACTIVE	PASSIVE	ACTIVE	PASSIVE
PRES.	vo'cō	vo'cor	mo'neō	mo'neor
PAST	vocā'bam	vocā'bar	monē'bam	monē'bar
FUT.	voca'bō	vocā'bor	monē'bō	monē'bor

IMPERATIVE

PRES.	vo'cā	vocā're	mo'nē	monē're

INFINITIVE

PRES.	vocā're	vocā'rī	monē're	monē'rī

THIRD CONJUGATION   THIRD CONJUGATION (-iō verbs)

INDICATIVE

	ACTIVE	PASSIVE	ACTIVE	PASSIVE
PRES.	re'gō	re'gor	ca'piō	ca'pior
PAST	regē'bam	regē'bar	capiē'bam	capiē'bar
FUT.	re'gam	re'gar	ca'piam	ca'piar

[1] Motto of the state of North Carolina, adapted from Sallust.

IMPERATIVE

PRES.   re'ge   re'gere   ca'pe   ca'pere

INFINITIVE

PRES.   re'gere   re'gī   ca'pere   ca'pī

Fourth Conjugation

INDICATIVE

ACTIVE		PASSIVE
PRES.	au'diō	au'dior
PAST	audiē'bam	audiē'bar
FUT.	au'diam	au'diar

IMPERATIVE

PRES.   au'dī   audī're

INFINITIVE

PRES.   audī're   audī'rī

DĒ MALŌ MAGISTRŌ LŪDĪ

First learn the special vocabulary, page 367.

292. Ōlim (*once upon a time*) Rōmānī cum fīnitimō oppidō
bellum gerēbant. Camillus, vir clārus, cōpiās Rōmānās
dūcēbat. In eō oppidō erat quīdam magister lūdī.[1] Eum
puerī amābant et virī oppidī eī[2] crēdēbant. Saepe magister
puerōs ex oppidō per agrōs proximōs ēdūcēbat, nec puerī in 5
perīculō erant, nam oppidum ā Rōmānīs nōndum (*not yet*)
oppugnābātur. Sed dēnique magister puerōs in media castra
Rōmāna indūcit et dīcit: " Spectā, Camille, eōs puerōs. Eī
erunt captīvī tuī." Sed Camillus dīcit: " Malum animum,

magister, habēs. Nōn cum puerīs Rōmānī bellum gerunt." 10 Tum suīs[3] dīcit, "Rapite et ligāte (*bind*) eum." Tum puerīs virgās (*rods*) dat et dīcit, "Iam agite, puerī meī, eīs

MALUS MAGISTER LŪDĪ POENAM DAT

virgīs eum malum magistrum in oppidum vestrum." Id factum erat grātum virīs eius oppidī et mox amīcitiam Rōmae petunt.   15

1. **quīdam magister lūdī**, *a school teacher.* 2. **eī**, dative with **crēdēbant** (§ 224). 3. *To his men.*

293. Derivation. What is the meaning of the following English words and to what Latin words are they related?

dictate	clarify	capacity	repeat	retard
regulate	regent	factory	sediment	rapture

Fifth Review, Lessons XXXIII–XL, §§ 755-761

LESSON XLI

Equō nē crēdite — Do not trust the horse[1]

THE ABLATIVE DENOTING *FROM*

294. One of the relations covered by the ablative case is expressed in English by the preposition *from* (cf. § 65). This relation is represented in Latin by a number of special constructions. One of these, the *ablative of personal agent*, has been already discussed (§ 261). Two others of importance are the *ablative of the place from*, many instances of which have occurred in the preceding exercises, and the *ablative of separation*.

295. Rule for Ablative of Place From. *The place from which is expressed by the ablative with the prepositions* **ā** (*ab*), **dē**, **ē** (*ex*).

Agricolae ex agrīs veniunt, *the farmers come from the fields*

a. **Ā** or **ab** denotes *from near* a place ; **ē** or **ex**, *out from* it ; and **dē**, *down from* it. This may be represented graphically as follows :

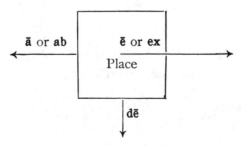

---

[1] This is taken from Vergil's Æneid, and refers to the famous wooden horse by means of which the Greeks took Troy after they had besieged it in vain for ten years. Used in a general way, the expression is a warning against the tricks of an enemy.

296. Rule for Ablative of Separation. *Words express-*
ing separation or taking away are followed by the abla-
tive, often with the prepositions ā (ab), dē, ē (ex).

1. Thēseus patriam ā Mīnōtaurō līberat, *Theseus frees his country*
from the Minotaur
2. Thēseus patriam perīculō līberat, *Theseus frees his country*
from peril

a. When there is actual separation of one material thing from
another, as in 1, the preposition is usually present. When the separation is figurative, as in 2, the preposition is usually omitted.

EXERCISES

First learn the special vocabulary, page 367

297. 1. Gallī crēbrīs proeliīs Germānōs ab agrīs suīs pro-
hibēbunt. 2. Factō[1] Camillī puerī ex castrīs Rōmānīs celeriter
dīmittentur. 3. Ibi ab amīcīs suīs longē aberant. 4. Memoria
eius factī animīs nostrīs numquam longē aberit. 5. Cūr vir
malus puerōs ā mūrīs oppidī abdūcit? 6. Vir malus amīcitiam
Camillī petēbat. 7. Lībera fīliōs nostrōs perīculō, Camille.
8. Certē eōs līberābō et vir malus poenam dabit. 9. Factō[1]
malō eum ex castrīs meīs agam.

1. Ablative of cause.

298. 1. The Roman camp was far distant from that place.
2. We shall be freed from the memory of those wrongs. 3. Depart from this place, my friends, and attack their towns. 4. My
men will lead them away from the walls. 5. Keep[1] the savages
out of your towns, Romans. 6. Seize that man, my son, and
send him away. 7. The boys are not dull, are they[2]?

1. Imperative of **prohibeō**. 2. Review § 251.

Nōn or.ɪne quod nitet aurum est — All is not gold that glitters

PRINCIPAL PARTS · VERB STEMS · THE PERFECT STEM
THE ENDINGS OF THE PERFECT

299. Principal Parts. Certain forms of the verb are important because we cannot inflect the verb without knowing them. These are called the *principal parts*.

In English, the principal parts are the present indicative, the past indicative, and the past participle : as, *go, went, gone.*

In Latin, the principal parts are the first person singular of the present indicative, the present infinitive, the first person singular of the perfect indicative, and the past participle : as,

| vo'cō | vocā're | vocā'vī | vocā'tus |

300. Verb Stems. From the principal parts we get three verb stems, from which we construct the entire conjugation. These are the *present stem*, formed from the present infinitive (§ 154), the *perfect stem*, and the *participial stem*.

301. The *perfect stem* is found by dropping final -ī from the first person singular of the perfect : as, **vocāv-** from **vocā'vī,** perfect of **vocō.**

302. The *participial stem* is found by dropping final -us from the past participle : as, **vocāt-** from **vocā'tus,** past participle of **vocō.**

303. From the perfect stem are formed
>The Perfect Indicative Active
>The Past Perfect Indicative Active
>The Future Perfect Indicative Active

304. Endings of the Perfect. The perfect is inflected by adding the following endings to the perfect stem :

1. -ī, *I*   -imus, *we*
2. -istī, *you*   -istis, *you*
3. -it, *he, she, it*   -ērunt or -ēre, *they*

The endings of the perfect are different from those found in any other tense. They are the same in all conjugations.

305. Practically all the verbs of the first conjugation have regular principal parts : as,

vo'cō   vocā're   vocā'vī   vocā'tus

Following the model, give the principal parts of **amō, nārrō, portō, parō, occupō, pugnō, superō, spectō, līberō.**

EXERCISES

First learn the special vocabulary, page 367

306. 1. Barbarī magnam cōpiam frūmentī comparābunt et ex agrīs suīs discēdent. 2. Multa oppida fīnitimōrum oppugnābunt. 3. Ea oppida mūrīs altīs et fossīs lātīs mūniuntur et fortiter dēfendentur. 4. Quam longē ab Italiā absunt ea oppida? Nōn longē absunt. 5. Nōnne Rōmānī auxilium ad ea oppida mittent? Certē, nam populī eōrum oppidōrum sunt sociī Rōmānōrum. 6. Amplae cōpiae Rōmānōrum animōs timidōs sociōrum cōnfīrmābunt. 7. Rōmānī firma praesidia in eīs oppidīs locābunt. 8. Itaque barbarī iniūriīs prohibēbuntur et cōpiās suās dīmittent.

307. 1. The cowardly allies will be defended by the Romans. 2. How far distant were those places[1] from their[2] camp? 3. Prepare an abundant supply[3] of grain, Marcus, and place it in our town. 4. Because of the memory[4] of your deeds, we shall be neither slow nor cowardly. 5. Their[2] hearts were encouraged, and so they seized their arms and bravely assaulted the lofty walls. 6. Why are you sitting there? Depart and quickly free those captives.

1. What is there irregular about the plural of **locus**? 2. Not **suus** (cf. §§ 135, 209). 3. **cōpia.** 4. Ablative of cause.

LESSON XLIII

Dīmidium factī est coepisse — Well begun is half done[1]

THE PERFECT, PAST PERFECT, AND FUTURE PERFECT INDICATIVE OF *SUM*

308. The irregular verb **sum** is inflected in the perfect, past perfect, and future perfect indicative as follows:

PRIN. PARTS: **sum, esse, fuī** (perf. stem **fu-**)

PERFECT

fu'ī, *I have been, I was*	**fu'imus,** *we have been, we were*
fuis'tī, *you have been, you were*	**fuis'tis,** *you have been, you were*
fu'it, *he has been, he was*	**fuē'runt** or **fuē're,** *they have been, they were*

PAST PERFECT (TENSE SIGN **-erā-**)

fu'eram, *I had been*	**fuerā'mus,** *we had been*
fu'erās, *you had been*	**fuerā'tis,** *you had been*
fu'erat, *he had been*	**fu'erant,** *they had been*

FUTURE PERFECT (TENSE SIGN **-eri-**)

fu'erō, *I shall have been*	**fue'rimus,** *we shall have been*
fu'eris, *you will have been*	**fue'ritis,** *you will have been*
fu'erit, *he will have been*	**fu'erint,** *they will have been*

[1] From Horace, the greatest Roman lyric poet and still the most widely read. The literal translation of the Latin is *Half of an achievement is to have begun it.*

a. The past perfect may be formed by adding **eram**, the past of **sum**, to the perfect stem. The tense sign is **-erā-**.

b. The future perfect may be formed by adding **erō**, the future of **sum**, to the perfect stem. But the third person plural ends in **-erint**, not **-erunt**. The tense sign is **-eri-**.

c. The perfect, past perfect, and future perfect of all active verbs are formed on the perfect stem. They are all inflected like **sum**.

SEXTUS, QUĪNTUS, MĀRCUS

First learn the special vocabulary, page 367

309. MĀRCUS. Ubi fuistis, Sexte et Quīnte?

SEXTUS. Ego (*I*) in nostrā vīllā fuī, et Quīntus in suā vīllā fuit. Diū in agrīs nostrīs fuimus. Officia agricolārum sunt multa. Habēsne bonōs servōs?

M. Habeō. Diū exempla ēgregiae dīligentiae fuērunt. Eīs ampla praemia mox dabō et eōs līberābō.

S. Sine sapientiā fueris. Tenē bonōs servōs et līberā eōs numquam. Sed quid spectās, Quīnte?

QUĪNTUS. Spectō eum pulchrum librum. Estne tuus?

M. Meus est. Semper bonīs librīs[1] studēbam. Is liber erat Galbae[2] et iam diū in casā suā erat. Liber est nōtus et de bellīs Rōmānōrum Gallōrumque nārrat. Dēnique Gallī pācantur, sed iam per septem[3] annōs Rōmānī in Galliā fuerant.

1. Dative. See § 224. 2. Genitive of the possessor, § 150. 3. Can you count seven in Latin?

310. 1. Where had the farmers been? They had been on their farms. 2. Have you not been examples of remarkable industry, O slaves? Yes. 3. Soon, Romans, we shall have been in Gaul for[1] seven years. 4. How long[2] have we been absent from our duties? 5. Finally the Gauls will be subdued, but they will have been neither stupid nor cowardly. 6. Encourage the loyal hearts of their[3] allies with an abundant supply of money.

1. **per.** 2. Distinguish between **quam diū,** *how long,* and **quam longē,** *how far.* 3. Not **suus** (cf. §§ 135, 209).

LESSON XLIV

Nōn ministrārī, sed ministrāre — Not to be ministered unto,
but to minister [1]

USE AND INFLECTION OF THE PERFECT INDICATIVE ACTIVE

311. Use of the Perfect. The perfect indicative has two distinct meanings; according to its translation, it is called the *present perfect* or the *past absolute*.

312. As *present perfect*, the perfect is translated by the English present perfect with *have*, and denotes the action as completed at the time of speaking: as, *I have now finished my work.*

313. As *past absolute*, the perfect is translated by the English past tense, and denotes that the action took place sometime in the past: as, *I finished my work.*

314. Translation of the English Past. The English past is expressed sometimes by the Latin perfect and sometimes by the Latin past. In telling a story the perfect is used to mark its successive forward steps, and the past to describe past situations and past circumstances that attended those steps.

What tenses would be used in a Latin translation of the following passage?

> I sailed the seas for many years. Once a school of whales surrounded our ship. The whales were swimming slowly along and were not terrified by our presence. Spouts of water arose on every side and some of the passengers were greatly alarmed. Then the monsters suddenly vanished.

[1] Motto of Wellesley College.

315. Inflection of the Perfect. The perfect indicative active of the four conjugations is inflected like **fuī** (cf. § 308), and is as follows :

FIRST CONJUGATION

vocā'vī (perf. stem **vocāv-**),
I have called, I called

1. vocā'vī   vocā'vimus
2. vocāvis'tī   vocāvis'tis
3. vocā'vit   vocāvē'runt or -ē're

SECOND CONJUGATION

mo'nuī (perf. stem **monu-**),
I have advised, I advised

mo'nuī   monu'imus
monuis'tī   monuis'tis
mo'nuit   monuē'runt or -ē're

THIRD CONJUGATION

rē'xī (perf. stem **rēx-**),
I have ruled, I ruled

1. re'xī   rē'ximus
2. rēxis'tī   rēxis'tis
3. rē'xit   rēxē'runt or -ē're

FOURTH CONJUGATION

audī'vī (perf. stem **audīv-**),
I have heard, I heard

audī'vī   audī'vimus
audīvis'tī   audīvis'tis
audī'vit   audīvē'runt or -ē're

a. In vocabularies the first person of the perfect is always given as the third of the principal parts. Principal parts must be learned thoroughly. With principal parts and the rules for tense formation well in mind, the conjugation of verbs becomes easy.

EXERCISES

316. Nearly all perfects of the first conjugation are formed by adding **-vī** to the present stem. Like **vocā'vī**, inflect **amā'vī**, **nārrā'vī**, **pācā'vī**.

317. Like **monuī**, inflect **habuī, tenuī, patuī**.

318. Like **rēxī**, inflect **dīxī** (perfect of **dīcō**), **dūxī** (perfect of **dūcō**), **mīsī** (perfect of **mittō**), and **cēpī** (perfect of **capiō**).

319. Like **audīvī**, inflect **mūnīvī**.

CURIUS DENTATUS AND THE SAMNITE AMBASSADORS

DĒ CURIŌ DENTĀTŌ

First learn the special vocabulary, page 368. See if you can explain the use of the past and perfect tenses in this story.

320. In numerō clārōrum Rōmānōrum erat Curius Dentātus. Saepe magna proelia faciēbat, saepe inimīca castra oppidaque capiēbat. Sed in mediīs victōriīs vīta eius erat vēra et integra. Nec in vīllā amplā, sed in casā parvā habitābat, et cum officia pūblica nōn prohibēbant, magnā dīligentiā 5 in parvō agrō labōrābat. Ōlim Samnītēs,[1] fīnitimī Rōmānōrum, quī amīcitiam Dentātī petēbant, ad eum lēgātōs mīsērunt. Lēgātī multa praemia pulchra et cōpiam aurī (*gold*) portābant et ad agrum Dentātī properāvērunt.

1. *The Samnites*, living west and south of Latium, conquered by the Romans after a great struggle, in which Dentatus played a prominent part.

LESSON XLV

Ut sēmentem fēceris, ita metes — As you sow, so shall you reap [1]

PRINCIPAL PARTS OF VERBS

321. The following verbs include the three irregular verbs and all verbs of the second conjugation previously used. Review the meanings and drill on the inflection of the perfect.

322. Principal Parts of Irregular Verbs. Learn the principal parts of the following irregular verbs :

PRES. INDIC.	PRES. INF.	PERFECT	PAST PART.	
sum	esse	fuī	— —	*be*
ab'sum	abes'se	ā'fuī	——	*be away*
dō	dare	dedī	datus	*give*

a. **Sum** and **absum** have the future participles **futūrus** and **āfutūrus**.

323. Principal Parts of Second Conjugation. Learn the principal parts of the following verbs of the second conjugation :

fa'veō	favē're	fāvī	fautū'rus	*favor*
ha'beō	habē're	ha'buī	ha'bitus	*have*
mo'neō	monē're	mo'nuī	mo'nitus	*advise*
no'ceō	nocē're	no'cuī	nocitū'rus	*injure*
pā'reō	pārē're	pā'ruī	——	*obey*
pa'teō	patē're	pa'tuī	——	*extend*
persuā'deō	persuādē're	persuā'sī	persuā'sus	*persuade*
prohi'beō	prohibē're	prohi'buī	prohi'bitus	*prevent*
respon'deō	respondē're	respon'dī	respōn'sus	*reply*
se'deō	sedē're	sēdī	sessus	*sit*
stu'deō	studē're	stu'duī	——	*be eager*

[1] From Cicero, Rome's greatest orator and generally considered her first man of letters.

te'neō	tenē're	te'nuī	———	*hold*
ti'meō	timē're	ti'muī	———	*fear*
vi'deō	vidē're	vīdī	vīsus	*see*

a. Note that all these verbs have the infinitive ending **-ēre**. This marks them as belonging to the second conjugation. Further, observe that the formation of the perfect varies in different verbs and that the past participle is sometimes lacking. Occasionally a verb that has no past participle will have a future participle ending in **-ūrus**, and this is then given in the principal parts. There are two examples of this in the above list. Do you see them? In dealing with verbs make it a rule to look at the infinitive first of all to determine the conjugation, and do not be surprised to find irregularities in the formation of the perfect and the participle.

DĒ CURIŌ DENTĀTŌ (CONCLUDED)

First learn the special vocabulary, page 368

324. Nōn in agrō sed in casā lēgātī Dentātum invēnērunt. Vir clārus ante mēnsam [1] sedēbat. Ibi cēnam [2] rāpulōrum [3] edēbat.[4] Tum lēgātī casam intrāvērunt [5] et dīxērunt : "Factīs tuīs ēgregiīs et officiīs pūblicīs, Dentāte, Samnītēs amīcitiam tuam petunt. Ea praemia et id aurum (*gold*) sunt tua." 5 Tum Dentātus respondit : "Minimē, Samnītēs, nātūram meam tenētis.[6] Vērus Rōmānus nōn studet aurō sed imperiō in (*over*) eōs quī aurum habent. Iam discēdite."

1. **mēnsa, -ae,** F., *table.* 2. **cēna, -ae,** F., *dinner.* 3. **rāpulum, -ī,** N., *young turnip.* 4. **edō, -ere,** *eat.* 5. **intrō, -āre,** *enter.* 6. *Understand.*

LESSON XLVI

Amīcus certus in rē incertā cernitur — A friend in need is
a friend indeed [1]

Pluperfect

~~PAST PERFECT~~ INDICATIVE · PRINCIPAL PARTS (Continued)

325. Past Perfect Indicative. The tense sign of the past perfect indicative active is **-erā-**. This is added to the perfect stem. The personal endings are the same as in the past indicative, and the inflection is like that of **fueram** (§ 308).

326. The past perfect indicative active of the four conjugations is inflected as follows:

FIRST CONJUGATION

vocā'veram (perf. stem **vocāv-**),
I had called

1. vocā'veram   vocāverā'mus
2. vocā'verās   vocāverā'tis
3. vocā'verat   vocā'verant

SECOND CONJUGATION

monu'eram (perf. stem **monu-**),
I had advised

monu'eram   monuerā'mus
monu'erās   monuerā'tis
monu'erat   monu'erant

THIRD CONJUGATION

rē'xeram (perf. stem **rēx-**),
I had ruled

1. rē'xeram   rēxerā'mus
2. rē'xerās   rēxerā'tis
3. rē'xerat   rē'xerant

FOURTH CONJUGATION

audī'veram (perf. stem **audīv-**),
I had heard

audī'veram   audīverā'mus
audī'verās   audīverā'tis
audī'verat   audī'verant

327. Principal Parts of Third Conjugation. Learn the principal parts of the following verbs of the third conjugation. The list includes all previously used. Review the meanings and drill on the inflection of the perfect and the past perfect.

[1] From Ennius, the most famous of the early Latin poets. More literally, *The faithful friend is revealed when all is unfaithful.* Note the play on words.

Pres. Indic.	Pres. Inf.	Perfect	Past Part.	
abdū'cō	abdū'cere	abdū'xī	abduc'tus	*lead away*
agō	a'gere	ēgī	āctus	*drive*
ca'piō	ca'pere	cēpī	captus	*take*
crēdō	crē'dere	crē'didī	crē'ditus	*believe*
dēfen'dō	dēfen'dere	dēfen'dī	dēfēn'sus	*defend*
dīcō	dī'cere	dīxī	dictus	*say*
dīmit'tō	dīmit'tere	dīmī'sī	dīmis'sus	*send away*
discē'dō	discē'dere	disces'sī	disces'sus	*go away*
dūcō	dū'cere	dūxī	ductus	*lead*
ēdū'cō	ēdū'cere	ēdū'xī	ēduc'tus	*lead out*
fa'ciō	fa'cere	fēcī	factus	*make*
gerō	ge'rere	gessī	gestus	*carry on, wage*
indū'cō	indū'cere	indū'xī	induc'tus	*lead in*
mittō	mit'tere	mīsī	missus	*send*
petō	pe'tere	petī'vī or petī'tus	petī'tus	*seek*
ra'piō	ra'pere	ra'puī	raptus	*seize*
regō	re'gere	rēxī	rēctus	*rule*
resis'tō	resis'tere	re'stitī	——	*resist*
vincō	vin'cere	vīcī	victus	*conquer*

EXERCISES

328. 1. Ēgerāmus, mīsistī, vīcit. 2. Capiet, gessērunt, resti-terat. 3. Rēxit, indūxerant, faciēmus. 4. Vocāverās, monuit, petiērunt. 5. Habēbit, rapuistis, ēdūxerātis. 6. Crēdideram, ēgistī, pāruit. 7. Fēcit, dēfenderat, persuāsimus. 8. Mittit, mittet, mīsit. 9. Dūxērunt, dīmīserāmus, nocēbit. 10. Dīxistī, discesserant, ēdūxistis.

329. 1. We have conquered, he will favor, he had made. 2. You (*sing.*) have waged, they will extend, lead thou. 3. He has seized, they had departed, you (*plur.*) had taken. 4. He has said, we were defending, we shall reply.

THE FORUM, THE CAPITOLINE, AND ADJACENT BUILDINGS (RESTORED)

The left corner shows a small part of the Palatine and the palaces of the Cæsars. The right side is filled with the Fora of the emperors. The Roman Forum lies in the middle, and is bounded at the end by the Capitoline Hill, with the Arx, or Citadel, on its right summit and the temple of Jupiter Capitolinus on its left. The long building between is the Tabularium, or Record Building. Compare this picture with the one facing page 66

LESSON XLVII

Vēnī, vīdī, vīcī — I came, I saw, I conquered[1]

FUTURE PERFECT INDICATIVE AND PERFECT INFINITIVE ACTIVE · PRINCIPAL PARTS (CONCLUDED)

330. Future Perfect Indicative Active. The tense sign of the future perfect indicative active is -eri-. This is added to the perfect stem. The personal endings are the same as in the future, and the inflection is like that of fuerō (§ 308).

331. The future perfect indicative active of the four conjugations is inflected as follows:

FIRST CONJUGATION

vocā'verō (perf. stem vocāv-),
I shall have called

1. vocā'verō   vocāve'rimus
2. vocā'veris   vocāve'ritis
3. vocā'verit   vocā'verint

SECOND CONJUGATION

monu'erō (perf. stem monu-)
I shall have advised

monu'erō   monue'rimus
monu'eris   monue'ritis
monu'erit   monu'erint

THIRD CONJUGATION

rē'xerō (perf. stem rēx-),
I shall have ruled

1. rē'xerō   rēxe'rimus
2. rē'xeris   rēxe'ritis
3. rē'xerit   rē'xerint

FOURTH CONJUGATION

audī'verō (perf. stem audīv-),
I shall have heard

audī'verō   audīve'rimus
audī'veris   audīve'ritis
audī'verit   audī'verint

332. Perfect Infinitive Active. The perfect infinitive active is also part of the perfect system and is easily learned in this connection. It is formed by adding -isse to the perfect stem.

[1] A famous dispatch of Cæsar at the conclusion of a short and brilliant campaign. He was a man of quick decision and tireless energy.

CONJ.	PERFECT STEM	PERFECT INFINITIVE
I	vocāv-	vocāvis'se, *to have called*
II	monu-	monuis'se, *to have advised*
III	rēx-	rēxis'se, *to have ruled*
IV	audīv-	audīvis'se, *to have heard*
sum	fu-	fuis'se, *to have been*

333. Principal Parts of Fourth Conjugation. The following list comprises the verbs of the fourth conjugation thus far used. Learn the principal parts, review the meanings, and drill on the perfect, past perfect, and future perfect indicative and the perfect infinitive.

PRES. INDIC.	PRES. INF.	PERFECT	PAST PART.	
au'diō	audī're	audī'vī	audī'tus	*hear*
inve'niō	invenī're	invē'nī	inven'tus	*find*
mū'niō	mūnī're	mūnī'vī	mūnī'tus	*fortify*
ve'niō	venī're	vēnī	ventus	*come*

EXERCISES

334. Give the present and perfect infinitives of dō, mūniō, faciō, crēdō, dīcō, mittō, teneō, videō, persuādeō, portō, absum, pācō.

335. Inflect the following verbs in the perfect, past perfect, and future perfect : nārrō, timeō, veniō, agō, locō, mittō, pugnō, mūniō, sum.

336. 1. You (*sing.*) have had, they have believed, they had sent. 2. He has seen, you (*sing.*) will have said, to have led. 3. You (*plur.*) have sent, they have obeyed, we had departed. 4. He has attacked, I had given, I shall have sent. 5. We shall have feared, he has extended, to have been. 6. You (*sing.*) had given, you (*plur.*) will have made, to have sent. 7. You (*sing.*) had come, you (*plur.*) had given, he will have carried.

LESSON XLVIII

Forsan et haec ōlim meminisse iuvābit — Perhaps some day you
will take pleasure in remembering even this [1]

REVIEW OF THE ACTIVE VOICE

337. Formation of Tenses of Indicative. A review of the
tenses of the indicative active shows the following formation:

PRESENT	First of the principal parts
PAST	Present stem + -ba-m
FUTURE	Present stem + { -bō, Conj. I and II ; -a-m, Conj. III and IV
PERFECT	Third of the principal parts
PAST PERF.	Perfect stem + -era-m
FUT. PERF.	Perfect stem + -erō

338. Synopsis of *vocō*. The synopsis of the active voice of
vocō, as far as we have learned the conjugation, is as follows:

PRINCIPAL PARTS: **vocō, vocā′re, vocā′vī, vocā′tus**

(pres. stem **vocā-**, perf. stem **vocāv-**)

INDIC-ATIVE	PRESENT	vocō	INDIC-ATIVE	PERFECT	vocā′vī
	PAST	vocā′bam		PAST PERF.	vocā′veram
	FUTURE	vocā′bō		FUT. PERF.	vocā′verō

PRES. IMPER. **vocā**

PRES. INFIN. **vocā′re**   PERF. INFIN. **vocāvis′se**

---

[1] From Vergil, author of the Ǣnē′id, the greatest Latin epic. The sentiment is appropriate when a person is beset by difficulties and dangers. Of
similar import are his words, " Revocāte animōs, maestumque timōrem mittite,"
Recall your courage and banish gloomy fear.

EXERCISES

339. Following § 338 as a model, learn to write and to recite rapidly the principal parts and the synopsis of the following verbs in any person or number : **parō, dō, habeō, videō, dīcō, dūcō, capiō, mūniō, veniō,** and other verbs selected from the lists in §§ 161, 323, 327, 333.

340. Read again the story about Curius Dentatus and answer the following questions in Latin :

1. Quō Samnītēs lēgātōs mīserant?
2. Cūr Samnītēs lēgātōs ad eum mīserant?
3. Quid lēgātī comparāverant et ad Dentātum portāverant?
4. Num Dentātus amplam vīllam habuit?
5. Nōnne vīta Dentātī vēra et integra fuerat?
6. Labōrāveratne Dentātus in agrō?
7. Ubi lēgātī Dentātum invēnērunt?
8. Cēpitne Dentātus praemia pulchra lēgātōrum?
9. Quid dīxit?

Sixth Review, Lessons XLI–XLVIII, §§ 762–767

A CHARIOT RACE IN THE CIRCUS MAXIMUS

The Circus Maximus was among the most magnificent structures of the Roman world, and held nearly 400,000 people

LESSON XLIX

Tempus fugit — Time flies

WORD FORMATION

341. Something has been said in §§ 238 and 258 concerning Latin and English prefixes. Those mentioned before are here reviewed and three new ones are added.

ā, ab, *from*, as in **abdūcō**, *lead away*; English, *abduct*

ad, *to*, as in **addūcō**, *lead to*; English, *adduce*

con- (com-, co-), *together*, as in **condūcō**, *lead together*; English, *conduct*. Often with intensive force, as in **convincō**, *conquer completely*; English, *convince*

dē, *down from*, as in **dēdūcō**, *lead down*; English, *deduce*

ē, ex, *out from*, as in **ēdūcō**, *lead out*; English, *educe*

in, *in, into*, as in **indūcō**, *lead in*; English, *induce*

prō, *forth, forward*, as in **prōdūcō**, *lead forward*; English, *produce*

re- (red-), *back* or *again*, as in **redūcō**, *lead back*; English, *reduce*

trāns (trā-), *across*, as in **trādūcō**, *lead across*; English, *traduce*

All these prefixes, excepting **con-** and **re-**, are also used alone as prepositions.

NOTE. An English derivative from a Latin compound often loses the literal meaning of the Latin and is used only in a figurative sense. This is well illustrated by the derivatives given above. For example, *traduce* never means to *lead across*, but is used only in the figurative sense of to *make a parade of, dishonor, slander*. The Latin student has the advantage of being able to trace the figurative meaning back to its literal source.

342. Derivation. Write a list of English derivatives from the verbs **servō, locō, vocō, videō, mittō, dīcō, spectō**, selecting the proper prefixes from § 341, and adding such English suffixes as you may know. Use the English dictionary.

NOTE. Students should keep derivation notebooks. See page 382.

GALLĪ RŌMAM OPPUGNANT

First learn the special vocabulary, page 368

343. Ōlim Gallī Italiam vāstābant. Iam agricolās miserōs ex agrīs lātīs ēgerant et equōs pulchrōs eōrum rapuerant. Iam multa oppida expugnāverant. Iam Rōmam petēbant. Tum Rōmānī magnopere perterrēbantur et in Capitōlium[1] fūgērunt. Mānlius, vir ēgregius bellī, Capitōlium firmō 5 praesidiō tenuit nec Gallōs timuit. Capitōlium erat in locō altō et magnīs mūrīs mūniēbātur. Diū populus nātūrā locī et praesidiō dēfendēbātur et Gallī frūstrā (in vain) labōrābant. Victōria longē aberat. Sed dēnique barbarī novum cōnsilium cēpērunt.[2] Nocte[3] magnō silentiō[4] saxa[5] alta 10 ascendērunt. Nec audiēbantur nec prohibēbantur. Iam mūrōs Capitōlī tenēbant. Sed erant in Capitōliō sacrī ānserēs.[6] Eī ānserēs Gallōs audīvērunt et Capitōlium servāvērunt. Nam clāmōre[7] suō Mānlium ex somnō[8] excitāvērunt.[9] Mānlius arma rapuit, suōs vocāvit, Gallōs dē saxīs 15 altīs iēcit.

1. The Capitolium was the citadel of Rome. It was located on the Capitoline Hill, which was steep and rocky. 2. **cōnsilium capere**, *to form a plan*. 3. *By night*. 4. **silentium, silentī,** N., *silence*. 5. **saxum, -ī,** N., *rock*. 6. *Geese.* These were sacred to Juno, whose temple was on the Capitoline. 7. **clāmōre suō**, *by their cackling*. 8. **somnus, -ī,** M., *sleep*. 9. **excitō, -āre,** *arouse*.

A ROMAN MARKET PLACE

THE SACRED GEESE SAVE THE CAPITOL

LESSON L

Vincit quī sē vincit — He conquers who conquers himself[1]
perfect passive

THE PAST PARTICIPLE · THE PASSIVE PERFECTS

344. Participles Defined. A participle is a verbal adjective, and takes its name from the fact that it participates in the uses of both verb and adjective. As a verb, it has tense and voice, and may be either transitive or intransitive. As an adjective, it is declined, and agrees with its noun in gender, number, and case. Thus, in "He, seeing the enemy, fled," *seeing* is a participle, present, active, and transitive, with *enemy* as its direct object. This is its verbal side. As an adjective, it agrees with *he* in gender, number, and case.

345. Participles in English. In English the chief classes of participles are *present* and *past*. The present participle ends in *-ing*. It usually describes an action as taking place at the same time with some other action : as, "*Reaching* for the boat I lost my balance." The past participle expresses completed action. In the passive it has the same form as the past tense : as, "The floors are *swept,*" "The chairs are *mended.*" The active past participle is formed by putting *having* before the passive past participle : as, "*Having swept* the floors, I rested," "*Having mended* the chairs, I sold them." Sometimes *having* is used also in passive participial expressions : as, "The floors *having been swept*, I rested." Participles with *having* are often called perfect participles.

perfect

346. Past Participles in English and Latin. English has both an active and a passive past participle : as, *having called*

---

[1] From Publilius Syrus. Born a slave and educated by his master, he was granted his freedom and became a noted writer.

124

(active), (*having been*) *called* (passive). Latin has only a passive past participle, and this participle is of special importance because, as we have seen (§ 299), it is the fourth and last of the principal parts.

347. Participial Stem. The participial stem is found, as will be recalled, by dropping -us from the past participle. From this stem are formed the future active infinitive and all passive perfects.

348. Perfect, Past Perfect, Future Perfect Indicative Passive. In English the perfect, past perfect, and future perfect tenses of the indicative passive are made up of forms of the auxiliary verb *to be* and the past participle: as, *I have been called, I had been called, I shall have been called.*

Very similarly in Latin the perfect, past perfect, and future perfect passive use the present, past, and future of **sum** as an auxiliary verb with the past participle: as,

Perfect passive, **vocā'tus sum**, *I have been called* or *was called*
Past perfect passive, **vocā'tus eram**, *I had been called*
Future perfect passive, **vocā'tus erō**, *I shall have been called*

349. The past participle is declined like **bonus, bona, bonum.** When making part of a verb form, it agrees in gender, number, and case with the subject of the verb, as shown below:

EXAMPLES IN THE SINGULAR

Vir vocātus est, *the man was called* or *has been called*
Puella vocāta est, *the girl was called* or *has been called*
Praesidium vocātum est, *the garrison was called* or *has been called*

EXAMPLES IN THE PLURAL

Virī vocātī sunt, *the men were called* or *have been called*
Puellae vocātae sunt, *the girls were called* or *have been called*
Praesidia vocāta sunt, *the garrisons were called* or *have been called*

350. In all the conjugations the *perfect, past perfect*, and *future perfect* indicative passive are formed and inflected in the same way. Study these inflections, §§ 832–835.

EXERCISES

351. Inflect the perfect, past perfect, and future perfect indicative, active and passive, of **vocō, moneō, regō**, and **audiō**.

352. 1. Agricolae frūmentum in oppidum sacrum portāvērunt. 2. Frūmentum ab agricolīs in oppidum sacrum portātum est. 3. Rēgīna Lesbiae pecūniam dederat. 4. Pecūnia ā rēgīnā Lesbiae data erat. 5. Mānlius dē mūrō sacrō Gallōs iēcerit. 6. Gallī ā Mānliō dē mūrō sacrō iactī erunt. 7. Dentātus lēgātōs dīmīserat. Lēgātī ā Dentātō dīmissī erant. 8. Puellae exemplum ēgregium vērae amīcitiae vīderant. 9. Exemplum ēgregium vērae amīcitiae ā puellīs vīsum erat. 10. Animī timidī eōrum factīs vestrīs cōnfirmātī sunt. 11. Gallī ab agrīs nostrīs armīs Rōmānīs prohibitī erant.

353. 1. Greece had been freed from danger. 2. Fresh troops had been put before the sacred town by the Romans. 3. The girls had been greatly terrified and had fled. 4. The fields had been laid waste, but, because of the nature of the place, the camp had not been taken by storm. 5. Did the Gauls climb your walls? Not at all, but they laid waste the fields.

ROMAN HAIRPINS, POWDER BOXES, AND OTHER TOILET ARTICLES

THE TIBER, CASTLE OF ST. ANGELO, AND ST. PETER'S

Navigation on the Tiber, now of little account, was of great importance to ancient Rome. There are ruins of great docks in the city and of still greater ones at Ostia, at the river's mouth, sixteen miles downstream. The Castle of St. Angelo is the tomb of the Emperor Hadrian. Concerning St. Peter's, compare the note and picture facing page 12

LESSON LI

THE PERFECT INFINITIVE PASSIVE AND THE FUTURE INFINITIVE ACTIVE · PREPOSITIONS

354. As the perfect infinitive passive and the future infinitive active are also formed from the participial stem, they are most easily learned at this point.

355. Perfect Infinitive Passive. The perfect infinitive passive is formed by adding **esse** to the past participle: as, **vocātus esse,** *to have been called.* Similarly in the other conjugations we have **monitus esse,** *to have been advised*; **rēctus esse,** *to have been ruled*; **audītus esse,** *to have been heard.*

356. Future Infinitive Active. The future infinitive active of **vocō** is **vocātū'rus esse,** *to be about to call.* This is formed by adding -**ūrus esse** to the participial stem. Similarly in the other conjugations we have **monitū'rus esse,** *to be about to advise*; **rēctū'rus esse,** *to be about to rule*; **audītū'rus esse,** *to be about to hear.*

357. We have now completed the infinitive, active and passive. The synopsis of the infinitives of **vocō** is as follows:

	ACTIVE	PASSIVE
Pres.	vocā're, *to call*	vocā'rī, *to be called*
Perf.	vocāvis'se, *to have called*	vocā'tus esse, *to have been called*
Fut.	vocātū'rus esse, *to be about to call*	(Rare and hence omitted)

---

[1] From Vergil. Literally, *Give your right (hand) to an unfortunate (man).*

a. The infinitives of the other conjugations are similarly formed; but do not forget the peculiar formation of the present infinitive passive in the third conjugation (§ 285).

358. Prepositions. We learned in § 77 that only the accusative and ablative are used with prepositions. Those prepositions which we have had before are here summarized and three more added.

a. Prepositions expressing ablative relations (*from, with, in,* etc.) govern the ablative case. Learn the following list:

ā or ab, *from, by*	ē or ex, *out from, out of*
cum, *with*	in, *in* or *on*
dē, *down from, concerning, about*	prō, *in behalf of, for*
sine, *without*	

b. Prepositions not expressing ablative relations must govern the accusative. Among these are

ad, *to, towards*	per, *through*
ante, *before, in front of*	post, *after*
in, *into, to, against*	trāns, *across*

There are many others; but learn the list above of prepositions taking the ablative, and use the accusative after all others.

EXERCISES

First learn the special vocabulary, page 368

359. 1. Imperium Rōmānum Germānīs quī trāns Rhēnum habitābant nōn grātum erat. 2. Itaque per multōs annōs Germānī Rōmānōs ab rēgnīs suīs prohibuērunt. 3. Fīrmīs et[1] vērīs animīs prō patriā fortiter pugnāvērunt. 4. Rēgna Germānōrum longē trāns Rhēnum patēbant. 5. Germānī cōpiās integrās ex silvīs oppidīsque ēvocābant. 6. Numerus virōrum erat magnus et animī eōrum bellō studēbant. 7. Sed fortūna bellī erat inīqua Germānīs ac Rōmānīs victōriam dedit. 8. Anteā

Germānī fuerant līberī, sed post victōriam Rōmānam multī in magnās silvās fūgērunt. 9. Multī raptī sunt atque in Italiam missī sunt. 10. Quam misera erat fortūna eōrum captīvōrum! 1. What are the three Latin words for *and*?

360. 1. The Roman power did not formerly extend across the Rhine. 2. When you are in the realm of the Germans, you will see great forests. 3. The nature of the place was certainly unfavorable for the battle. 4. They will fight bravely and many will give their lives [1] for their country.[2] 5. After the unfavorable battle grain was provided and many fresh troops were called out.

1. Singular. 2. Not the dative.

361. Give the infinitives, active and passive, of the following verbs : **pācō, habeō, teneō, agō, gerō, capiō, iaciō, audiō, mūniō.**

LESSON LII

Dulce et decōrum est prō patriā morī — Sweet and fitting it is to die for one's country [1]

THE CONJUGATION OF *POSSUM*

362. Possum, *I am able, I can*, is a compound of the adjective **potis,** *able*, and **sum,** *I am*. It is inflected in the indicative and infinitive as follows :

PRINCIPAL PARTS : **possum, posse, potuī, ——**

INDICATIVE MOOD

PRESENT

possum, *I am able, I can*	**pos'sumus,** *we are able, we can*
potes, *you are able, you can*	**potes'tis,** *you are able, you can*
potest, *he is able, he can*	**possunt,** *they are able, they can*

[1] From one of the Odes of Horace, Rome's greatest lyric poet.

PAST

po'teram, *I was able, I could*;   poterā'mus, *we were able, we*
etc.   *could*; etc.

FUTURE

po'terō, *I shall be able*; etc.   pote'rimus, *we shall be able*;
etc.

PERFECT

po'tuī, *I have been able, I*   potu'imus, *we have been able,*
could; etc.   *we could*; etc.

PAST PERFECT

potu'eram, *I had been able*;   potuerā'mus, *we had been able*;
etc.   etc.

FUTURE PERFECT

potu'erō, *I shall have been able*;   potue'rimus, *we shall have*
etc.   *been able*; etc.

INFINITIVE MOOD

PRESENT   PERFECT

posse, *to be able*   potuis'se, *to have been able*

a. This verb has no imperative and no future infinitive. The perfect infinitive, as in all verbs, is formed by adding -isse to the perfect stem (§ 332).

EXERCISES

DĒ MŪCIŌ SCAEVOLĀ

First learn the special vocabulary, page 369

363. Ōlim Porsenna, quī rēgnum Etrūscōrum[1] tum obtinēbat, cum Rōmānīs dē imperiō Italiae pugnāvit et Rōmam māgnīs cōpiīs oppugnāvit. Iam Rōmānī inopiā frūmentī labōrābant[2] et magnopere perterrēbantur. Erat in numerō Rōmānōrum ēgregius iuvenis[3] Mūcius Scaevola.[4] Is 5 timidōs animōs eōrum cōnfirmāvit atque dīxit: " In castra

Etrūscōrum prōcēdam et Porsennam interficiam. Itaque patriam perīculō līberābō." Fortiter negōtium suscēpit, sed vīsus captusque est. Tum ante Porsennam prōductus est.

1. **Etrūscī, -ōrum,** M., *the Etruscans*, neighbors of the Romans to the north and their most powerful enemies in the early years of the city. 2. Used here in the sense of *suffer*. 3. *Youth.* 4. The English pronunciation is *Sev′o-la.*

364. 1. They had held the sovereignty across the Rhine for **(per)** many years. 2. Because of the scarcity of grain the men had not advanced. 3. That matter had been undertaken by Mucius. 4. The captives had been led before your camp. 5. After the battle a large supply of money was found there.

LESSON LIII

Possunt quia posse videntur — They can because they think they can [1]

THE INFINITIVE USED AS IN ENGLISH

365. Nature of the Infinitive. The uses of the infinitive are much the same in Latin as in English. Being a *verbal noun* it is used sometimes as a verb and sometimes as a noun. As a verb, it has tense and voice, may govern a case, and may be modified by an adverb. As a noun, it may have the construction of a noun. For example, in *To cross the marsh quickly was difficult,* the infinitive *to cross* is a noun, for it is the subject of *was*; but it is also a verb, for it takes an object (*marsh*) and is modified by an adverb (*quickly*).

366. Infinitive Clause as Object. In English, verbs of *commanding, wishing, forbidding,* and the like may be followed by a clause consisting of a noun or pronoun in the objective

[1] From Vergil. Literally, *They are able because they seem (think themselves) to be able.*

case and an infinitive : as, *the slave commanded the men to flee.* The same construction is used in Latin.

Servus virōs fugere iussit, *the slave commanded the men to flee*
Eōs fābulam audīre cupit, *he wishes them to hear the story*
Eum dīcere vetat, *he forbids him to speak*

367. Rule for the Infinitive Object Clause. *The verbs iubeō,* command; *cupiō,* wish; *vetō,* forbid, *and the like are often followed by an infinitive clause as object.*

368. Rule for Subject of Infinitive. *The subject of the infinitive is in the accusative.*

369. Complementary Infinitive. In English, and also in Latin, an infinitive without a subject may be added to many verbs as an adverbial modifier to complete their meaning. Such verbs are called *verbs of incomplete predication,* and the added infinitive is called a *complementary infinitive.* Among such verbs are the following :

> **incipiō,** *I begin*   **possum,** *I am able, I can*
> **properō,** *I hasten*   **studeō,** *I am eager*

Fugere incipiunt, *they begin to flee*
Oppidum capere properat, *he hastens to take the town*
Nōn pugnāre potes, *you are not able to fight* or *you can't fight*
Eum invenīre studeō, *I am eager to find him*

370. Infinitive as Noun. In English, and also in Latin, the infinitive is often a pure noun, being used as the subject of a sentence or as a predicate noun : as,

> **Vidēre est crēdere,** *seeing (to see) is believing (to believe)*
> **Vincere est grātum,** *to conquer is pleasing*

a. An infinitive used as a noun is neuter singular, as is shown in the sentence above by **grātum,** a neuter adjective in agreement with **vincere,** the subject.

EXERCISES

First learn the special vocabulary, page 369

371. 1. Vincere Rōmānōs erat grātum inimīcīs fīnitimīs. 2. Mūcius Porsennam interficere studēbat. 3. Rōmānī eum suscipere id negōtium cupīvērunt. 4. Populus eum in castra inimīca prōcēdere nōn vetuit. 5. Rōmānī imperium Italiae obtinēre incēpērunt. 6. Inopiā frūmentī Rōmānī diū resistere nōn poterant. 7. Porsenna Mūcium prōdūcī iussit. 8. Porsennam interficere erat officium pūblicum vērī Rōmānī.

372. 1. To possess power was pleasing to Dentatus. 2. The ambassadors were eager to give him [1] money. 3. But they could not persuade him.[2] 4. They began to speak, but Dentatus commanded them to depart. 5. He wished them to see an example of a true Roman. 6. Therefore he did not desire them to give him the money. 7. Dentatus forbade them to seek his friendship with money.[3]

1. Indirect object. 2. What case? See § 224. 3. Ablative of means.

THE ROMAN FORUM, A.D. 400
Note the Capitoline Hill with its two summits in the background

LESSON LIV

Oleum et operam perdidī — I have wasted time and labor[1]

WORD FORMATION

373. One of the most important of the Latin prefixes is **in** We have already learned something of its use with verbs. It is then the same as the preposition **in**, and has the same meanings of *in*, *on*, *into*, *against*, and has the same force in related English words : as, Latin **indūcō**, *lead into* ; English *induce*, meaning to lead one into some course of action.

374. But there is another prefix **in-**, identical in form but of a different origin, which may be combined with an adjective or an adverb. This **in-** negatives the word to which it is attached : thus, **fīrmus**, *firm* or *strong*, but **īnfīrmus**, *infirm* or *weak*. The same prefix is similarly used in English : as, *insecure*, *in-sincere*, *in-valid*, etc. In English the prefix often changes its form to *un-*, as in *unsafe*, *unmoved*, etc. This **in-** is never used as a Latin preposition, but only as a prefix.

375. Latin prefixes before a consonant may change their final consonant to a similar letter or one more easily pronounced. This is called assimilation. Thus, **in- + mātūrus = immātūrus**, *immature* ; **in- + mortālis = immortālis**, *immortal* ; **con- + rēctiō = correctiō**, *correction*. Compare also such English words as *impossible* (**in- + possum**), *irresponsible* (**in- + respondeō**), *illiberal* (**in- + līberālis**), etc.

376. Another important point is that Latin simple verbs having a short **a** in the first syllable followed by a single consonant (as in **capiō**) generally change **a** to **i** in the present, and

---

[1] From Plautus. Literally, *I have wasted oil* (i. e. *lamp oil*) *and labor.*

MŪCIUS SCAEVOLA

to **e** in the past participle, when the simple verb is compounded
with a prefix. So **in-** + **capiō** becomes **incipiō** in the present and
inceptus in the past participle. The same change in spelling
follows in English ; from **capiō** we have *capture*, but **incipiō**
gives us *incipient*, and **inceptus**, *inception*. So **recipiō** gives us
recipient, *recipe*, and **receptus**, *reception*, *receptive*.

EXERCISES

377. Derivation. Name ten English words in the composition
of which the prefix **in-** is used, and state the force of the prefix.

378. Give the synopsis, active and passive, of **iaciō, cupiō,
iubeō, vāstō.**

DĒ MŪCIŌ SCAEVOLĀ (Concluded)

First learn the special vocabulary, page 369

379. Porsenna in mediis castrīs sedēbat et magnopere per-
terrēbātur, nam suum perīculum ex animō agere nōn poterat.
Spectāvit Mūcium et dīxit : "Vītam meam petere, Rōmāne,
parābās. Meō iūdiciō sine auxiliō sociōrum id negōtium nōn
suscēpistī. Nārrā malum cōnsilium ac cōnservā vītam tuam. 5
Sī nōn ita faciēs, ignī [1] cremāberis." [2] Mūcius respondit :
" Nōn vītam sed patriam cōnservāre est officium Rōmānum.
Poenās tuās minimē timeō. Vītam Rōmānam rapere potes,
sed animō [3] Rōmānō nocēre nōn potes." Tum statim dex-
tram [4] mediō ignī, [5] quī nōn longē aberat, iniēcit, [6] nec dolōrc [7] 10
superābātur. Post id factum ēgregium Porsenna vetuit eum
interficī et iussit eum ad Rōmānōs remittī. Posteā Mūcius
appellātus est Scaevola. [8]

1. *By fire.* 2. **cremō, -āre,** *burn, consume.* 3. Why dative? See § 224.
4. **dextra, -ae,** F., *right hand.* 5. **mediō ignī,** *into the midst of a fire.*
6. **iniēcit,** *he thrust.* 7. *By the pain.* 8. **Scaevola,** *left-handed.*

LESSON LV

SENTENCES AND CLAUSES · RELATIVE PRONOUNS

380. Sentences and Clauses. Sentences are *simple, compound,* or *complex.*

381. A *simple* sentence makes but one statement, and has but one subject and one predicate : as,

Columbus discovered America

382. A *compound* sentence contains two or more independent statements : as,

Columbus discovered America | and | he thereby won immortal fame

383. A *complex* sentence contains one independent statement and one or more dependent statements : as,

When Columbus discovered America | he won immortal fame

384. The separate statements in a compound or complex sentence are called *clauses.* An independent statement is called a *main clause* ; a dependent statement, a *subordinate clause.*

385. Subordinate clauses may be used as nouns, adjectives, or adverbs. Hence we have *noun clauses, adjective clauses,* and *adverb clauses.*

386. Relative Pronouns. Examine the following sentences :

1. *This is the wounded soldier.*
2. *This is the soldier who has been wounded.*
3. *This is the soldier, and the soldier has been wounded.*

[1] Motto of Brown University.

Number 1 is a simple sentence. Number 2 is complex, the adjective *wounded* in number 1 being represented in number 2 by the subordinate adjective clause *who has been wounded.* The word *who* is a pronoun, taking the place of *soldier,* as shown by number 3, and it also connects the subordinate adjective clause *who has been wounded* with the noun *soldier.* A pronoun that connects an adjective clause with a noun or pronoun is called a *relative pronoun,* and the noun or pronoun is called its *antecedent.* In English the relative pronouns are *who, whose, whom, which, what, that.*

387. Declension of Relative Pronoun quī. The relative pronoun in Latin is quī, quae, quod. It is declined as follows:

	MASC.	FEM.	NEUT.	MASC.	FEM.	NEUT.
NOM.	quī	quae	quod	quī	quae	quae
GEN.	cuius	cuius	cuius	quōrum	quārum	quōrum
DAT.	cui	cui	cui	quibus	quibus	quibus
ACC.	quem	quam	quod	quōs	quās	quae
ABL.	quō	quā	quō	quibus	quibus	quibus

a. Review the declension of is, § 203, and note the similarity in the endings. The forms quī, quae, and quibus are the only forms showing new endings.

NOTE. The genitive **cuius** is pronounced *cŏŏ'yŏŏs*, and the dative **cui** is pronounced *kwee.*

388. Translation. The relative quī is translated as follows:

	MASC. AND FEM.	NEUT.
NOM.	*who, that*	*which, what, that*
GEN.	*of whom, whose*	*of which, of what, whose*
DAT.	*to* or *for whom*	*to* or *for which,* *to* or *for what*
ACC.	*whom, that*	*which, what, that*
ABL.	*from,* etc., *whom*	*from,* etc., *which* or *what*

389. Agreement of Relative Pronoun. Note the following sentences :

Puer quem vidēs est Mārcus, *the boy whom you see is Mark*
Puella quam vidēs est Lesbia, *the girl whom you see is Lesbia*

The relatives **quem** and **quam** agree with their antecedents **puer** and **puella** in gender and number, but not in case. The antecedents are nominatives, subjects of **est,** and the relatives are accusatives, objects of **vidēs.** The rule for the agreement of the relative is, therefore, as follows :

390. Rule for Agreement of Relative Pronoun. *The relative agrees with its antecedent in gender and number, but its case is determined by its use in its own clause.*

EXERCISES

First learn the special vocabulary, page 370

391. 1. Mūcius, quī ā Porsennā in iūdicium vocātus est, animum vērum habēbat. 2. Rōma, quam Porsenna expugnāre cupiēbat, inopiā frūmentī labōrābat. 3. Vir cuius vīta prō patriā datur ēgregiam fāmam obtinēbit. 4. Porsenna, quem Mūcius interficere studēbat, magnopere perterritus est. 5. Factum quō Mūcius vītam suam cōnservāre potuit ā multīs poētīs nārrātum est. 6. Quid dē Mūciō putās ? Vir clārus meō iūdiciō erat Mūcius. 7. Cūr appellātus est Scaevola ?

392. 1. Afterwards the camp was moved from that unfavorable place. 2. Only a few hurled their spears, the rest immediately fled. 3. The baggage which was captured was placed in our camp. 4. Will he begin to send back the grain which they have found ? I don't think so. 5. He will command the troops which he has summoned to move the baggage across the Rhine.

LESSON LVI

Iacta est ālea — The die is cast[1]

INTERROGATIVE PRONOUNS AND ADJECTIVES · THE ABLATIVE ABSOLUTE

393. Interrogatives in English. Interrogative pronouns and adjectives are used in asking questions. In English the interrogative pronouns are *who? which?* and *what? Which* and *what* are used also as interrogative adjectives.

> *Who is your friend?* (*Who*, interrogative pronoun)
> *What friends have you?* (*What*, interrogative adjective)

394. Interrogatives in Latin. The Latin interrogative pronoun is **quis** (*who?*), **quid** (*what?*). It is declined in the singular as follows :

	MASC. AND FEM.	NEUT.
NOM.	**quis,** *who?*	**quid,** *what? which?*
GEN.	**cuius,** *whose?*	**cuius,** *whose?*
DAT.	**cui,** *to* or *for whom?*	**cui,** *to* or *for which* or *what?*
ACC.	**quem,** *whom?*	**quid,** *what? which?*
ABL.	**quō,** *from,* etc., *whom?*	**quō,** *from,* etc., *which* or *what?*

The plural forms are the same as those of the relative (§ 387).

> **Quis est amīcus tuus,** *who is your friend?*
> **Quī sunt amīcī tuī,** *who are your friends?*

395. The Latin interrogative adjective is **quī** (or **quis**), **quae, quod.** It is declined like the relative (§ 387).

> **Quōs librōs habēs,** *what books have you?*

---

[1] Words of Julius Cæsar when he crossed the river Rubicon, the boundary of his province, with an armed force. This act amounted to a declaration of war against the Roman government.

140

396. Ablative Absolute. In English a noun with a participle attached is often used to make a phrase grammatically independent of the main clause : as,

The town having been captured
With the town captured } *the lieutenant fled*

The independent phrase is called the absolute construction. The noun is in the nominative case, and is called the *nominative absolute*.

397. In Latin a noun with attached participle in the absolute construction is put in the ablative, and the construction is called the *ablative absolute* : as,

Oppidō captō, lēgātus fūgit

a. The ablative absolute denotes the circumstances accompanying the action of the main verb, a fundamental ablative relation often expressed in English by the preposition *with*. Note the second form in § 396 : *With the town captured, the lieutenant fled.*

398. There is no present participle "being" in Latin. In consequence we often have two nouns, or a noun and an adjective, in the ablative absolute with no participle : as,

fīliā rēgīnā, *his daughter being queen*
puerīs tardīs, *the boys being slow*

399. Translation of Ablative Absolute. The absolute construction, rather rare in English, is very common in Latin, and is often best translated by a clause introduced by *when, after, since, though*, etc. Use the form of clause that will best express the thought. Note the following translations of **oppidō captō, lēgātus fūgit** :

when, since, after, although, etc. { *the town was captured, the lieutenant fled*

400. Rule for Ablative Absolute. *The ablative of a noun and a participle, a noun and an adjective, or two nouns may be used in the absolute construction to denote attendant circumstances.*

EXERCISES

401. 1. Castrīs mōtīs, crēbra tēla nostrīs [1] nocēre nōn potuē-runt. 2. Eō locō occupātō, reliquae cōpiae perīculō līberātae sunt. 3. Agrīs vāstātīs et cquīs raptīs, inopiā frūmentī mox labōrābimus. 4. Sociīs nostrīs interfectīs, ā quibus auxilium petēmus? 5. Eō proeliō factō, paucī prōcēdere studēbant. 6. Quōrum [2] erat imperium Italiae? Imperium Italiae erat Rōmānōrum. 7. Quī Germānōs cōpiās integrās dūcere trāns Rhēnum vetuērunt? Rōmānī. 8. Quibus bona rēgīna pecūniam darī iussit? Miserīs captīvīs. 9. Lēgātō in iūdicium vocātō, populus bellum gerī nōn cupīvit.

1. Why dative? See § 224.   2. Predicate genitive of possession, § 150.

402. 1. After the battle was fought,[1] to what famous place did they wish the lieutenant to move the camp? 2. How far away was the camp which you saw? 3. Did the battle rage [2] a long time? I think so. 4. Whose money did you find? Galba's. 5. After the town had been stormed, did not the people suffer [3] the penalty due the state [4]? 6. Who can tell the story of Dentatus? I can.

1. Not **pugnō**.   2. Literally, *was it fought*, the word *battle* not being expressed. See § 259, note 3.   3. **dō, -āre**.   4. *Due the state*, **pūblicus, -a, -um**.

Seventh Review, Lessons XLIX–LVI, §§ 768–773

THE ARCH OF TITUS AND THE COLOSSEUM

The Arch of Titus was erected in the first century of our era to commemorate the destruction of Jerusalem by Titus. To the same period belongs the Colosseum, the most impressive ruin in Rome, covering about five acres. In it gladiatorial combats were held for nearly five hundred years. There were seats for almost 100,000 spectators and several hundred gladiators or wild beasts could fight in the arena at the same time

SECOND HALF YEAR

Classes should have reached at least this point at the beginning of the second half year. This is suggested not as a maximum, however, but as a minimum. Go as far beyond it as you can consistently with good work, so as to have more time for the reading of the stories at the end of the book before the close of the year.

LESSON LVII

Salūs populī suprēma lēx estō — The safety of the people shall be the supreme law [1]

THE THIRD DECLENSION · CONSONANT STEMS

403. Nouns that end in **-is** in the genitive singular are of the Third Declension. They may be masculine, feminine, or neuter.

CLASSES OF NOUNS IN THE THIRD DECLENSION

404. Nouns of the third declension are divided into two classes, known as *consonant stems* and *i-stems*.

a. The *stem* is the body of a word to which the terminations are added. When the stem ends in a consonant, the stem is the same as the base. In vowel stems the stem is formed by adding the stem vowel to the base: thus, the base of **hostis**, *enemy*, is **host-**, and the stem is **host + i = hosti-**. Consonant stems and i-stems differ somewhat in declension, so the distinction is an important one.

[1] Motto of the state of Missouri, quoted from a famous code of Roman laws.

143

CONSONANT STEMS, MASCULINES AND FEMININES

405. Masculines and feminines are declined alike. The nominative is often the same as the base or nearly so. Often it is formed by adding -s to the base. In that case the added -s causes various changes in spelling. Always learn the genitive along with the nominative, for the genitive gives the key to all the other forms.

	cōnsul, M., *consul* (base cōnsul-)	legiō, F., *legion* (base legiōn-)	pater, M., *father* (base patr-)	TERMINATIONS
NOM.	cōn'sul	le'giō	pa'ter	—
GEN.	cōn'sulis	legiō'nis	pa'tris	-is
DAT.	cōn'sulī	legiō'nī	pa'trī	-ī
ACC.	cōn'sulem	legiō'nem	pa'trem	-em
ABL.	cōn'sule	legiō'ne	pa'tre	-e
NOM.	cōn'sulēs	legiō'nēs	pa'trēs	-ēs
GEN.	cōn'sulum	legiō'num	pa'trum	-um
DAT.	cōnsu'libus	legiō'nibus	pa'tribus	-ibus
ACC.	cōn'sulēs	legiō'nēs	pa'trēs	-ēs
ABL.	cōnsu'libus	legiō'nibus	pa'tribus	-ibus

	prīnceps, M., *chief* (base prīncip- [1])	mīles, M., *soldier* (base mīlit- [1])	rēx, M., *king* (base rēg-)	
NOM.	prīn'ceps	mīles	rēx	-s
GEN.	prīn'cipis	mī'litis	rēgis	-is
DAT.	prīn'cipī	mī'litī	rēgī	-ī
ACC.	prīn'cipem	mī'litem	rēgem	-em
ABL.	prīn'cipe	mī'lite	rēge	-e

[1] An i in the last syllable of the base is often changed in the nominative to e: as, prīnceps, base prīncip-; mīles, base mīlit-.

Nom.	prīn'cipēs	mī'litēs	rēgēs	-ēs
Gen.	prīn'cipum	mī'litum	rēgum	-um
Dat.	prīnci'pibus	mīli'tibus	rē'gibus	-ibus
Acc.	prīn'cipēs	mī'litēs	rēgēs	-ēs
Abl.	prīnci'pibus	mīli'tibus	rē'gibus	-ibus

a. The nominative case termination s combines with a final c or g of the base and makes x : thus, rēg + s gives rēx, *king*; and duc + s gives dux, *leader*. A final d or t is dropped before s : thus, lapid + s gives lapis, *stone*; mīlet + s gives mīles, *soldier*.
b. The base or stem is found by dropping -is in the genitive singular.
c. Review § 108 and apply the rules to this declension.

EXERCISES

First learn the special vocabulary, page 370

406. 1. Sī mīlitēs rēgis oppidum nostrum oppugnābunt, ab legiōnibus Rōmānīs vincentur. 2. Cum tēla nostra iacere incipiēmus, paucī resistent; reliquī statim fugient. 3. Mīlitēs nostrī ā patre cōnsulis dūcēbantur. 4. Multīs interfectīs, rēx prīncipēs rēgnī lēgātōs[1] mīsit et pācem petiit. 5. Lēgātīs audītīs, pāx rēgī data est. 6. Pater cōnsulis iussit rēgem in suum rēgnum discēdere nec iniūriam agrīs nostrīs facere. 7. Rēx, quī legiōnēs nostrās magnopere timuit, imperiō[2] Rōmānō pāruit et statim discessit. 8. Numquam posteā bellum cum legiōnibus nostrīs gerere poterit.

1. In apposition with **prīncipēs**. 2. Why dative? See § 224.

407. 1. The consul commanded the soldiers to move the camp quickly from that unfavorable place. 2. The legions could not fight bravely there. 3. The king, who was eager to make peace, sent ambassadors. 4. After peace had been made,[1] the chiefs forbade the king's father to call out the legions.

1. Ablative absolute.

LESSON LVIII

Sī quaeris pēnīnsulam amoenam, circumspice — If you are
seeking a charming peninsula, look about you [1]

THE THIRD DECLENSION, CONSONANT STEMS (CONTINUED)

408. Neuter Consonant Stems. There are many neuter consonant stems. The nominative singular generally differs from
the base. Thus, bases in -in- have final -en in the nominative,
and bases in -er- or -or- generally have -us.

	flūmen, N., *river* (base flūmin-)	tempus, N., *time* (base tempor-)	caput, N., *head* (base capit-)	TERMINA- TIONS
Nom.	flū'men	tem'pus	ca'put	—
Gen.	flū'minis	tem'poris	ca'pitis	-is
Dat.	flū'minī	tem'porī	ca'pitī	-ī
Acc.	flū'men	tem'pus	ca'put	—
Abl.	flū'mine	tem'pore	ca'pite	-e
Nom.	flū'mina	tem'pora	ca'pita	-a
Gen.	flū'minum	tem'porum	ca'pitum	-um
Dat.	flūmi'nibus	tempo'ribus	capi'tibus	-ibus
Acc.	flū'mina	tem'pora	ca'pita	-a
Abl.	flūmi'nibus	tempo'ribus	capi'tibus	-ibus

a. These neuter nouns, like all other neuters, have the nominative
and accusative alike, which in the plural end in -a (§ 108. *a*).

b. Some neuters of this class have passed into English without
change : as, *acumen, omen, specimen.* A few have kept the Latin form
also in the plural : as, *genus,* plural *genera* ; *stamen,* plural *stamens*
and *stamina,* with a difference in meaning. Note, too, the plurals
viscera and *capita.*

---

[1] Motto of the state of Michigan.

146

MĀRCUS ET QUĪNTUS

First learn the special vocabulary, page 370

409. QUĪNTUS. Quid audīvistī, Mārce, dē magnō bellō quod cōnsul noster in Germāniā nunc gerit? Diū patria in perīculīs mediīs fuit et timidī animī perterrērī incipiunt.

MĀRCUS. Bona fāma vēnit. Cōnsul magnās cōpiās Germānōrum crēbrīs proeliīs superāvit atque eōs trāns flūmen Rhēnum ēgit. Rēx Germānōrum, vir barbarus et inimīcus, in silvās fūgit. Et[1] māter et soror eius, quae in castrīs Germānīs erant, captae sunt.

Q. Certē ea fāma, sī vēra est, grāta populō Rōmānō erit. Quō modo (*how*) dē victōriā audīvistī?

M. Et pater et frāter meus cum legiōnibus pugnant. Hodiē[2] litterās[3] ā patre accēpimus.

Q. Certē animum meum cōnfīrmāvistī. Sed tempus fugit. Valē.[4]

1. et . . . et, *both . . . and.* 2. *Today.* 3. **litterae, -ārum,** F., *letter.* 4. *Good-by.*

410. 1. When kings ruled the Romans, the times were evil. 2. Rome, the capital of Italy, has a well-known river. 3. After the king was killed,[1] both his son and his brother begged for peace. 4. Did not the Romans capture both his mother and his sister?[2] I think so. 5. After the ambassadors had been received,[1] the chiefs who were eager for war[3] fled.

1. Ablative absolute. 2. See § 251. 3. What case? See § 223.

LESSON LIX

Cēdant arma togae — Let arms yield to peace[1]

RŌMULUS ET REMUS

First learn the special vocabulary, page 371. Decline all the nouns, adjectives, and pronouns in the story, and give the principal parts of all the verbs.

411. Rōmulus et Remus erant fīliī Mārtis,[1] deī bellī. Eōrum māter erat Rhea Silvia, fīlia Numitōris,[2] quī rēx Albānōrum[3] anteā fuerat, sed ā malō frātre Amūliō pulsus erat. Itaque Amūlius, quī rēgnum Albānōrum tum obtinēbat, puerōs magnopere timuit et eōs interficere cōnsilium cēpit. 5 Rhea vītam fīliōrum suōrum cōnservāre studēbat, sed rēx iussit servum eōs in flūmen dēicere. Imperiō rēgis autem servus nōn pāruit, sed puerōs in arcā ligneā[4] posuit, quae aquā[5] flūminis sine perīculō vehī[6] poterat. Mox puerī ad rīpam flūminis vectī sunt.[6] Ibi lupa,[7] quae nōn longē aberat, 10 puerōs audīvit atque cūrāvit.[8] Posteā pāstor[9] benignus[10] eōs invēnit et in casam parvam portāvit.

Post longum tempus Rōmulus et Remus, quī virī nunc erant, et malum rēgem interfēcērunt et rēgnum Numitōrī reddidērunt. Tum auxiliō sociōrum suōrum novum oppidum 15 ad (*near*) flūmen posuērunt. Eius flūminis nōmen est Tiberis.[11] Eius oppidī nōmen est Rōma. Rōma posita est in eō locō ubi (*where*) Rōmulus et Remus inventī erant.

1. **Mārs**, genitive **Mārtis**. 2. Numitor, brother of Amulius, was the dethroned king of Alba, at that time the largest town in Latium. 3. **Albānī, -ōrum**, M., *the Albans*. 4. **in arcā ligneā**, *in a wooden chest*. 5. Ablative of means. 6. **vehō, -ere**, *carry*. 7. **lupa, -ae**, F., *wolf*. 8. **cūrō, -āre**, *care for*. 9. **pāstor, -ō'ris**, M., *shepherd*. 10. **benignus, -a, -um**, *kind*. 11. **Tiberis**, *the Tiber*.

[1] Motto of the state of Wyoming. Literally, *Let arms yield to the toga.* The toga, the dress of the civilian, was a sign of peace.

LESSON LX

THE THIRD DECLENSION, *I*-STEMS, MASCULINES AND FEMININES

412. Masculine and feminine i-stems are declined alike. As distinguished from consonant stems, they have **-ium** in the genitive plural and **-īs** or **-ēs** in the accusative plural.

<table>
<tr><td colspan="3">caedēs, F., slaughter
(stem caedi-, base caed-)</td><td colspan="2">hostis, M., enemy
(stem hosti-, base host-)</td></tr>
<tr><td>Nom.</td><td>caedēs</td><td>caedēs</td><td>hostis</td><td>hostēs</td></tr>
<tr><td>Gen.</td><td>caedis</td><td>cae'dium</td><td>hostis</td><td>hos'tium</td></tr>
<tr><td>Dat.</td><td>caedī</td><td>cae'dibus</td><td>hostī</td><td>hos'tibus</td></tr>
<tr><td>Acc.</td><td>caedem</td><td>caedīs, -ēs</td><td>hostem</td><td>hostīs, -ēs</td></tr>
<tr><td>Abl.</td><td>caede</td><td>cae'dibus</td><td>hoste</td><td>hos'tibus</td></tr>
</table>

<table>
<tr><td colspan="3">urbs, F., city
(stem urbi-, base urb-)</td><td colspan="2">cohors, F., cohort
(stem cohorti-, base cohort-)</td></tr>
<tr><td>Nom.</td><td>urbs</td><td>urbēs</td><td>co'hors</td><td>cohor'tēs</td></tr>
<tr><td>Gen.</td><td>urbis</td><td>ur'bium</td><td>cohor'tis</td><td>cohor'tium</td></tr>
<tr><td>Dat.</td><td>urbī</td><td>ur'bibus</td><td>cohor'tī</td><td>cohor'tibus</td></tr>
<tr><td>Acc.</td><td>urbem</td><td>urbīs, -ēs</td><td>cohor'tem</td><td>cohor'tīs, -ēs</td></tr>
<tr><td>Abl.</td><td>urbe</td><td>ur'bibus</td><td>cohor'te</td><td>cohor'tibus</td></tr>
</table>

a. A few nouns have either -**ī** or -**e** in the ablative singular: as, **cīvis** (abl. **cīvī** or **cīve**), **ignis** (abl. **ignī** or **igne**), **nāvis** (abl. **nāvī** or **nāve**).

b. A number of Latin and Greek nouns ending in **-is** or **-x** have passed into English without change and form their plural in **-es**: as, *analysis, analyses*; *appendix, appendices*; *axis, axes*; *basis, bases*; *crisis, crises*; *hypothesis, hypotheses*; *index, indices*; *oasis, oases*; *parenthesis, parentheses*; *thesis, theses*; *vertex, vertices*.

---

[1] Motto of the University of Mississippi.

413. Masculine and feminine i-stems include the following :

a. Nouns in -ēs or -is with the same number of syllables in the genitive as in the nominative. Thus **caedēs, caedis,** is an i-stem, but **mīles, mīlitis,** is a consonant stem.

b. Nouns of more than one syllable in -ns or -rs: as, **cliēns, cohors.**

c. Nouns of one syllable in -s or -x preceded by a consonant: as, **urbs, arx.**

RŌMĀNĪ ET SABĪNĪ

First learn the special vocabulary, p. 371

414. Erant in urbe novā multī virī, sed mulierēs paucae. Itaque Rōmulus spectācula[1] pūblica comparāvit et Sabīnōs,[2] fīnitimōs suōs, invītāvit.[3] Magnus numerus Sabīnōrum cum fīliābus ad spectācula Rōmāna vēnērunt. Tum signō datō[4] Rōmānī fīliās Sabīnōrum rapuērunt. Statim Sabīnī cohortēs 5 ad bellum ēvocāvērunt, et iam caedēs misera nōn longē aberat. Sed mulierēs, fīliae Sabīnōrum, quās Rōmānī in mātrimōnium dūxerant, in medium proelium properāvērunt et bellum prohibuērunt.

1. **spectāculum, -ī,** N., *spectacle, game.* 2. **Sabīnī, -ōrum,** M., *the Sabines,* the nearest neighbors of Rome. 3. **invītō, -āre,** *invite.* 4. Ablative absolute.

415. 1. The king had been driven from his realm by his wicked brother. 2. Where did Romulus build the new city? 3. After the city was built,[1] whose daughters did the Romans marry? 4. The neighbors commanded the Romans to give back the women, but could not persuade them.[2] 5. The cohorts of the enemy were thrown down from the rampart with great slaughter.[3]

1. Ablative absolute. 2. What case? See § 224. 3. What construction? See § 168.

MULIERĒS BELLUM PROHIBUĒRUNT

LESSON LXI

Deus dītat — God enriches [1]

THE THIRD DECLENSION, *I*-STEMS, NEUTERS

416. Neuter i-stems end in -e, -al, or -ar in the nominative singular, in -ī in the ablative singular, and have an -i- in every form of the plural. They are declined as follows:

	mare, N., *sea* (stem mari-, base mar-)	animal, N., *animal* (stem animāli-, base animāl-)	calcar, N., *spur* (stem calcāri-, base calcār-)	TERMINATIONS
NOM.	ma′re	an′imal	cal′car	—
GEN.	ma′ris	animā′lis	calcā′ris	-is
DAT.	ma′rī	animā′lī	calcā′rī	-ī
ACC.	ma′re	an′imal	cal′car	—
ABL.	ma′rī	animā′lī	calcā′rī	-ī
NOM.	ma′ria	animā′lia	calcā′ria	-ia
GEN.	——	animā′lium	calcā′rium	-ium
DAT.	ma′ribus	animā′libus	calcā′ribus	-ibus
ACC.	ma′ria	animā′lia	calcā′ria	-ia
ABL.	ma′ribus	animā′libus	calcā′ribus	-ibus

a. In the nominative and accusative singular the final -i of the stem is either dropped or changed to -e.

EXERCISES

First learn the special vocabulary, page 371

417. Equitēs Rōmānī calcāria magna gerēbant et equī eōrum erant pulchra animālia. 2. Ōra Galliae maribus et īnsulīs continētur. 3. Gallia multās cīvitātēs et multās linguās habet.

[1] Motto of the state of Arizona, whose wealth consists of minerals.

4. Prīncipēs cīvitātis, quī bellō semper studēbant, lēgātōs ad Rōmānōs remittī vetuērunt. 5. Vīdistīne animālia magna quae in mediō marī habitant? Pauca vīdī. 6. Num calcāria quae eques gerit equō nocēbunt? Nōn nocēbunt. 7. Barbarī cōpiās suās trāns flūmen dūxērunt, sed lēgātus iussit cohortēs castrīs[1] continērī. 8. Linguae Latīnae magnā dīligentiā studēmus. 9. Pōnite castra celeriter, hostēs impedīmenta iam cēpērunt.

1. Latin, *by camp*, ablative of means.

418. 1. Do their horsemen wear spurs? I think so. 2. If the danger is great, we can keep the soldiers in camp.[1] 3. We saw many large animals in the forests of Germany. 4. To sail through the deep seas is pleasing to sailors.[2] 5. The Romans found savage peoples and strange[3] languages in those states.

1. Compare § 417. 7. 2. See § 130. 3. **novus, -a, -um.**

THE TIBER AT THE FOOT OF THE AVENTINE

LESSON LXII

Nīl sine nūmine — Nothing without divine guidance [1]

THE THIRD DECLENSION, IRREGULAR NOUNS

419. A few nouns of the third declension are somewhat irregular in inflection. Among these are the following:

	homō, M., *man*	vīs, F., *force*	iter, N., *march*
Nom.	ho'mō	vīs	iter
Gen.	ho'minis	vīs (*rare*)	iti'neris
Dat.	ho'minī	vī (*rare*)	iti'nerī
Acc.	ho'minem	vim	iter
Abl.	ho'mine	vī	iti'nere
Nom.	ho'minēs	vī'rēs	iti'nera
Gen.	ho'minum	vī'rium	iti'nerum
Dat.	homi'nibus	vī'ribus	itine'ribus
Acc.	ho'minēs	vī'rīs, -ēs	iti'nera
Abl.	homi'nibus	vī'ribus	itine'ribus

a. The accusative plural **vīrīs** may be distinguished from the dative and ablative plural **virīs** (from **vir**) by the length of the **i** in the first syllable.

EXERCISES

First learn the special vocabulary, page 372

DĒ BRŪTŌ PRĪMŌ CŌNSULE

420. Ōlim Rōmānī ā rēgibus regēbantur, sed post multōs annōs rēgēs vī et armīs pulsī sunt atque cōnsulibus imperium commissum est. Prīmus cōnsul erat Brūtus, quem ēgregiā virtūte populus amābat. Tamen erant in urbe quīdam [1] malī

---

[1] Motto of the state of Colorado.

154

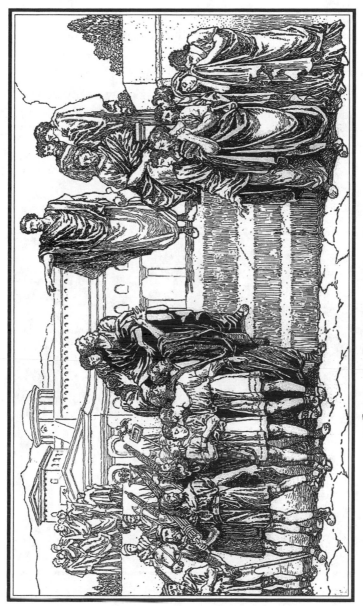

BRŪTUS FĪLIŌS SUŌS INTERFICĪ IUBET

hominēs quī imperiō cōnsulis inimīcī erant ac rēgēs redūcī cupiēbant. In eōrum numerō erant fīliī Brūtī. Itaque Brūtus fīliōs suōs in iūdicium vocāvit et iussit eōs interficī. Quid dē eō exemplō virtūtis Rōmānae putās?

   1. **quīdam**, *some, certain.*

421. 1. The men who were in the boat were overcome by the violence of the sea. 2. A few who were saved will march to the nearest city. 3. After the battle had begun,[1] our soldiers by their great valor quickly conquered the remainder of the enemy.[2] 4. Nevertheless, the enemy did not flee, but led their forces back into camp.

   1. Ablative absolute. 2. Latin idiom, *the remaining enemy.*

ORPHEUS AND EURYDICE

LESSON LXIII

Iūstitia omnibus — Justice to all[1]

ORPHEUS ET EURYDICĒ

First learn the special vocabulary, page 372

422. Poētae multās fābulās dē Orpheō, sacrō vāte,[1] nārrant. Eum etiam animālia et arborēs[2] libenter[3] audiēbant. Orpheus puellam pulchram, Eurydicēn,[4] in mātrimōnium dūxerat, sed mors eam rapuit et Orpheus vir miser relictus est. Tum Orpheus dolōrem[5] suum continēre nōn poterat et ausus est 5 ad īnferōs[6] dēscendere.[7] Ibi Plūtōnem,[8] rēgem īnferōrum, petiit et dīxit: "Cūr, Plūtō, eam iniūriam miserō virō fēcistī? Certē nōn aequum est Eurydicēn mortī darī. Eam redūcere studeō." Tum dulcissimē[9] cecinit[10] et etiam Plū-tōnī persuāsit. Tamen Plūtō eum spectāre Eurydicēn vetuit 10 et dīxit, "Sī in eō locō eam spectābis, posteā eam vidēbis numquam." Iam salūs nōn longē aberat. Sed Orpheus resistere nōn potuit et Eurydicēn spectāvit. Statim magnā vī Eurydicē rapta est et numquam est reddita.

1. **vātēs, -is,** M. and F., *bard, inspired singer.* 2. **arbor, -oris,** F., *tree.* 3. *Gladly.* 4. *Eu-ryd'i-ce.* This is the accusative case. 5. **dolor, -ōris,** M., *grief.* 6. **īnferī, -ōrum,** M., *shades, lower world.* 7. **dēscendō, -ere,** *descend.* 8. **Plūtō, -ōnis,** M., *Pluto.* 9. *Very sweetly.* 10. Perfect of **canō, -ere,** *sing.*

423. Answer the following questions in Latin:

1. Quī dē Orpheō fābulās nārrant?
2. Quam puellam Orpheus in mātrimōnium dūxit?
3. Cūr mala erat fortūna Orpheī?
4. Quid Orpheus facere studuit?
5. Quid Plūtō vetuit?
6. Num Orpheus puellam servāre potuit?

[1] Motto of the District of Columbia.

LESSON LXIV

Ālīs volat propriīs — She flies with her own wings [1]

WORD FORMATION

424. Selecting appropriate prefixes from § 341, write a list of English derivatives from the following verbs. Define the derivatives, looking them up in the English dictionary if necessary.

putō	agō	habeō
moveō	parō	pellō
capiō	pugnō	teneō

425. Latin Suffixes. Many Latin words are formed from others by means of suffixes. Thus:

cīvis, *citizen*	cīvitās, *state*
adveniō, *come to*	adventus, *arrival*
capiō, *take*	captīvus, *captive*
aequus, *level*	aequō, *make level*
līber, *free*	lībertās, *freedom*
magnus, *great*	magnitūdō, *greatness*
pecus, *cattle*	pecūnia, *wealth*
vir, *man*	virtūs, *manliness, courage*

We see, too, that by the use of suffixes different parts of speech are derived from each other, such as verbs from nouns, nouns from verbs, nouns from adjectives, etc. Some of the suffixes are readily recognized and have a uniform and easily defined meaning. We shall study some of the more important ones later on (§§ 626–629). A knowledge of prefixes and suffixes will greatly increase your Latin and English vocabulary, as it will enable you to grasp the meaning of many words without consulting a dictionary.

---

[1] Motto of the state of Oregon.

426. English Suffixes. Suffixes are equally important in English. Many of them are of Latin origin and have the same meaning as in Latin. As an illustration of the part that suffixes play in the making of English words, note the following combinations of *port-*, 'carry,' from Latin **portō** :

porter portly portage portal portable

Using prefixes as well, we get a much larger number : as,

comport	unexportable	importation
comportable	exportation	importer
deport	exporter	reimport
deportable	reëxport	report
deportation	import	reportable
deportment	importable	unreportable
export	important	reporter
exportable	unimportant	etc.

Eighth Review, Lessons LVII–LXIV, §§ 774–777

A ROMAN STREET SCENE

LESSON LXV

Tē Deum laudāmus — We praise Thee, O God

ADJECTIVES OF THE THIRD DECLENSION, THREE ENDINGS

427. All adjectives are either of the first and second declensions (like **bonus, pulcher, līber**) or of the third declension.

428. Nearly all adjectives of the third declension have i-stems and are declined like nouns with i-stems (§ 412).

429. Classes of Adjectives. Adjectives of the third declension are classified as follows:

Class I. Adjectives of three endings — a different form in the nominative for each gender.

Class II. Adjectives of two endings — the nominative of the masculine and feminine alike, the neuter different.

Class III. Adjectives of one ending — the nominative masculine, feminine, and neuter all alike.

430. Adjectives of the third declension in -er have three endings; those in -is have two; the others have one.

CLASS I

431. Adjectives of three endings are declined as follows:

ācer, ācris, ācre (stem ācri-, base ācr-), *sharp, keen, eager*

	MASC.	FEM.	NEUT.	MASC.	FEM.	NEUT.
NOM.	ācer	ācris	ācre	ācrēs	ācrēs	ācria
GEN.	ācris	ācris	ācris	ācrium	ācrium	ācrium
DAT.	ācrī	ācrī	ācrī	ācribus	ācribus	ācribus
ACC.	ācrem	ācrem	ācre	ācrīs, -ēs	ācrīs, -ēs	ācria
ABL.	ācrī	ācrī	ācrī	ācribus	ācribus	ācribus

160

EXERCISES

First learn the special vocabulary, page 372

432. 1. Rōmānī ācre proelium cum cōpiīs pedestribus equestribusque hostium facient. 2. Prōcliō commissō equitēs nostrī cōpiās equestrēs hostium in fugam dare cupient. 3. Hostēs magnā virtūte pugnābunt, tamen vincentur. 4. Mulierēs puellaeque, quae proclium opectant, aut capientur aut salūtem fugā petent. 5. Castra nostra in aequō locō posita sunt. 6. Fīrmum praesidium ante castra locātum erat. 7. Cōpiae pedestrēs per silvās magnīs itineribus[1] reductae erant. 8. Hominēs eius cīvitātis bona tēla habēbant et vāllum magnā vī oppugnāvērunt.

1. **magna itinera,** *forced marches.*

433. 1. The sailors of Britain are not timid, and do not fear death. 2. But with eager hearts they dare to sail even through the midst of the perils of the sea. 3. Leaving safety behind,[1] they put the enemy to flight. 4. The spurs which the cavalry forces wore[2] were sharp. 5. The men had swift horses, and sought safety in flight.[3] 6. Either kill the captive or let him go.[4]

1. Ablative absolute. 2. **gerō, -ere.** 3. Latin, *by flight.* 4. Imperative of **dīmittō, -ere.**

434. Derivation. Define the following English words and give the Latin word to which each is related:

dislocate	dependent	disintegrate	dispute
prohibition	project	legation	temporal
amplify	official	minimize	invincible

LESSON LXVI

Chrīstō et Ecclēsiae — For Christ and the Church[1]

ADJECTÍVES OF THE THIRD DECLENSION, TWO ENDINGS

CLASS II

435. Adjectives of two endings are declined as follows:

omnis, omne (stem omni-, base omn-), *every, all*[2]

	M. AND F.	NEUT.	M. AND F.	NEUT.
Nom.	omnis	omne	omnēs	omnia
Gen.	omnis	omnis	omnium	omnium
Dat.	omnī	omnī	omnibus	omnibus
Acc.	omnem	omne	omnīs, -ēs	omnia
Abl.	omnī	omnī	omnibus	omnibus

EXERCISES

First learn the special vocabulary, page 373

436. 1. Brūtus, prīmus cōnsul, suōs fīliōs in iūdicium vocāvit. 2. Brūtus eōs ad certam mortem dūcī iussit. 3. Fīliī cōnsulis in[1] salūtem commūnem cōnsilia facere incēperant. 4. Itaque coāctī sunt grave supplicium dare. 5. Brūtus erat certus amīcus patriae et omnia[2] prō bonō pūblicō faciēbat. 6. Etiam Rōmānīs id grave supplicium nōn grātum erat. 7. Nōn omnēs Brūtō similēs esse possunt. 8. Rōmānī omnibus terrīs multa exempla virtūtis vērae dedērunt.

1. *Against.* 2. Adjective used as a noun. This usage is very common.

[1] Motto of Harvard University.
[2] **Omnis** is usually translated *every* in the singular and *all* in the plural.

437. I. The languages of Gaul and of Italy were not at all similar. 2. The wars which the Romans waged with the Gauls were long and severe. 3. The fortune of war is not always sure. 4. All men are compelled to defend the common safety, or the country cannot be preserved. 5. Our courageous soldiers with their swift horses will keep[1] the violence of the enemy from our towns.

1. prohibeō, -ēre.

LESSON LXVII

Parēs cum paribus facillimē congregantur — Birds of a feather
flock together[1]

ADJECTIVES OF THE THIRD DECLENSION, ONE ENDING

CLASS III

438. Adjectives of one ending are declined as follows:

pār (stem pari-, base par-), *equal*

	M. AND F.	NEUT.	M. AND F.	NEUT.
NOM.	pār	pār	parēs	paria
GEN.	paris	paris	parium	parium
DAT.	parī	parī	paribus	paribus
ACC.	parem	pār	parīs, -ēs	paria
ABL.	parī	parī	paribus	paribus

a. Some adjectives of one ending have -e in the ablative singular.

b. Adjectives declined like pār do not always end in -r, but have various other endings, such as -x, -ns, -es, etc. The final letter of the base is shown by the genitive: as, fēlix, fēlīcis; āmēns, āmentis; etc.

[1] Literally, *Equals most easily assemble with equals.* A Latin proverb, quoted by Cicero in his well-known essay on old age.

MIDAS, THE KING OF THE GOLDEN TOUCH [1]

First learn the special vocabulary, page 373

439. Ōlim erat rēx cuius nōmen erat Midās. Eī deus Bacchus erat amīcus et dīxerat: "Tibi,[1] rēx, beneficium dare studeō. Id quod maximē petis, tibi dabō." Sed sapientia rēgis pār bonae fortūnae nōn erat et respondit, "Cupiō omnia quae corpore meō tangam [2] in aurum [3] mū- 5 tārī." [4] Statim rēx accēpit dōnum [5] quod petīverat. Saxum [6] tangit et saxum in aurum solidum [7] mūtātur. Tum arborem [8] tangit, et arbor est similis aurō. Rēx gaudet [9] et deō grātiās agit. Sed cum cibum [10] et aquam tangit, et cibus et aqua in aurum mūtantur. Magnopere perterritus Midās mortem 10 certam timuit et deum vocāvit: "Servā, servā, Bacche. Dā auxilium miserō. Dōnum [5] tuum nōn est beneficium, sed grave supplicium." Bacchus audīvit et iussit eum in flūmine corpus suum lavere.[11] Rēx pāruit et līberātus est. Etiam nunc harēna [12] eius flūminis est aurea.[13] 15

1. tibi, *to you.* 2. Future of tangō, -ere, *touch.* 3. aurum, -ī, N., *gold.* 4. mūtō, -āre, *change.* 5. dōnum, -ī, N., *gift.* 6. saxum, -ī, N., *stone.* 7. solidus, -a, -um, *solid.* 8. arbor, -oris, F., *tree.* 9. gaudeō, -ēre, *rejoice.* 10. cibus, -ī, M., *food.* 11. lavō, -ere, *wash.* 12. harēna, -ae, F., *sand.* 13. aureus, -a, -um, *golden.*

440. Give the principal parts of all the familiar verbs used in § 439. Decline the nouns **aqua, beneficium, rēx, nōmen, mors, corpus.** Decline the adjectives **certus, similis.**

[1] Read "The Golden Touch" in Hawthorne's "The Wonder-Book."

ROMAN SILVER CUPS

LESSON LXVIII

Excelsior — Higher[1]

REGULAR COMPARISON OF ADJECTIVES · THE COMPARATIVE WITH *QUAM*

441. Comparison of Adjectives in English. In English, adjectives regularly change their form to express quality in different degrees. This is called comparison. There are three degrees of comparison : the *positive*, the *comparative*, and the *superlative*. The usual way of comparing an adjective is by using the suffix *-er* for the comparative and *-est* for the superlative : as, positive *high*, comparative *higher*, superlative *highest*. Sometimes we use the adverbs *more* and *most* : as, positive *beautiful*, comparative *more beautiful*, superlative *most beautiful*.

442. Comparison of Adjectives in Latin. In Latin, as in English, adjectives are regularly compared by adding suffixes. From the base of the positive the comparative is formed by adding **-ior**, masculine and feminine, and **-ius**, neuter ; the superlative, by adding **-issimus, -issima, -issimum.** Thus, **altus** (base **alt-**), *high*, and **gravis** (base **grav-**), *heavy*, are compared as follows :

altus, -a, -um,	**altior, altius,**	**altissimus, -a, -um,**
high	*higher*	*highest*
gravis, grave,	**gravior, gravius,**	**gravissimus, -a, -um,**
heavy	*heavier*	*heaviest*

443. Adjectives in **-er** form the comparative regularly, but the superlative is formed by adding **-rimus, -rima, -rimum** to the nominative masculine of the positive. Thus, **ācer** (base **ācr-**),

[1] Motto of the state of New York.

165

sharp; **pulcher** (base **pulchr-**), *pretty*; and **līber** (base **līber-**), *free*, have the following comparative and superlative forms:

ācer, ācris, ācre, *sharp*	**ācrior, ācrius,** *sharper*	**ācerrimus, -a, -um,** *sharpest*
pulcher, pulchra, pulchrum, *pretty*	**pulchrior, pulchrius,** *prettier*	**pulcherrimus, -a, -um,** *prettiest*
līber, lībera, līberum, *free*	**līberior, līberius,** *freer*	**līberrimus, -a, -um,** *freest*

444. The superlative is often translated by *very* : as, **altissimus,** *very high.*

445. Comparative with *quam.* In English two objects are compared by the use of a comparative followed by the conjunction *than* : as, *the ditch is wider than the wall.* In this sentence *ditch* is nominative, subject of *is*; and *wall* is also nominative, subject of *is* understood. That is to say, the two objects compared are in the same case. In Latin the word for *than* is **quam** and the usage is the same. Thus the sentence above becomes **fossa est lātior quam mūrus.**

<u>**446.**</u> **Rule for Comparative with** *quam. In comparisons with* **quam** *the two objects compared are in the same case.*

EXERCISES

First learn the special vocabulary, page 373

447. 1. Cōnsul est aequior quam rēx. 2. Supplicium rēgis erat gravissimum. 3. Equus est celerior quam homō. 4. Sed equus nōn est omnium animālium celerrimum.[1] 5. Virtūs Scaevolae, quī ignem et mortem nōn timēbat, erat clārissima. 6. Quis erat fortior quam Thēseus, quī puerōs puellāsque patriae servāvit? 7. Viae Rōmānae erant longissimae et per multās terrās patēbant. 8. Iter quod per silvās dūcēbat erat difficile. 9. Castra in locō inīquissimō posita erant.   10. Id iter erat brevius et facilius.   11. Mare est altius quam flūmen.

1. Neuter, agreeing with **animal** understood.

448. 1. The wall of that town was very high.   2. Galba's horse is more beautiful and swifter than mine.   3. Those spears are very sharp.   4. That route was longer and more difficult.   5. The longest rivers are not always the deepest.   6. The fire which the goddess gave to the queen was very sacred.

449. Compare the adjectives **brevis, fortis, nōtus, gravis, crēber, miser, grātus, longus, tardus, integer.**

LESSON LXIX

Silent lēgēs inter arma — Laws are silent amid arms [1]

DECLENSION OF COMPARATIVES · THE ABLATIVE OF THE MEASURE OF DIFFERENCE

450. Declension of Comparatives. Comparatives are adjectives of the third declension. They are of two endings (§ 429) and are declined as follows:

altior, *higher*

	MASC. AND FEM.	NEUT.	MASC. AND FEM.	NEUT.
Nom.	altior	altius	altiōrēs	altiōra
Gen.	altiōris	altiōris	altiorum	altiōrum
Dat.	altiōrī	altiōrī	altiōribus	altiōribus
Acc.	altiōrem	altius	altiōrēs	altiōra
Abl.	altiōre	altiōre	altiōribus	altiōribus

451. Ablative of Measure of Difference.   In the sentence *Sextus is a foot taller than Julia* the word *foot* expresses the measure of difference in height between Sextus and Julia.

[1] From Cicero, the greatest Roman orator.

The Latin form of expression would be *Sextus is taller by a foot than Julia,* Sextus est longior pede quam Iūlia, and the ablative pede is called the *ablative of the measure of difference.*

452. Rule for Ablative of Measure of Difference. *With comparatives and words implying comparison the ablative is used to denote the measure of difference.*

a. The neuter ablatives multō, *by much*; nihilō, *by nothing*; and paulō, *by a little,* are very common in this construction.

EXERCISES

First learn the special vocabulary, page 373

453. 1. Corpus hominis est multō levius quam corpus equī. 2. Inter ea oppida iter est nihilō facilius. 3. Puellae sunt paulō breviōrēs quam puerī. 4. Mea poena est multō gravior quam tua. 5. Cōpiae pedestrēs erant nihilō fortiōrēs quam cōpiae equestrēs. 6. Nihil grātius quam fābulam dē virtūte Dentātī audīvimus. 7. Estne tua soror brevior quam mea? Longior pede ea est. 8. Animālia vīdimus quae multō tardiōra sunt quam equī. 9. Urbe expugnātā, fīlia pulcherrima rēgīnae inter ignēs et arma relicta est. 10. Oppidum vestrum ab eō locō magnō spatiō abest.

454. 1. The marches which the commander made were neither very long nor very swift. 2. The commander thanked the bravest legion most of all. 3. Your spears are no[1] longer and no lighter than mine. 4. Between the Gauls and the Germans very frequent wars were waged. 5. That river is no[1] wider, but a foot[1] deeper. 6. Nothing is more beautiful than Rome, the capital of Italy. 7. We are a long distance[2] from Italy.

1. Ablative of measure of difference. 2. Latin, *distant by a great space.*

455. Decline the comparatives occurring in § 453.

LESSON LXX

Lūx et vēritās — Light and truth[1]

IRREGULAR COMPARISON OF ADJECTIVES · THE DECLENSION OF *PLŪS*

456. Irregular Comparison of Adjectives. Some adjectives in English have irregular comparison : as, *good, better, best*; *much, more, most*. So some Latin adjectives are compared irregularly. Among these are the following :

POSITIVE	COMPARATIVE	SUPERLATIVE
bonus, -a, -um, *good*	melior, melius	optimus, -a, -um
magnus, -a, -um, *great*	maior, maius	maximus, -a, -um
malus, -a, -um, *bad*	peior, peius	pessimus, -a, -um
multus, -a, -um, *much*	——, plūs	plūrimus, -a, -um
parvus, -a, -um, *small*	minor, minus	minimus, -a, -um

457. The following adjectives, with regular comparative, form the superlative by adding -limus to the base of the positive :

POSITIVE	COMPARATIVE	SUPERLATIVE
facilis, -e, *easy*	facilior, -ius	facillimus, -a, -um
difficilis, -e, *hard*	difficilior, -ius	difficillimus, -a, -um
similis, -e, *like*	similior, -ius	simillimus, -a, -um
dissimilis, -e, *unlike*	dissimilior, -ius	dissimillimus, -a, -um

458. Declension of *plūs*. Plūs, *more*, in the singular is a neuter noun. The plural (*more, many, several*) is used as an adjective. It is declined as follows :

---

[1] Motto of Yale University, the University of Indiana, the University of North Carolina, and the University of Montana.

169

170 IRREGULAR COMPARISON OF ADJECTIVES

	SINGULAR	PLURAL	
	NEUT. NOUN	MASC. AND FEM. ADJ.	NEUT. ADJ.
NOM.	plūs	plūrēs	plūra
GEN.	plūris	plūrium	plūrium
DAT.	——	plūribus	plūribus
ACC.	plūs	plūrīs, -ēs	plūra
ABL.	plūre	plūribus	plūribus

EXERCISES

First learn the special vocabulary, page 374

459. 1. Reliquī hostēs, quī proelium committere audēbant, cōpiīs nostrīs nōn parēs erant atque in maximam silvam fūgērunt. 2. Lībertās est multō melior quam servitūs. 3. Nihil peius quam servitūs esse potest. 4. Lēgēs quibus¹ pārēmus sunt lēgibus² Rōmānīs nōn dissimillimae. 5. Dux vetuit plūrēs captīvōs dīmittī. 6. Linguae Galliae et Britanniae erant simillimae. 7. Fortēs mulierēs difficillimum iter aut perīcula plūrima silvārum nōn timuērunt. 8. Rēx pessimus ampliōrem pecūniam petiit, sed populus plūs dare nōn potuit. 9. Minōrēs prīncipēs cīvitātis maximam auctōritātem nōn habēbant. 10. Agrīs³ ignī vāstātīs, dux oppida maxima oppugnāre incēpit.

1. What case? See § 224. 2. Dative, § 130. 3. Ablative absolute.

460. Among the Romans the consuls had the greatest authority. 2. After the kings¹ were driven out, greater liberty was given to the people. 3. The smallest states often have the bravest men and the best women. 4. The shortest route was much more difficult than the longest. 5. After that time the captives feared either certain death or the worst slavery. 6. Your laws and your languages are very different.²

1. Ablative absolute. 2. Latin, *different by much.*

LESSON LXXI

Omnia praeclāra rāra — All the best things are rare[1]

FORMATION AND COMPARISON OF ADVERBS

461. Formation of Adverbs. An adverb is a word that modifies a verb, an adjective, or another adverb, and generally answers the question *How? Where? When? Why? To what extent?*

462. Rule for Adverbs. *Adverbs modify verbs, adjectives, and other adverbs.*

463. Adverbs are generally derived from adjectives. In English they usually end in *-ly*: as, adjective *brave*, adverb *bravely*. Latin adverbs, too, have certain endings. They are compared, but not declined.

464. Adverbs derived from adjectives of the first and second declensions are formed by adding **-ē** to the base of the adjective.

ADJ.	lātus, *wide*	pulcher, *beautiful*	līber, *free*
ADV.	lātē, *widely*	pulchrē, *beautifully*	lībere, *freely*

465. Adverbs derived from adjectives of the third declension are generally formed by adding **-iter** to the base of the adjective.

ADJ.	ācer, *sharp*	celer, *swift*	brevis, *brief*
ADV.	ācriter, *sharply*	celeriter, *swiftly*	breviter, *briefly*

466. Comparison of Adverbs. Adverbs are compared like the adjectives from which they are derived, except that the comparative ends in **-ius** and the superlative in **-ē**.

[1] From Cicero, Rome's foremost man of letters.

171

POSITIVE	COMPARATIVE	SUPERLATIVE
lātē, *widely*	lātius	lātissimē
pulchrē, *beautifully*	pulchrius	pulcherrimē
līberē, *freely*	līberius	līberrimē
ācriter, *sharply*	ācrius	ācerrimē
similiter, *similarly*	similius	simillimē

467. Using the regular terminations, form adverbs from the following adjectives, and compare them :

longus	brevis	altus	gravis	celer
tardus	similis	malus	levis	fortis

EXERCISES

First learn the special vocabulary, page 374

468. 1. Dux tardissimē prōcessit quod nihil dē nātūrā locī cognōverat. 2. Tum iussit equitēs celerrimē discēdere et hominēs ex proximō oppidō rapere. 3. Post breve tempus equitēs septem[1] hominēs cēpērunt et eōs ad ducem addūxērunt. 4. Dux cupīvit captīvōs nārrāre omnia quae cognōverant. 5. Is captīvīs dīxit : " Dīcite līberrimē, hominēs. Si ita nōn faciētis, gravissimum supplicium dabitis." 6. Tamen septem captīvī nihil respondērunt et certam mortem fortissimē exspectāvērunt.

1. Count seven in Latin ; see § 283.

469. 1. When that plan[1] became known, their[2] allies quickly deserted the city and sought safety in flight.[3] 2. The commander had been very severely wounded by a spear. 3. The soldiers advanced more slowly because they were waiting for fresh troops. 4. The captives were quickly brought to the commander. 5. He wished to learn the nature of the place. 6. A few[1] being lightly wounded, the rest did not advance farther.

1. Ablative absolute. 2. Not **suus**. 3. Latin, *by flight*.

LESSON LXXII

FORMATION AND COMPARISON OF ADVERBS (CONCLUDED)

470. Case Forms used as Adverbs. The accusative or the ablative neuter singular of some adjectives is used adverbially. Thus the comparative adverb in -ius is really the accusative neuter singular of the comparative adjective. Other examples are the following:

> **facile,** *easily,* accusative of **facilis,** *easy*
> **plūrimum,** *very much,* accusative of **plūrimus,** *most*
> **prīmum,** *first,* accusative of **prīmus,** *first*
> **prīmō,** *at first,* ablative of **prīmus,** *first*

471. The following adverbs are formed irregularly and have irregular comparison:

bene, *well*	**melius,** *better*	**optimē,** *best*
diū, *long* (time)	**diūtius,** *longer*	**diūtissimē,** *longest*
magnopere, *greatly*	**magis,** *more*	**maximē,** *most*
saepe, *often*	**saepius,** *oftener*	**saepissimē,** *oftenest*

a. Note the difference in meaning between **diū,** *long* in time, and **longē,** *long* in space.

472. In English, adverbs and adjectives are often compared by means of *more* and *most.* So some Latin adverbs and adjectives are compared by means of **magis,** *more,* and **maximē,** *most*: as, **idōneus,** *suitable*; **magis idōneus,** *more suitable*; **maximē idōneus,** *most suitable.*

a. The Latin comparative sometimes means *quite* or *somewhat,* and the superlative is often best translated by *very* or *exceedingly.*

---

[1] Motto of the University of Missouri.

COLLOQUIUM — DUO DISCIPULĪ

First learn the special vocabulary, page 374

473. PRIMUS. Habēsne multās fābulās in tuō librō?
SECUNDUS. Plūrimās fābulās habeō. Omnēs fābulae sunt bonae ; sed optima fābula, meō iūdiciō, est fābula dē Thēseō. Quam facile et bene perīcula maxima superāvit!

P. Certē facta Thēseī sunt nōtissima, tamen fābula Mānlī, virī clārissimī, meum animum magis tenet. Is Rōmam ā Gallīs quī mūrōs ascenderant servāvit. Facta Mānlī sunt maiōra quam facta Thēseī.

S. Minimē ita putō. Quid autem dē Scaevolā dīcam? Nōnne eius virtūs multō magis ēgregia?

P. Id est vērum, nam is ignem mortemque nōn timēbat. Tamen Dentātus maiōra negōtia, prīmō in bellō deinde in pāce, suscēpit ac saepius patriam servāvit. Itaque Dentātus erat maior quam Scaevola.

S. Iam dē quattuor virīs fāmae nōtissimīs dīximus. Prīmus [1] erat Thēseus, secundus erat Mānlius, tertius erat Scaevola, quārtus erat Dentātus. Dē Brūtō autem, prīmō cōnsule, nōn dīximus. Sed dē omnibus dīcere nōn possumus. Diūtius manēre nōn possum. Frāter meus mē [2] exspectat et vīllā nostrā magnō spatiō absum.

1. Learn the ordinal numerals, *first, second, third, fourth,* as they appear here. 2. *Me.*

474. Derivation. Using prefixes previously studied (§§ 341, 373, 374) and such suffixes as appear in § 426, and any others you know, make a list of at least twenty-five English derivatives from the verbs **nāvigō, timeō, sedeō, vincō, faciō.**

Ninth Review, Lessons LXV–LXXII, §§ 778–782

THE ROMAN CAMPAGNA AND THE ALBAN MOUNT

The great plain surrounding Rome, known as the Campagna, now nearly bare, was in ancient times a terrestrial paradise of villas and gardens. After the fall of the Roman Empire it was laid waste by barbarian invaders and has never been reclaimed. The Alban Mount was the sacred mountain of the Latins. On its slope was built Alba Longa, Rome's mother city

LESSON LXXIII

Ad maiōrem Deī glōriam — To the greater glory of God[1]

THE FOURTH DECLENSION

475. Nouns that end in -ūs in the genitive singular are of the Fourth Declension.

476. Nouns of the fourth declension are either masculine or neuter. The nominative singular of masculine nouns ends in -us; of neuters, in -ū.

a. Feminines, by exception, are **domus,** *house*; **manus,** *hand*; and a few others.

477. Nouns of the fourth declension are declined as follows :

	adventus, M., *arrival* (base advent-)	cornū, N., *horn* (base corn-)	TERMINATIONS MASC.	NEUT.
Nom.	adventus	cornū	-us	-ū
Gen.	adventūs	cornūs	-ūs	-ūs
Dat.	adventuī (-ū)	cornū	-uī (-ū)	-ū
Acc.	adventum	cornū	-um	-ū
Abl.	adventū	cornū	-ū	-ū
Nom.	adventūs	cornua	-ūs	-ua
Gen.	adventuum	cornuum	-uum	-uum
Dat.	adventibus	cornibus	-ibus	-ibus
Acc.	adventūs	cornua	-ūs	-ua
Abl.	adventibus	cornibus	-ibus	-ibus

a. The base is found, as in other declensions, by dropping the ending of the genitive singular.

b. **Cornū** is the only neuter in common use.

[1] Motto of the Jesuits.

EXERCISES

First learn the special vocabulary, page 374

478. 1. Ante adventum Caesaris equitātus hostium magnā celeritāte ācerrimum impetum in castra fēcit. 2. Continēre exercitum ā proeliō difficile erat. 3. Post adventum suum Caesar iussit legiōnēs ex castrīs ēdūcī. 4. Ā dextrō cornū equitātum Rōmānum, ā sinistrō cornū equitātum sociōrum posuit. 5. Signō datō, proelium commissum est. 6. Diū et ācriter in eō locō pugnātum est.[1] 7. Dēnique multīs [2] interfectīs et vulnerātīs, hostēs fugere incēpērunt ad castra quae trāns flūmen posita erant. 8. Hāc victōriā cognitā, cīvitātēs proximae, prīmum minōrēs, deinde eae quae plūrimum poterant, pācem petiērunt.

1. See § 259, note 3. 2. Adjective used as a noun, ablative absolute.

479. 1. After Cæsar's arrival [1] was known, the cavalry fought well. 2 First on the right wing, then on the left, the signal was given. 3. The swiftness of our attack terrified the army most of all. 4. Lesbia remained a little [2] longer,[3] because she was expecting her sister. 5. The farmer held the animal by the horn. 6. He very easily led it to the shore.

1. Ablative absolute. 2. Ablative of measure of difference. 3. Why not longius?

OFFERING A SACRIFICE

LESSON LXXIV

In lūmine tuō vidēbimus lūmen — In thy light we shall see light[1]

EXPRESSIONS OF PLACE

480. Regular Expressions of Place. The place *to which*, the place *from which*, and the place *at* or *in which* are regularly expressed by prepositions with their proper cases. From this general principle we deduce the following rules:

481. Rule for Accusative of Place to Which. *The place to which is expressed by* **ad** *or* **in** *with the accusative, and answers the question* **Whither ?**

> Galba ad casam properat, *Galba hastens to his cottage*

482. Rule for Ablative of Place from Which. *The place from which is expressed by* **ā** *or* **ab**, **dē**, **ē** *or* **ex**, *with the ablative, and answers the question* **Whence ?** (Cf. § 295.)

> Galba ā casā properat, *Galba hastens from his cottage*

483. Rule for Ablative of Place at or in Which.[2] *The place at or in which is expressed by the ablative with* **in**, *and answers the question* **Where ?**

> Galba in casā habitat, *Galba lives in his cottage*

484. Important Exceptions. Names of towns and small islands, **domus**, *home*,[3] and **rūs**, *country*, omit the preposition in expressions of place.

> Galba Athēnās properat, *Galba hastens to Athens*
> Galba Athēnīs properat, *Galba hastens from Athens*

---

[1] Motto of Columbia University.
[2] This is often called the locative ablative (from **locus**, *place*).
[3] When **domus** means *house*, the preposition is used.

177

> Galba Athēnīs habitat, *Galba lives at* (or *in*) *Athens*
> Galba domum properat, *Galba hastens home*
> Galba rūs properat, *Galba hastens to the country*
> Galba domō properat, *Galba hastens from home*
> Galba rūre properat, *Galba hastens from the country*

a. Names of *countries*, like **Germānia, Italia**, etc., do not come under these exceptions. With them prepositions must be used.

485. Locative Case. Names of towns and small islands that are singular and belong to the first or second declension express the place *at which* by the so-called *locative* case. This is like the genitive singular in form. Other locatives are **domī**,[1] *at home*, and **rūrī**, *in the country*.

> Galba Rōmae habitat, *Galba lives at Rome*
> Galba Corinthī habitat, *Galba lives at Corinth*
> Galba domī habitat, *Galba lives at home*
> Galba rūrī habitat, *Galba lives in the country*

a. When the name of the town is *plural*, there is no special locative form and the ablative must be used (§ 483).

> Galba Athēnīs habitat, *Galba lives at Athens*

EXERCISES

First learn the special vocabulary, page 375

486. 1. Num[1] frāter tuus iter in Galliam cum exercitū Caesaris fēcit? 2. Minimē. Frāter meus domī mānsit. 3. Ubi est domus tua? 4. Anteā rūrī habitābāmus, nunc in urbe domum habēmus. 5. Habitāsne Rōmae? 6. Nōn Rōmae sed Athēnīs[2] habitō, quae urbs est in Graeciā. Mox ab Italiā nāvigābō et domum celerrimē contendam. Nōnne cupis Athēnās, urbem Minervae, nāvigāre? 7. Cupiō, sed nōn possum. Officia pūblica mē[3] prohibent. Meliōra tempora exspectō.

---

[1] For the declension of **domus** see § 813.

ATHĒNAE, URBS MINERVAE

Tum in nāvem ascendam atque prīmum Athēnās, deinde ad reliquās urbēs clārās, quae magnō spatiō absunt, contendam.

1. See § 251. 2. **Athēnae, -ārum,** F., *Athens.* 3. *Me.*

487. 1. The cavalry was on the right wing, the infantry on the left. 2. Ambassadors of the king hastened to Rome and thanked[1] the consul. 3. In the country we saw an ample supply of grain. 4. The men who were the most powerful remained at Rome. 5. They were waiting for the arrival of a ship. 6. When an attack[2] had been made on the city, the consul fled from Rome into the country.

1. **grātiās agere,** followed by the dative. 2. Ablative absolute.

LESSON LXXV

Rēgnant populī — The peoples rule[1]

THE FIFTH DECLENSION · THE ABLATIVE OF TIME

488. Fifth Declension. Nouns that end in -ēī in the genitive singular are of the Fifth Declension. The nominative singular ends in -ēs.

489. Nouns of the fifth declension are feminine, except **diēs,** *day,* which is usually masculine.

490. Nouns of the fifth declension are declined as follows:

diēs (base di), M., *day*   rēs (base r-), F., *thing*   TERMINA-
                                                           TIONS

	diēs	diēs	rēs	rēs	-ēs	-ērum
Nom.	diēs	diēs	rēs	rēs	-ēs	-ērum
Gen.	diēī	diērum	reī	rērum	-ĕī	-ēs
Dat.	diēī	diēbus	reī	rēbus	-ĕī	-ēbus
Acc.	diem	diēs	rem	rēs	-em	-ēs
Abl.	diē	diēbus	rē	rēbus	-ē	-ēbus

1 Motto of the state of Arkansas.

a. The vowel e which appears in every form is regularly long. But it is shortened in the ending -eī after a consonant, as in rĕī; and before -m in the accusative singular, as in diem. (Cf. § 194. 2.)

b. Only diēs and rēs are declined throughout. Other nouns of this declension lack all or a part of the plural.

c. What do the abbreviations A. M. and P. M. stand for? (Cf. p. 292.)

491. Declension shown by Genitive. The key to the declension of a noun is the ending of its genitive singular. Review the five distinctive genitive endings given below.

DECLENSION	GENITIVE ENDING
I	-ae
II	-ī
III	-is
IV	-ūs
V	-ĕī

492. Ablative of Time When. The ablative relation of *at, in,* or *on* (§ 65) may refer to *time* as well as to place: as, *at noon, in summer, on the first day.* The ablative expressing this relation is called the *ablative of time.*

493. Rule for Ablative of Time When. *The time when or within which anything happens is expressed by the ablative without a preposition.*

a. Occasionally the preposition in is found. Compare the English *The next day we started* and *On the next day we started.*

EXERCISES

First learn the special vocabulary, page 375

494. 1. Hieme diēs sunt multō breviōrēs quam aestāte. 2. Prīmā lūce agricolae labōrāre incēpērunt. 3. Populus oppidum nocte relīquit quod diūtius manēre timuit. 4. Hieme Rōmae habitāmus, aestāte rūrī. 5. Omnēs rēs quās hominēs pessimī fēcerant clāriōrēs erant quam lūx. 6. Proximō[1] annō in Italiā domī eram. 7. Eīs rēbus cognitīs, omnēs paulō ācrius contendere incēpērunt. 8. Dux iussit legiōnem prīmam mediā nocte discēdere. 9. Eō diē vīdimus multōs ignēs quī agrōs hostium vāstābant. 10. Ignēs magnō spatiō aberant.

1. *Last.* It may also mean *next* if the sense demands that translation.

495. 1. Galba, who lives in the country, is a remarkable example of industry. 2. For he begins to work at daylight. 3. Neither does he leave the fields before night. 4. In summer he works longer[1] than in winter. 5. But even at that time many things claim[2] his attention. 6. And he does not often sit[3] idly at home.

1. Not **longius.** 2. **animum tenēre,** *claim attention.* 3. **sedēre,** *sit idly.*

LESSON LXXVI

Est modus in rēbus — There is a proper measure in things[1]

GENDER IN THE THIRD DECLENSION · WORD FORMATION

496. Gender in Third Declension. In all the declensions except the third the gender of nouns is easy to determine. In the third, however, the rules for gender are numerous and present many exceptions. The subject has therefore been postponed to prevent confusion during the learning of the case forms. We take it up at this point, confining it to a few rules that are of great practical service and have few exceptions.

[1] From Horace, the great lyric poet. The sentiment teaches the value of the golden mean. One of the sayings of one of the seven sages of Greece was, "Nothing too much." The Latin equivalent, *nē quid nimis,* quoted from Terence, will be found on the title-page of this book.

a. *Masculine* are most nouns in -or and -es (genitive -itis).

b. *Feminine* are most nouns in -dō, -iō, -tās, -ūs, and in -s preceded by a consonant.

(1) Exception: masculine are

> dēns, *a tooth*, and mōns, *a mountain*,
> pōns, *a bridge*, and fōns, *a fountain*.

c. *Neuter* are most nouns in -e, -al, -ar, -n, -ŭs.

497. Word Formation. To the prefixes that you have learned (ā, ab, ad, con-, dē, ē, ex, in, in-, prō, re-, trāns) we now add four more : inter, per, prae, and sub. Two of these, inter and per, you have already learned as prepositions.

a. **Inter,** *between* or *among,* also used as a preposition with the accusative: as, **intermittō,** *send between* or *among,* hence *interrupt, suspend*; English derivatives, *intermission, intermittent*; **intericiō** (**inter + iaciō,** *throw*), *throw between*; English derivatives, *interject, interjection,* etc.

b. **Per,** *through,* also used as a preposition with the accusative: as, **permittō,** *send through,* hence *give leave, permit*; English derivatives, *permission, permissible,* etc. As a prefix **per** often has the force of *through and through, thoroughly*: as, **terreō,** *frighten*; **perterreō,** *frighten thoroughly*; **moveō, permoveō**; etc.

c. **Prae,** *before,* also used as a preposition with the ablative, but more common as a prefix: as, **praemittō,** *send ahead.* In English this prefix usually appears as *pre-,* as in the word *prefix* itself, which means to *fix* or *fasten before* or *in front.* Compare also such words as *predict* (**prae + dīcō**), *prepare* (**prae + parō**), *precede* (**prae + cēdō,** *move*), *preoccupy* (**prae + occupō**), etc.

d. **Sub,** *under,* also used as a preposition, generally with the ablative: as, **submittō,** *send under,* hence *yield, submit*; English derivatives, *submission, submissive,* etc. The prefix also takes the form *suc-, suf-, sug-, sup-,* and *sus-,* as in *suc-cumb, suf-fer, sug-gest, sup-port, sus-tain.* Look up these words in the English dictionary and note the force of the prefix and the meaning of the root word.

EXERCISES

498. Derivation. What should you judge to be the meaning of **inter + veniō, per + veniō, prae + veniō, sub + veniō** ?

499. Derivation. With **veniō** as the root word, write a list of twenty-five English derivatives, using prefixes and suffixes, and define each derivative.

500. With the aid of the rules in § 496 give the gender of the following nouns :

mare	aestās	animal
mors	nōmen	legiō
pedes	virtūs	corpus

501. Give the rules for gender in the five declensions. See §§ 86, 97, 496, 476, 489.

LESSON LXXVII

Non omnia possumus omnēs — We cannot all do all things [1]

THE NINE IRREGULAR ADJECTIVES

502. Nine adjectives of the first and second declensions have the genitive singular in -īus and the dative in -ī in all genders. The rest of the singular and all the plural forms are regular. Learn the meaning of each :

alius, alia, aliud, *other, another* (of several)

alter, altera, alterum, *the one, the other* (of two)

neuter, neutra, neutrum, *neither* (of two)

nūllus, -a, -um, *none, no*

sōlus, -a, -um, *alone*

tōtus, -a, -um, *all, whole, entire*

ūllus, -a, -um, *any*

ūnus, -a, -um, *one, alone*; (in the plural) *only*

uter, utra, utrum, *which?* (of two)

[1] From Lucilius, a famous writer of Latin satire.

503. Declension of nūllus and alius.

	MASC.	FEM.	NEUT.	MASC.	FEM.	NEUT.
NOM.	nūllus	nūlla	nūllum	alius	alia	aliud
GEN.	nūllī'us	nūllī'us	nūllī'us	alī'us	alī'us	alī'us
DAT.	nūllī	nūllī	nūllī	aliī	aliī	aliī
ACC.	nūllum	nūllam	nūllum	alium	aliam	aliud
ABL.	nūllō	nūllā	nūllō	aliō	aliā	aliō

The plural is regular.

504. Alius and alter are frequently used in pairs as follows:

alius . . . alius, *one . . . another*
alter . . . alter, *the one . . . the other*
aliī . . . aliī, *some . . . others*
alterī . . . alterī, *the one party . . . the other party*
alter iubet, alter pāret, *the one commands, the other obeys*
aliī terram, aliī aquam amant, *some love the land, others the water*

505. Alius repeated in another case expresses briefly a double statement.

alius aliud petit, *one seeks one thing, another another* (literally, *another seeks another thing*)
aliī aliam urbem occupant, *some seize one city, others another* (literally, *others seize another city*)

EXERCISES

506. 1. Utra domus est Caesaris? Neutra domus est Caesaris. 2. Ea cīvitās nec ūllī lēgī [1] nec. ūllī imperiō [1] pārēbit. 3. Exercitus duo cornua habet; alterum appellātur dextrum, alterum sinistrum. 4. Aliī aliās rēs portābant. 5. Aliī hieme, aliī aestāte ācrius labōrant. 6. Gallī sōlī impetum eōrum prohibēre nōn poterant. 7. Alius aliam rem spectāvit. 8. Aliī equī sunt celerēs, aliī tardī. 9. Omnia in ūnō locō locāta erant.

1. Why dative? See § 224.

507. 1. Some horses are slower than others. 2. The king had seized the sovereignty of the entire island. 3. Some live on one street, others on another. 4. At night we could see many fires; some were large, others small. 5. At daylight neither commander was at home. 6. At no time of the year have I seen any ships in that sea. 7. You can make that journey without any danger.

LESSON LXXVIII

Nec tēcum possum vīvere, nec sine tē — I can live neither with you nor without you [1]

CLASSES OF PRONOUNS · PERSONAL AND REFLEXIVE PRONOUNS

508. Classes of Pronouns. The classes of pronouns are the same in Latin as in English.

a. **Personal pronouns,** which show the person speaking, spoken to, or spoken of : as, **ego,** *I*; **tū,** *you.* (Cf. § 509.)

b. **Possessive pronouns,** which denote possession : as, **meus,** *my*; **tuus,** *your*; **suus,** *his, her, its, their*; etc. (Cf. § 133.)

c. **Reflexive pronouns,** used in the predicate to refer back to the subject : as, **sē vīdit,** *he saw himself.* (Cf. § 511.)

d. **Intensive pronouns,** used to emphasize a noun or pronoun : as, **ipse id vīdī,** *I myself saw it.* (Cf. § 516.)

e. **Demonstrative pronouns,** which point out persons or things : as, **is,** *this, that.* (Cf. § 203.)

f. **Relative pronouns,** which connect a subordinate adjective clause with an antecedent : as, **quī,** *who.* (Cf. § 386.)

g. **Interrogative pronouns,** which ask a question : as, **quis?** *who?* (Cf. § 394.)

h. **Indefinite pronouns,** which point out indefinitely : as, **aliquis,** *someone, anyone*; **quīdam,** *some, certain ones*; etc. (Cf. § 528.)

[1] From Martial, a Roman poet, famous for his epigrams.

509. Personal Pronouns. The personal pronouns of the first person are **ego**, *I*, and **nōs**, *we* ; of the second person, **tū**, *thou* or *you*, and **vōs**, *ye* or *you*. They are declined as follows :

SINGULAR

	FIRST PERSON	SECOND PERSON
NOM.	**ego,** *I*	**tū,** *you*
GEN.	**meī,** *of me*	**tuī,** *of you*
DAT.	**mihi,** *to* or *for me*	**tibi,** *to* or *for you*
ACC.	**mē,** *me*	**tē,** *you*
ABL.	**mē,** *with, from,* etc., *me*	**tē,** *with, from,* etc., *you*

PLURAL

NOM.	**nōs,** *we*	**vōs,** *you*
GEN.	**nostrum** or **nostrī,** *of us*	**vestrum** or **vestrī,** *of you*
DAT.	**nōbīs,** *to* or *for us*	**vōbīs,** *to* or *for you*
ACC.	**nōs,** *us*	**vōs,** *you*
ABL.	**nōbīs,** *with, from,* etc., *us*	**vōbīs,** *with, from,* etc., *you*

a. The nominatives, **ego, tū, nōs, vōs,** are used only to express emphasis or contrast.

510. The personal pronoun of the third person (*he, she, it, they,* etc.) is regularly expressed by the demonstrative pronoun **is, ea, id** (§ 205).

511. Reflexive Pronouns. The reflexives of the first person (*myself, ourselves*) and of the second person (*yourself, yourselves*) are expressed by the forms of **ego** and **tū** : as,

videō mē, *I see myself*	**vidēmus nōs,** *we see ourselves*
vidēs tē, *you see yourself*	**vidētis vōs,** *you see yourselves*

512. The reflexive pronoun of the third person (*himself, herself, itself, themselves*) has a special form, declined alike in the singular and plural.

SINGULAR AND PLURAL

NOM. lacking

GEN. **suī**, *of himself, herself, itself, themselves*

DAT. **sibi**, *to* or *for himself, herself, itself, themselves*

ACC. **sē** or **sēsē**, *himself, herself, itself, themselves*

ABL. **sē** or **sēsē**, *with, from,* etc., *himself, herself, itself, themselves*

EXAMPLES

Puer sē videt, *the boy sees himself*
Puella sē videt, *the girl sees herself*
Animal sē videt, *the animal sees itself*
Iī sē vident, *they see themselves*

513. Enclitic Use of *cum*. The preposition **cum**, when used
with the ablatives **mē, tē, sē, nōbīs, vōbīs**, is joined to them :
as, **mēcum**, *with me*; **nōbīs'cum**, *with us*; etc. **Cum** is likewise
joined to **quō, quā**, and **quibus**, the ablative forms of the relative
and interrogative : as,

Vir quōcum puer venit, *the man with whom the boy is coming*
Quibuscum bellum gerunt, *with whom do they carry on war?*

EXERCISES

First learn the special vocabulary, page 375

514. 1. Mea patria est mihi nōta, et tua patria est tibi nōta.
2. Vestrī amīcī sunt nōbīs grātī, et nostrī amīcī sunt vōbīs grātī.
3. Lēgātī pācem amīcitiamque sibi et sociīs suīs petiērunt. 4. Sī
tū [1] arma capiēs, ego [1] rēgnum tuum occupābō. 5. Uter vestrum
est cīvis Rōmānus? Neuter nostrum. 6. Quibus [2] rēbus cognitīs, multī sēsē in fugam dedērunt. 7. Timōre servitūtis com-
mōtae, multae mulierēs sēsē interfēcērunt. 8. Quōcum imperātor
iter faciet? Mēcum.

1. Personal pronouns in the nominative are emphatic. 2. *These.* The
relative is often used at the beginning of a sentence with the force of a
demonstrative.

515. 1. You cannot see yourself. 2. The queen is pleasing to herself, but not to her kingdom. 3. The general, alarmed by your arrival, fled.[1] 4. You will suffer[2] punishment on that day, but not I.[3] 5. Many things alarmed us, but most of all the fear of the cavalry.

1. Latin, *gave himself into flight.* 2. Latin, *give.* 3. The pronouns *you* and *I*, being emphatic, must be expressed.

LESSON LXXIX

Nīl sine magnō vīta labōre dedit mortālibus — Life has given
nothing to mortals without great labor [1]

THE INTENSIVE PRONOUN *IPSE* · THE DEMONSTRATIVE PRONOUN *ĪDEM*

516. Intensive Pronoun *ipse*. The intensive **ipse, ipsa, ipsum,** is used both as a pronoun and as an adjective. It is usually an adjective and emphasizes the noun or pronoun with which it agrees, and is translated *himself, herself, itself, myself, yourself,* etc.: as,

    Homō ipse venit, *the man himself is coming*
    Puella ipsa venit, *the girl herself is coming*
    Puerī ipsī veniunt, *the boys themselves are coming*
    Ego ipse veniō, *I myself am coming*

a. In English the pronouns *himself* etc. are used both intensively (as, *Galba will come himself*) and reflexively (as, *Galba will kill himself*); in Latin the former would be translated by the adjective **ipse,** the latter by the pronoun **sē**:

    Galba ipse veniet   **Galba sē interficiet**

b. **Ipse** is sometimes translated by *very*: as, **eō ipsō diē,** *on that very day.*

                    [1] From Horace.

517. The intensive pronoun **ipse** is declined like the nine irregular adjectives (§ 502).

	Masc.	Fem.	Neut.	Masc.	Fem.	Neut.
Nom.	ipse	ipsa	ipsum	ipsī	ipsae	ipsa
Gen.	ipsī'us	ipsī'us	ipsī'us	ipsōrum	ipsārum	ipsōrum
Dat.	ipsī	ipsī	ipsī	ipsīs	ipsīs	ipsīs
Acc.	ipsum	ipsam	ipsum	ipsōs	ipsās	ipsa
Abl.	ipsō	ipsā	ipsō	ipsīs	ipsīs	ipsīs

518. Demonstrative Pronoun *īdem*. The demonstrative pronoun **īdem**, *the same*, is a compound of **is**, and is declined as follows :

	Masc.	Fem.	Neut.
Nom.	īdem	e'adem	idem
Gen.	eius'dem	eius'dem	eius'dem
Dat.	eī'dem	eī'dem	eī'dem
Acc.	eun'dem	ean'dem	idem
Abl.	eō'dem	eā'dem	eō'dem

	Masc.	Fem.	Neut.
Nom.	iī'dem / eī'dem	eae'dem	e'adem
Gen.	eōrun'dem	eārun'dem	eōrun'dem
Dat.	iīs'dem / eīs'dem	iīs'dem / eīs'dem	iīs'dem / eīs'dem
Acc.	eōs'dem	eās'dem	e'adem
Abl.	iīs'dem / eīs'dem	iīs'dem / eīs'dem	iīs'dem / eīs'dem

a. The forms **iidem** and **iisdem** are often spelled and pronounced with one **i**.

b. The demonstrative **īdem** is used both as a noun and as an adjective.

c. **Īdem** is sometimes best rendered *also, at the same time* : as, **ego īdem dīxī**, *I also said*.

EXERCISES

First learn the special vocabulary, page 376

519. 1. Ego et tū [1] eandem urbem incolimus. 2. Iter ipsum nōn timēmus, sed aliīs rēbus commōtī sumus. 3. Ōlim nōs ipsī idem iter fēcimus, sed aliō tempore annī. 4. Rōmānī in maximam spem adventū imperātōris adductī erant. 5. Iam tōtam spem salūtis dēposuērunt, quod pars exercitūs capta est et imperātor ipse est in manibus hostium. 6. Tamen vōs ipsī eōsdem saepissimē vīcistis. 7. Imperātor suā manū fīliam servāvit, sed sē ipse [2] servāre nōn potuit.

1. Latin says *I and you*, not *you and I*. 2. The intensive **ipse** here agrees with the subject, though in English the emphasis falls on the predicate.

520. 1. The general himself gave a part of the army the right of way through the same kingdom. 2. After all hope [1] of safety was left behind, the citizens themselves laid down their arms. 3. The same great fear seized [2] the hearts of all.

1. Ablative absolute. 2. **occupō, -āre.**

LESSON LXXX

Nōn sibi, sed suīs — Not for herself, but for her own [1]

THE DEMONSTRATIVE PRONOUNS *HIC, ISTE, ILLE*

521. Use of *hic*, *iste*, and *ille*. The demonstrative pronoun **is, ea, id**, makes no definite reference to place or time (§ 203); but **hic** (*this, he*) refers to a person or thing near the speaker, **iste** (*that, he*) to a person or thing near the person addressed, and **ille** (*that, he*) to a person or thing remote from both.

Amāsne hunc equum, *do you like this horse* (of mine)?

Istum equum amō, sed illum equum nōn amō, *I like that horse* (of yours), *but that horse* (yonder) *I don't like*

[1] Motto of Tulane University.

522. The demonstratives **hic**, **iste**, and **ille** are used both as pronouns and as adjectives. When used as adjectives, they regularly precede their nouns.

523. Declension of *hic*, *iste*, and *ille*. Hic is declined as follows :

	MASC.	FEM.	NEUT.	MASC.	FEM.	NEUT.
NOM.	hic	haec	hoc	hī	hae	haec
GEN.	huius	huius	huius	hōrum	hārum	hōrum
DAT.	huic	huic	huic	hīs	hīs	hīs
ACC.	hunc	hanc	hoc	hōs	hās	haec
ABL.	hōc	hāc	hōc	hīs	hīs	hīs

a. **Huius** is pronounced *hŏŏ'yŏŏs*, and **huic** is pronounced *hweek* (one syllable).

524. The demonstrative pronouns **iste, ista, istud**, and **ille, illa, illud**, except for the nominative and accusative singular neuter forms **istud** and **illud**, are declined like **ipse, ipsa, ipsum.** (See § 517.)

A GALLIC CHIEFTAIN ADDRESSES HIS FOLLOWERS

First learn the special vocabulary, page 376

525. Ille fortis Gallōrum prīnceps suōs convocāvit et hōc modō[1] animōs eōrum cōnfirmāvit : "Vōs, quī hōs fīnēs incolitis, in hunc locum convocāvī,[2] quod mēcum dēbētis istōs agrōs atque istās domōs ā manibus Rōmānīs līberāre. Hoc nōbīs nōn difficile erit, quod illī hostēs hās silvās, hōs montēs 5 timent. Sī fortēs erimus, deī ipsī nōbīs viam salūtis dēmōn-strābunt. Itaque dēpōnite istum timōrem. Magnam spem victōriae habeō. Iam magnam partem exercitūs Rōmānī superāvimus."[2]

1. Ablative of manner. 2. Translate by the present perfect (§ 312).

526. 1. Is that spear (of yours [1]) heavy? No, this spear (of mine [1]) is light. 2. That spear of Mark's is much longer than mine. 3. You ought to show us the road that leads across this mountain. 4. That road which extends through our territory is much shorter. 5. The very manner of life of those savages is not the same.

1. English words in parentheses are not to be translated.

LESSON LXXXI

Labor omnia vincit — Labor conquers all things [1]

INDEFINITE PRONOUNS

527. Indefinite pronouns do not, like demonstratives, point out definite persons or things, but refer to them indefinitely : as, *someone, anyone, something, some, any.*

528. Indefinite pronouns, like demonstratives, are used both as pronouns and as adjectives. The simple indefinite pronoun is **quis**, *someone, anyone,* and the indefinite adjective is **quī, quae, quod**, *some, any.*[2] Far more common are the compounds **aliquis**, *someone* ; **quisque**, *each one* ; and **quīdam**, *a certain one.* The forms of these indefinites are as follows :

1. Substantive forms :

MASC. AND FEM.	NEUT.
aliquis, *someone, anyone*	**aliquid**, *something, anything*
quisque, *each one, everyone*	**quidque**, *each thing, everything*

MASC.	FEM.	NEUT.
quīdam, *a certain man*	**quaedam**, *a certain woman*	**quiddam**, *a certain thing*

---

[1] Motto of the state of Oklahoma.

[2] The indefinites **quis** and **quī** are the same in form and declension as the interrogatives (§§ 394, 395).

2. Adjective forms :

MASC.	FEM.	NEUT.
aliquī	aliqua	aliquod, *any*
quisque	quaeque	quodque, *each*
quīdam	quaedam	quoddam, *a certain*

529. Declension of Indefinites. Indefinites are declined, in general, like the interrogatives **quis** and **quī**. An **m** coming before a **d** is changed to **n** : as, **quendam**, not **quemdam**.[1]

EXERCISES

First learn the special vocabulary, page 376

530. 1. Hōc proeliō factō, Gallī suam quisque [1] domum properāvērunt. 2. Quīdam hominēs, quī amīcī illīus rēgis exīstimābantur, ab imperātōre retentī sunt. 3. Est in vītā cuiusque aliqua adversa (*ill*) fortūna. 4. Aliquis dēbet tibi viam dēmōnstrāre. 5. Quisque nostrum illī fortī mīlitī aliquid dare dēbet. 6. Ego quendam rūrī vīdī quī per illōs fīnēs iter fēcerat.

1. In apposition with **Gallī**.

531. 1. If you see a certain Quintus at Rome, send him to me. 2. Even I said something to someone. 3. Some who were considered very brave did not retain their arms. 4. Each citizen ought to uphold the state and obey the laws.[1] 5. Certain cities are considered equal to Rome itself.

1. Dative, § 224.

Tenth Review. Lessons LXXIII–LXXXI, §§ 783–787

[1] The declension of the indefinites is given in § 831, but demands little special study.

LESSON LXXXII

Quot hominēs, tot sententiae — As many men, so many minds [1]

CARDINAL NUMERALS AND THEIR DECLENSION

532. Cardinal Numerals. Cardinal numerals answer the question *How many?* The first twelve cardinals are as follows: [2]

1, ūnus	*5*, quīnque	*9*, novem
2, duo	*6*, sex	*10*, decem
3, trēs	*7*, septem	*11*, ūndecim
4, quattuor	*8*, octō	*12*, duodecim

a. The word for 100 is **centum**; for 200, **ducentī**; for 1000, **mīlle**.

533. Declension of Cardinals. Of the cardinals, only **ūnus, duo, trēs,** the hundreds above one hundred, and **mīlle** used as a noun, are declined.

534. Ūnus, *one,* is one of the nine irregular adjectives, and is declined like **nūllus** (§ 503).

535. Learn the declension of **duo,** *two,* and of **trēs,** *three.* See § 824.

536. Mīlle, *thousand,* in the singular is an indeclinable adjective. In the plural it is a neuter noun, and is declined like the plural of **mare**:

Nom.	mīlia
Gen.	mīlium
Dat.	mīlibus
Acc.	mīlia
Abl.	mīlibus

[1] From Terence, the famous writer of comedies. The motto means that every man has his opinion.

[2] A fuller table of numerals is given in § 823.

537. Ducentī, *two hundred*, and other hundreds above one hundred are declined like the plural of **bonus**: as,

ducentī	ducentae	ducenta
ducentōrum	ducentārum	ducentōrum
ducentīs	ducentīs	ducentīs
etc.	etc.	etc.

THE CONTEST OF THE HORATII AND THE CURIATII

Try to translate this at sight

538. Ōlim Rōmānī cum Albānīs [1] bellum gerēbant. Erant in duōbus exercitibus trigeminī [2] frātrēs, trēs Horātiī in exercitū Rōmānō, trēs Curiātiī in exercitū Albānō. Ducibus convocātīs, quīdam ex eīs dīxit: "Cūr omnēs nōs pugnāmus? Melius est paucōs [3] prō omnibus contendere et reliquōs [3] esse 5

SO-CALLED TOMB OF THE HORATII AND CURIATII

PATER IPSE TRIBUS FĪLIĪS ARMA NOVA DEDIT

integrōs. Cūr nōn iubēmus trēs Horātiōs cum tribus Curiātiīs pugnāre et hōc modō bellum diiūdicāmus [4]?" Hōc
cōnsiliō omnibus [5] persuāsit, et pater ipse Horātiōrum filiis
fortibus suīs nova arma dedit.

Et Horātiī et Curiātiī certāminī [6] studēbant et manūs cōn- 10
seruērunt.[7] Prīmō impetū trēs Albānī ā tribus Rōmānīs
vulnerātī sunt, duo Rōmānī ā tribus Albānīs interfectī sunt,
ūnus Rōmānus integer erat. Iam tōtus Albānōrum exercitus certam victōriam exspectābat. Rōmānus autem fugam
simulāvit [8] et illō modō trēs vulnerātōs Albānōs sēparāvit.[9] 15
Tum subitō [10] revertit [11] et singulōs [12] superāvit atque interfēcit. Posteā Rōmānī in [13] Albānōs multōs annōs imperium
tenēbant.

1. **Albānī, -ōrum,** *the Albans,* who lived near Rome. 2. *Triplet.*
3. **paucōs** is the subject accusative of **contendere,** and **reliquōs** of **esse.**
The infinitive clauses are the subjects of **est.** 4. **diiūdicō, -āre,** *decide.*
5. Why dative? See § 224. 6. **certāmen, -inis,** N., *contest.* 7. **manūs cōn-
seruērunt,** *joined in a hand-to-hand struggle.* 8. **simulō, -āre,** *pretend.*
9. **sēparō, -āre,** *separate.* 10. *Suddenly.* 11. **revertō, -ere,** *turn back.*
12. **singulī,** *one at a time.* 13. *Over.*

VILLA OF A WEALTHY ROMAN

LESSON LXXXIII

Ēnse petit placidam sub lībertāte quiētem — With the sword she
seeks calm repose in freedom [1]

ORDINAL NUMERALS · THE GENITIVE OF THE WHOLE, OR THE PARTITIVE GENITIVE

539. Ordinal Numerals. Ordinal numerals answer the question *In what order?* The first twelve are as follows:

first, prīmus, -a, -um	*seventh*, septimus, -a, -um
second, secundus, -a, -um	*eighth*, octā'vus, -a, -um
third, tertius, -a, -um	*ninth*, nōnus, -a, -um
fourth, quārtus, -a, -um	*tenth*, decimus, -a, -um
fifth, quīntus, -a, -um	*eleventh*, ūndecimus, -a, -um
sixth, sextus, -a, -um	*twelfth*, duodecimus, -a, -um

The ordinals are all declined like **bonus.**

540. Genitive of the Whole, or Partitive Genitive. In the sentence *Of all these the Belgæ are the bravest*, the phrase *of all these* represents the whole number of whom the Belgæ are the bravest part. This sentence is expressed similarly in Latin : as,

Hōrum omnium fortissimī sunt Belgae

and the genitive **hōrum omnium** is called the genitive of the whole, or the partitive genitive.

541. Rule for Genitive of the Whole. *A genitive denoting the whole is used with words denoting a part, and is known as the genitive of the whole, or the partitive genitive.*

[1] Motto of the state of Massachusetts.

198

542. Mīlle, singular, is an indeclinable adjective : as, **mīlle mīlitēs,** *a thousand soldiers.* **Mīlia,** plural, is a neuter noun, and is followed by the genitive : as, **decem mīlia mīlitum,** *ten thousand soldiers* (literally, *ten thousands of soldiers*).

543. Cardinal numbers, except **mīlia,** are followed by the ablative with **ex** or **dē,** instead of the genitive : as, **ūnus ex puerīs,** *one of the boys.*

EXERCISES

First learn the special vocabulary, page 377

544. Annus quattuor tempora [1] et duodecim mēnsēs [2] continet. Aestās est omnium temporum grātissimum. Nunc mēnsis prīmus annī est Iānuārius, sed antīquīs [3] temporibus Mārtius [4] prīmus mēnsis existimābātur. Quā dē causā September erat septimus mēnsis antīquī [3] annī, Octōber erat 5 octāvus mēnsis, November erat nōnus mēnsis, December erat decimus mēnsis. Omnium mēnsium Februārius erat brevissimus. Urbs Rōma plūs quam mīlle annōs permānsit [5] et multa mīlia hominum habet.

1. Here used in the sense of *seasons.*   2. **mēnsis, -is,** M., *month.*
3. **antīquus, -a, -um,** *ancient.*   4. *March.*   5. Present perfect, § 312.

545. The Romans had seven kings. The first king was Romulus, the second king was Numa, the third king was Tullus Hostilius, the fourth king was Ancus Marcius, the fifth king was Tarquinius Priscus, the sixth king was Servius Tullius, the seventh king was Tarquinius Superbus. Of all the kings Tarquinius Superbus was the worst. For this reason he was driven out by Brutus, the first consul.

LESSON LXXXIV

Cīvī et reī pūblicae — For the citizen and the commonwealth[1]

THE ACCUSATIVE OF DURATION OF TIME OR EXTENT OF SPACE

546. The questions *How long?* and *How far?* are answered in English by an adverbial objective expressing duration of time or extent of space. This relation is similarly expressed in Latin by the Latin objective, or accusative : as,

> Gallī sex diēs pugnāvērunt, *the Gauls fought for six days*
> Aqua centum pedēs alta est, *the water is a hundred feet deep*

547. Rule for Accusative of Duration or Extent. *Duration of time and extent of space are expressed by the accusative.*

548. The accusative of time *how long* and the ablative of the time *when* or *within which* (§ 493) must be carefully distinguished. Select what would be accusatives of time or space and ablatives of time in the following passage if it were in Latin :

At midnight I went on deck. For many hours I had been tossing sleepless in my bunk. In the first place, the storm which began on Monday had now been raging for five days. Furthermore, in a few hours we should be in the channel; only a few miles from safety, to be sure, but also in the most dangerous zone of our voyage. The night was clear, and once I thought I saw a periscope, but it was only a floating spar extending several feet above the water. I was distinctly nervous, and did not care to repeat my former experience when I spent forty-eight hours in a leaky boat, which we rowed forty-seven miles before we were saved.

[1] Motto of the University of Oklahoma.

CÆSAR IN GAUL

First learn the special vocabulary, page 377

549. Caesar bellum in Galliā septem annōs gessit. Prīmō annō Helvētiōs superāvit, et eōdem annō Germānōs, quī magnum numerum hominum trāns Rhēnum trādūxerant, ex Galliā expulit. Multōs iam annōs Germānī magnam partem Galliae obtinēbant.[1] Quā dē causā prīncipēs Galliae lēgātōs 5 ad Caesarem mīserant et auxilium petierant. Lēgātīs audītīs, Caesar brevī tempore cōpiās suās coēgit. Magnō itinere cōnfectō, aciem īnstrūxit et prīmā lūce proelium cum Germānīs commīsit. Tōtum diem ācriter pugnātum est. Caesar ipse ā dextrō cornū aciem dūxit. Dēnique post magnam caedem 10 Germānī aliī aliam in partem trāns Rhēnum fugam cēpērunt.

1. Translate as if past perfect.

550. 1. The battle began at daylight and part of the army fought all[1] day. 2. That bridge is two hundred feet long. 3. The enemy's camp was twelve miles[2] distant. 4. Those mountains are three hundred feet high. 5. In a short time the queen had collected five thousand men. 6. That forest extended a great distance.

1. Not **omnis**. 2. Latin, *twelve thousands of paces.*

A GATE OF POMPEII (RESTORED)

LESSON LXXXV

Amīcitia nisi inter bonōs esse nōn potest — Friendship cannot
exist except between the good [1]

THE ABLATIVE OF RESPECT · THE GENITIVE WITH ADJECTIVES

551. Ablative of Respect. Note the following sentences:

Cīvēs erant paucī numerō, *the citizens were few in number*
Mārcus frātrem virtūte superat, *Mark excels his brother in valor*

The ablatives **numerō** and **virtūte** answer the question *In
what respect?* and are called ablatives of respect.

552. Rule for Ablative of Respect. *The ablative is used
to denote in what respect something is true.*

553. Genitive with Adjectives. Compare the following sentences:

Rēx bellum cupit, *the king desires war*
Rēx bellī cupidus est, *the king is desirous of war*

The relation between the verb **cupit** and its direct object
bellum is clearly similar to that between the adjective **cupidus**
and its genitive **bellī**. Genitives used as the object of the action
or feeling implied in certain adjectives are therefore called
objective genitives.

554. Rule for Genitive with Adjectives. *The adjectives*
***cupidus**, desirous; **perītus**, skilled; **imperītus**, ignorant, and
others of similar character are followed by the objective
genitive.*

[1] From Cicero's famous essay on friendship.

EXERCISES

First learn the special vocabulary, page 377

555. 1. Aciem īnstruere nōn poterat, quod erat imperītus reī mīlitāris. 2. Sapientiā Minerva reliquās deās superābat. 3. Signō datō, legiō decima, cupidior laudis quam vītae ipsīus, prōcēdere incēpit. 4. Gallī et Germānī dissimillimī linguā ac lēgibus erant. 5. Quīdam ex prīncipibus, quod pācis cupidī erant, lēgātōs ad nōs mīsērunt. 6. Dux reī mīlitāris perītus in locō inīquō nōn permanēbit. 7. Servī lībertātis cupidissimī aliī aliam in partem fūgērunt. 8. Quīdam imperātor, Galba nōmine, timōre commōtus iter intermittī iussit. 9. Oppidum, nūllō spatiō intermissō, mūrō vīgintī [1] pedēs altō dēfendēbātur. 10. Cūr in eādem lībertāte quam ā patribus nostrīs accēpimus permanēre nōn possumus?

1. *Twenty.*

556. 1. Few men were equal to Cæsar either [1] in wisdom or in valor. 2. The men are unskilled in languages. 3. These ought not to sail to other lands. 4. Cæsar was king in fact,[2] but not in name. 5. Some work because they are desirous of praise, others because they are desirous of money. 6. The commander himself is skilled in the art of war. 7. He will not let several days elapse without good cause.

1. *Either . . . or*, aut . . . aut. 2. rēs.

ANCIENT COINS

LESSON LXXXVI

Nōn omnis moriar — I shall not wholly die [1]

DEPONENT VERBS · THE GENITIVE OR ABLATIVE OF DESCRIPTION

557. Deponent Verbs. A deponent verb is one that is passive in form but active in meaning.

558. The principal parts of deponents are, of course, passive.

hortor, hortārī, hortātus sum, *urge*

a. A few verbs are deponent in the perfect system only : as,

audeō, audēre, ausus sum, *dare*

559. Deponent verbs are conjugated in the passive :

hortor, hortārī, hortātus sum (*urge*), like vocor (§ 832)
vereor, verērī, veritus sum (*fear*), like moneor (§ 833)
sequor, sequī, secūtus sum (*follow*), like regor (§ 834)
patior, patī, passus sum (*suffer*), like capior (§ 836)
partior, partīrī, partītus sum (*share*), like audior (§ 835)

560. Besides having all the forms of the passive, deponent verbs have also the future active infinitive, the active participles, and a few other active forms which will be noted later.[2]

561. Genitive or Ablative of Description. English and Latin employ similar expressions of quality or description. Thus we may say either *Cæsar was a man of great courage* or *Cæsar was a man with great courage.* Similarly in Latin we may use the genitive in the first case and the ablative in the second : as,

Caesar erat vir magnae virtūtis
Caesar erat vir magnā virtūte

---

[1] From Horace, the poet laureate of the Augustan age.
[2] The complete synopsis of deponent verbs is given in § 837.

562. Rule for Genitive or Ablative of Description. *The genitive or the ablative, with a modifying adjective, is used in expressions of quality or description.*

a. Numerical descriptions of measure are in the genitive, and descriptions of physical characteristics are usually in the ablative.

fossa decem pedum, *a ditch of ten feet,* or *a ten-foot ditch*
puella parvīs manibus, *a girl with small hands*

CÆSAR AND THE HELVETIANS

First learn the special vocabulary, page 378

563. 1. Helvētiī, quī nec deōs nec hominēs verēbantur, magnum dolōrem patiēbantur quod ex omnibus partibus[1] magnae altitūdinis montibus continēbantur. 2. Quā dē causā cōnsilium cēpērunt ex suīs fīnibus cum omnibus cōpiīs excēdere. 3. Hīs rēbus cognitīs, Caesar, vir ēgregiā virtūte et reī mīlitāris perītissimus, magnīs itineribus in Galliam contendit. 4. Nōn passus est Helvētiōs iter per fīnēs Rōmānōs facere, sed plūrēs[2] diēs eōs secūtus est. 5. Dēnique Helvētiī, itinere intermissō, aciem īnstrūxērunt. 6. Helvētiī Rōmānīs erant parēs virtūte, sed nōn armīs. 7. Tum Caesar mīlitēs hortātus est, et, proeliō commissō, magnam partem hostium interfēcit.

1. **ex omnibus partibus,** *on all sides.* 2. *Several.*

564. 1. Cæsar constructed[1] a ten-foot rampart.[2] 2. The rampart was many miles[3] long. 3. Men of no wisdom suffer pain because they do not fear the laws. 4. One man urges one thing, another another.[4] 5. But we shall follow Cæsar's authority. 6. In height your mountains are not equal to ours.

1. **dūcō.** 2. Latin, *a rampart of ten feet.* 3. Latin, *many thousands of paces.* 4. Translate the sentence by three Latin words. See § 505.

LESSON LXXXVII

Vōx clāmantis in dēsertō — The voice of one crying in the wilderness [1]

PARTICIPLES

565. The nature of the participle has been already discussed (§ 344). Latin has four participles, the present and the future in the active voice, and the past and the future (also called the gerundive) in the passive voice.[2]

I. **Present Active Participle.** Present Stem + -ns or -ēns

- vocāns, *calling*
- monēns, *advising*
- regēns, *ruling*
- audiēns, *hearing*

II. **Future Active Participle.** Participial Stem + -ūrus, -a, -um

- vocātūrus, *about to call*
- monitūrus, *about to advise*
- rēctūrus, *about to rule*
- audītūrus, *about to hear*

III. **Past Passive Participle.** Participial Stem + -us, -a, -um

- vocātus, *having been called*
- monitus, *having been advised*
- rēctus, *having been ruled*
- audītus, *having been heard*

IV. **Future Passive Participle or Gerundive.** Present Stem + -ndus or -endus, -a, -um

- vocandus, *to be called*
- monendus, *to be advised*
- regendus, *to be ruled*
- audiendus, *to be heard*

566. Declension of Participles. All participles ending in -us are declined like **bonus** (§ 120). Present participles are declined like adjectives of one ending; see the declension of **vocāns**, § 817.

---

[1] Motto of Dartmouth College. From the Latin translation of the Bible.

[2] It is to be noted that Latin, unlike English, has no past active participle (*having called*) or present passive participle (*being called*).

206

567. Past and Future Participles. We have made frequent use of the past passive participle as the last of the principal parts (§ 299), and in the formation of the perfect passive system (**vocātus sum,** etc.). We have also used it frequently in agreement with a noun in the ablative absolute (§ 400) : as,

> **Gallīs superātīs, Caesar in Italiam contendit,** *after the Gauls had been overcome, Cæsar hastened into Italy*

The future active participle with **esse** makes the future active infinitive (§ 356): as, **vocātūrus esse,** *to be about to call.*

568. Present Active Participle. The present active participle, as well as the past passive, is often used with a noun or pronoun in the ablative absolute.

> **Caesare dūcente, nihil timēmus,** *Cæsar leading* (or *when Cæsar leads*), *we fear nothing*

569. Participles of Deponent Verbs. Deponent verbs have four participles, of the same form as those of other verbs : as,

> **hortāns,** *urging*
> **hortātūrus,** *about to urge*
> **hortātus,** *having urged*
> **hortandus,** *to be urged* [1]

But note that the past participle of deponents is *active* in meaning, and that only deponent verbs have an *active* past participle. Compare

> **hortātus,** *having urged* (active), from **hortor,** deponent
> **vocātus,** *having been called* (passive), from **vocō,** not deponent

570. Give the participles of the following verbs :

portō	mittō	mūniō	vereor
iaciō	dūcō	moveō	patior

[1] The future passive participle, or gerundive, of deponent verbs is passive in meaning as well as in form.

EXERCISES

First learn the special vocabulary, page 378

571. 1. Caesar sequēns Helvētiōs nec nocte nec diē iteɪ intermīsit. **2.** Magnam multitūdinem hostium fugientium interfēcit et grave supplicium dē captīvīs sūmpsit. **3.** Magnitūdine et altitūdine illud flūmen omnia alia superat. **4.** In [1] eō flūmine imperātor pontem mīlle pedum fēcit. **5.** His bellīs cōnfectīs, imperātor librum dē rē mīlitārī scrīpsit. **6.** Ubi Lesbiam vīdistī? Lesbiam sedentem ante casam Galbae vīdī. **7.** Tertiā hōrā explōrātōrēs, quī praemissī erant, locum idōneum castrīs dēlēgērunt. **8.** Illō imperātōre dūcente, certissima esse victōria dēbet. **9.** Dux tuus est celerior corpore quam animō. **10.** Veritī fortūnam pessimam, grātiās deīs iam ēgimus quod cōnservātī erāmus.

1. Where we say "build a bridge *over*," the Romans said "build a bridge *in*," because bridges were often built of boats.

572. 1. When our country calls,[1] we ought to take up arms. **2.** The king, fearing the multitude, did not dare to send ahead spies. **3.** After suffering[2] wrongs for many years, the allies were eager for war. **4.** At the fourth hour suitable scouts were chosen and sent forward. **5.** Cæsar inflicted punishment on that king. **6.** Many books have been written concerning the size of Rome. **7.** After drawing up[3] the line of battle, the commander waited for two hours.

1. Express by the present participle in the ablative absolute. 2. Past participle. 3. Express by the past participle in the ablative absolute, and note that, as this participle is regularly passive in Latin, the voice of the English verb must be changed, and thus the English becomes *after the line of battle had been drawn up*. Never fail to change an English past participle from the active to the passive before translating, unless the Latin verb is deponent (cf. § 569).

LESSON LXXXVIII

Scientia sōl mentis — Knowledge the sun of the mind[1]

WORD FORMATION

573. Spelling of English Words in *-ant* and *-ent*. Many English nouns and adjectives ending in *-ant* and *-ent* are derived from the Latin present participle, and have the same form as its base. Thus:

LATIN VERB	PRESENT PARTICIPLE	ENGLISH WORD
occupō	occupāns, -antis	*occupant*
servō	servāns, -antis	*servant*
importō	importāns, -antis	*important*
studeō	studēns, -entis	*student*
agō	agēns, -entis	*agent*
contineō	continēns, -entis	*continent*

English words of this kind derived from Latin verbs of the first conjugation end in *-ant*; from verbs of other conjugations, in *-ent*.

a. Exceptions to this rule are words of Latin origin that have come into English through the medium of Norman French, where the present participle of verbs of all conjugations ends regularly in *-ant*. Thus, from **teneō** (present participle **tenēns**) the English derivative is not *tenent*, as we should expect, but *tenant* (cf. French *tenant*).

574. Nouns in *-or* denoting the Agent or Doer. Many Latin nouns denoting the *agent* or *doer* are formed from Latin verbs by changing **-us** of the past participle to **-or.** These nouns have generally passed into English with no change of form. Thus:

---

[1] Motto of Delaware College.

Verb	Past Participle	Latin Noun	English Noun
agō	āctus	āctor	*actor*
audiō	audītus	audītor	*auditor*
capiō	captus	captor	*captor*
inveniō	inventus	inventor	*inventor*
līberō	līberātus	līberātor	*liberator*
moneō	monitus	monitor	*monitor*
nārrō	nārrātus	nārrātor	*narrator*
nāvigō	nāvigātus	nāvigātor	*navigator*
spectō	spectātus	spectātor	*spectator*
vincō	victus	victor	*victor*

The number of these nouns, both in Latin and English, is very great. Some of the Latin nouns have a feminine form in -trīx : as, administrātrīx, victrīx, etc. The same suffix is used in English : as, *administrator*, M. ; *administratrix*, F.

EXERCISES

First learn the special vocabulary, page 378

575. 1. Rōmānī bellum cum Albānīs gerentēs omnēs nōn pugnāvērunt. 2. Nam imperātōrēs melius cōnsilium docēbant. 3. Trēs frātrēs, virtūtis magnae et reī mīlitāris perītī, utrimque (*from each side*) dēlēctī sunt. 4. Apud duōs exercitūs ācerrimē pugnātum est. 5. Curiātiīs interfectīs, cīvitās Rōmāna maiōrem potestātem habuit. 6. Albānī vērō dolōrem magnum passī sunt.

576. Derivation. Using prefixes previously studied (§ 497) and such suffixes as appear in § 426, and any others you know, make a list of at least twenty English derivatives from the verbs scrībō, sūmō, iaciō, audiō, pōnō.

Eleventh Review. Lessons LXXXII–LXXXVIII, §§ 788–792

THE GATE OF ST. SEBASTIAN

Rome is still a walled town. The wall built about 600 B.C. by King Servius Tullius sufficed for nine hundred years though the city had spread far beyond it on every side. But about A.D. 300 the danger of barbarian invasion became so great that the present wall was constructed. It is nearly twelve miles in circuit and has fifteen gates. The gate in the picture is the Porta Appia, now called the Gate of St. Sebastian, through which passes the Appian Way

LESSON LXXXIX

Scientia crēscat, vīta colātur — Let knowledge grow, let
life be enriched [1]

THE SUBJUNCTIVE MOOD · PRESENT SUBJUNCTIVE OF THE
FIRST AND SECOND CONJUGATIONS · THE INDICATIVE AND
SUBJUNCTIVE COMPARED

577. Subjunctive Mood. Besides the indicative and imperative, Latin has a third mood, called the subjunctive.

578. Tenses of Subjunctive. The subjunctive has four tenses :
present, past, perfect, and past perfect.

The personal endings, active and passive, are the same as in
the indicative.

a. The meaning of the subjunctive varies in different constructions to
such a degree that it is not practical to translate the subjunctive forms in
the paradigms.

579. Present Subjunctive of First Conjugation. The sign of
the present subjunctive in the first conjugation is -ē-, which
takes the place of -ā, the final vowel of the present stem : as,

ACTIVE	PASSIVE
voc(ā) + ē + m = vocem	voc(ā) + ē + r = vocer

580. In the subjunctive, as elsewhere, a long vowel is
shortened before nt and final -m, -t, or -r (see § 194). The
present subjunctive is inflected as follows :

ACTIVE VOICE		PASSIVE VOICE	
1. vo'cem	vocē'mus	vo'cer	vocē'mur
2. vo'cēs	vocē'tis	vocē'ris (-re)	vocē'minī
3. vo'cet	vo'cent	vocē'tur	vocen'tur

[1] Motto of The University of Chicago.

211

581. Present Subjunctive of Second Conjugation. The sign of the present subjunctive in the second conjugation is -ā-, which is added to the present stem and is followed by the personal endings: as,

ACTIVE monē + ā + m = moneam   PASSIVE monē + ā + r = monear

Long vowels are shortened in the usual places (§ 194).

ACTIVE VOICE		PASSIVE VOICE	
1. mo′neam	moneā′mus	mo′near	moneā′mur
2. mo′neās	moneā′tis	moneā′ris (-re)	moneā′minī
3. mo′neat	mo′neant	moneā′tur	monean′tur

582. Indicative and Subjunctive Compared. The indicative mood asserts facts or inquires after facts. The subjunctive, on the other hand, expresses *desires, wishes, purposes, possibilities, expectations,* and the like. The following sentences illustrate the difference between indicative and subjunctive ideas.

INDICATIVE IDEAS	SUBJUNCTIVE IDEAS
1. *We call him* Eum vocāmus	1. *Let us call him* Eum vocēmus (desire)
2. *You see the city* Urbem vidēs	2. *May you see the city* Urbem videās (wish)
3. *Scouts come who warn you* Explōrātōrēs veniunt quī tē monent	3. *Scouts come to warn* (or *who are to warn*) *you* Explōrātōrēs veniunt quī tē moneant (purpose)
4. *They fight bravely* Fortiter pugnant	4. *They would fight bravely* Fortiter pugnent (possibility)
5. *He waits at Rome until the enemy are overcome* Rōmae exspectat dum hostēs superantur	5. *He waits at Rome until the enemy shall be overcome* Rōmae exspectat dum hostēs superentur (expectation)

EXERCISE

583. Which verbs in the following paragraph would be in the indicative, and which in the subjunctive, in a Latin translation?

And we won't come back till it's over over there.

How splendidly our soldiers made good the words of their song. Who would have expected so speedy and so glorious a victory? They were young. They were fine. They were brave. But they had not been tested. "Let us hope, let us have confidence," was the best one could say. The crisis was at hand. At Paris, less than forty miles away, one might hear the thunder of the guns. And still the enemy pressed on and the brave French were forced back. American forces were rushed to the front. The French urged retreat to a stronger position. "We came to fight, not to retreat," said the Yanks. Then in plunged the Marines. May their glory ever shine! And what they did thrilled the world. From that day onward the Stars and Stripes blazed the victorious trail.

'Tis the Star-Spangled Banner, O long may it wave
O'er the land of the free, and the home of the brave!

584. Inflect the present subjunctive, active and passive, of **vāstō, moveō, servō, iubeō.**

GREEK VASES

LESSON XC

PRESENT SUBJUNCTIVE, THIRD AND FOURTH CONJUGA-
TIONS · SUBJUNCTIVE OF PURPOSE

585. Present Subjunctive of Third Conjugation. The sign
of the present subjunctive of the third conjugation is -ā-. This
-ā- takes the place of -e, the final vowel of the present stem,
and is followed by the personal endings:

ACTIVE   reg(e)+ā+m = regam   PASSIVE   reg(e)+ā+r = regar

ACTIVE VOICE		PASSIVE VOICE	
1. re′gam	regā′mus	re′gar	regā′mur
2. re′gās	regā′tis	regā′ris (-re)	regā′minī
3. re′gat	re′gant	regā′tur	regan′tur

a. In like manner inflect **capiam**, the present subjunctive of **capiō**,
and other -iō verbs of the third conjugation (see § 836).

586. Present Subjunctive of Fourth Conjugation. The sign
of the present subjunctive of the fourth conjugation is -ā-.
This is added to the present stem and is followed by the
personal endings:

ACTIVE   audī + ā + m = audiam   PASSIVE   audī + ā + r = audiar

ACTIVE VOICE		PASSIVE VOICE	
1. au′diam	audiā′mus	au′diar	audiā′mur
2. au′diās	audiā′tis	audiā′ris (-re)	audiā′minī
3. au′diat	au′diant	audiā′tur	audian′tur

[1] Motto of the state of Maryland. From the Latin translation of the Bible.

587. Subjunctive of Purpose. Observe the following sentence:

Explōrātōrēs veniunt quī tē moneant, *scouts come to warn you*

The verb **moneant** in the dependent clause is in the subjunctive because it expresses the scouts' purpose. This use of the subjunctive is called the *subjunctive of purpose*. In English the purpose is often expressed, as here, by the infinitive. *It is never so expressed in good Latin prose.*

588. Rule for Subjunctive of Purpose. *A clause expressing purpose takes the subjunctive.*

589. A clause of purpose is introduced by the relative pronoun **quī** (as above), or by **ut,** *in order that, that*; or, if negative, by **nē,** *in order that not, that not, lest.*

> **Caesar mittit mīlitēs quī agrōs vāstent,** *Cæsar sends soldiers to lay waste* (literally, *who should lay waste*) *the fields*
> **Mīlitēs veniunt ut agrōs vāstent,** *soldiers come to lay waste* (literally, *in order that they may lay waste*) *the fields*
> **Agricolae pugnant nē agrī vāstentur,** *the farmers fight that their fields may not be laid waste*

EXERCISES

First learn the special vocabulary, page 379

590. 1. Dux, vir summae virtūtis, praemittit explōrātōrēs quī locum idōneum castrīs dēligant. 2. Iubet eōs celerrimē properāre nē tempus āmittant. 3. Interim quīdam prīnceps, vir summā potestāte apud Gallōs, ducem quaerit ut condiciōnēs pācis petat. 4. Sed dux eum rapit ut dē eō supplicium sūmat. 5. Tum vērō suōs (*his men*) convocat ut ratiōnem proelī doceat.

591. 1. The soldier asks for better arms that he may not lose his life. 2. The king sends his son to hear the conditions of peace. 3. He follows this plan lest he lose the supreme power. 4. An army is hastening to inflict punishment on him.

LESSON XCI

Et docēre et rērum exquīrere causās — Both to teach and to search
out the reasons of things [1]

PAST SUBJUNCTIVE, FIRST AND SECOND CONJUGATIONS
SEQUENCE OF TENSES

592. Inflection of Past Subjunctive. The past subjunctive of
any verb may be formed by adding the personal endings to
the present infinitive active. The past subjunctive of **vocō** and
moneō is inflected as follows:

ACTIVE VOICE

1. vocā′rem	vocārē′mus	monē′rem	monērē′mus
2. vocā′rēs	vocārē′tis	monē′rēs	monērē′tis
3. vocā′ret	vocā′rent	monē′ret	monē′rent

PASSIVE VOICE

1. vocā′rer	vocārē′mur	monē′rer	monērē′mur
2. vocārē′ris (-re)	vocārē′minī	monērē′ris (-re)	monērē′minī
3. vocārē′tur	vocāren′tur	monērē′tur	monēren′tur

593. Sequence of Tenses Defined. Tenses referring to present
or future time are called *primary* tenses. Tenses referring to
past time are called *secondary* tenses. As a rule, the tenses of
the verbs used in the principal and the dependent clause of
a complex sentence harmonize; that is, all are primary or all
are secondary. For example, in *He says that he is coming* both
of the verbs are present and in a primary tense; but if we
change *He says* to *He said*, a corresponding change takes place
in the verb in the dependent clause, and we say *He said that he
was coming*, both of the verbs being in a secondary tense. This
harmony between the tenses is called the *sequence of tenses.*

[1] Motto of the University of Georgia.

216

594. Primary and Secondary Tenses. In the following table the primary tenses are marked (1) and the secondary tenses (2):

INDICATIVE	SUBJUNCTIVE
(1) Present	(1) Present
(2) Past	(2) Past
(1) Future	(1) Perfect
(2) Perfect	(2) Past Perfect
(2) Past Perfect	
(1) Future Perfect	

When indicatives and subjunctives are used in the same sentence, the tenses generally harmonize.

595. Rule for Sequence of Tenses. *In a complex sentence a primary tense of the indicative in the principal clause is followed by a primary tense of the subjunctive in the dependent clause, and a secondary by a secondary.*

596.   EXAMPLES

I. Primary tenses in principal and dependent clauses:

Present   **Mittit** ⎫
Future   **Mittet** ⎬ hostēs ut agrōs vāstent (Pres. Subjv.)
Fut. Perf. **Mīserit** ⎭

He ⎧ *sends* ⎫ *foes* ⎧ *that they may,* ⎫ *lay waste the fields*
⎨ *will send* ⎬ ⎨ *in order to,* or ⎬
⎩ *will have sent* ⎭ ⎩ *to* ⎭

II. Secondary tenses in principal and dependent clauses:

Past   **Mittēbat** ⎫
Perfect   **Mīsit** ⎬ hostēs ut agrōs vāstārent (Past Subjv.)
Past Perf. **Mīserat** ⎭

He ⎧ *was sending* ⎫ *foes* ⎧ *that they might,* ⎫ *lay waste the fields*
⎨ *sent* or *has sent* ⎬ ⎨ *in order to,* or ⎬
⎩ *had sent* ⎭ ⎩ *to* ⎭

EXERCISES

First learn the special vocabulary, page 379

597. 1. Partem impedīmentōrum relinquit ut ad illud oppidum celerius perveniat. 2. Interim imperātor trēs legiōnēs remīserat quae illōs fīnēs statim pācārent. 3. Propter nātūram eius locī nēmō excēdere potuit quī fortūnam miseram nostram nūntiāret. 4. Hostēs vāllum decem mīlia passuum longum et fossam octō pedum perdūxerant ut itinere nostrōs prohibērent. 5. Hōc proeliō nūntiātō, multī perītī reī mīlitāris domum contendērunt ut prō rē pūblicā pugnārent. 6. Ampliōrēs cōpiās exspectābimus nē hostēs summum montem [1] obtineant. 7. Propter vulnera imperātor in castrīs manēre dēbet atque mittere aliquem quī animōs mīlitum hortētur. 8. Quīdam vir laudis cupidissimus librum dē suīs victōriīs scrīpsit. 9. Quīdam vērō cīvēs, timōre summō permōtī, Caesarem quaerunt ut eum dē ratiōne bellī cōnsulant.

1. **summum montem**, *the top of the mountain.*

598. 1. Cæsar forbade the Germans to advance farther, lest they should settle in Gaul. 2. After all things [1] had been prepared, he climbed to the top of the mountain to storm the camp. 3. I shall arrive at Rome [2] at daybreak [3] that I may undertake this serious business of the republic immediately. 4. Scævola came to put [4] the king to death. 5. Because of his supreme valor no one inflicted punishment on him.

1. Ablative absolute. 2. Accusative without a preposition. 3. Latin, *first light*, ablative of time. 4. Latin, *give the king to death.*

LESSON XCII

PAST SUBJUNCTIVE, THIRD AND FOURTH CONJUGATIONS
NOUN CLAUSES OF PURPOSE

599. Inflection of Past Subjunctive. The past subjunctive of **regō** and **audiō** is inflected as follows:

ACTIVE VOICE

1. re'gerem	regerē'mus	audī'rem	audīrē'mus
2. re'gerēs	regerē'tis	audī'rēs	audīrē'tis
3. re'geret	re'gerent	audī'ret	audī'rent

PASSIVE VOICE

1. re'gerer	regerē'mur	audī'rer	audīrē'mur
2. regerē'ris (-re)	regerē'minī	audīrē'ris (-re)	audīrē'minī
3. regerē'tur	regeren'tur	audīrē'tur	audīren'tur

a. Like **regerem** inflect **caperem**, the past subjunctive of **capiō**, and other -iō verbs of the third conjugation (see § 836).

600. Noun Clause Defined. A clause is often used as a part of speech, and is then named after the part of speech to which it is equivalent (cf. § 385). Thus we saw in § 386 that a relative clause has the force of an adjective and hence is called an adjective clause. A clause may modify a verb like an adverb, and is then called an adverbial clause : as, **vēnērunt ut pācem peterent**, *they came to seek peace* (adverbial clause of purpose). Similarly, a clause that is used as a noun is called a *noun* clause. Such a clause is often the subject or object of a verb : as,

> *That we should agree seems impossible* (clause used as subject)
> *Cæsar commanded that the captives should be let go* (clause used as object)

[1] Motto of the University of Michigan.

601. Noun Clauses of Purpose. In English, verbs of *asking*, *commanding*, *urging*, etc. are usually followed by an infinitive clause as object: as,

> They asked
> They commanded ⎱ *me to come*
> They urged

Verbs of this kind denote a purpose or desire that something be done, and the infinitive expresses what that something is. But in Latin, as we have learned (§ 582), a purpose or desire is not expressed by the infinitive, but by the subjunctive. Compare the following English and Latin sentences:

> *They urged me to come*
> **Hortābantur mē ut venīrem** (lit. *that I should come*)

602. Rule for Noun Clauses of Purpose. *Verbs denoting a purpose or desire that something be done are followed by a subjunctive clause as object, introduced by* **ut** *or* **nē**.

603. The following common verbs are regularly followed by a noun clause with **ut** or **nē** and the subjunctive:

hortor, *urge*
imperō, *order* (with the dative of the *person* ordered and a subjunctive clause of the *thing* ordered)
moneō, *advise*
persuādeō, *persuade* (with the same construction as **imperō**)
petō, rogō, *beg, ask*
postulō, *demand, require*

a. Remember that **iubeō,** *order*, takes the infinitive as in English (§ 367). Compare the following sentences:

> **Iubeō eum venīre,** *I order him to come*
> **Imperō eī ut veniat,** *I give orders to him that he come*

EXERCISES

First learn the special vocabulary, page 379

604. 1. Maximē lēgātōs hortātus est ut dē rē frūmentāriā prōvidērent. 2. Imperātor rēgī imperat nē sociīs populī Rōmānī noceat. 3. Gallī, timōre servitūtis permōtī, postulāvērunt ut exercitus reī pūblicae ex finibus suīs excēderet. 4. Plūrimīs vulneribus acceptīs, quīdam nōbīs persuāsit ut fugam temptārēmus. 5. Propter inopiam reī frūmentāriae imperātor monuit ut castra in alium locum movērentur. 6. Petimus et hortāmur ut nōs ab iniūriīs dēfendās. 7. Ad urbem tertiā hōrā pervēnī, sed nēmō mē rogāvit ut ūnum (*even one*) diem manērem. 8. Proximō diē magna multitūdō vēnit ut mē cōnsuleret et dē condiciōnibus pācis quaereret. 9. Hīs rēbus gestīs, lēgātus cum tribus legiōnibus relictus est ut dē rē frūmentāriā prōvidēret.

605. 1. Because of [1] your wounds I urge you not to try[2] that long journey. 2. You asked him to look out[2] for[3] the grain supply, didn't you[4]? Not at all. 3. Seek for the general and demand that he lead his forces out of my territory. 4. He ordered[5] the captives not to attempt[2] flight. 5. The woman demanded that the money be found.

1. The ablative of cause might be used, but the accusative with **propter** is more common. 2. Not infinitive. 3. **dē.** 4. On this form of question, review § 251. 5. What construction follows **iubeō**? What **imperō**?

GLADIATORS' HELMETS

LESSON XCIII

Deī sub nūmine viget — She flourishes under the will of God [1]

THE SUBJUNCTIVE OF *SUM* AND *POSSUM*

606. Subjunctive of *sum*. The subjunctive of **sum** is inflected as follows:

PRESENT		PAST	
1. sim	sīmus	essem	essē′mus
2. sīs	sītis	essēs	essē′tis
3. sit	sint	esset	essent

PERFECT		PAST PERFECT	
1. fu′erim	fue′rimus	fuis′sem	fuissē′mus
2. fu′eris	fue′ritis	fuis′sēs	fuissē′tis
3. fu′erit	fu′erint	fuis′set	fuis′sent

607. Subjunctive of *possum*. The subjunctive of **possum** is inflected as follows:

PRESENT		PAST	
1. possim	possī′mus	possem	possē′mus
2. possīs	possī′tis	possēs	possē′tis
3. possit	possint	posset	possent

PERFECT		PAST PERFECT	
1. potu′erim	potue′rimus	potuis′sem	potuissē′mus
2. potu′eris	potue′ritis	potuis′sēs	potuissē′tis
3. potu′erit	potu′erint	potuis′set	potuis′sent

a. Compare the perfect subjunctive with the future perfect indicative. Note that the past subjunctive may be formed by adding **m** to the present active infinitive (**posse + m**), and the past perfect subjunctive by adding **m** to the perfect active infinitive (**potuisse + m**).

[1] Motto of Princeton University.

EXERCISES

First learn the special vocabulary, page 380

608. 1. Sī exercitus vester fīnibus nostrīs appropinquābit, magnam multitūdinem mittēmus quae iter vestrum vī et armīs impediat. 2. Imperātor reliquās cōpiās prōdūxit nē rē frūmentāriā interclūderētur. 3. Hāc ōrātiōne[1] habitā,[2] nē tardissimī quidem rogant ut inīquae condiciōnēs pācis accipiantur. 4. Caesar quidem trēs legiōnēs cōnscrīpserat ac postulāverat ut iter hostium maximē impedīrētur. 5. Anteā nē eius quidem ōrātiō cīvibus persuādēre potuerat ut rem pūblicam cōnservāre dēbērent. 6. Nunc vērō nēmō ausus est rogāre nē legiōnēs novae cōnscrīberentur. 7. Caesar vāllum longum perdūxit nē aquā ab hostibus interclūderētur. 8. Tum suōs,[3] gravibus vulneribus impedītōs, hortātus est ut sēsē in castrīs continērent.

1. Ablative absolute. 2. **ōrātiōnem habēre** = *deliver an oration.* 3. Possessive adjective used as a noun, *his men.*

609. 1. As winter[1] was approaching, he ordered[2] two cohorts to look out for a grain supply. 2. Someone urged the chief to make[3] a speech. 3. He asked the citizens to hinder[3] the march of the enemy. 4. He demanded of them (**ab eīs**) that they shut the enemy off from the river. 5. Yet not even he could persuade the timid citizens to enroll[3] new legions.

1. Ablative absolute with present participle. 2. Write with both **iubeō** and **imperō.** 3. Not infinitive.

FINGER RINGS WITH ENGRAVED SETTINGS

LESSON XCIV

Lūx sit — Let there be light[1]

THE PERFECT AND PAST PERFECT SUBJUNCTIVE OF *VOCŌ, MONEŌ, REGŌ*, AND *AUDIŌ*

610. Inflection of Perfect Subjunctive. Learn the inflection of the following perfect subjunctives :

	ACTIVE	PASSIVE
CONJ. I	vocā′verim	vocā′tus (-a, -um) sim (§ 832)
CONJ. II	monu′erim	mo′nitus (-a, -um) sim (§ 833)
CONJ. III	rē′xerim	rēc′tus (-a, -um) sim (§ 834)
CONJ. IV	audī′verim	audī′tus (-a, -um) sim (§ 835)

611. Inflection of Past Perfect Subjunctive. Learn the inflection of the following past perfect subjunctives :

	ACTIVE	PASSIVE
CONJ. I	vocāvis′sem	vocā′tus (-a, -um) essem (§ 832)
CONJ. II	monuis′sem	mo′nitus (-a, -um) essem (§ 833)
CONJ. III	rēxis′sem	rēc′tus (-a, -um) essem (§ 834)
CONJ. IV	audīvis′sem	audī′tus (-a, -um) essem (§ 835)

a. Note that the formation and inflection of the perfect and past perfect subjunctive active are like **fuerim** and **fuissem**, the corresponding tenses of **sum**; and that in the passive **sim** and **essem** take the place of **sum** and **eram** of the indicative passive.

EXERCISES

612. Inflect the complete subjunctive, active and passive, of **pācō, moveō, rapiō, mittō, mūniō.**

---

[1] Motto of the University of Washington. Compare the following verse in the Latin Bible : " Dīxitque Deus: Fīat lūx. Et facta est lūx."

HĒRŌ ET LĒANDER

The story of Hero and Leander has been the subject of many poems, both ancient and modern. See Leigh Hunt, Tom Hood, Moore, Tennyson.

First learn the special vocabulary, page 380

613. Iūdiciō multōrum poētārum nēmō apud puellās Graecās [1] erat pulchrior quam Hērō, sacerdōs [2] templī [3] quod Sēstī [4] positum est. Eam Lēander, adulēscēns [5] nōbilissimus, tōtō animō amāvit et in mātrimōnium ducere cupīvit, sed lēgēs vetuērunt. Lēander autem nec lēgēs sacrās nec deōs 5 inīquōs veritus est. Tamen ut amor [6] eius cēlārētur,[7] Lēander numquam diē sed tantum [8] nocte vēnit ut eam vidēret. Nec sine summā difficultāte erat hoc iter, nam mare angustum,[9] Hellēspontus nōmine,[10] inter Sēstum et Abȳdum, urbem Lēandrī, interfluit.[11] Sed nē mare quidem eum interclūdere 10 poterat. Omnī [12] nocte Lēander Hellēspontum trānābat [13]; omnī nocte Hērō in summā turrī dīligenter locābat lucernam [14] quae adulēscentem per aquās perdūceret.

1. **Graecus, -a, -um,** *Greek.* 2. **sacerdōs, -ōtis,** M. and F., *priest* or *priestess.* 3. **templum, -ī,** N., *temple.* 4. **Sēstus, -ī,** F., *Sestos,* a city on the Hellespont at its narrowest point, opposite Aby'dos. The form **Sēstī** is locative; see § 485. 5. **adulēscēns, -entis,** M., *youth.* 6. **amor, -ōris,** M., *love.* 7. **cēlō, -āre,** *conceal.* 8. *Only.* 9. **angustus, -a, -um,** *narrow.* 10. Ablative of respect, § 552. 11. **interfluō, -ere,** *flow between.* 12. **omnis** in the singular often means *every.* 13. **trānō, -āre,** *swim across.* The Hellespont at this point is about a mile wide, but there is a dangerous current. Byron's successful attempt to swim across is well known. 14. **lucerna, -ae,** F., *lamp.*

614. 1. Many reasons urged Leander not to expose [1] himself to death. 2. Not even Hero could persuade him [2] not to attempt [3] that journey. 3. He asked her to put [3] a lamp on top of the tower. 4. She listened [4] attentively that she might save his life. 5. She ought to advise him to remain [3] at home.

1. **committō.** Not infinitive.   2. Dative.   3. Not infinitive.   4. **audiō.**

LESSON XCV

SUBJUNCTIVE OF RESULT

615. Observe the following sentence :

The danger was so great that all fled, **perīculum erat tantum ut omnēs fugerent**

The principal clause names a cause, and the dependent clause states the result of this cause. In English the verb *fled* in the dependent clause is indicative, but in Latin this clause is introduced by **ut** (*so that*), and **fugerent** is subjunctive. This construction is called the *subjunctive of result.*

616. Rule for Subjunctive of Result. *Clauses of result are introduced by* **ut** (*negative* **ut nōn**) *and have the verb in the subjunctive.*

617. Result is sometimes expressed by a noun clause used as object : as,

Perīculum fēcit ut omnēs fugerent, *the danger caused all to flee* (literally, *made so that all fled*)

618. Rule for Object Clauses of Result. *Object clauses of result introduced by* **ut** (*negative* **ut nōn**) *are used after verbs of effecting or bringing about.*

619. Purpose and Result Clauses Compared. Affirmative clauses of purpose and result are similar ; but a negative purpose clause is introduced by **nē**, while a negative result clause has **ut nōn.**

---

[1] Motto of Johns Hopkins University. From the Latin Bible.

HERO AND LEANDER

Leander! Leander! Speak to me!
Speak to me! Leander! Leander!

MARTIN SCHÜTZE — Hero and Leander

a. When **tam, ita, sīc** (all meaning *so*), **tālis** (*such*), or **tantus** (*so great*) appears in the main clause, the dependent clause denotes result.

b. Do the following sentences denote purpose or result?

Celeriter fūgit nē caperētur, *he fled swiftly that he might not be taken*
Tam celeriter fūgit ut servārētur, *he fled so swiftly that he was saved*
Celeriter fūgit ut servārētur, *he fled swiftly that he might be saved*
Tam celeriter fūgit ut nōn caperētur, *he fled so swiftly that he was not taken*

HĒRŌ ET LĒANDER (Concluded)

First learn the special vocabulary, page 380

620. Hāc in condiciōne rēs diū permanēbant. Sed nihil est certum hominī,[1] nec ūlla fortūna semper aequa. Ōlim tanta tempestās[2] coörta est[3] ut etiam maximae nāves impetum maris sustinēre nōn possent ac summā celeritāte ad ōrās fīnitimās fugerent. Tamen Lēander suā cōnsuētūdine[4] ad .5 ōram prīmā nocte pervēnit ut iter faceret. Mare quidem erat turbidum,[5] sed is lūcem turris trāns mare vidēre poterat ibique[6] erat Hērō ipsa. Itaque omnī timōre dēpositō adulēscēns[7] nōbilis vītam suam aquīs commīsit. Statim autem summīs difficultātibus ita premēbātur ut vī ipsā maris 10 superārētur.

Interim Hērō eum multās hōrās exspectābat. Tālī timōre commōta est ut mēns cōnsistere nōn posset. Prīmā lūce vērō ad ōram contendit ut eum quaereret. Dēnique dīligenter quaerēns corpus eius invēnit. Eō vīsō[8] sēsē in mare coniēcit. 15 Nam dolor ipse fēcerat[9] ut puella miserrima mentem suam āmitteret.

1. *Man is sure of nothing.* 2. **tempestās, -ātis,** F., *storm.* 3. **coörior, -īrī,** deponent verb, *rise.* 4. *According to his custom.* 5. **turbidus, -a, -um,** *stormy.* 6. Two words, **ibi + que.** 7. **adulēscēns, -entis,** M., *youth.* 8. Ablative absolute. Translate, *on seeing this.* 9. *Had caused.*

621. 1. So great was the violence of the sea that no one dared to sail. 2. The timid sailors stood on the shore. 3. They warned him not to throw [1] himself into such a sea. 4. Leander was so hard pressed that he abandoned all hope of safety. 5. Hero, according to her custom, was waiting for him. 6. What caused [2] her to lose her mind?

1. Not infinitive. 2. Latin idiom, *made that she lost.*

LESSON XCVI

Commūne vinculum omnibus artibus — The common bond for all the arts [1]

THE DATIVE WITH COMPOUNDS

622. The dative is the case of the indirect object (§ 58). Many intransitive verbs take an indirect object (§ 222), and some transitive verbs take both a direct object and an indirect object: as, **Mārcus puerō tēlum dedit,** *Marcus gave a spear to the boy.* Whether or not a verb will have an indirect object depends on its meaning. A number of verbs, some transitive and some intransitive, which in their simple form do not take an indirect object, have a meaning, when compounded with certain prepositions, that calls for one. This indirect object is called the *dative with compounds.*

623. Rule for Dative with Compounds. *Some verbs compounded with ad, ante, con, dē, in, inter, ob, post, prae, prō, sub, and super take the dative of the indirect object. Transitive compounds may take both an accusative and a dative.*

1 Motto of the University of Minnesota.

Potestās rēgī nōn deërat, *power was not lacking to the king*
Caesar equitātuī lēgātum praefēcit, *Cæsar placed the lieutenant in
command of the cavalry*

a. Many verbs compounded with these prepositions *do not take the
dative*, because their meaning forbids : as,

Caesar cōpiās ad montem prōdūxit, *Cæsar led forth the troops to
the mountain*

EXERCISES

First learn the special vocabulary, page 381

624. 1. Cōnsul optimōs cīvēs ēvocāre incēpit ut eīs praemia
ampla prōpōneret. 2. Magna multitūdō convēnerat nē amplus
exercitus imperātōrī deësset. 3. Quem nāvibus senātus prae-
ficiet? Senātus virum summae virtūtis dēliget. 4. Barbarī ita
premēbantur ut oppida reliqua incenderent. 5. Aciē īnstrūctā,
imperātor iussit Mārcum dextrō cornū praeesse. 6. Peditēs
tantum numerum tēlōrum coniēcērunt ut paucī in mūrō cōnsistere possent. 7. Cōnsuētūdine populī Rōmānī et iūre bellī
senātus dēbet illī imperātōrī imperāre ut. cīvitātēs inimīcās
pācet. 8. Altitūdō vāllī fēcit ut paucī vulnerārentur.

625. 1. The senate ordered that the remaining captives be led
away into slavery. 2. Heretofore, according to the law of war, the
towns had been set on fire. 3. The senate assembled to place[1]
someone in command of the infantry forces. 4. These things he
set forth that money might not be lacking to the commonwealth.
5. Is not[2] your mind in command of your body[3]? Yes.

1. Express *place in command* by one word. 2. See § 251. 3. Not genitive.

~~~~~~~~~~

Twelfth Review. Lessons LXXXIX-XCVI, §§ 793-797

LESSON XCVII

Cīvium in mōribus reī pūblicae salūs — In the character
of its citizens lies the safety of the commonwealth [1]

WORD FORMATION

626. Many abstract nouns are formed from adjectives by
the suffixes **-ia, -tia, -tās, -tūdō.**

memor-ia, *memory*	memor, *mindful*
inop-ia, *want*	inops, *poor*
sapient-ia, *wisdom*	sapiēns, *wise*
amīci-tia, *friendship*	amīcus, *friendly*
celeri-tās, *swiftness*	celer, *swift*
līber-tās, *freedom*	līber, *free*
magni-tūdō, *greatness*	magnus, *great*
alti-tūdō, *height*	altus, *high*

627. Adjectives denoting *quality* or *state* are formed from
verbs by the suffix **-idus.**

cup-idus, *desirous*	cupere, *desire*
tim-idus, *fearful*	timēre, *fear*

628. Adjectives denoting *fullness* are formed from nouns by
the suffix **-ōsus** (the English suffix *-ous*).

perīcul-ōsus, *dangerous*	perīculum, *danger*
studi-ōsus, *zealous*	studium, *zeal*

629. Adjectives denoting *capability* in a passive sense are
formed from verbs by the suffixes **-ilis** and **-bilis.**

fac-ilis, *easy* (able to be done)	facere, *do*
crēdi-bilis, *credible* (able to be believed)	crēdere, *believe*
amā-bilis, *lovable*	amāre, *love*

---

[1] Motto of the University of Florida.

231

630. Hints on Spelling. When in doubt as to whether an English word should end in *-able* or *-ible*, remember that derivatives from Latin verbs of the first conjugation end in *-able*, those from other conjugations end in *-ible*.

portable	**portāre**	*visible*	**vidēre**
vulnerable	**vulnerāre**	*reducible*	**redūcere**
comparable	**comparāre**	*audible*	**audīre**
habitable	**habitāre**	*possible*	**posse**

A few common words are exceptions : as, *tenable, movable, capable, preventable.*

631. Most English words ending in *-tion* or *-sion* are derived from Latin verbs. If the Latin past participle ends in **-tus,** use the suffix *-tion* ; if in **-sus,** use *-sion.*

ENGLISH WORD	LATIN PARTICIPLE
exception	**exceptus**
contention	**contentus**
monition	**monitus**
ascension	**ascēnsus**
admission	**admissus**
session	**sessus**

EXERCISES

632. Derivation. From your knowledge of prefixes what should you judge to be the meaning of the following compounds of **iaciō,** *throw* ?

adiciō	**dēiciō**	**iniciō**	**prōiciō**	**subiciō**
coniciō	**ēiciō**	**obiciō**	**reiciō**	**trāiciō**

633. See how many English derivatives you can write from **iaciō** and its compounds.

LESSON XCVIII

Litterīs dēdicāta et omnibus artibus — Dedicated to letters and all the arts [1]

THE IRREGULAR VERBS *VOLŌ, NŌLŌ,* AND *MĀLŌ*

634. Learn the inflection of **volō**, *wish*; **nōlō**, *be unwilling*; and **mālō**, *prefer* (§ 840), and note that the indicative and subjunctive are inflected like **regō** except in the present indicative and the present and past subjunctive. These verbs have no passive voice.

635. Constructions with *volō, nōlō,* and *mālō.* In English we say *I wish to write* or *I wish him to write.* In the first sentence *I wish* is followed by the complementary infinitive *to write,* and the subject of the two verbs is the same. In the second, *I wish* is followed by the object clause *him to write,* and the subjects are different.

Similarly, in Latin, **volō, nōlō,** and **mālō** are used with the complementary infinitive when the subject remains the same; and with the infinitive with subject accusative when the subjects are different (§§ 367–369).

> **Volō scrībere,** *I wish to write*
> **Volō eum scrībere,** *I wish him to write*

EXERCISES

First learn the special vocabulary, page 381

636. 1. Potestās Caesarī nōn deërat et mālēbat rē [1] esse rēx quam nōmine. 2. Hostēs, cum prīmī ōrdinēs sē ostendunt, nē cōnsistunt quidem, sed in fīnēs suōs sē recipiunt. 3. Cōpiae enim quae praemissae erant ut impetum nostrum prohibērent

---

[1] Motto of the University of Nebraska.

233

satis fīrmae nōn erant. 4. Hās rēs lēgātī prōposuerant ut hae cīvitātēs in fidem[2] ac potestātem populī Rōmānī venīre vellent. 5. Oportuit Rōmānōs urbem vāllō fossāque circummūnīre ut fidēs[3] pūblica servārētur. 6. Illa silva, quae ab flūmine ad mare pertinet, multa genera animālium habet quae in aliīs locīs nōn videntur. 7. Nōnne illa legiō cui fīlius tuus praeerat parāvit omnia quae ad salūtem cīvium pertinent? Parāvit. 8. Tanta multitūdō convēnerat ut cōpia frūmentī satis[4] nōn esset.

1. **rē,** *in reality,* ablative of respect, § 552. 2. **in fidem,** *under the protection.* 3. **fidēs pūblica,** *the promise given by the state.* 4. The word **satis** may be an adverb, as in 3; or an adjective, as in 8; or a noun, as, **satis suppli'cī,** *enough (of) punishment;* **satis facere,** *to give satisfaction;* etc.

637. 1. The senate is not willing to give satisfaction[1] to our enemies. 2. We wish war rather than that kind of peace. 3. For it is necessary to keep the faith which we received from our fathers. 4. Display hope, citizens, and not fear. 5. Fortify[2] the city all about with walls and ditches. 6. For the senate does not wish us to withdraw without a battle. 7. But it wishes us to prepare all things that pertain to war.

1. See § 636, note 4. 2. *Fortify all about* is expressed by one word.

A ROMAN STOVE WITH HOT-WATER BOILER

LESSON XCIX

Vīta hominum lūx — Light, the life of men[1]

VOCABULARY REVIEW · CONSTRUCTIONS WITH *CUM*

638. Review the word lists in §§ 732, 733, 737, 738.

639. Constructions with *cum*. The conjunction **cum** has three meanings : *when, since,* and *although.*

640. Clauses introduced by **cum** are of four kinds : *temporal, descriptive, causal,* and *concessive.*

641. Cum meaning *when* is temporal or descriptive,[2] and is usually followed by the indicative if the tense is present or future, otherwise by the subjunctive.

> **Veniam cum poterō,** *I will come when I can*
> **Cum Rōmānī sē ostenderent, hostēs fūgērunt,** *when the Romans appeared (showed themselves), the enemy fled*

642. Cum causal (*since*) and **cum** concessive (*although*) are followed by the subjunctive.

> **Cum pācem peterent, Caesar in eōs impetum nōn fēcit,** *since they were seeking peace, Cæsar did not make an attack on them*
> **Cum prīmī ōrdinēs fūgissent, tamen reliquī fortiter cōnsistēbant,** *though the first ranks had fled, yet the rest bravely stood their ground*

---

[1] Motto of the University of New Mexico.
[2] A descriptive clause describes the circumstances under which the main action took place : as, *The farmer found the money when he was plowing.* It is, furthermore, implied that but for the circumstances stated, the action expressed in the main clause would not have taken place. Thus, in the sentence above, if the farmer had not been plowing, he would not have found the money.

643. **Rule for Constructions with *cum*.** *Cum means when, since, or although, and takes the subjunctive except in a temporal or descriptive clause of present or future time.*

EXERCISES

644. 1. Cum rēgīna novās grātāsque condiciōnēs pācis prōposuisset, nē sociī quidem, quī inimīcī anteā fuerant, arma ac frūmentum dare nōlēbant. 2. Cum[1] via tam longa sit, tamen oportet puerōs puellāsque iter facere. 3. Cum[2] aqua satis alta esset, nautae sine ūllā difficultāte ad īnsulam parvam nāvigāvērunt. 4. Cum nāvēs omnī genere convocātae essent, rēgīna iussit servōs cōpiam frūmentī ex agrīs proximīs ad ōram maris portāre. 5. Cum ōrdinēs nostrī sē ostenderent, hostēs in oppidum sē recipiēbant. 6. Cum Rōmānī in fīnēs Gallōrum venīrent, Gallī magnopere commōtī sunt. 7. Cum imperātor lēgātōs videt, rogat, "Cūr, lēgātī, vēnistis? Quid quaeritis?" 8. Lēgātī respondent, "Volumus in fidem et potestātem populī Rōmānī venīre."

1. **cum** = *though.* The concessive use of **cum** is often indicated by the presence of **tamen** in the main clause. 2. **cum** = *since.*

645. 1. Since the money is not sufficient, why do you not demand more? 2. Though you prepare all kinds of arms, you cannot overcome my allies. 3. When I was living at Rome, I often heard and saw famous Romans. 4. When you call me, I will hasten. 5. When the enemy appeared, we withdrew.

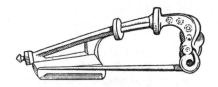

GOLDEN FIBULA, OR BROOCH

The Romans were familiar with the principle of the modern safety pin

LESSON C

Mediō tūtissimus ībis — In the middle course you will go safest[1]

VOCABULARY REVIEW · THE IRREGULAR VERB EŌ

646. Review the word lists in §§ 743, 744.

647. Irregular Verb eō. Learn the inflection of the irregular verb eō, *go* (§ 842), and the declension of the present participle iēns, *going* (§ 817).

EXERCISES

648. Derivation. The irregular verb eō has a large number of compounds. Using your knowledge of prefixes, give the meaning of the following common words : **adeō, exeō, ineō, redeō, trānseō.**

649. 1. Cum[1] exercitus rē frūmentāriā premerētur, dux ad oppidum īre contendit. 2. Castrīs positīs, nostrī equitēs crēbra proelia cum barbarīs fēcērunt, sed legiōnēs sēsē in castrīs continēbant. 3. Germānī cum magnīs cōpiīs ex fīnibus suīs ierant ut agrōs meliōrēs occupārent. 4. Multī Germānōs ita timēbant ut cum eīs pugnāre nōllent et domum īre vellent. 5. Imperātor, cum hanc fāmam audīvisset, dīxit, " Īte domum, sī vultis, atque ego sōlus in hostēs ībō." 6. Tum tanta virtūs animōs omnium occupāvit ut manēre quam īre māllent. 7. Cum ad Galliam īrēmus, ōram īnsulae Britanniae vidēre poterāmus. 8. Sine ūllā spē praemī aut victōriae et cum summō perīculō pugnāvī, nē amīcitiam tuam āmitterem. 9. Puerī miserī, quī per silvam euntēs raptī erant, numquam posteā vīsī sunt.

1. **cum** causal.

[1] From Ovid, a famous poet of the Augustan age. The words are often quoted to urge the value of moderation in all things.

650. 1. The senate persuaded the general[1] not to go[2] to Britain. 2. Though we have toiled many days, yet you wish us to go home without any reward. 3. When you have plenty of money, I advise you to go[2] to Rome. 4. Since you fear frequent wars, why do you not make peace? 5. Go into battle with good arms if you wish to conquer.

1. Not accusative. 2. Not infinitive.

LESSON CI

Lūx et lēx — Light and law[1]

VOCABULARY REVIEW · INDIRECT STATEMENTS

651. Review the word lists in §§ 749, 750.

652. Indirect Statements in English. Direct statements are those which the speaker or writer makes himself or which are quoted in his exact language. Indirect statements are those reported in a different form of words from that used by the speaker or writer. Compare the following direct and indirect statements :

Direct statements
- 1. *The Gauls are brave*
- 2. *The Gauls were brave*
- 3. *The Gauls will be brave*

Indirect statements after a verb in the present tense
- 1. *He says* that the Gauls *are brave*
- 2. *He says* that the Gauls *were brave*
- 3. *He says* that the Gauls *will be brave*

Indirect statements after a verb in a past tense
- 1. *He said* that the Gauls *were brave*
- 2. *He said* that the Gauls *had been brave*
- 3. *He said* that the Gauls *would be brave*

When an English direct statement becomes indirect,

[1] Motto of the University of North Dakota.

a. The indirect statement becomes a dependent clause introduced by the conjunction *that.*

b. The verb remains finite and its subject is in the nominative.

c. The tenses of the verbs originally used are changed after the past tense, *He said.*

653. Indirect Statements in Latin. In Latin the direct and indirect statements above would be expressed as follows :

Direct statements
1. **Gallī sunt fortēs,** *the Gauls are brave*
2. **Gallī erant fortēs,** *the Gauls were brave*
3. **Gallī erunt fortēs,** *the Gauls will be brave*

Indirect statements
1. **Dīcit** or **Dīxit Gallōs esse fortīs** (*he says* or *he said the Gauls to be brave*)[1]
2. **Dīcit** or **Dīxit Gallōs fuisse fortīs** (*he says* or *he said the Gauls to have been brave*)[1]
3. **Dīcit** or **Dīxit Gallōs futūrōs esse fortīs** (*he says* or *he said the Gauls to be about to be brave*)[1]

Comparing these Latin indirect statements with the English in the preceding section, we observe three marked differences :

a. There is no conjunction corresponding to *that.*

b. The verb is in the infinitive and its subject is in the accusative.

c. The tenses of the infinitive are not changed after a past tense of the principal verb.

654. Rule for Indirect Statements. *When a direct statement becomes indirect, the principal verb is changed to the infinitive and its subject nominative becomes subject accusative of the infinitive.*

655. Tenses of Infinitive. When the sentences in §653 were changed from the direct to the indirect form of statement, **sunt** became **esse**, **erant** became **fuisse**, and **erunt** became **futūrōs esse.**

---

[1] These parenthetical renderings are not inserted as translations, but merely to show the literal meaning of the Latin.

656. Rule for Tenses of Infinitive in Indirect Statements.
A present indicative of a direct statement becomes present infinitive of the indirect, a past indicative becomes perfect infinitive, and a future indicative becomes future infinitive.

657. Rule for Verbs followed by Indirect Statements.
The accusative-with-infinitive construction in indirect statements is found after verbs of **saying, telling, knowing, thinking,** *and* **perceiving.**

658. Verbs regularly followed by indirect statements are

a. Verbs of saying and telling:

dīcō, dīcere, dīxī, dictus, *say, tell*
negō, negāre, negāvī, negātus, *deny, say not*
nūntiō, nūntiāre, nūntiāvī, nūntiātus, *announce*
respondeō, respondēre, respondī, respōnsus, *reply*

b. Verbs of knowing:

cognōscō, cognōscere, cognōvī, cognitus, *learn,* (in the perfect) *know*
sciō, scīre, scīvī, scītus, *know*

c. Verbs of thinking:

exīstimō, exīstimāre, exīstimāvī, exīstimātus, *think, believe*
iūdicō, iūdicāre, iūdicāvī, iūdicātus, *judge, decide*
putō, putāre, putāvī, putātus, *reckon, think*
spērō, spērāre, spērāvī, spērātus, *hope*

d. Verbs of perceiving:

audiō, audīre, audīvī, audītus, *hear*
sentiō, sentīre, sēnsī, sēnsus, *feel, perceive*
videō, vidēre, vīdī, vīsus, *see*
intellegō, intellegere, intellēxī, intellēctus, *understand, perceive*

Most of these verbs you know. Learn the new ones, and use the list for reference.

EXERCISES

659. 1. Caesar per explōrātōrēs cognōverat hostēs inopiā frūmentī premī. 2. Rōmānī audīvērunt Helvētiōs proximā aestāte ex fīnibus suīs excessūrōs esse. 3. Lēgātī cum pervēnissent, respondērunt frātrem rēgis exercituī praefutūrum esse. 4. Prīncipēs Gallōrum negābant sē oppida sua incendisse. 5. Rēx respondit pecūniam esse rēgīnae.[1] 6. Poētae exīstimābant potestātem deōrum esse maiōrem quam deārum. 7. Hīs rēbus[2] cognitīs, spērāvimus aliquem missūrum esse nāvigium quod nōs servāret.[3] 8. Cum urbī appropinquārēmus, intellēximus mediam partem altīs et lātīs mūrīs mūnītam esse. 9. Hāc ōrātiōne[2] habitā, sēnsimus animum fīnitimōrum esse nōbīs inimīcum.

1. **rēgīnae**, predicate genitive of possessor (§ 150). 2. Ablative absolute (§ 400). 3. Subjunctive in a relative clause of purpose (§ 589).

660. Using five of the verbs in § 658, write five Latin sentences, each one containing an indirect statement.

A STREET IN POMPEII

The street is paved with blocks of lava. Note the stepping-stones for crossing the street in wet weather. Vesuvius looms in the distance

LESSON CII

Quī trānstulit sustinet — He who transplanted sustains [1]

VOCABULARY REVIEW · THE IRREGULAR VERB *FERŌ*

661. Review the word lists in §§ 755, 756.

662. Irregular Verb *ferō*. Learn the inflection of **ferō**, *bear* (§ 841). Its principal parts are very irregular, but the different tenses are formed on the three stems as usual.

a. The verb **ferō** has many compounds. One of these is **īnferō** in the idiom **bellum īnferō**, *I make war on*, with the dative. Learn also the idiom **graviter** or **molestē ferō**, *I am annoyed*, followed by the accusative and infinitive.

EXERCISES

663. Derivation. Note the prefixes and give the meanings of the following compounds : **ad'ferō, cōn'ferō, dē'ferō, īn'ferō, trāns'ferō.** Name ten English derivatives from these words.

664. I. 1. Māvis, nōn vultis, vīs, nōlumus. 2. Ut nōlit, nē vellēmus, nōlīte, māvultis. 3. It, īmus, ut eant, eunt. 4. Fer,[1] tulisse, ferent, tulerant. 5. Ut ferrent, lātus esse, nē ferant.

1. **Dīc, dūc, fac,** and **fer** are the four short imperatives. Cf. p. 100, footnote.

II. 1. Rōmānī molestē ferēbant illam cīvitātem sociīs bellum īnferre. 2. Explōrātōrēs nūntiāvērunt summum montem circummūnītum esse et fīrmō praesidiō tenērī. 3. Caesar respondit senātum graviter ferre magnam multitūdinem Germānōrum in optimīs partibus Galliae sedēre. 4. Nōs iūdicāmus vōs nōbīs bellum īnferre nōn oportēre. 5. Rēx dīxit memoriā patrum

1 Motto of the state of Connecticut.

242

Helvētiōs proelium cum Rōmānīs commīsisse et eōs [1] magnā caede in fugam dedisse. 6. Cum impedīmenta rapta essent, barbarī impetum nostrōrum diūtius ferre nōn poterant.

1. eōs refers to the Romans and is the object of dedisse.

665. 1. We are annoyed that the Gauls are making war on our allies. 2. The king denied that his son had gone. 3. The captives hastened to go that they might observe [1] the battle. 4. When the towers had been moved [2] to the walls, all who bore arms were led out.

1. spectō, -āre. 2. agō, -ere, ēgī, āctus.

LESSON CIII

Virtūs omnibus rēbus anteit — Virtue surpasses all things [1]

VOCABULARY REVIEW · THE SUBJUNCTIVE IN INDIRECT QUESTIONS

666. Review the word lists in §§ 762, 763.

667. Indirect Question Defined. When we report a question instead of asking it directly, we have an indirect question.

DIRECT QUESTION | INDIRECT QUESTION
Who conquered the Gauls? | *He asked who conquered the Gauls*

An indirect question is a noun clause and is usually the object of a verb of *asking, saying, knowing,* or *feeling.*

668. Moods in Questions. In English, as the example shows, the indicative is used in both direct and indirect questions.

1 From Plautus, a dramatic poet.

669. In Latin, verbs in direct questions are in the indicative; verbs in indirect questions are in the subjunctive.

DIRECT QUESTION	INDIRECT QUESTION
Quis Gallōs vīcit?	Rogāvit quis Gallōs vinceret
Who conquered the Gauls?	*He asked who conquered the Gauls*
Ubi est Rōma?	Rogat ubi sit Rōma
Where is Rome?	*He asks where Rome is*

a. Compare indirect *questions* and indirect *statements.* An indirect question is interrogative in form and has its verb in the subjunctive, as shown above. An indirect statement is introduced in English by the conjunction *that,* and its verb in Latin is in the infinitive: as, *He says that Cæsar conquered the Gauls,* dīcit Caesarem Gallōs vīcisse.

670. Indirect questions are introduced by the same interrogative words as direct questions. *Whether* is usually rendered by **num.**

671. Rule for Indirect Questions. *In an indirect question the verb is in the subjunctive, and its tense is determined by the rule for the sequence of tenses* (§ 595).

672.   IDIOMS

memoriā tenēre, *to remember* (literally, *to hold by memory*)
novīs rēbus studēre, *to be eager for a revolution* (literally, *new things*)
in reliquum tempus, *for the future*

EXERCISES

673. 1. Rēx rogāvit cūr lēgātī excessissent atque cūr ad sē nōn vēnissent. 2. Imperātor, vir ēgregiae virtūtis, amplās et integrās cōpiās mīsit quae oppidum dēfenderent et cognōscerent quae esset nātūra locī. 3. Gallī, quī semper novīs rēbus [1] studēbant, quaesīvērunt quid Rōmānī armīs facere possent. 4. Moneō tē nē in reliquum tempus petās quid agam. 5. Tenētisne memoriā

INDIRECT QUESTIONS 245

quae sint pūblica officia cōnsulis? 6. Omnibus rēbus comparā-
tīs, dux exspectāvit² quid hostēs facerent. 7. Hī mīlitēs erant
tam timidī ut imperiō¹ ducis pārēre nōn audērent.³

1. Why dative? See § 224. 2. *Waited to see.* 3. Why subjunctive?
See § 616.

674. 1. How far distant is the villa? 2. He asks how far distant the villa is. 3. Do you remember the story about Brutus?
4. They asked whether he remembered the story about Brutus.
5. Whither do you wish to go? 6. Do you know whither you
wish to go?

Thirteenth Review. Lessons XCVII–CIII, §§ 798–803

A MUSICAL RECITAL

The woman at the left is reciting a poem to the accompaniment of a lyre and
two pipes. The pipes are fitted into a band across the piper's mouth, enabling
him to blow on both pipes at the same time

LESSON CIV

Mēns agitat mōlem — Mind moves the mass [1]

VOCABULARY REVIEW · THE IRREGULAR VERB *FĪŌ*

675. Review the word lists in §§ 768, 769.

676. Irregular Verb *fīō*. Learn the inflection of **fīō**, *be made, happen* (§ 843). In the present system this verb serves as the passive of **faciō**. The rest of the passive of **faciō** is regular.

677.   IDIOMS

Aliquem certiōrem faciō, *I inform someone* (literally, *I make someone more certain*), followed by an infinitive with subject accusative or by an indirect question.

Certior fīō, *I am informed* (literally, *I am made more certain*), followed by the same construction as above.

Helvētiīs in animō est, *the Helvetii intend* (literally, *it is in mind to the Helvetii*), followed by the complementary infinitive.

EXERCISES

678. 1. Tuā linguā intellegō tē esse Gallum, et certior factus sum tibi in animō esse ratiōnem nostram bellī hostibus nūntiāre. 2. Quā dē causā tē rapī iubēbō ut supplicium pūblicum dē tē sūmam. 3. Multa beneficia ā populō Rōmānō anteā accēpistī, itaque tē rogō cūr tē gravissimam poenam dare nōn oporteat. 4. Iūre[1] bellī tē ad mortem dūcī statim oportet. 5. Magnā parte impedīmentōrum relictā, hostēs aliī aliam in partem fūgērunt. 6. Sciēbant nec quō īrent nec quid facerent. 7. Explōrātor lēgātum certiōrem fēcit quae[2] cōpiae castra obtinērent.

1. *In accordance with the right.* 2. *What forces*, introducing an indirect question.

[1] Motto of the University of Oregon.

246

679. 1. Don't you know why I am unwilling to undertake this business? 2. He asked why they were terrified. 3. He perceived why the camp had been moved. 4. Someone informed the senate that the town could not be taken. 5. We think that you will receive this state under[1] your protection. 6. He had been informed that the army had been led forward. 7. Do you know what the Helvetii intend to do?

1. **in** with the accusative.

LESSON CV

Litterae sine mōribus vānae — Letters without morals are vain[1]

VOCABULARY REVIEW · PREDICATE ACCUSATIVE
DATIVE OF PURPOSE

680. Review the word lists in §§ 774, 775.

681. Predicate Accusative. In English, verbs of *making*, *choosing*, *calling*, *naming*, and the like may take two objects referring to the same person or thing. The first of these is the direct object, and the second completes the sense of the predicate, and is called the predicate objective or the objective attribute.

> *The Romans made* **him consul**
> *The senate called the* **king friend**

682. Similarly, in Latin, **faciō**, *make*; **dēligō**, *choose*; **vocō** and **appellō**, *call*, and the like may take two accusatives : the first, the direct object; the second, referring to the same person or thing, known as the predicate accusative.

> **Rōmānī eum cōnsulem fēcērunt,** *the Romans made him consul*
> **Senātus rēgem amīcum appellāvit,** *the senate called the king friend*

1 Motto of the University of Pennsylvania.

683. When the verb is changed to the passive, both the accusatives become nominatives ; the direct object becoming the subject, and the predicate accusative the predicate nominative.

> Rēx amīcus ā senātū appellātus est, *the king was called friend by the senate*

a. Note that senātus, the subject of the active verb, becomes ā senātū, ablative of agent, when the verb is changed to the passive.

684. Rule for Predicate Accusative. *Verbs of making, choosing, calling, and the like may take. a predicate accusative along with the direct object. With the passive voice the two accusatives become nominatives.*

685. Dative of Purpose. Observe the following sentence :

> Explōrātōrēs locum castrīs dēlēgērunt, *the scouts chose a place for a camp*

Note that the dative castrīs expresses the purpose for which the place was intended. Such a dative is called the *dative of purpose* or *end for which*. It is often followed by a second dative denoting the person or thing affected : as,

> Hoc erat magnō impedīmentō Gallīs, *this was (for) a great hindrance to the Gauls*

686. Rule for Dative of Purpose. *The dative is used to denote the purpose or end for which, often with another dative denoting the person or thing affected.*

687.   IDIOMS

> iniūriās alicui īnferre, *to inflict injuries upon someone*
> nihil posse, *to have no power*
> praesidiō cīvitātī esse, *to be a defense to the state*

688. 1. Omnibus temporibus exercitus erat firmissimō prae-sidiō cīvitātī. 2. Lēgātus nōs certiōrēs fēcit tē cōnsulem appellātum esse. 3. Rogāvī cūr senātus mihi iniūriās intulisset. 4. Rēx voluit vōbīs auxiliō esse, sed nihil poterat. 5. Certior factus eram tibi in animō esse domum sine mē contendere. 6. Magnō impedimentō hostibus erit sī hunc locum castrīs dēli-gēmus. 7. Scīsne cūr Rōmānī urbem Rōmam appellāverint?

EXERCISE

689. 1. Men like you are a great defense to any common-wealth. 2. The consul called the woman's sister queen of the island. 3. The new city was called Rome by Romulus. 4. It will be a great hindrance [1] to your safety if the citizens make you king. 5. The chiefs dared to inflict injuries upon the king because he had no power. 6. He asked where the horseman had left his spurs.

1. Latin, *for a great hindrance.*

LESSON CVI

Crēscit eundō — She grows as she goes [1]

VOCABULARY REVIEW · THE GERUND AND GERUNDIVE

690. Review the word lists in §§ 778, 779.

691. Gerund. A verbal noun is the name of an action : as, *Talking is useless.*

692. English has many verbal nouns ending in -*ing.* When these are in the nominative case, they are expressed in Latin by the infinitive : as,

Seeing is believing, **vidēre est crēdere**

693. When the English verbal noun is not a nominative, it is expressed in Latin by a verbal noun called a *gerund.*

1 Motto of the state of New Mexico. Literally, *She grows by going.*

694. The Latin gerund is used only in the genitive, dative, accusative, and ablative singular, and is formed by adding -ndī, -ndō, -ndum, -ndō to the present stem : as,

GEN. vocandī, *of calling*
DAT. vocandō, *for calling*
ACC. vocandum, *calling*
ABL. vocandō, *by calling*

Learn the gerunds of the other model verbs, **moneō, regō, capiō, audiō** (§§ 833–836). Deponent verbs have the gerund of the active voice.

695. Uses of Gerund. The gerund has the construction of a noun ; but, being verbal in character, it may have an object : as,

gerendō bellum, *by waging war*

Here **gerendō** is ablative of means and **bellum** is its direct object.

696. Gerund denoting Purpose. The accusative of the gerund with **ad,** or the genitive of the gerund followed by **causā** (*for the sake of*), is often used to express purpose.

Hominēs ad videndum vēnērunt, *the men came for the purpose of seeing, to see* (literally, *for seeing*)
Hominēs videndī causā vēnērunt, *the men came for the sake of seeing, to see*

697. Gerundive. The future passive participle (§ 565) is called the *gerundive* when it takes the place of the gerund. The gerund, being a noun, may be used either alone or with an object ; but the gerundive, being an adjective, must agree with a noun. Observe the following sentences :

1. **Urbem videndī causā vēnērunt,** *they came to see the town*
2. **Urbis videndae causā vēnērunt,** *they came to see the town* (literally, *they came for the sake of the town to be seen*)

In sentence 1, we have the gerund **videndī** and its direct object **urbem.** In 2, we have the gerundive **videndae** in agreement with **urbis.**

Note that the sentences are translated alike. *The gerund with a direct object must not be used except in the genitive or in the ablative without a preposition.* Even then the gerundive construction is more common.

SUMMARY OF IMPORTANT POINTS

1. The gerund is a noun. The gerundive is an adjective.
2. The gerund may stand alone or with an object.
3. The gerundive construction is more frequently used than the gerund with an object.
4. The gerund with an object may be used only in the genitive or in the ablative without a preposition.
5. The accusative of the gerund or gerundive after **ad**, or the genitive preceding **causā**, may be used to denote purpose.

EXERCISES

698. 1. Omnēs mulierēs ōrātiōnem audiendī [1] causā mānsērunt. 2. Omnēs mulierēs ad ōrātiōnem audiendam [1] mānsērunt. 3. Fuga erat tam celeris ut nūllum spatium ad novās cōpiās cōgendās darētur. 4. Multīs vulnerātīs, reliquī adventum ducis exspectāvērunt, minimē diūtius resistendī causā sed pācis petendae causā. 5. Spatium neque arma capiendī neque auxilī petendī datum est. 6. Haec cīvitās, auctōritāte et grātiā rēgis adducta, cōpiās pedestrēs ad iter nostrum prohibendum mīserat. 7. Maximae rēs nōn exspectandō sed agendō cōnficiuntur.

1. Which of these expressions is gerund and which gerundive?

699. 1. You will make your death more certain by remaining among the Gauls. 2. He made the journey much [1] shorter by building [2] a bridge. 3. They sent ambassadors to seek [3] peace. 4. The cavalry battle was very severe, since [4] the place was unfavorable for fighting. 5. Cæsar learned, by inquiring, what [5] the nature of the island was.

1. Latin, *by much*, ablative of measure of difference, § 452. 2. Use both the gerund and the gerundive construction. 3. Use the genitive with **causā**. 4. **cum** causal, § 642. 5. What kind of question? See § 671.

LESSON CVII

Disciplīna praesidium cīvitātis — Training, the defense of the state [1]

VOCABULARY REVIEW · REVIEW OF AGREEMENT AND OF THE GENITIVE AND DATIVE

700. Review the word lists in §§ 783, 784.

701. The Four Agreements.

1. Agreement of the predicate noun and appositive (§§ 61, 104).
2. Agreement of the adjective, adjective pronoun, and participle (§§ 91, 134).
3. Agreement of the verb with its subject (§ 48).
4. Agreement of the relative pronoun with its antecedent (§ 390).

702. The Genitive Case.

1. Genitive of the Possessor $\begin{cases} a. \text{ As attributive (§ 34).} \\ b. \text{ As predicate (§ 150).} \end{cases}$
2. Genitive of the Whole, or Partitive Genitive (§ 541).
3. Genitive with Adjectives (§ 554).
4. Genitive of Description (§ 562).

703. The Dative Case.

1. The Indirect Object $\begin{cases} a. \text{ With intransitive verbs, and with transitive verbs in connection with a direct object in the accusative (§ 58).} \\ b. \text{ With special intransitive verbs (§ 224).} \\ c. \text{ With verbs compounded with ad, ante, con, dē, in, inter, ob, post, prae, prō, sub, and super (§ 623).} \end{cases}$
2. Dative with Adjectives (§ 130).
3. Dative of Purpose (§ 686).

[1] Motto of the University of Texas.

EXERCISES

704. 1. Fortissimī mīlitum quōs vīdimus exīstimāvērunt imperium bellī essc Caesaris imperātōris. 2. Sociī, timōre commōtī, quendam reī mīlitāris perītissimum exercituī praefēcerant. 3. Num senātus memoriam iniūriārum quās nōbīs intulistī dēpōnere dēbet? 4. Nōn virtūs sed sapientia rēgī deërat. 5. Mīlitēs cum diūtius impetum sustinēre nōn possent, aliī aliam in partem fūgērunt. 6. Aciē īnstrūctā, imperātor proelium ā dextrō cornū commīsit. 7. Cum Rōmae essem, aliquis dēmōnstrāvit domum ubi ille incolēbat. 8. Magna pars equitātus, hostēs sequendī cupida, summā celeritāte contendit. 9. Decima legiō erat maximae virtūtis. Quā dē causā Caesar huic legiōnī maximē favēbat.

705. 1. Marcus is not desirous of living[1] in the city. 2. Which of you is a Roman citizen? Neither of us. 3. You alone could persuade me to hold[2] back the army. 4. Whom did the general place in command of the left wing? 5. A wall of great height was a strong defcnse[3] to the town. 6. A certain man inflicted these injuries on me. 7. He was desirous of your friendship.

1. Genitive of the gerund. 2. Not infinitive. 3. Dative of purpose.

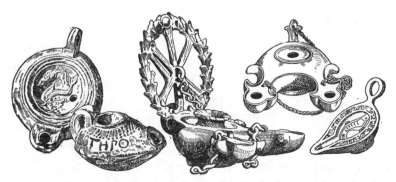

ROMAN LAMPS

LESSON CVIII

Studiīs et rēbus honestīs — For studies and honorable pursuits[1]

VOCABULARY REVIEW · REVIEW OF THE ACCUSATIVE AND ABLATIVE

706. Review the word lists in §§ 788, 789.

707. The Accusative Case.

1. The Accusative as Direct Object (§ 35).
2. The Predicate Accusative (§ 684).
3. The Accusative as Subject of an Infinitive (§ 368).
4. The Accusative of Duration or Extent (§ 547).
5. The Accusative denoting the Place to Which (§ 481).

708. The Ablative Case.

I. Ablative rendered *with* (or *by*):
  1. Cause (§ 165).
  2. Means (§ 166).
  3. Accompaniment (§ 167).
  4. Manner (§ 168).
  5. Measure of Difference (§ 452).
  6. Ablative Absolute (§ 400).
  7. Description (§ 562).
  8. Respect (§ 552).
II. Ablative rendered *from* (or *by*):
  1. Place from Which (§§ 295, 482).
  2. Separation (§ 296).
  3. Personal Agent with a Passive Verb (§ 261).
III. Ablative rendered *in* (or *at*):
  1. Place at or in Which (§ 483).
  2. Time When or within Which (§ 493).

---

[1] Motto of the University of Vermont.

EXERCISES

709. 1. Dux trēs cohortēs praemīsit quae vāllum fossamque duo mīlia passuum per eōrum fīnīs perdūcerent. 2. Aliquae cīvitātēs scrīpsērunt sē mālle in fidē populī Rōmānī permanērc. 3. Paucīs praesidiō castrīs relictīs, barbarī tertiā hōrā aciem instruere incēpērunt. 4. Plūrēs diēs iter intermissum est ut mīlitēs oppida hostium expugnārent. 5. Plūrimum vērō apud Gallōs haec cīvitās et virtūtc et hominum numerō poterat. 6. Illa victōria nōbīs erat grātior quam omnēs aliae. 7. Imperātor captīvum rogāvit quā dē causā salūtem fuga petīsset. 8. Hōc proeliō cōnfectō, lēgātus suīs laudcm idōneam dedit quod summā virtūte pugnāverant. 9. Rēx cum ā senātū amīcus appellātus esset, tamen erat animō inimīcō.

710. 1. The Gauls, meanwhile, seize the bridge that they may prevent[1] our march. 2. On hearing this,[2] Cæsar hastened from Rome into Gaul with three legions. 3. The citizens informed[3] me that a certain man had called Cæsar king. 4. Because of the greatness of the crowd no one could hear the oration. 5. Some towns are much larger than others. 6. The next day he went home to see[4] his son.

1. Latin, *keep us from the march.* 2. Latin, *these things having been heard,* ablative absolute. 3. Latin, *made more certain.* 4. Why not infinitive?

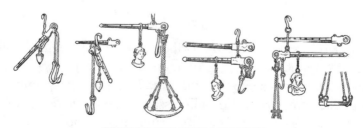

STEELYARDS FROM POMPEII

These seem to havc been a Roman invention. Nearly all the scales found at Pompeii are of this pattern

LESSON CIX

Ecce quam bonum — Behold how good[1]

VOCABULARY REVIEW · REVIEW OF THE GERUND AND GERUNDIVE, THE INFINITIVE, AND THE SUBJUNCTIVE

711. Review the word lists in §§ 793, 794.

712. The Gerund and Gerundive.

1. The Gerund and its Construction (§§ 691–696).
2. The Gerundive and its Construction (§ 697).

713. Constructions of the Infinitive.

I. The Infinitive used as in English:
  1. As Subject or Predicate Nominative (§ 370).
  2. As Object with Subject Accusative (§ 367).
  3. Complementary Infinitive (§ 369).
II. The Infinitive in Indirect Statements (§§ 654, 656, 657).

714. Constructions of the Subjunctive.

1. The Subjunctive of Purpose (§§ 588, 602).
2. The Subjunctive of Result (§§ 616, 618).
3. The Subjunctive with **cum** (§ 643).
4. The Subjunctive in Indirect Questions (§ 671).

EXERCISES

715. 1. Caesar ab explōrātōribus certior factus est Gallōs novīs rēbus studēre. 2. Lēgātī cum pervēnissent, petēbant nē Rōmānī oppidum suum incenderent. 3. Dux mihi imperāvit ut cognōscerem quae ratiō bellī esset. 4. Nōs quidem molestē ferimus sociōs nostrōs dē rē frūmentāriā nōn prōvīdisse. 5. Propter multitūdinem tēlōrum erat difficillimum in vāllō cōnsistere. 6. Tam ācriter ab utrāque parte pugnābātur ut

[1] Motto of the University of the South.

multa mīlia hominum vulnerārentur. 7. Nōnne cōpiās integrās praemittēmus ad Rōmānōs itinere intcrclūdendōs? 8. Cum oppidō¹ mediā nocte appropinquārēmus, tamen omnēs. cīvēs nōs cxspectābant. 9. Cum pācem iam petātis, hās condiciōnēs prōpōnam. 10. Inopia aquae fēcit ut nōs omnēs premerēmur.

1. Dative with **appropinquārēmus**.

716. 1. Such terror seized the hearts of all that not even the bravest were willing to remain. 2. Hc asked whu was in command of the ships.¹ 3. He demanded that² for the future the army should not be led through our terriluiy. 4. Cæsar built a bridge for the purpose³ of terrifying thc Germans. 5. Someone said that you had been placed in command of the army.¹

1. Not genitive. See § 623. 2. *That* ... *not*, nē. 3. Use **causa** with the gcnitive of the gerund or gerundive. See § 696.

LESSON CX

Iamque opus exēgī — And now I have finished my work¹

VOCABULARY REVIEW · REVIEW OF WORD FORMATION

717. Review the word lists in §§ 798, 799.

718. Review of Prefixes.

1. Illustrate the force of each of the following prefixes by a Latin word (§§ 341, 497):

ā (ab)	dē	inter	prō	sub
ad	ē (ex)	per	re-	trāns
con- (com-, co-)	in	prae		

2. What is meant by assimilation? (§ 375.)

3. What changes in spelling occur in compounds of words like **capiō, faciō**, etc.? (§ 376.)

¹ From the olooing lincs of Ovid's gieat pōēm, the " Metamorphoses."

4. What is the force of **in-** (**im-**) when prefixed to an adjective or adverb? Illustrate. (§ 374.)

719. Review of Suffixes.

1. What can you say in general about the use of suffixes in Latin and in English? (§§ 425, 426.)

2. How are Latin nouns like **rēctor, victor,** etc. formed, and how are the corresponding English words derived? (§ 574.)

3. By means of what suffixes are abstract nouns formed from adjectives? Illustrate. (§ 626.)

4. Explain the force of the suffix in the following adjectives: **cupidus, perīculōsus, facilis, crēdibilis.** (§§ 627–629.)

720. Hints on Spelling.

1. What generally determines whether an English word should end in *-ant* or *-ent*? Illustrate. (§ 573.)

2. What is the rule for the spelling of English words in *-able* or *-ible*? in *-tion* or *-sion*? Illustrate. (§§ 630, 631.)

THE GAULS IN SIGHT OF ROME

OPTIONAL LESSONS

OPTIONAL LESSON A

Ēmollit mōrēs nec sinit esse ferōs — She refines character and does not allow it to be untrained [1]

THE SUBJUNCTIVE OF CHARACTERISTIC OR DESCRIPTION

721. A relative clause with its verb in the indicative states a fact concerning the antecedent : as,

> Caesar erat imperātor quī Gallōs superāvit, *Cæsar was the general who overcame the Gauls*

722. A relative clause with its verb in the subjunctive is often used to *describe* an antecedent. Such a clause is called a relative clause of characteristic or description : as,

> Quondam erat imperātor quī Gallōs superāret, *once there was a general who overcame the Gauls*

a. A relative clause is descriptive when the antecedent is indefinite or general and the relative may be translated by the words *of such a character that*, as in the following expressions :

> sunt quī sciant, *there are some who know* (i.e. of such a character that they know)
> quis est quī sciat, *who is there who knows?*
> nēmō est quī sciat, *there is no one who knows*
> ūnus est quī sciat, *he is the only one who knows*

723. Rule for Subjunctive of Characteristic. *A relative clause with the subjunctive may be used to describe an antecedent. This is called the subjunctive of characteristic or description.*

---

[1] From Ovid. Motto of the University of South Carolina.

EXERCISES

724. 1. Erant duo itinera quibus Helvētiī domō discēdere possent. 2. Erat nūllum oppidum quod sē armīs dēfendere vellet. 3. Quis est quī viam meliōrem nōbīs ostendere possit? 4. Ille est ūnus quī sciat nātūram illīus locī. 5. Cum Rōmānī oppidum rē frūmentāriā interclūserint, nihil habēmus quō diūtius sustinēre possīmus. 6. Aliī Gallōrum pācis petendae cupidī erant. 7. Erant aliī quī novīs rēbus studērent. 8. Erant quī molestē ferrent novās legiōnēs in nostrīs fīnibus cōnscrībī. 9. Nēmō est quī neget rem pūblicam cōnservārī dēbēre. 10. Dentātus cum imperium summum tenēret, tamen rūrī vīvere mālēbat. 11. Quis est quī nōn audīverit Rōmulum urbem suam Rōmam appellāvisse?

725. 1. Once there was a consul who inflicted the severest punishment on his own sons. 2. Who is there that does not remember that man's name? 3. There were some who said that the consul's sons made war upon their country. 4. It is the business [1] of the consul to look out for the safety [2] of the commonwealth. 5. He is the only one who has sufficient authority.[3]

1. Omit. 2. Not dative. 3. Latin, *sufficient of authority*, partitive genitive.

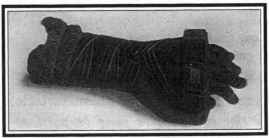

ROMAN CAESTUS, OR BOXING GLOVE
This consisted of thongs of leather bound around the hand and forearm.
It was often loaded with lead and was a terrible weapon

OPTIONAL LESSON B

Dē gustibus nōn est disputandum — There is no disputing about tastes [1]

THE PERIPHRASTIC CONJUGATIONS AND THE DATIVE OF AGENT

726. The future active participle in -ūrus is often combined with the forms of **sum** to denote future or intended action : as,

vocātūrus sum, *I am about to call, I intend to call*
audītūrus eram, *I was about to hear, I intended to hear*

This is known as the *active periphrastic conjugation.*

727. The future passive participle (gerundive) in -ndus is similarly combined with the forms of **sum** to denote obligation or necessity in the passive voice : as,

vocandus sum, *I ought to be called, I must be called*
audiendus sum, *I ought to be heard, I must be heard*

This is known as the *passive periphrastic conjugation.*

728. The personal agent is regularly expressed by the ablative with **ā** or **ab** (§ 261) : as, **castra ā mīlitibus mūnīta sunt,** *the camp was fortified by the soldiers* ; but with a passive periphrastic form the person by whom something ought to be done or must be done is expressed by the *dative.* This is called the *dative of agent* : as,

Castra mīlitibus mūnienda sunt, *the camp must be fortified by the soldiers*

729. Rule for Dative of Agent. *With the passive periphrastic conjugation agency is expressed by the dative.*

[1] Or *Everyone to his own taste.* Both of these translations are free. Literally, *It ought not to be disputed about tastes,* **disputandum est** being an impersonal passive periphrastic form.

EXERCISES

730. 1. Caesarī omnia ūnō tempore erant agenda. 2. Signum proelī imperātōrī dandum erat. 3. Mīlitēs quī aberant ducibus convocandī erant. 4. Legiōnēs quae pugnātūrae erant Caesarī hortandae erant. 5. Hīs omnibus rēbus cōnfectīs, aciēs erat instruenda. 6. Sed tam breve erat tempus et tantus erat impetus hostium ut magna pars hārum rērum eīs intermittenda esset. 7. Eō diē erant quī putārent Rōmānōs nōn victūrōs esse. 8. Quis est quī crēdat illud proelium nōn faciendum fuisse? 9. Mox audītūrī sumus dē aliīs bellīs quae ā Rōmānīs gesta sunt. 10. Longa itinera magnō impedīmentō Rōmānīs futūra sunt.

731. 1. Many things had to be done by Theseus to save [1] the boys and girls of Greece. 2. That famous man intended to kill the Minotaur. 3. First a long journey to Crete had to be made by him. 4. Then help had to be given by someone. 5. When he had arrived at [2] Crete, he told the king's daughter what [3] he intended to do. 6. Without much difficulty he persuaded her to give [4] him [5] aid.

1. Not infinitive (§ 588). 2. **ad.** 3. An indirect question (§ 671). 4. Not infinitive (§ 602). 5. **sibi.**

THE ROMANS STORM THE ENEMY'S STRONGHOLD

ORIGINAL STORIES

Study each of the following pictures. Where is the scene laid? What objects do you see? What characters are present? What are they doing? Attention to these details will give you the material for writing a short Latin story or, at least, for composing some disconnected sentences. The vocabulary below each picture will help you.

I. In times ancient as well as modern, women by their patriotic service have saved the state when men were ready to despair.

argentum, -ī, *n.*, silver
aurum, -ī, *n.*, gold
computō, -āre, -āvī, -ātus, compute
dēsum, -esse, -fuī, -futūrus, be lacking, *w. dat.*
dōnum, -ī, *n.*, gift
mātrōna, -ae, *f.*, matron, lady
mēnsa, -ae, *f.*, table
ōrnāmentum, -ī, *n.*, jewel

patria, -ae, *f.*, country, native land
pecūnia, -ae, *f.*, money
perīculum, -ī, *n.*, danger
scrība, -ae, *m.*, clerk
sedeō, -ēre, sēdī, sessūrus, sit; ante mēnsam sedēre, sit before a table
sine, *prep. w. abl.*, without
summa, -ae, *f.*, sum total
tabula, -ae, *f.*, writing tablet

II. Roman women were famous for their devotion to their children, whom they valued far above beauty or personal adornment.

ancilla, -ae, *f.*, maidservant

ānulus, -ī, *m.*, ring

arcula, -ae, *f.*, jewel casket

armilla, -ae, *f.*, bracelet

aurum, -ī, *n.*, gold

Cornēlia, -ae, *f.*, Cornelia, *the woman on the left*

ēducō, -āre, -āvī, -ātus, train, bring up

fōrma, -ae, *f.*, beauty

Gāius, Gāī, *m.*, Gaius, *the younger son of Cornelia*

gemma, -ae, *f.*, gem, jewel

laudō, -āre, -āvī, -ātus, praise

līberī, -ōrum, *m. pl.*, children

margarīta, -ae, *f.*, pearl

mātrōna, -ae, *f.*, matron

maximē, *adv.*, most of all, especially

mēnsa, -ae, *f.*, table

optimus, -a, -um, best

ōrnāmentum, -ī, *n.*, ornament, jewel

ostentō, -āre, -āvī, -ātus, display, show off

pretiōsus, -a, -um, expensive, fine

rogō, -āre, -āvī, -ātus, ask

splendidus, -a, -um, glittering

superbus, -a, -um, proud

Tiberius, Tibe′rī, *m.*, Tiberius, *the older son of Cornelia*

vīcīna, -ae, *f.*, neighbor

visitō, -āre, -āvī, -ātus, call on, go to see

III. This picture is clearly of a religious character. The Romans were very faithful in their worship. The household gods comprised the Lares (the spirits of the ances-tors), the Pena'tes (the gods guarding the family stores), and the Genius (the guardian spirit of the master of the house). The family shrine was often a niche, containing images of the gods, with an altar before it. In the picture the niche is closed by a metal screen. The serpents painted on the wall are a symbol of the protecting divinities. Incense was burned to the gods; and wine, oil, and food were offered. Family worship was usually conducted by the father. He is not present in this case. Perhaps he is fighting with the Gauls, and is in danger of his life.

absum, abesse, āfuī, āfutūrus, be away, be absent
adōrō, -āre, -āvī, -ātus, worship
ampulla, -ae, f., bottle
ante, prep. w. acc., before
āra, -ae, f, altar
cotīdiē, adv., daily
cremō, -āre, -āvī, -ātus, burn
dōnum, -ī, n., gift, offering
ēducō, -āre, -āvī, -ātus, train, educate
fūmō, -āre, ——, ——, smoke
invocō, -āre, -āvī, -ātus, invoke, call upon
larārium, -ī, n., household shrine

Larēs, -um, m. pl., the Lares
mātrōna, -ae, f., matron, wife
oleum, -ī, n., oil
optō, -āre, -āvī, -ātus, wish for, pray for
pavīmentum, -ī, n., pavement, floor
Penātēs, -ium, m. pl., the Pena'tes
peristȳlum, -ī, n., the peristyle, the inner court of a Roman house
sacrificō, -āre, -āvī, -ātus, offer sacrifice
sellula, -ae, f., low stool
stō, -āre, stetī, stātūrus, stand
trochus, -ī, m., hoop
tūs, tūris, n., incense

IV. Among the Greek heroes none was more famous than Hercules. He went about destroying the huge and fierce monsters that laid waste the land. One of the most dangerous of these was an immense hydra, or water serpent, with seven heads.

cauda, -ae, *f.*, tail
clāva, -ae, *f.*, club
cupiō, -ere, -īvī, -ītus, desire, wish
exspīrō, -āre, -āvī, -ātus, breathe
   out
feriō, -īre, ——, ——, strike, hit
flamma, -ae, *f.*, flame, fire
fortissimus, -a, -um, bravest
fūmus, -ī, *m.*, smoke
Herculēs, -is, *m.*, Hercules
hērōs, -ōis, *acc.* hērōa (*a Greek
   noun*), *m.*, hero, demigod

hydra, -ae, *f.*, hydra, water serpent
mōnstrum, -ī, *n.*, monster
necō, -āre, -āvī, -ātus, kill
petō, -ere, -iī, -ītus, seek, attack
rapiō, -ere, -uī, -tus, seize
saevus, -a, -um, savage
timeō, -ēre, -uī, ——, fear
validissimus, -a, -um, strongest
vāstō, -āre, -āvī, -ātus, lay waste,
   destroy
vāstus, -a, -um, huge, immense
vulnerō, -āre, -āvī, -ātus, wound

V. Among the most beautiful surviving works of ancient art are the Greek vases. Besides their grace of form, they are adorned with artistic designs and pictures drawn from legends of gods and heroes. Often, too, there are scenes from the classic drama. The colors used are chiefly black, red, and white. How absorbed the young Greek is in his painting! Does the girl seem interested? What do you think the artist will do with the vase after he has finished it?

admīror, -ārī, -ātus sum, admire
adulēscēns, -entis, *m.*, youth
albus, -a, -um, white
artificium, artifi'cī, *n.*, work of art
āter, ātra, ātrum, black
color, -ōris, *m.*, color
ērudītus, -a, -um, skillful
iānua, -ae, *f.*, door, doorway
lapis, -idis, *m.*, stone
laudō, -āre, -āvī, -ātus, praise
mūrus, -ī, *m.*, wall

patella, -ae, *f.*, saucer
pēnicillus, -ī, *m.*, paint brush
pictor, -ōris, *m.*, artist, painter
pictūra, -ae, *f.*, picture
pingō, -ere, pīnxī, pictus, paint
pōcillum, -ī, *n.*, little cup
ruber, -bra, -brum, red
spectō, -āre, -āvī, -ātus, look at
teneō, -ēre, -uī, ——, hold the attention of, interest
vās, vāsis, *n.*, *pl.* vāsa, -ōrum, vase

VI. Many stories are told about Dædalus (*ded'a-lus*), the Athenian, famed for his skill as an inventor, artist, and builder. Once, accompanied by his son Icarus (*ik'a-rus*), he visited the island of Crete and by his marvelous works won the king's favor. Later the king became angry with him and refused to let him leave the island. All the ships were seized and all the ports guarded. Longing for home, Dædalus and his son seemed without means of escape. But Dædalus had genius and a courage equal to any deed of daring. What did he do?

āla, -ae, *f.*, wing
audāx, -ācis, bold
avis, -is, *f.*, bird
cēra, -ae, *f.*, wax
dēcidō, -ere, dēcidī, ——, fall down
dēsīderō, -āre, -āvī, -ātus, long for
doceō, -ēre, -uī, -tus, teach
fuga, -ae, *f.*, flight
fugiō, -ere, fūgī, fugitūrus, flee
incipiō, -ere, -cēpī, -ceptus, begin
interclūdō, -ere, -clūsī, -clūsus, shut
  off, cut off
īrātus, -a, -um, angry
ligō, -āre, -āvī, -ātus, bind, tie
liquefaciō, -ere, ——, -factus, melt

mare, -is, *n.*, sea
monitum, -ī, *n.*, advice
opus, operis, *n.*, work
pāreō, -ēre, -uī, ——, obey, *w. dat.*
penna, -ae, *f.*, feather
pōnō, -ere, posuī, positus, put
recūsō, -āre, -āvī, -ātus, refuse
reditus, -ūs, *m.*, return
reperiō, -īre, repperī, repertus, in-
  vent
sōl, sōlis, *m.*, sun
submergō, -ere, -mersī, -mersus,
  drown
umerus, -ī, *m.*, shoulder
volō, -āre, -āvī, -ātūrus, fly

VII. The Romans were devoted to their children and trained them very carefully. They taught them to be obedient and respectful, to have reverence for all things sacred, to be truthful and honorable, and to be courageous and self-reliant. Every Roman boy was destined to be a soldier, and so from earliest childhood he learned to despise danger and to regard cowardice as worse than death.

ancilla, -ae, *f.*, maidservant
collum, -ī, *n.*, neck
columna, -ae, *f.*, column
domus, -ūs, *f.*, house
fortis, forte, brave
ignāvia, -ae, *f.*, cowardice
ignāvus, -a, -um, cowardly
leō, -ōnis, *m.*, lion
ligō, -āre, -āvī, -ātus, bind, tie
lūdō, -ere, -sī, -sus, play
manus, -ūs, *f.*, hand
māter, -tris, *f.*, mother

pavīmentum, -ī, *n.*, pavement
quod, *conj.*, because
restis, -is, *f.*, rope
rīdeō, -ēre, -sī, -sus, laugh
saevus, -a, -um, savage
scutica, -ae, *f.*, whip
sedeō, -ēre, sēdī, sessus, sit
stō, -āre, stetī, stātūrus, stand
timeō, -ēre, -uī, ——, fear
timor, -ōris, *m.*, fear
verberō, -āre, -āvī, -ātus, beat, whip
virtūs, -ūtis, *f.*, courage

VIII. This picture might be called "What happened at Lucia's Party." Lucia is having a party on the porch. Refreshments are being served by two maids. But the children in the adjoining room, drawn from their play by the tempting sights and smells, are getting nothing. What do you suppose they did about it?

ancilla, -ae, *f.*, maidservant

bibō, -ere, bibī, ——, drink

callidus, -a, -um, crafty, sly

cēlō, -āre, -āvī, -ātus, hide, conceal

cibus, -ī, *m.*, food

conclāve, -is, *n.*, room

convīva, -ae, *m. and f.*, guest

convīvium, -ī, *n.*, party

convīvor, -ārī, -ātus sum, give a party

crūstulum, -ī, *n.*, confectionery

dēsīderō, -āre, -āvī, -ātus, long for

edō, -ere, ēdī, ēsus, eat

ēripiō, -ere, -ripuī, -reptus, snatch away

ēsuriēns, -entis, hungry

frūctus, -ūs, *m.*, fruit

lateō, -ēre, latuī, ——, lie hid

līberī, -ōrum, *m. pl.*, children

lībum, -ī, *n.*, cake

mel, mellis, *n.*, honey

mēnsa, -ae, *f.*, table

occultus, -a, -um, hidden, secret

pānis, -is, *m.*, bread

pōculum, -ī, *n.*, cup

porticus, -ūs, *f.*, porch

post, *prep. w. acc.*, behind

sella, -ae, *f.*, chair

vīnum, -ī, *n.*, wine

virgō, -inis, *f.*, young girl

IX. Roman towns had many shops. These resembled our stalls or booths. They were open in front with the exception of a low wall forming the counter, and were closed at night by wooden shutters. The wares stood or hung about the shop or were placed on shelves within easy reach of the shopkeeper as he stood behind the counter. This is a provision shop. There are eatables of different kinds, and jars of wine. Do you see the sign? What does it advertise? Give Latin names to the characters, and tell what they are doing or make up a story about them. Do not forget the donkey.

altilēs, -ium, *f. pl.*, poultry
alveus, -ī, *m.*, trough
amphora, -ae, *f.*, wine jar
asinus, -ī, *m.*, donkey
bibō, -ere, bibī, ——, drink
cāseus, -ī, *m.*, cheese
cibāria, -ōrum, *n. pl.*, provisions
dēfessus, -a, -um, weary
edō, -ere, ēdī, ēsus, eat
emō, -ere, ēmī, ēmptus, buy
farcimen, -inis, *n.*, sausage
fundō, -ere, fūdī, fūsus, pour
holus, -eris, *n.*, vegetables

īnsigne, -is, *n.*, sign
mēnsa, -ae, *f.*, table, counter
oleum, -ī, *n.*, oil
pendeō, -ēre, pependī, ——, hang, be suspended
pōculum, -ī, *n.*, cup
quiēs, -ētis, *f.*, rest
recreō, -āre, -āvī, -ātus, refresh
sitiō, -īre, -īvī, ——, be thirsty
taberna, -ae, *f.*, shop
tabernārius, -ī, *m.*, shopkeeper
vēndō, -ere, -didī, -ditus, sell
vīnum, -ī, *n.*, wine

THE RETURN OF PERSEPHONE

From the painting by Sir Frederick Leighton. Used by permission of the Art
Gallery Committee of the Corporation of Leeds. (See story of Ceres and
Proserpina, page 275)

SELECTIONS FOR SIGHT READING

A BRITISH CHIEF URGES RESISTANCE TO THE ROMAN INVASION

(AFTER LESSON XXIII)

Est fāma bellī, Britannī, novī et magnī. Iam Rōmānī agrōs miserōrum Gallōrum tenent. Iam ōrās Galliae proximās nostrae īnsulae tenent. Nunc Britannia est in perīculō. Iam Rōmānī cōpiās suās convocant. Mox ad īnsulam nostram nāvigābunt et oppida nostra occupābunt. Sed sumus Britannī; Britannī nihil 5 (*nothing*) timent. Numquam Rōmānīs oppida nostra, filiās nostrās, fīliōs nostrōs dabimus. Ad arma! Ad arma! Pugnābimus, pugnābimus. Numquam liberī virī erunt servī. Superābimus Rōmānōs et magna erunt praemia nostra.

A FATHER'S LETTER TO HIS SON

(AFTER LESSON XLIII)

Quam grāta mihi (*to me*), Mārce, erat epistula magistrī tuī! Nam magister dīligentiam tuam laudat (*praise*) et dīcit: "Fīlius tuus est bonus et industrius. Numquam officium suum neglegit (*neglect*) et semper ēgregium exemplum tardīs dat." Māter ad tē (*you*) librum pulchrum, praemium dīligentiae tuae, mox mittet. 5 Soror (*sister*) tua hodiē (*today*) sex annōs habet. Saepe rogat (*ask*): "Ubi est frāter Mārcus? Diū āfuit. Quandō (*when*) revertet (*return*)?" Valē.

FABLE — THE LION'S SHARE

(AFTER LESSON LXI)

Animālia leō, equus, capra (*goat*), ovis (*sheep*), societātem faciunt. Multam praedam capiunt et in ūnum locum comportant. Tum in quattuor partēs praedam dīvidunt. Praedā dīvīsā, leō dīxit: "Prīma

pars mea est, nam leō est rēx animālium. Et mea est secunda pars
meīs labōribus. Tertiam partem vindicō (*claim*), nam magnam 5
famem habeō. Dēnique quārtam partem rapiam et sī quis (*anyone*)
prohibēbit, eum interficiam."

ARI'ON'S GOOD FORTUNE

(AFTER LESSON LXXX)

ARI'ON SAVED BY A DOLPHIN

*Ari'on, the noted singer, after an enthusiastic reception in foreign
lands, embarks for home laden with treasures*

Ōlim Ariōn,[1] vātēs[2] nōtissimus, domō longissimē aberat ac
patriam petēbat. Eī rēgēs multārum terrārum praemia amplissima
dederant. Ariōn omnēs rēs quās accēperat in nāve posuerat et
domum sēcum portābat. Iam nāvis in mediō marī erat, neque ūlla
terra vidērī poterat.   5

1. In English, *A-rī'on*. 2. **vātēs, -is**, M. and F., *bard, singer*.

The crew conspire to drown him and seize his wealth

Tum nautae, homines pessimī, barbarum consilium cepērunt atque inter sē[1] dixērunt : " Certē hic vir ex manibus nostrīs numquam dīmittētur.[2] Eum interficiēmus et omnia quae habet nostra erunt." Deinde vātem corripiunt[3] et in mare dēiciunt.

He is miraculously saved by a huge dolphin

Arīōn tōtam spem salūtis dēposuerat et mortem certam exspec- 10 tāvit. Sed deī ipsī vītam eius conservāvērunt. Nam subitō[4] Arīōn in tergō[5] magnī delphīnī[6] sedēre vīsus est, quī ad ōram proximam eum celeriter vexit.[7]

CERES AND PROSERPINA

(AFTER LESSON LXXXVIII)

This is one of the most beautiful of the Greek myths. Proser'pina's abduction signifies the disappearance of vegetation in the autumn, when the vital forces of nature are drawn deep into the earth. Thus Pluto steals Proserpina. When vegetation reappears in the spring, Proserpina is restored to her mother. Read Tennyson's " Deme'ter and Perseph'one."

Pluto, king of the lower world, falls in love with Proserpina and carries her down to his gloomy realm

Verō, Venus,[8] tua potestās est maxima. Nam tū docuistī etiam Plūtōnem,[9] deum inferōrum,[10] amāre. Ōlim deus per īnsulam Siciliam[11] currum[12] agēbat. Ibi Prōserpinam,[13] fīliam pulcherrimam Cereris,[14] deae agricultūrae,[15] vīdit et adamāvit.[16] Eam statim rapuit et equōs hortātus ē conspectū[17] fūgit.   5

1. **inter sē**, *to each other* (literally, *between themselves*). 2. *Allowed to escape.* 3. **corripiō, -ere**, *seize.* 4. *Suddenly.* 5. **tergum, -ī**, N., *back.* 6. **delphīnus, -ī**, M., *dolphin.* 7. **vehō, -ere**, *carry.* 8. **Venus, -eris**, F., *Venus*, the goddess of love and beauty. 9. **Plūtō, -ōnis**, M., *Pluto*, king of the lower world. 10. **inferī, -ōrum**, M., *the shades, the lower world.* 11. **Sicilia, -ae**, F., *Sicily.* 12. **currus, -ūs**, M., *chariot.* 13. **Prōserpina, -ae**, F., *Proser'pina*, daughter of Ceres. 14. **Cerēs, -eris**, F., *Ceres*, goddess of agriculture. 15. **agricultūra, -ae**, F., *agriculture.* 16. **adamō, -āre**, *fall in love with.* 17. **conspectus, -ūs**, M., *sight.*

Ceres, after a long search, discovers where her daughter is. Then she goes to Jupiter and demands that her daughter be returned

Tum vērō Cerēs, gravī dolōre ac timōre commōta, fīliam diem noctemque sine fīne petēbat. Interim Plūtō Prōserpinam in mātrimōnium dūxerat. Iam dea erat rēgīna īnferōrum.[1] Dēnique Cerēs omnia cognōverat, et inīquō animō apud Iovem [2] causam [3] ita dīxit: "Fīliam meam, quam per omnēs terrās mariaque petē- 10 bam, invēnī. Eam Plūtō rapuit. Etiam nunc ea in manū eius est. Plūtō mihi magnam iniūriam fēcit. Iubē eum fīliam meam reddere. Sūme dē eō gravissimum supplicium."

Jupiter compromises the matter so that Proserpina spends six months with her mother and six months with her husband

Iuppiter respondit: "Ita, Cerēs, dīcere nōn dēbēs. Hoc factum meō iūdiciō nōn est iniūria, sed certus *(true)* amor.[4] Sed tibi petentī 15 hanc veniam [5] dabō. Sex mēnsēs cuiusque annī Prōserpina in rēgnō Plūtōnis manēbit atque sex mēnsēs tēcum erit." Itaque hieme Prōserpina est apud īnferōs,[1] et aestāte, īnferīs relictīs, cum mātre terram incolit.

CINCINNATUS CALLED FROM THE PLOW

(AFTER LESSON CV)

The early Romans were devoted to agriculture

Omnibus temporibus vīta rūstica [6] summō auxiliō virtūtī ac fīrmissimō praesidiō cīvitātī fuit.[7] Hanc rem etiam Rōmānī crēdēbant, et multī eōrum vīllās habēbant et agrōs manibus suīs colēbant.[8]

Cincinnatus was an example of this fine old type

Apud hōs erat Cincinnātus, vir bellō ēgregius et agricola minimē tardus. Ōlim cum quīdam hostēs urbī appropinquārent et iam multī 5 timidī salūtem patriae dēspērāre inciperent, mentēs omnium ad Cincinnātum versae [9] sunt. Ille autem nōn in urbe sed rūrī erat.

1. See p. 275, n. 10. 2. **Iovem**, accusative of **Iuppiter, Iovis**, M., *Jupiter*, king of the gods. 3. **causam dīcere**, *plead a cause*. 4. **amor, -ōris**, M., *love*. 5. **venia, -ae**, F., *favor*. 6. **rūsticus, -a, -um**, *of the country, rustic*. 7. A present perfect, § 312. 8. **colō, -ere**, *till*. 9. **vertō, -ere**, *turn*.

CINCINNATUS CALLED FROM THE PLOW

On one occasion the senate, having appointed Cincinnatus dictator,
sent lictors to escort him from his farm to the city

Tum senātus Cincinnātum dictātōrem fēcit et mīsit līctōrēs [1] quī
eum in urbem dēdūcerent. Līctōrēs rūs contendērunt et ad vīllam
parvam Cincinnātī celeriter pervēnērunt. Ille tunicātus [2] agrum 10
arābat [3] et, cum līctōrēs vidēret, rogāvit quid vellent. Līctōrēs
respondērunt senātum eum dictātōrem fēcisse ut patriam ex summō
perīculō līberāret, et sē vēnisse ut eum in urbem dēdūcerent.

Cincinnatus, though reluctant to leave his work, went with them,
but as soon as possible returned to finish his plowing

Agrum relinquere Cincinnātō nōn grātum erat, tamen senātuī
pārēre oportēbat. Itaque pulvere [4] ac sūdōre absterso, optimus vir 15
induit [5] togam quam līctōrēs ferēbant et Rōmam prōcessit. Bellō
paucīs diēbus cōnfectō, Cincinnātus domum properāvit ut arāret.

THE LORD'S PRAYER

Pater noster, quī es in caelīs, sānctificētur nōmen tuum. Adveniat
rēgnum tuum; fīat voluntās tua, ut in caelō, ita etiam in terrā.
Pānem nostrum cotīdiānum dā nōbīs hodiē. Et remitte nōbīs dēbita
nostra, sīcut et nōs remittimus dēbitōribus nostrīs. Et nē nōs indū-
cās in tentātiōnem, sed līberā nos ab illō improbō. Quia tuum est 5
rēgnum, et potentia, et glōria, in saecula. Āmēn. — Matt. 6. 9–13

THE GOLDEN RULE

Omnia ergō quaecumque vultis ut faciant vōbīs hominēs, et vōs
facite illīs. Haec est enim lēx et prophētae. — Matt. 7. 12

THE STRAIT GATE

Intrāte per angustam portam : quia lāta porta, et spatiōsa via
est quae dūcit ad perditiōnem, et multī sunt quī intrant per eam. —
Matt. 7. 13

1. The lictors were the official attendants of a magistrate and carried a
bundle of rods (**fascēs**), sometimes with an ax in the middle standing for the
power of the state to punish. Note the fasces on the American dime. 2. **tunicātus, -a, -um,** *dressed in his tunic.* Compare *in his shirtsleeves* or *in his
overalls.* 3. **arō, -āre,** *plow.* 4. **pulvere . . . absterso,** *wiping off the dust and
sweat.* 5. **induō, -ere,** *put on.*

A LATIN PLAY

PERSEUS AND ANDROMEDA

This may be used at any time after Lesson LXXX is finished

CHARACTERS

CEPHEUS, king of Ethiopia
CASSIOPEIA, queen of Ethiopia
ANDROMEDA, daughter of Cepheus and Cassiopeia
PERSEUS, the Greek hero

SACERDOS, priestess of the oracle
Three citizens of Ethiopia
Friends of the royal family and attendants

SCENE I

A room in the palace. CEPHEUS and CASSIOPEIA are sitting at a table. An ATTENDANT stands at the right near the stage entrance

CEPHEUS. Cūr, Cassiopeia mea, faciem tuam sine fīne laudās? Audācia tua mē terret. Nōnne deōrum invidiam verēris?

CASSIOPEIA. Nōn magis dīcō quam vērum est. Spectā mē. Nōnne sum pulchrior quam ūlla dea? Nē nymphae maris quidem sunt pulchriōrēs.

CEPHEUS (*raising his hand in solemn protest*). Tacē, mulier, tacē! Etiam nunc deī supplicium fortasse parant.

CASSIOPEIA. Minimē tacēbō. Supplicia deōrum nōn timeō. Nōn crēdō . . . (*She is interrupted by a loud rapping on the door.*)

ATTENDANT. Aliquis pulsat, rēgīna.

CASSIOPEIA. Aperī ōstium.

ATTENDANT (*after opening the door*). Trēs cīvēs rēgī dīcere cupiunt.

CEPHEUS. Iubē eōs intrāre.

Enter three men in great excitement

CITIZENS (*all speaking at once*). Perīmus, rēx! Quid faciēmus? Quid faciēmus?

CEPHEUS. Quid est, cīvēs? Quis dolor vōs permovet?

279

First Citizen. Ingēns mōnstrum ex marī vēnit atque agrōs meōs vāstāvit.

Second Citizen. Idem mōnstrum omne pecus meum dēvorāvit.

Third Citizen. Heu mē miserum! Saevum mōnstrum coniugem līberōsque meōs interfēcit.

Cassiopeia (*rising and raising both arms to heaven*). Quid dīcitis? Quid audiō? Mea est culpa. Ō verba stultissima! Ō mala superbia! Cepheus. Ūna salūs relicta est. Ad ōrāculum properābō et auxilium petam.

Scene II

At the seat of the oracle. A veiled Priestess is seated on a high stool

Attendant. Cēpheus, rēx Aethiopiae, sacerdōs, aditum petit.

Sacerdos. Dūc eum ante mē. Eum audiam. (*The attendant leads in* Cepheus, *who kneels before the priestess.*) Cūr, rēx, ad mē vēnistī? Cepheus. Tē cōnsulere, sacerdōs, cupiō. Saevum mōnstrum agrōs nostrōs vāstat et populum meum perterret. Quis hoc mōnstrum mīsit? Cūr missum est?

Sacerdos. Neptūnus, deus maris, mōnstrum mīsit. Deus est inimīcus propter superbiam rēgīnae tuae. Illa ausa est sē ante nymphās ipsās pōnere.

Cepheus. Obsecrō, sacerdōs, quō modō mōnstrum ex patriā agere possum?

Sacerdos. Expiāre culpam rēgīnae oportet. Dā Andromedam, fīliam tuam, mōnstrō et patria tua cōnservābitur. Discēde et pārē.

Cepheus *rises and with bowed head leaves the stage*

Scene III

Room in the palace, as in Scene I. Cassiopeia and Andromeda are seated at a table

Andromeda. Quae mora patrem tenet?

Cassiopeia. Iam diū eum exspectō. In diēs perīcula nostra crēscunt. Pectus meum est plēnum sollicitūdinis et timōris. (Cepheus *enters with slow step and sad countenance. The queen and* Andromeda *rise to greet him.*) Salvē, coniūnx. Vultus tuus mē terret. Quid ōrāculum dīxit?

A LATIN PLAY 281

CEPHEUS. Gravissima est fortūna nostra. Neptūnus, inimīcus propter superbiam tuam, hoc supplicium dē populō nostrō sūmit. Sī patriam cōnservāre cupimus, Andromedam mōnstrō dare oportet. CASSIOPEIA. Quid! Andromedam dare! (*Clasps* ANDROMEDA *in her arms.*) Numquam, numquam hoc faciam. (*Buries her face on* ANDROMEDA'S *shoulder and weeps.*)

ANDROMEDA. Audī, māter cārissima, melius est mē perīre quam omnēs dare poenās. Parāta sum, pater, pārēre ōrāculō.

SCENE IV

On the seashore. ANDROMEDA stands bound to a rock [1] in the center of the background. CEPHEUS and CASSIOPEIA, dressed in black robes, are seated on the ground at the right. Friends of the royal family appear at the left, some sitting and some standing. All exhibit signs of grief

CASSIOPEIA. Periī; hunc dolōrem tolerāre nōn possum. Cūr illa stultissima verba dīxī? Ego, nōn Andromeda, mōnstrō darī dēbeō. CEPHEUS. Vērum dīcis, coniūnx ; sed verba ōrāculī scīs. (*A distant roaring is heard.*) Audīsne illum sonitum terribilem? Sine dubiō mōnstrum appropinquat.

FIRST FRIEND. Heu! Heu! Iam mors imminet.

SECOND FRIEND. Etiam Andromeda sonitum audit. Ecce, quam pallidus est vultus eius!

PERSEUS, *wearing helmet and breastplate and grasping a sword, makes a sudden entrance. All look at him in amazement*

CEPHEUS. Quis es, hospes? Quō modō in fīnēs nostrōs pervēnistī? PERSEUS. Perseus sum, fīlius Iovis. Alīs per aurās iter faciō. Unde istae lacrimae? Cūr illa virgō vincula gerit?

CEPHEUS. Illa virgō est fīlia mea. Imperiō ōrāculī dabitur mōnstrō saevō quod Neptūnus ex marī cotīdiē ēmittit. Mōnstrum hōc modō pācātum nōbīs parcet. Prō patriā Andromeda vītam suam dat. PERSEUS. Per deōs, rēx, ego ipse hoc mōnstrum interficiam sī mihi fīliam tuam in mātrimōnium dabis.

[1] A large box, four or five feet high, covered with gray cloth, will serve as a rock.

CEPHEUS (*with great eagerness*). Libenter, hospes, hanc condiciōnem accipiō. Sed brevissimum est tempus. Etiam nunc mōnstrum adest. (*A loud roaring is heard.*)
PERSEUS (*calling loudly*). Pelle timōrem ex animō tuō, Andromeda. Tē servābō. (*Rushes from the stage.*)
THIRD FRIEND. Magna spēs mē iam tenet.
FOURTH FRIEND (*pointing to the sky*). Ecce, hospes per aurās altē volat.
FIFTH FRIEND. Iam dēscendit et mōnstrum petit.

All stand gazing toward the scene of combat. The sound of blows is heard mingled with roars of rage and pain. Then PERSEUS *reënters and all greet him with shouts of* " Iō triumphe." *He goes to* AN-DROMEDA, *frees her from her bonds, and, taking her by the hand, leads her to her father*

PERSEUS. Ecce, rēx, fīlia tua. Meā virtūte eam servāvī. Praemium meum postulō.
CEPHEUS. Tua est Andromeda, hospes. Tū es servātor domūs meae.

Curtain falls while all shout " Fēlīciter "

PERSEUS ANDROMEDAM SERVAT

BACULUS THE CENTURION

(Use after completing the Lessons)

Publius Sextius Baculus, a centurion, served in Cæsar's army and won his general's highest praise for his courage and fidelity. The incidents here related are partly based on Cæsar's narrative[1] and are partly fiction. They make no claim to historic accuracy.

Baculus on the march

"Venī, māter, celeriter venī! Multitūdō mīlitum appropinquat. Iam prīmum agmen vidēre possum." Ita magnā vōce clamāvit iuvenis quī ante casam stābat et intentīs oculīs mīlitēs prōcēdentēs spectābat. Verbīs audītīs, māter ex casā properāvit ac prope fīlium cōnstitit.   5

Iuvenis erat Mārcus Caecilius Metellus,[2] fīlius imperātōris nōtissimī quī plūribus ante annīs[3] vītam prō rē pūblicā dederat. Iam Mārcus et Līvia māter in vīllā patris habitābant. Illa vīlla posita erat in viā Flāminiā quae ad Galliam dūcit.

Iam cōpiae multō propius vēnerant. Prīmum equitēs prōcēde-   10
bant, tum peditēs, multa mīlia hominum, sequēbantur; dēnique magnus numerus equōrum et carrōrum, quī impedīmenta ferēbant, agmen claudēbat. Apud centuriōnēs erat quīdam corpore magnō, humerīs lātīs, speciē ēgregiā, quī sē inūsitātā auctōritāte gerēbat. Eum[4] simul atque Līvia cōnspēxit, vehementer permōta 15
clamāvit, "Obsecrō, quem videō? Ecce, mī fīlī, Baculus centuriō, amīcus patrī tuō amīcissimus, quem iam post multōs annōs videō. Quam gaudeō! Sine dubiō in Galliam ad castra Caesaris cōpiās dūcit." "Crēdō, māter cārissima," inquit[5] Mārcus, "deōs

1. See Cæsar's Gallic War, II. 25; III. 5; VI. 38. 2. A Roman regularly had three names: the first, his given name; the second the name of his clan (gēns); and the third the name of his family. 3. See § 452. 4. *As soon as Livia perceived him.* Eum is placed first as the connecting word. See § 198. a. N. 5. inquit Mārcus, *said Marcus.* The verb inquit is used with a direct quotation and is followed by its subject.

283

Baculum ad nōs mīsisse. Scīs mē[1] iam diū cupere nōmen dare
et vestīgia patris sequī. Quis melius quam Baculus prīma[2] castrōrum rudīmenta docēre potest?" "Bene dīcis," inquit Līvia.
"Castra Baculī nōn longē aberunt. Adī ad eum et dā eī epistulam
quam statim scrībam." 5

Marcus goes to the Roman camp and is kindly received by Baculus

Plūribus[3] post hōrīs Mārcus ad castra Rōmāna pervēnit. Prō
portīs castrōrum armātī stābant. Ex hīs ūnus Mārcum rogāvit
quid vellet[4] et quem peteret.[4] Tum Mārcus, cum respondisset[5] sē
Baculum centuriōnem petere, ad praetōrium[6] dēductus est.

Baculus, vir reī[7] mīlitāris perītissimus, propter ēgregiam virtūtem 10
ā Caesare saepe laudātus erat et prīmus pīlus creātus erat. Hōc
tempore, imperātōre et reliquīs ducibus superiōribus absentibus,
tōtī legiōnī[8] praeerat. Is, cum Mārcum nōn nōvisset,[9] tamen eum
benignē accēpit. Eī tum Mārcus dedit epistulam mātris. Baculus,
epistulā acceptā et apertā, haec verba lēgit. 15

Livia's letter to Baculus

Līvia Baculō salūtem[10] dīcit. Sī[11] valēs, bene est; ego valeō.
Haec epistula sine dubiō tibi[12] admīrātiōnem movēbit; nam post
mortem coniugis meī ad tē nōn scrīpsī. Sed sciō tē memoriam
amīcitiae nostrae adhūc tenēre. Iuvenis quī ad tē hanc epistulam
adfert est fīlius meus. Is tibi omnēs fortūnās nostrās nārrābit. 20
Pectus eius studiō reī mīlitāris flagrat. Iam aetātem mīlitārem habet.
Tibi eum commendō. Nōmen[13] dare vult. Valē.

Baculus makes Marcus his aide-de-camp

"Hercle," inquit Baculus, "esne tū fīlius Mārcī Metellī? Certē
fuit nēmō nōbilior aut generōsior umquam. Amantissimē tē accipiō.

1. mē ... dare, *that I have long been desiring to enlist* (literally, *to give my
name*). 2. prīma castrōrum rudīmenta, *the first principles of military service*.
3. plūribus post hōrīs, *several hours later*; literally, *afterwards by several hours*.
See § 452. 4. See § 671. 5. For the mood see § 643. 6. See § 221. 7. See § 554.
8. See § 623. 9. In a **cum** clause of concession. See § 613. 10. salūtem
dīcit, *sends greetings*. 11. Roman letters often begin with this sentence. 12. tibi
... movēbit, *will cause you surprise*. 13. Cf. note 1 above.

Tū es patrī simillimus et corpore et animō. Māter tua, optima Līvia, dīcit tē velle cursum mīlitārem scquī." " Vērum dīcis,"inquit Mārcus, " et sub tuīs signīs mīlitāre [1] maximē cupiō." Baculus rīsit et respondit, " Nihil mihi grātius erit et tē optiōnem [2] cōnstituam."

Baculus resumes the march to Gaul

Proximō diē sonitus tubae Mārcum ex somnō prīmā lūce susci- 5 tāvit. Baculus iam surrēxerat et iusserat castra sine morā movērī. Celeriter cōpiae profectae sunt, nec tōtō diē iter intermissum est. Sub occāsum sōlis mīlitēs dēfessī castra posuērunt. Ita quattuor diēs magnīs itineribus contendērunt. Quīntō diē intra fīnēs Gallōrum ingressī sunt. 10

Gaul and its people [3]

Gallia est omnis dīvīsa in partēs trēs; quārum ūnam partem incolunt Belgae, aliam Aquītānī, tertiam eī quī ipsōrum linguā Celtae appellantur. Hī omnēs linguā,[4] īnstitūtīs, lēgibus inter sē differunt. Hōrum omnium fortissimī sunt Belgae, quod proximī sunt Germānīs quī trāns Rhēnum incolunt, quibuscum continenter 15 bellum gerunt.[5] Quā [6] dē causā Helvētiī quoque reliquōs Gallōs virtūte praecēdunt, quod fere cotīdiānīs proeliīs cum Germānīs contendunt.

The Helvetian migration

Hōc ipsō tempore Helvētiī, hominēs vagandī [7] et bellandī [7] cupidī, dē fīnibus suīs cum omnibus cōpiīs exīre volēbant ut lātiōrēs 20 agrōs peterent. Molestē ferēbant sē nātūrā locī undique continērī. Erant omnīnō itinera duo quibus domō exīre possent,[8] ūnum angustum et difficile per fīnēs Sēquanōrum, alterum multō facilius per Prōvinciam Rōmānam. Hōc itinere ēgredī cōnstituērunt.

1. The infin. of mīlitō. 2. An **optiō** had duties resembling those of an aide-de-camp. The office involved little responsibility or military skill. 3. See map, p. 49. 4. **linguā** and the next two words are ablatives of respect. See § 552. 5. That is, the Belgæ have developed their courage by their constant warfare with the Germans. 6. **quā dē causā**, *for this reason.* 7. Gen. of the gerund with **cupidī**. See § 554. 8. See § 723.

Cæsar resolves to stop them

Hīs rēbus audītīs, Caesar, prōcōnsul Galliae, Genāvam, oppidum Helvētiīs proximum, contendit ut eōs prohibēret. Simul Baculō imperāvit ut cōpiās cōgeret et quam[1] celerrimē in Galliam iter faceret. Quā dē causā, ut dictum est, Baculus cursū incitātō prōcesserat. Iam celerius[2] omnī opīniōne castrīs Caesaris appropin- 5 quābat. Interim Helvētiī convēnerant ad rīpam Rhodanī, quod flūmen inter prōvinciam et fīnēs Helvētiōrum fluit. Nē Helvētiī Rhodanum trānsīrent, Caesar rīpam mūrō fossāque mūnīvit et praesidia disposuit. Tum exspectāvit[3] sī sē invītō trānsīre cōnārentur.

The Helvetii try to cross the Rhine. Baculus brings needed help

Brevī tempore postquam Caesar hās mūnītiōnēs perfēcit, Hel- 10 vētiī perrumpere cōnātī sunt. Prīmum impetum Caesar facile sustinuit, sed Helvētiī nōn numquam interdiū, saepius noctū, cōnātū[4] nōn dēstitērunt. Rōmānī, cum[5] numerō hominum multō īnferiōrēs essent, dēfessī proeliīs vigiliīsque paene cōnfectī sunt. In hōc discrīmine rērum Baculus cum cōpiīs suīs ad castra 15 pervēnit et maximō gaudiō acceptus est. Quem[6] cum imperātor vidēret, " Peropportūnē," inquit, " Bacule, ades. Sine tuō subsidiō diūtius sustinēre vix poterāmus. Quis tandem est iuvenis quī propter[7] tē adstat?" " Hic iuvenis," inquit Baculus, " est Mārcus Mārcī fīlius Metellus. Ego et pater eius ā puerīs amīcī 20 erāmus. Illum mors abstulit, sed relīquit fīlium quem in rē mīlitārī exerceō." Caesar manum Mārcō porrigēns, " Salvē," inquit, " Mārce. Dē rēbus gestīs patris tuī, virī clārissimī, saepe audīvī. Laetus tē accipiō. Posteā noster eris."

1. **quam celerrimē,** *as quickly as possible.* 2. **celerius omnī opīniōne,** *quicker than any one would suppose.* 3. **exspectāvit sī** etc., *he waited to see whether they would try to cross against his will.* **sē invītō** is ablative absolute. On **cōnārentur** see § 671. 4. Abl. of Separation. See § 296. 5. **cum,** *since.* See § 643. 6. **quem ... vidēret,** *when the general saw him.* **quem** is the object of **vidēret;** literally, *whom when the general saw.* This use of the relative is very common in Latin. 7. **propter tē adstat,** *stands near you.*

The Helvetii, unable to break through Cæsar's lines, follow the other route through the country of the Sequani

Illā ipsā nocte Helvētiī, aliī nāvibus aliī vadīs Rhodanī, cum omnibus cōpiīs flūmen trānsiērunt et summā vī mūnītiōnēs Rōmānās perrumpere cōnātī sunt. Sed tanta commūtātiō adventū Baculī et novārum cōpiārum facta est ut hostēs facile repelleren- tur et plūrimī tēlīs occīderentur aut in flūmine perīrent. Post hanc 5 calamitātem Helvētiī adversā fortūnā superātī illō itinere sē āver- tērunt et cōnstituērunt alteram viam per fīnēs Sēquanōrum sequī.

Cæsar follows them

Caesar, cum certior factus esset Helvētiōs ab illō locō profectōs esse et iam cōpiās suās per fīnēs Sēquanōrum trādūxisse, eōs cum omnibus cōpiīs secūtus est. Interim Helvētiī agrōs vāstābant et 10 oppida expugnābant. Multae gentēs, sociī populī Rōmānī, sē ad Caesarem recipiēbant ut auxilium rogārent. Quibus rēbus adductus Caesar, neque diurnō neque nocturnō itinere intermissō, mātūrāvit.

The end of the pursuit

Dēnique propter inopiam reī frūmentāriae Caesar iter ā Hel- vētiīs āvertit et Bibracte, oppidum Haeduōrum maximum et cōpiō- 15 sissimum, quod nōn longē aberat, īre contendit. Quod[1] cum hostibus nūntiātum esset, Helvētiī exīstimābant Rōmānōs timōre perterritōs discēdere. Itaque itinere[2] conversō Rōmānōs ā no- vissimō agmine lacessere incipiēbant. Baculus, quī cum suīs agmen[3] claudēbat, mīsit Mārcum quī Caesarī novam hostium ratiō- 20 nem nūntiāret. Hīs rēbus cognitīs Caesar in proximō colle aciem īnstrūxit et cōpiam[4] pugnandī hostibus fēcit.

The Helvetii are defeated in a great battle

Helvētiī cum omnibus suīs carrīs secūtī impedīmenta in ūnum locum contulērunt; ipsī confertissimā aciē sub[5] prīmam aciem

1. **quod cum,** *when this.* See p. 286, l. 16, and note. 2. **itinere conversō,** *changing their course.* 3. **agmen claudēbat,** *was bringing up the rear.* 4. **cōpiam ... fēcit,** *gave the enemy an opportunity of fighting.* 5. **sub ... successērunt,** *advanced close to the Roman battle front.*

Rōmānōrum successērunt. Caesar hortātus suōs proelium commīsit. Mīlitēs, ē locō superiōre tēlīs missīs, facile aciem hostium
perfrēgērunt. Tum gladiīs dēstrictīs in eōs impetum fēcērunt. Ab
septimā hōrā ad vesperum ācriter pugnātum est, et nēmō āversum [1]
hostem vidēre potuit. Tandem vulneribus dēfessī pedem rettulē- 5
runt. Hostibus superātīs, Rōmānī et impedīmenta et castra Helvētiōrum cēpērunt. Helvētiī omnium rērum inopiā adductī lēgātōs
ad Caesarem mīsērunt, et, omnibus armīs trāditīs et obsidibus datīs,
in dēditiōnem acceptī sunt. Praetereā Caesar iussit eōs in fīnēs
suōs, unde erant profectī, revertī. Dē numerō hōrum Caesar ipse 10
dīcit mīlia CCCLXVIII hominum domō exīsse et mīlia CX revertisse.

Baculus seriously wounded

Hōc proeliō Baculus grave vulnus accēpit. Nam cum iam plūrēs
hōrās pugnātum esset et rēs [2] esset in perīculō, Baculus magnā
vōce clāmāns " Quis sequētur ? " in mediōs hostēs sē iniēcit. In-
fēlīx autem inīquo locō vestīgia [3] nōn tenuit et graviter in terram 15
concidit. Eum hostēs statim circumsistunt. Tum vērō cum gemitū
Rōmānī ad eum servandum prōcurrunt. Dēnique, plūribus utrimque
interfectīs, Baculus graviter vulnerātus ē manibus hostium ēripitur.

Baculus and Marcus return to Italy

Post proelium, cum Mārcus vulnerātō amīcō [4] adsidēret, imperātor ipse vēnit ut virum fortissimum vidēret. Postquam virtūtem 20
eius amplissimīs verbīs laudāvit," Brevī tempore," inquit,"mihi est in
animō bellum cum Ariovistō, saevissimō rēge Germānōrum, gerere.
Ille multa mīlia Germānōrum trāns Rhēnum trādūxit et sociīs populī
Rōmānī gravēs iniūriās intulit. Sed sine tē, Bacule, hoc bellum
gerendum erit.[5] Moneō ut in Italiam revertāris, et operam valē- 25
tūdinī dēs. Post paucōs mēnsēs, ut spērō, in armīs rūrsus eris."
" Mēcum itūrus est,[6] Caesar," inquit Mārcus. " Quis enim melius
quam māter mea, Līvia, eum cūrāre potest ? " Itaque ūsque ad
proximum annum Baculus cum Mārcō et Līvia erat.

1. *in flight*; literally, *turned away.* 2. rēs . . . perīculō, *the situation was
critical.* 3. vestīgia nōn tenuit, *did not keep his footing.* 4. Dative with adsidēret.
See § 623. 5. gerendum erit, *will have to be waged*, passive periphrastic. See
§ 727. 6. itūrus est, *he intends to go*, active periphrastic. See § 726.

Baculus receives a letter from Cæsar

Initā aestāte Baculus, iam optimā valētūdine, hanc epistulam a
Caesare accēpit. " Caesar Baculō salūtem dīcit. Sī valēs, bene est;
ego valeō. Spērō tē integrīs vīribus parātum esse arma sūmere.
Certior factus sum omnēs Belgās contrā populum Rōmānum coniū-
rāre. Venī ad castra et dūc tēcum Mārcum. Valē." 5

War with the Belgæ

Cum Baculus et Mārcus in Galliam pervenīrent, Caesar cum exercitū iam profectus erat, et, multīs gentibus superātīs, per Nerviōrum
fīnēs iter faciēbat. Omnium Belgārum fortissimī Nerviī erant. In-
cūsābant reliquōs Belgās quī sē populō Rōmānō dēdiderant, et dīcēbant sē neque lēgātōs missūrōs [1] neque ūllam condiciōnem pācis 10
acceptūrōs.[1] Iam cum multīs sociīs adventum Rōmānōrum ex-
spectābant.

The Nervii plan their attack

Cum Baculus et Mārcus exercitum Caesaris cōnsequerentur,
castra Nerviōrum nōn longē aberant. Quīdam inimīcī Gallī, cōnsuētūdine itineris exercitūs Rōmānī perspectā, Nerviōs certiōrēs 15
fēcerant inter [2] singulās legiōnēs impedīmentōrum magnum numerum intercēdere, et facile futūrum esse, cum prīma [3] legiō castra
pōneret reliquaeque legiōnēs longē abessent, in hanc impetum facere.
Hoc [4] cōnsilium Nerviī exīstimāvērunt sibi nōn omittendum esse.

A desperate battle is fought

Locus, quem Rōmānī castrīs dēlēgerant, erat in summō colle 20
quī ā quōdam flumine nascebātur. Trāns flūmen hostēs in silvās
sē abdiderant. Peropportūnē [5] accidit quod Caesar ratiōnem agminis mūtāverat, nec ūnam sed sex legiōnēs dūcēbat. Post eās tōtīus

1. Future infinitive with **esse** omitted as it often is. 2. **inter ... intercēdere,**
between every two legions a very long baggage train intervened. 3. The first legion
that reached the camp site began at once to lay it out and fortify it. 4. **Hoc ...
esse,** *this plan the Nervii thought ought not to be left untried by them.* See §§ 727,
729. 5. **peropportūnē accidit quod,** etc., *very opportunely it happened that,* etc. ;
the change in the order of march gave Cæsar six legions with which to meet
the attack instead of only one. That fact alone saved the day for Cæsar.

exercitūs impedīmenta conlocāverat. Nerviī, cum prīma impedīmenta Rōmānōrum vidērent, putābant tempus exspectātum adesse.
Subitō incrēdibilī celeritāte cum omnibus cōpiīs ē silvā prōvolāvē-
runt, et, flūmen trānsgressī, eādem celeritāte adversō[1] colle ad
castra Rōmāna contendērunt. Caesarī[2] omnia ūnō tempore erant 5
agenda : vēxillum[3] prōpōnendum, signum tubā[4] dandum, ab opere[5]
revocandī mīlitēs, aciēs īnstruenda, mīlitēs hortandī, signum[6] dandum ; quārum rērum magnam partem temporis brevitās et hostium
celeritās impediēbant. Dīversae legiōnēs aliae[7] aliā in parte hostibus resistēbant. Undique ācerrimē pugnābātur, praesertim ā dextrō 10
cornū. Ibi duodecima legiō, in quā Baculus ascrīptus est, ab hostibus urgēbātuɪ. Iam omnēs ferē centuriōnēs aut vulnerātī aut occīsī
erant, in hīs Baculus ipse quī tot et tam gravibus vulneribus est
cōnfectus ut sē sustinēre nōn posset.

Cæsar to the rescue

In hōc discrīmine rērum Caesar, scūtō mīlitī[8] dētrāctō, quod ipse 15
sine scūtō vēnerat, in prīmam aciem prōcessit. Imperātōris cōnspectus mīlitibus spem īnferēbat et paulum hostium impɕtus tardātus est.
Interim reliquae legiōnēs, quae aliīs in partibus vīcerant, cum cog-
nōvissent quō[9] in locō rēs esset, subsidium ferēbant. Dēnique Nerviī
magnā caede superātī sunt. Post proelium Mārcus invenīrī nōn 20
poterat. Multā autem nocte incolumis ad castra revertit ; captus
ab hostibus effūgit. Nec Baculus vulneribus mortuus est, sed post
breve tempus arma sūmere poterat.

The twelfth legion in the Alps

Belgīs superātīs, legiō duodecima in Alpēs in oppidum quod
appellābātur Octodūrus[10] hiemandī causā dūcēbātur. Hoc oppidum 25

---

1. **adversō colle**, *up the opposite hill.* 2. Dat. of agent with the passive periphrastic **agenda erant**. See § 729. A number of periphrastics follow with
omitted auxiliary. 3. This was red in colʊr and the signal for arming. 4. This
was the signal to take their places in the ranks. 5. The work of fortifying the
camp. 6. The battle signal. 7. **aliae aliā in parte,** *some in one place, others in
another.* See § 505. 8. **mīlitī,** dat. with **dētrāctō.** See § 623. **mīlitibus,** in
the next line but one, is in the same construction. 9. **quō . . . esset,** *in what
a state the situation was.* See § 671. 10. See p. 49.

altissimīs montibus undique continēbātur. Galba lēgātus, quī legiōnī praeerat, Baculō[1] negōtium dedit ut hīberna mūnīret. Itaque Baculus negōtium suscipit et iubet[2] locum mūrō altō mūnīrī. Hōc opere·nōndum pcrfcctō, maxima multitūdō barbarōrum ex omnibus partibus impetum facit. Cum iam multās hōrās pugnārē- 5 tur ac nōn sōlum vīrēs sed etiam tēla Rōmānōs dēficerent, Baculus et quīdam tribūnus mīlitum, vir magnac virtūtis, ad Galbam accurrunt. "Rēs est in perīculō, lēgāte," inquiunt.[3] " Ēruptiō est ūna spēs salūtis." Hōc cōnsiliō captō, mīlitēs ex castrīs subitō ērūpērunt. Hāc ēruptiōne imprōvīsā hostēs ita commōtī sunt ut tertiā parte 10 interfectā reliquī fugerent. Quō proeliō factō Galba, alterum impetum timēns, incolumem legiōnem in fīnēs Allobrogum dūxit ibique hiemāvit.

A letter from Britain

Illō tempore Britannia erat Rōmānīs terra incognita. Nē Gallīs quidcm crat īnsula nōta praeter eam partem quae est contrā Galliam. Multīs dē causīs Caesar īnsulam adīre cupiēbat, et quārtō 15 annō prōcōnsulātūs profectus est. Et Baculus et Mārcus hoc iter fēcērunt. Dē hīs rēbus Mārcus hanc epistulam ad Līviam mātrem scrīpsit: " Mārcus Līviae mātrī suae salūtem plūrimam dīcit. In Britanniā Caesar castra nunc pōnit. Haec īnsula ā Galliā nōn longē abest. Nactī idōneam ad nāvigandum tempestātem tertiā 20 ferē vigiliā[4] solvimus, et quārtā[4] hōrā diēī Britanniam attigimus. Ibi in omnibus collibus armātās hostium cōpiās cōnspēximus. Cuius locī haec erat nātūra ut[5] mare montibus angustē continērētur. Cum locus ad ēgrediendum idōneus nōn esset, circiter mīlia passuum vii ab eō locō prōgressus imperator contrā[6] apertum et 25 plānum lītus nāvēs cōnstituit. Sed barbarī secūtī nostrōs[7] nāvibus ēgredī prohibēre cōnābantur. Nostrī autem, altitūdine maris

---

1. **Baculō** ... **mūnīret**, *commissioned Baculus to fortify the winter quarters.*
ut ... **mūnīret** is a clause of purpose. 2. See frontispiece. 3. **inquiunt**, *they say.* 4. The Romans divided the night into four watches, and the day from sunrise to sunset into twelve hours. 5. **ut** ... **continērētur**, *that the sea is closely bounded by mountains*, the cliffs of Dover. See picture, p. 61. 6. **contrā** ...
cōnstituit, *brought the ships to anchor opposite to an open and level beach.*
7. **nostrōs** ... **cōnābantur**, *attempted to keep our men from disembarking.*

perterritī et illīus generis pugnandī imperītī, erant tardiōrēs,[1] cum simul dē nāvibus dēsiliendum et in fluctibus cōnsistendum et cum hostibus pugnandum esset. Tum aquilifer decimae legiōnis, vir fortissimus, sē ex nāve prōicit. ' Dēsilīte,' inquit, ' commīlitōnēs, nisi vultis aquilam hostibus prōdere,' et in hostēs aquilam ferre 5 incipit. Simul Baculus dēsilit clamāns, 'Venīte! Venīte, Rōmānī!' Tum vērō nostrī ūniversī ex nāvibus dēsiluērunt. Pugnātum est utrimque ācriter. Dēnique, barbarīs in fugam datīs, ōram occupāmus et castra pōnimus. Haec īnsula, remōtissima terrārum, est saevissima et asperrima. Omnia sunt terribilia et perīculī plēna. 10 Dēsīderō tē, māter cārissima. Ō quandō ego tē aspiciam! Vale."

Cæsar's sixth campaign

Sextō annō bellī Gallicī Caesar per prīmam partem aestātis in Germāniā rem gerēbat. Tum suōs in Galliam redūxit et castra in mediīs Eburōnum fīnibus posuit. Ibi impedīmenta omnium legiōnum contulit et praesidiō[2] impedīmentīs ūnam legiōnem relīquit. Ipse 15 et reliquae legiones aliī[3] aliās in partēs profectī sunt. Discēdēns monuit lēgātum ut mīlitēs in castrīs continēret.

The commanding officer, moved by the murmurs of his men who complain of being confined in camp without good cause, disregards Cæsar's advice

Plūrēs diēs post profectiōnem Caesaris lēgātus praeceptīs imperātōris summā dīligentiā pāruit ac nē cālōnem quidem ex vāllō ēgredī passus est. Sed septimō diē, permōtus vōcibus[4] mīlitum 20 quī molestē ferēbant sē, omnibus Gallīs superātīs, tam diū continērī, quīnque cohortēs et magnam multitūdinem cālōnum in agrōs proximōs frūmentandī[5] causā mīsit.

1. *more backward than usual.* 2. **praesidiō impedīmentīs**, two datives. See § 686. 3. **aliī . . . partēs**, *some in one direction and others in another.* **aliī** is masculine because it agrees not only with **legiōnēs** but also with **ipse.** An adjective agreeing with two or more nouns denoting persons of different genders is regularly masculine. 4. *murmurs.* 5. **frūmentandī causā**, *to gather grain.*

"VENĪTE! VENĪTE, RŌMANĪ!" CLĀMĀVIT BACULUS

A German force unexpectedly attacks the camp. A panic ensues

Hīs absentibus et castrīs paene sine praesidiō relictīs, duo mīlia
Germānōrum imprōvīsō perveniunt et castra capere cōnantur. Ex[1]
omnibus partibus hostēs castra circumveniunt. Vix Rōmānī prīmum
impetum sustinent et portās dēfendunt. Omnēs perterritī sciunt
neque quam in partem auxilium ferre neque quid facere dēbeant. 5
Nūllīs dēfēnsōribus in vāllō vīsīs, barbarī crēdunt nūllum praesidium intus esse. Quā dē causā ācrius perrumpere cōnantur.

Baculus to the rescue

Baculus centuriō, cum aeger esset, cum exercitū nōn profectus
est, sed in praesidiō relictus erat. Iam[2] diem quīntum cibō caruerat. Clāmōre audītō, surgit et ex tabernāculō prōdit. Videt hostēs 10
imminēre atque rem[3] esse summō in discrīmine. Capit arma a
proximīs atque in portā cōnsistit. Cōnsequuntur hunc centuriōnēs
eius cohortis quae in statiōne erat. Paulisper proelium sustinent.
Relinquit[4] animus Baculum, gravibus acceptīs vulneribus; vix per[5]
manūs trāditus servātur. Hōc spatiō interpositō, reliquī animīs 15
cōnfīrmātīs in mūnītiōnibus cōnsistere audent speciemque dēfēnsō-
rum praebent. Mox mīlitēs quī ex castrīs ēgressī erant revertērunt
et Germānī trāns Rhēnum sē recēpērunt. Ita virtūte Baculī castra
et impedīmenta cōnservāta sunt.

Dē rēbus gestīs Baculī hāctenus. 20

1. **ex omnibus partibus,** *on all sides.* 2. **Iam . . . caruerat,** *already for five
days he had gone without food*; on **cibō** see § 296. 3. **rem . . . discrīmine,** *that
the situation is extremely critical.* 4. **relinquit . . . Baculum,** *consciousness
fails Baculus* or *Baculus faints.* 5. **per manūs trāditus,** *passed along from
hand to hand.*

LATIN SONGS

INTEGER VITAE

The words are the first two stanzas of the twenty-second ode in Book I of the " Odes " of Horace (65–8 B.C.). The music is by Dr. F. F. Flemming (about 1811).

In - te - ger vi - tae sce - le - ris - que
Si - ve per Syr - tes i - ter aes - tu-

pu - rus Non e - get Mau - ris ia - cu - lis, nec
o - sas, Si - ve fac - tu - rus per in - hos - pi-

ar - cu, Nec ve - ne - na tis gra - vi - da sa-
ta - lem Cau - ca - sum, vel quae lo - ca fa - bu-

git - tis, Fus - ce, pha - re - tra,
lo - sus Lam - bit Hy - das - pes.

Fuscus, the man of life upright and pure
Needeth nor javelin nor bow of Moor,
Nor arrows tipped with venom deadly sure,
    Loading his quiver;

Whether o'er Afric's burning sands he rides,
Or frosty Caucasus' bleak mountain sides,
Or wanders lonely, where Hydaspes glides,
    That storied river.

THEODORE MARTIN

ADESTE FIDELES
(PORTUGUESE HYMN)

The words are by an unknown author of the seventeenth century. The tune, which is found in most of our hymnals, is generally ascribed to John Reading, who died in 1692. The name " Portuguese Hymn " comes from the melody's having been first used in the chapel of the Portuguese embassy in London. A translation under the title " O come, all ye Faithful " was made by F. Oakeley (1841).

Ad - es - te, fi - de - les, Lae - ti tri - um - phan - tes; Ve-
Can - tet nunc I - o! Cho - rus an - ge - lo - rum;
Er - go qui na - tus Di - e ho - di - er - na,

ni - te, ve - ni - te in Beth - le - hem;
Can - tet nunc au - la cae - les - ti - um,
Ie - su, ti - bi sit glo - ri - a;

Na - tum vi - de - te Re - gem an - ge - lo - rum: Ve-
Glo - ri - a, glo - ria In - ex - cel - sis De - o! Ve-
Pa - tris ae - ter - ni Ver - bum ca - ro fac - tum! Ve-

ni - te a - do - re - mus, ve - ni - te a - do - re - mus, ve-

ni - te a - do - re - mus Do - mi - num.

GAUDEAMUS

The second and third stanzas of this famous student song were known as early as 1267. The melody in its present form dates back to about the middle of the eighteenth century.

Gau-de-a-mus i-gi-tur,   Iu-ve-nes dum su - mus;
U - bi sunt, qui an-te nos   In mun-do fu - e - re?
Vi - ta nos-tra bre-vis est,   Bre-vi fi - ni - e - tur;

Post iu-cun-dam iu-ven-tu-tem, Post mo-les-tam se-nec-tu-tem,
Tran-se-as ad su-pe-ros,   A - be-as ad in - fe - ros,
Ve-nit mors ve - lo - ci - ter,   Ra-pit nos a - tro-ci - ter,

Nos ha-be - bit   hu - mus, Nos ha-be - bit   hu - mus.
Quos si vis vi - de - re, Quos si vis vi - de - re.
Ne-mi-ni par - ce - tur, Ne-mi-ni par - ce - tur.

Let us now in youth rejoice,
None can justly blame us ;
For when golden youth has fled,
And in age our joys are dead,
Then the dust doth claim us,
Then the dust doth claim us.

Where have all our fathers gone?
Here we'll see them never ;
Seek the gods' serene abode —
Cross the dolorous Stygian flood —
There they dwell forever,
There they dwell forever.

Brief is this our life on earth,
Brief — nor will it tarry —
Swiftly death runs to and fro,
All must feel his cruel blow,
None the dart can parry,
None the dart can parry.

A ROUND FOR THREE PARTS

A - mor vin - cit om - ni - a, A - mor vin - cit
om - ni - a, A - mor vin - cit om - ni - a, om - ni - a.

A ROUND FOR FOUR PARTS

Duc, duc, re - mos duc Flu - mi - ne se - cun - do;
Vi - vi - tur, vi - vi - tur, vi - vi - tur, vi - vi - tur Ve - lut in som - ni - o.

Row, row, row your boat, gently down the stream.
Merrily, merrily, merrily, merrily, life is but a dream.

REVIEWS[1]

I. REVIEW OF LESSONS I-VII

732. Give the English of the following words:

NOUNS

agricola	fābula	nauta	puella	terra
aqua	fīlia	pecūnia	rēgīna	

VERBS		PREPOSITIONS	
amat.	properat	ā *or* ab	in *with acc.*
dat	sunt	ad	in *with abl.*
est	vocat	cum	per
nārrat			

733. Give the Latin of the following words. Go through the entire list, checking the words you do not remember. Then drill on the words you have checked.

from	water	daughter	money	are	through
loves	gives	tells	hastens	calls	land
farmer	story	sailor	in *or* on	is	queen
to	with	into	girl		

734. Review Questions. What English letters does the Latin alphabet lack? When is i a consonant? What is the sound of c and of g? How many syllables has a Latin word? How are words divided into syllables? When is a syllable long? Give the rules of Latin accent. Name the parts of speech and give an English example of each. Define the subject, the predicate. What is a transitive verb? an intransitive verb? the copula? Define the direct object. What is inflection? declension? conjugation? What does the form of a noun show? Name the Latin cases. What case is used for the subject? the possessor? the indirect object? the direct

---

[1] It is suggested that each of the reviews be assigned for a written test.

object? Translate **filia rēgīnae pecūniam Lesbiae dat.** What is the ending of the verb in the third person, singular and plural? Give the rule for the agreement of the verb. What relations are expressed by the dative case? by the ablative case? Where does the verb generally stand? the subject? the possessive genitive? the direct object? the indirect object? What is a predicate noun? How many declensions are there? How is the declension to which a noun belongs determined? Decline **rēgīna, fābula, filia.** What cases are always alike? How is the ablative singular distinguished from the nominative? What Latin cases may be used with prepositions?

735. Derivation. Give ten English words related to the Latin words in § 732. Define these and illustrate each by an English sentence.

736. Fill out the following summary of the first declension:

1. Ending in the nominative singular
2. Rule for gender
3. Case terminations $\begin{cases} a. \text{ Singular} \\ b. \text{ Plural} \end{cases}$
4. Irregular nouns

II. REVIEW OF LESSONS VIII–XV

737. Give the English of the following words:

NOUNS OF THE FIRST DECLENSION

| casa | fāma | īnsula | via |

NOUNS OF THE SECOND DECLENSION

ager	auxilium	filius	populus	socius
amīcus	bellum	frūmentum	puer	tēlum
arma	equus	oppidum	servus	vir

ADJECTIVES OF THE FIRST AND SECOND DECLENSIONS

altus, -a, -um	līber, lībera, līberum	novus, -a, -um
amīcus, -a, -um	longus, -a, -um	parvus, -a, -um
bonus, -a, -um	magnus, -a, -um	proximus, -a, -um
grātus, -a, -um	multus, -a, -um	pulcher, pulchra, pulchrum
inimīcus, -a, -um	nōtus, -a, -um	

VERBS		INTERROGATIVE PRONOUNS	ADVERBS	
convocat	parat	quid	cūr	saepe
habitat	portat	quis	nōn	ubi
labōrat	nāvigat		quō	

CONJUNCTIONS

et   sed

738. Give the Latin of the following words:

where	rumor	war	free (*adj.*)
but	friend	horse	well-known
who	nearest	small	why
sail (*verb*)	whither	call together	much, many
toil (*verb*)	prepare	not	slave
cottage	road	pleasing	man
field	aid (*noun*)	son	spear, missile
high *or* deep	friendly	people	great
often	live (*verb*)	ally	long
and	island	new	grain
what	good	hostile	town
carry	pretty	boy	arms

739. Review Questions. What is meant by grammatical gender? Give the rule for the gender of nouns of the first declension. Decline **terra, filia.** What nouns belong to the second declension? Give the rule for gender in the second declension. Decline **amīcus, puer, ager, vir, oppidum.** Decline **socius** and **auxilium,** and explain the peculiarity in the genitive of nouns like these. When is the vocative not like the nominative? Give the general rules of declension. What is an adjective? Decline **magnus, -a, -um; līber, lībera, līberum; pulcher, pulchra, pulchrum.** Decline **agricola bonus.** Why is it not correct to say **agricola bona?** What is the position of adjectives? What is the position of vocatives? What are adverbs? Where do they stand? How are questions introduced in Latin? How are questions answered in the affirmative? How are questions answered in the negative? Name the possessive adjectives. What is the vocative singular masculine of **meus?** Why is **suus** called a reflexive possessive? Where are possessive adjectives placed when they are unemphatic? when they are emphatic?

740. Give the rules for the following constructions, and illustrate each by a Latin sentence:

1. Agreement of adjectives
2. Apposition
3. Dative with adjectives
4. Agreement of possessives

741. Derivation. Give fifteen English words related to the Latin words in § 737. Define these and illustrate each by an English sentence.

742. Fill out the following summary of the second declension:

1. Endings in the nominative
2. Rule for gender
3. Case terminations of nouns in **-us** { *a.* Singular *b.* Plural *c.* Vocative singular
4. Case terminations of nouns in **-um** { *a.* Singular *b.* Plural
5. Peculiarities of nouns in **-er**
6. Peculiarity of the genitive of nouns in **-ius** and **-ium**

III. REVIEW OF LESSONS XVI–XXIII

743. Give the English of the following words:

Nouns of the First Declension

amīcitia	dīligentia	Germānia	silva
Britannia	Gallia	ōra	victōria
cōpia			

Nouns of the Second Declension

barbarus	castrum	Germānus	praemium
Britannī	Gallus	perīculum	proelium

Adjectives of the First and Second Declensions

barbarus, -a, -um	miser, misera, miserum	suus, -a, -um
crēber, crēbra, crēbrum	noster, nostra, nostrum	tuus, -a, -um
meus, -a, -um	Rōmānus, -a, -um	vester, vestra, vestrum

VERBS

First Conjugation	Second Conjugation	
occupō, -ā're	habeō, -ē're	timeō, -ē're
pugnō, -ā're	moneō, -ē're	videō, -ē're
superō, -ā're	teneō, -ē're	

ADVERBS			PREPOSITIONS	CONJUNCTION
iam	numquam	semper	ē or ex	itaque
mox	nunc	tum	sine	

744. Give the Latin of the following words :

therefore	danger	seize	conquer, overcome
Gaul	my, mine	our, ours	then
out of	thick, frequent	already	reward, prize
plenty, forces	Roman	a savage	have
without	friendship	always	presently
a Gaul	never	fight (*verb*)	fear (*verb*)
his, her, its	thy, thine	forest	shore
industry	savage (*adj.*)	Britons	advise, warn
fort, camp	Britain	your, yours	a German
now	wretched	battle	victory
Germany	see	hold	

745. Review Questions. Define the active voice and the passive voice, and illustrate each by an English sentence. Name the moods. Name the English tenses and give an example of each. Define the three persons. Give the personal endings. What is their office? Define the indicative mood. Inflect the present, past, and future of **sum.** How many regular conjugations has Latin? What are the four distinguishing, or characteristic, vowels? What is the present stem and how may it be found? What is the tense sign of the past tense? of the future? What verbs belong to the first conjugation? to the second conjugation? Inflect **nārrō** and **nāvigō** in the present, past, and future. In what respect is the verb **dō** irregular? Inflect **habeō** and **videō** in the present, past, and future. What are the three meanings of the Latin present? What are the two uses of the Latin past tense? How does the meaning of **ē (ex)** differ from that of **ā (ab)**? Give the rules for the shortening of vowels. What are the general principles of Latin order?

REVIEWS
746. Give the rules for the following constructions, and illustrate each by a Latin sentence:

1. Predicate Genitive of Possession 3. Ablative of Means
2. Ablative of Cause 4. Ablative of Manner
5. Ablative of Accompaniment

747. Derivation. Give fifteen English words related to the Latin words in § 743. Define them and illustrate each by an English sentence.

748. Make a blank scheme, as shown here, of the first three tenses of the indicative, and, pointing rapidly with your pencil to the different spaces and using a variety of verbs, give the form required for each space. Drill until you can give the forms instantly. You do not know these three tenses well enough until you can give them complete, of any verb, in less than fifteen seconds.

INDICATIVE   INFINITIVE

Verb ------------   ------------

Present stem ------------

PRESENT
1. ------------   ------------
2. ------------   ------------
3. ------------   ------------

PAST (TENSE SIGN -bā-)
1. ------------   ------------
2. ------------   ------------
3. ------------   ------------

FUTURE (TENSE SIGN -bi-)
1. ------------   ------------
2. ------------   ------------
3. ------------   ------------

IV. REVIEW OF LESSONS XXIV–XXXII

749. Give the English of the following words:

NOUNS OF THE FIRST DECLENSION

dea	iniūria	poena	sapientia
fossa	patria	poēta	vīta

NOUNS OF THE SECOND DECLENSION

animus	deus	liber	nāvigium	vāllum
cōnsilium	fīnitimī	mūrus	numerus	

ADJECTIVES OF THE FIRST AND SECOND DECLENSIONS

clārus, -a, -um	lātus, -a, -um	medius, -a, -um
fīnitimus, -a, -um	malus, -a, -um	

VERBS

First Conj.	*Second Conj.*	*Third Conj.*		*Fourth Conj.*
nūntiō, -ā′re	pateō, -ē′re	capiō, -ere	indūcō, -ere	audiō, -ī′re
servō, -ā′re	respondeō, -ē′re	dīcō, -ere	mittō, -ere	mūniō, -ī′re
		dūcō, -ere	petō, -ere	veniō, -ī′re
		faciō, -ere	regō, -ere	
		gerō, -ere	vincō, -ere	

RELATIVE PRONOUN	PREPOSITION	CONJUNCTION	ADVERBS
quī	dē	cum	celeriter
			posteā

750. Give the Latin of the following words:

afterwards	conquer	lead into	take, seize
quickly	number (*noun*)	announce	say, speak
come	boat	goddess	adjoining, neighboring
fortify	life	plan (*noun*)	lead (*verb*)
answer	wide	famous	god
middle of	evil	wall	neighbors

rampart, wall	rule (*verb*)	make, do	down from, concerning
wisdom	seek	who	wrong, insult (*noun*)
hear	book	lie open, extend	wage, carry on
mind, heart	poet	save	send
when	punishment	ditch	country, native land

751. Review Questions. Define demonstrative pronouns and adjectives. Decline **is, ea, id.** Where do demonstrative adjectives stand? Explain the use of **is** in the sentence **videō eum.** Explain the difference in meaning between **Mārcus fīlium suum vocat** and **Mārcus fīlium eius vocat.** What verbs belong to the third conjugation? Inflect **dūcō, mittō,** and **gerō** in the present, past, and future. What is the tense sign in the future of the first and second conjugations? of the third and fourth conjugations? What verbs belong to the fourth conjugation? Inflect **faciō, veniō,** and **mūniō** in the present, past, and future. What are verbs like **faciō** called? What are the tenses of the imperative? How is the present imperative formed? Give the present imperative of **servō, respondeō, vincō, mittō, dīcō, dūcō, faciō,** and **veniō.**

752. Give the rules for the following constructions, and illustrate each by a Latin sentence:

    1. Agreement of a demonstrative with its noun
    2. Dative with special intransitive verbs

753. Derivation. What is the force of the Latin prefix **re-**? Illustrate by English or Latin words. What is the meaning of the Latin prepositions **ā (ab), ad, dē, ē (ex), in,** when used as prefixes? Illustrate by English or Latin words. Give fifteen English words related to the Latin words in § 749. Define them and illustrate each by an English sentence.

754. Continue to use the scheme of § 748, and drill with verbs of all four conjugations.

V. REVIEW OF LESSONS XXXIII–XL

755. Give the English of the following words :

NOUNS OF THE FIRST DECLENSION	NOUNS OF THE SECOND DECLENSION
Graecia memoria	captīvus factum praesidium

ADJECTIVES OF THE FIRST AND SECOND DECLENSIONS

fīrmus, -a, -um   tardus, -a, -um

VERBS

First Conjugation   *Second Conjugation*   *Third Conjugation*

oppugnō   spectō   sedeō   agō   ēdūcō   rapiō

CONJUNCTIONS	ADVERBS
nam neque (nec)	certē dēnique diū fortiter ibi

756. Give the Latin of the following words :

attack (*verb*)	bravely	a long time	memory
for	and not, neither	slow	lead out
certainly	finally, at last	Greece	deed
garrison	seize	strong, trusty	drive
there	look at	sit	captive

757. Review Questions. Define the active voice and the passive voice. Illustrate each by a Latin sentence. Name the personal endings of the passive. Do the tense signs differ from those used in the active? What are the tense signs of the past and future? Define the infinitive. Explain the formation of the present infinitive, active and passive. Explain the formation of the present imperative, active and passive. Inflect the verb **sum** through the first three tenses of the indicative, the present infinitive, and the imperative. Give the complete inflection, active and passive, as far as we have gone, of **portō, habeō, vincō, rapiō**, and **mūniō**. Give the synopsis of the active of **spectō, sedeō, agō, faciō**, and **veniō**, and also the synopsis of the passive of **servō, teneō, petō, rapiō**, and **audiō**.

758. Give the rules for the ablative of means and the ablative of the personal agent, and illustrate each by a Latin sentence.

759. Derivation. Define the following English words, giving the Latin root word and the force of the prefix in each case :

conserve	remit	convoke	comport	abduct
deserve	evoke	deport	report	deduce
emit	invoke	export	adduce	reduce
admit	revoke	import	induce	conduce

760. Give ten English words related to the Latin words in § 755. Define them and illustrate each by an English sentence.

761. Extend the scheme of § 748 so as to include all the verb inflection you have had, and use it as suggested with verbs of all four conjugations.

VI. REVIEW OF LESSONS XLI–XLVIII

762. Give the English of the following words :

NOUNS OF THE FIRST DECLENSION	NOUNS OF THE SECOND DECLENSION	
nātūra	annus	imperium locus
vīlla	exemplum	lēgātus officium

ADJECTIVES OF THE FIRST AND SECOND DECLENSIONS

amplus, -a, -um	integer, -gra, -grum	timidus, -a, -um
ēgregius, -a, -um	pūblicus, -a, -um	vērus, -a, -um

VERBS

First Conj.	*Second Conj.*	*Third Conj.*	*Fourth Conj.*
comparō locō	prohibeō	abdūcō discēdō	inveniō
cōnfīrmō pācō		dēfendō dīmittō	
līberō			

Irregular

absum

ADVERBS			PREPOSITION
longē	minimē	quam	ante

763. Give the Latin of the following words :

far away	farm	set free	hinder	how
nature	place (*noun*)	ambassador	defend	send away
year	put	lead away	find	ample
get together	subdue	cowardly	depart	public
remarkable	before	power	not at all	whole
example	duty	strengthen	be away	true

764. Review Questions. What are the principal parts of an English verb? of a Latin verb? What are the three verb stems? How is the present stem formed? the perfect stem? the participial stem? What tenses are formed from the perfect stem? Give the endings of the perfect. What is the tense sign of the past perfect? of the future perfect? Give the principal parts of **sum** and inflect it in all the moods and tenses you have learned. How is the perfect translated as perfect definite? as past absolute? How are the Latin past and Latin perfect used? Give the principal parts and the inflection in full of the indicative of **dō, nūntiō, habeō, gerō, faciō, mūniō.** Give also the present imperative active and the present and perfect infinitives of these verbs.

765. Give the rules for the ablative of the personal agent, the place from which, and separation, and illustrate each by a Latin sentence.

766. Derivation. Give ten English words related to the Latin words in § 762. Define them and illustrate each by an English sentence.

767. Extend the scheme of §§ 748 and 761, and continue its use.

VII. REVIEW OF LESSONS XLIX–LVI

768. Give the English of the following words :

NOUNS OF THE FIRST DECLENSION	NOUNS OF THE SECOND DECLENSION		
fortūna	impedīmentum	negōtium	Rhēnus
inopia	iūdicium	rēgnum	

ADJECTIVES OF THE FIRST AND SECOND DECLENSIONS

inīquus. -a, -um   paucī, -ae, -a   reliquus, -a, -um

VERBS

First Conj.		Second Conj.		Third Conj.	
appellō	putō	iubeō	ascendō	incipiō	prōdūcō
cōnservō	vāstō	moveō	cupiō	interficiō	remittō
ēvocō	vetō	obtineō	fugiō	prōcēdō	suscipiō
expugnō		perterreō	iaciō		

Irregular

possum

ADVERBS		PREPOSITIONS	CONJUNCTIONS	
anteā	magnopere	post	ac	atque
ita	statim	prō	sī	
		trāns		

769. Give the Latin of the following words:

across	desire, wish	kingdom	preserve
and	baggage	Rhine	advance
hindrance	storm (*verb*)	want, lack	kill
greatly	climb up	business, affair	lead forward
unfavorable	hurl	judgment	call, name
fortune	command	send back	possess, gain
be able, can	after, behind	undertake	forbid
move	at once	flee	for, in behalf of
think	thus, so	terrify	few, only a few
begin	remaining, rest	lay waste	heretofore
power	if	call out	

770. Review Questions. Give the principal parts of the verbs of the second and third conjugations used in § 768. Define a participle. What participles are lacking in Latin? What Latin forms are made from the participial stem? Why is **vir vocātae sunt** incorrect? Give the complete inflection in the passive indicative, imperative, and infinitive of the following verbs: **moveō, iaciō, iubeō, dūcō**. Give the complete inflection of **possum**. Give the list of prepositions that take the ablative. Decline the relative **quī** and the interrogative **quis**.

771. Define an infinitive. Give an example in Latin of an infinitive object clause, of a complementary infinitive, of the infinitive used as a noun. Define a simple sentence, a complex sentence, a compound sentence. What are the different kinds of clauses? Give the rule for the agreement of the relative pronoun, and illustrate by a Latin sentence. Give the rule for the ablative absolute, and illustrate by a Latin sentence. How is an ablative absolute best translated?

772. Derivation. Give fifteen English words related to the Latin words in § 768. Define them and illustrate each by an English sentence. Give the force of the prefixes **ab, ad, con-, dē, ē, in, prō, re-, trāns.** What is the force of **in-** prefixed to an adjective or adverb? What is meant by assimilation? What changes of spelling occur in words like **capiō** when compounded with a prefix?

773. Extend the scheme of §§ 748 and 761, so as to include all you have had of the passive, and continue to use it for drill.

VIII. REVIEW OF LESSONS LVII–LXIV

774. Give the English of the following words:

NOUN OF THE FIRST DECL.	NOUNS OF THE SECOND DECL.	
lingua	mātrimōnium	signum

NOUNS OF THE THIRD DECLENSION

animal	cohors	homō	mīles	pāx	soror
caedēs	cōnsul	iter	mors	prīnceps	urbs
calcar	eques	legiō	mulier	rēx	virtūs
caput	flūmen	mare	nōmen	salūs	vīs
cīvitās	frāter	māter	pater		

ADJECTIVE OF THE FIRST AND SECOND DECLENSIONS

aequus, -a, -um

VERBS

Second Conjugation	*Third Conjugation*			
audeō	accipiō	dēiciō	pōnō	reducō
contineō	committō	pellō	reddō	relinquō

312 REVIEWS

Conjunctions

autem et . . . et etiam tamen

775. Give the Latin of the following words:

equal, fair	drive, banish	father	cohort
even, also	put	peace	enemy
dare	return	chief	bound, restrain
tongue	nevertheless	king	city
man	however	head	woman
journey, march	both . . . and	river	spur (*noun*)
valor	intrust	brother	state (*noun*)
strength	consul	leave	animal
death	legion	time	horseman
safety	mother	sister	sea
receive	soldier	name (*noun*)	marriage
throw down	lead back	slaughter	signal (*noun*)

776. Review Questions. Define base and stem. Into what two classes are nouns of the third declension divided? Decline **caput, cīvitās, eques, flūmen, legiō, pater, tempus.** What masculine and feminine nouns have i-stems? In what cases do i-stems differ from consonant stems? What neuter nouns have i-stems? Decline **caedēs, hostis, cohors, mors, mare, animal.** Decline the irregular nouns **homō, iter, vīs.**

777. Derivation. Give fifteen English words related to the Latin words in § 774. Define them and illustrate each by an English sentence. How many Latin prefixes can you name? What is the force of each? Write all the English derivatives you can from the verb **mittō, -ere, mīsī, missus,** using both prefixes and suffixes.

IX. REVIEW OF LESSONS LXV–LXXII

778. Give the English of the following words:

NOUNS OF THE FIRST DECL.   NOUNS OF THE SECOND DECL.

fuga   grātia   beneficium   spatium

NOUNS OF THE THIRD DECL.   INDECLINABLE NOUN

auctōritās   dux   ignis   lēx   pēs   nihil

REVIEWS 313

ADJECTIVE OF THE FIRST AND SECOND DECLENSIONS

certus, -a, -um

ADJECTIVES OF THE THIRD DECLENSION

ācer, ācris, ācre	equester, equestris,	omnis, omne
brevis, breve	equestre	pār
celer, celeris, celere	facilis, facile	pedester, pedestris,
commūnis, commūne	fortis, forte	pedestre
difficilis, difficile	gravis, grave	similis, simile
dissimilis, dissimile	levis, leve	

VERBS

First Conjugation	*Second Conjugation*	*Third Conjugation*
exspectō	maneō	addūcō
vulnerō		cognōscō
		cōgō

ADVERBS   PREPOSITION   CONJUNCTIONS

bene	plūrimum	inter		aut
deinde	prīmō			quod
facile	prīmum			
maximē				

779. Give the Latin of the following words :

because	fire	brave	favor
between, among	slavery	easy	authority
certain	wound (*verb*)	short	easily
sharp	lead to	difficult	most of all
very much	nothing	well	equal
or	swift	next	common
flight	unlike	leader	all, every
kindness	on foot	foot	heavy
wait for	light	compel, collect	similar
remain	first	liberty	of cavalry
learn, know	at first	law	space
body			

780. Review Questions. Into what three classes are adjectives of the third declension divided? How can you tell to which class an adjective belongs? Decline **equester, gravis,** and **pār.** What is meant by comparison of adjectives? Compare the adjectives **longus, fortis, celer, crēber, bonus, magnus, malus, multus, parvus, facilis, similis.** Decline **melior** and **plūs.** Define an adverb. Give an English sentence containing an adjective and an adverb. How are adverbs formed from adjectives of the first and second declensions? of the third declension? Form adverbs from **altus, integer, celer, levis,** and compare them. What case forms are sometimes used adverbially? Illustrate. Compare **bene, diū, magnopere, saepe.**

781. Give an example in Latin of a comparative followed by **quam**; of the ablative of measure of difference.

782. Derivation. Give fifteen English derivatives from the words in § 778.

X. REVIEW OF LESSONS LXXIII-LXXXI

783. Give the English of the following words:

NOUNS

Second Declension	*Third Declension*		*Fourth Declension*	
modus	aestās	hiems	nox	adventus	exercitus
	Caesar	imperātor	pars	cornū	impetus
	celeritās	lūx	pedes	domus	manus
	cīvis	mōns	rūs	equitātus	
	fīnis	nāvis	timor		

Fifth Declension

diēs	rēs	spēs

ADJECTIVES OF THE FIRST AND SECOND DECLENSIONS

alius, -a, -ud	nūllus, -a, -um	ūllus, -a, -um
alter, -a, -um	sinister, -tra, -trum	ūnus, -a, -um
dexter, -tra, -trum	sōlus, -a, -um	uter, -tra, -trum
neuter, -tra, -trum	tōtus, -a, -um	

VERBS

First Conjugation	Second Conjugation		Third Conjugation	
dēmōnstrō	commoveō	retineō	contendō	incolō
exīstimō	dēbeō	sustineō	dēpōnō	

PRONOUNS

aliquis	īdem	iste	suī
ego	ille	quīdam	tū
hic	ipse	quisque	

784. Give the Latin of the following words :

I	hope (*noun*)	a certain	home, house
inhabit	no	that (*of yours*)	right
someone	light	alarm (*verb*)	point out
this (*of mine*)	general	hold up	army
hasten, strive	thou, you	self	that (*yonder*)
any	each	whole, all	attack (*noun*)
one	lay down	another	think, regard
which (*of two*)	left	the other	end, territory
fear (*noun*)	alone	ship	hand
country	thing	night	citizen
foot soldier	hold back	neither	same
part (*noun*)	mountain	owe, ought	of himself
summer	manner	speed	day
winter	arrival	horn	Cæsar

785. Review Questions. What nouns belong to the fourth declension? What is their gender? Decline **manus** and **cornū**. What nouns belong to the fifth declension? What is their gender? Decline **diēs** and **rēs**. Give the ending of the genitive singular in each of the five declensions. Give the rules for gender in the third declension. Name the nine irregular adjectives and decline **nūllus**. Name the classes of pronouns. Decline **ego, tū,** and **suī**. Explain the use of **ipse** and decline it. How do **hic, iste,** and **ille** differ in meaning? Decline them. Define an indefinite pronoun. What general rule can you give for the declension of indefinites?

786. Give the rules for the expression of the place to which, in which, and from which. What important exception do these rules have? Give the

Latin for *at Rome, at home, in the country*. What are these forms called? Give a Latin sentence containing an ablative of time. Translate **aliī terram aliī mare amant** and **aliī aliam in partem fugiunt**.

787. Derivation. Give fifteen English derivatives from the words in § 783. What is the force of the prefixes **inter, per, prae**, and **sub**? Give Latin and English words having these prefixes.

XI. REVIEW OF LESSONS LXXXII–LXXXVIII

788. Give the English of the following words :

NOUNS

First Decl.	Third Decl.		Fourth Decl.	Fifth Decl.
causa	altitūdō	laus	multitūdō	passus	aciēs
hōra	dolor	magnitūdō	pōns	
	explōrātor	mīlia	potestās	

ADJECTIVES

First and Second Declensions				Third Declension
cupidus	idōneus	prīmus	sextus	mīlitāris
decimus	imperītus	quārtus	tertius	trēs
ducentī	nōnus	quīntus	ūndecimus	
duo	octāvus	secundus	ūnus	
duodecimus	perītus	septimus		

Indeclinable

centum	mīlle	octō	quīnque	sex
decem	novem	quattuor	septem	ūndecim
duodecim				

VERBS

First Conj.	Second Conj.	Third Conj.			
hortor	doceō	cōnficiō	expellō	patior	sequor
	permaneō	dēligō	īnstruō	praemittō	sūmō
	vereor	excēdō	intermittō	scrībō	trādūcō

PREPOSITION

apud

ADVERBS

interim   vērō

789. Give the Latin of the following words :

pace	eleventh	draw up	cause (*noun*)
line of battle	third	leave off	hour
military	sixth	suffer	desirous
three	power	send ahead	tenth
seven	bridge	drive out	two hundred
six	crowd	go out from	two
eleven	praise (*noun*)	choose	twelfth
meanwhile	size	complete	hundred
truly	thousand	twelve	ten
take up, assume	first	skilled	height
lead across	fourth	eighth	among
follow	fifth	ninth	urge
write	second	unskilled	teach
five	seventh	suitable	last (*verb*)
four	nine	scout	fear (*verb*)
one	eight	pain (*noun*)	

790. Review Questions. Give the first twelve cardinals and decline the first three. Give the first twelve ordinals. How are ordinals declined? Decline **milia.** Define a deponent verb. Give the synopsis of **hortor, vereor,** and **sequor** in the indicative and subjunctive. Give the four participles of **veniō** and explain the formation of each. What participles that are found in English are lacking in Latin? Decline **portāns,** present participle of **portō.** Give the four participles of **hortor.** What important fact can you state concerning the meaning of the past participle of deponent verbs?

791. Give the rule for each of the following constructions, and illustrate each by a Latin sentence :

Genitive of the whole	Genitive with adjectives
Ablative of respect	Genitive or ablative of description
Accusative of duration of time and extent of space	

Give the Latin for *a thousand soldiers, ten thousand soldiers, five of the soldiers.* Translate " While the Helvetii were going forth from their boundaries, Cæsar was hastening from Rome," using the ablative absolute for the first clause.

792. Derivation. Give fifteen English words related to the Latin words in § 788. Define them and illustrate each by an English sentence. How can you generally tell whether a word should end in *-ant* or *-ent?* What can you say about the formation and meaning of Latin nouns like **victor, rēctor,** etc., and their appearance in English?

XII. REVIEW OF LESSONS LXXXIX-XCVI

793. Give the Latin of the following words:

NOUNS

Third Declension

condiciō	difficultās	mēns	ōrātiō	turris
cōnsuētūdō	iūs	nēmō	ratiō	vulnus

Fourth Declension   *Fifth Declension*

senātus   rēs pūblica

ADJECTIVES

First and Second Declensions   *Third Declension*

frūmentārius   summus   tantus   nōbilis   tālis

VERBS

First Conj.	*Second Conj.*	*Third Conj.*		*Fourth Conj.*
appropinquō	permoveō	āmittō	interclūdō	conveniō
imperō	prōvideō	coniciō	perdūcō	impediō
postulō		cōnscrībō	praeficiō	perveniō
rogō		cōnsistō	premō	
temptō		cōnsulō	prōpōnō	
		incendō	quaerō	

Irregular

dēsum   praesum

PREPOSITION   ADVERBS

propter   dīligenter   quidem

794. Give the Latin of the following words :

draw near	condition	mind (*noun*)	hurl
command	custom	no one	wound (*noun*)
move deeply	of grain	consult	seek
look out for	highest	set on fire	senate
enroll	so great	cut off	commonwealth
stand still	well-known	lead through	assemble
press hard	such	set over	hinder
set forth	difficulty	speech	arrive
be lacking	right (*noun*)	method	demand (*verb*)
on account of	be before *or* over	tower	ask
carefully	indeed	lose	try

795. Review Questions. Name the three moods and the tenses of the indicative and subjunctive. Inflect in full the indicative and subjunctive of **vāstō, moveō, agō, rapiō,** and **mūniō.** Inflect the indicative and subjunctive of **sum** and **possum.** How may the past and past perfect active subjunctive of any verb be formed?

796. Name the primary and secondary tenses, and give the rule for the sequence of tenses. In what expressions is the indicative used? In what the subjunctive? How is purpose often expressed in English? How is it usually expressed in Latin? Give an example of each. What is a noun clause? Give the rule for noun clauses of purpose, and illustrate by an example. Name five verbs that are regularly followed by ut or nē and the subjunctive. Give the rule for the subjunctive of result, and illustrate by an example. Translate " Many things caused the slave to fear," and explain the construction of the dependent clause. Give the rule for the dative with compounds, and illustrate by an example.

797. Derivation. Give ten English words related to the Latin words in § 793. Define them and illustrate each by an English sentence.

XIII. REVIEW OF LESSONS XCVII–CIII

798. Give the English of the following words :

circummūniō	genus	negō	ostendō	sciō
enim	intellegō	nōlō	pertineō	sentiō
eō	iūdicō	oportet	recipiō	spērō
ferō	mālō	ōrdō	satis	volō
fidēs				

799. Give the Latin of the following words :

kind (*noun*)	perceive	for	faith
be unwilling	be necessary	deny	reach, pertain
sufficient	know	prefer	take back
wish (*verb*)	feel	bear	judge
fortify around	rank	hope (*verb*)	go

800. Give the Latin of the following idioms :

To make war upon   To remember   To be eager for a revolution
To be annoyed   For the future   To give satisfaction

801. Inflect the verbs eō, ferō, mālō, nōlō, volō.

802. Review Questions. What constructions are used after volō, nōlō, and mālō? Give the rule for the constructions with cum. Write sentences illustrating (*a*) cum = *when*, (*b*) cum = *since*, (*c*) cum = *although*. What is an indirect statement? How are indirect statements introduced in English? What can you say about the mood and tense of the English verb in an indirect statement? What are the three marked differences between an English and a Latin indirect statement? What kind of verbs are followed by indirect statements? Give an English indirect statement and translate it into Latin. What is an indirect question? Give an example of an English indirect question and translate it into Latin.

803. Derivation. Give ten English words related to the Latin words in § 798. Define them and illustrate each by an English sentence. How are abstract nouns formed from adjectives? Illustrate. Explain the meaning and formation of cupidus. What is the force of the suffix -ōsus? of the suffixes -ilis, -bilis? What rule can you give for the spelling of English words ending in -*able* or -*ible*? in -*tion* or -*sion*?

SUMMARY OF RULES OF SYNTAX

FIRST HALF YEAR

Agreement

1. The verb agrees with its subject in person and number (§ 48).
2. A predicate noun agrees with the subject in case (§ 61).
3. An appositive agrees in case with the noun which it explains (§ 104).
4. Adjectives agree with their nouns in gender, number, and case (§ 91).
5. The relative agrees with its antecedent in gender and number, but its case is determined by its use in its own clause (§ 390).

Nominative Case

6. The subject of a finite verb is in the nominative (§ 33).

Genitive Case

7. The word denoting the owner or possessor of something is in the genitive (§ 34).
8. The possessive genitive often stands in the predicate and is connected with its noun by a form of the verb **sum** (§ 150).

Dative Case

9. The indirect object of a verb is in the dative (§ 58).
10. The dative of the indirect object is used with the intransitive verbs **crēdō, faveō, noceō, pāreō, persuādeō, resistō, studeō**, and others of like meaning (§ 224).
11. The dative is used with adjectives to denote the object toward which the given quality is directed. Such are those meaning *near*, also *fit, friendly, pleasing, like*, and their opposites (§ 130).

Accusative Case

12. The direct object of a transitive verb is in the accusative (§ 35).
13. The subject of the infinitive is in the accusative (§ 368).

321

Ablative Case

14. *Cause* is denoted by the ablative, usually without a preposition (§ 165).
15. *Means* is denoted by the ablative without a preposition (§ 166).
16. *Accompaniment* is denoted by the ablative with **cum** (§ 167).
17. *Manner* is denoted by the ablative with **cum. Cum** may be omitted if an adjective is used with the ablative (§ 168).
18. The place from which is expressed by the ablative with the prepositions **ā (ab), dē, ē (ex)** (§ 295).
19. Words expressing separation or taking away are followed by the ablative, often with the prepositions **ā (ab), dē, ē (ex)** (§ 296).
20. The ablative with the preposition **ā** or **ab** is used with passive verbs to indicate the person by whom the act is performed (§ 261).
21. The ablative of a noun and a participle, a noun and an adjective, or two nouns may be used in the absolute construction to denote attendant circumstances (§ 400).

Infinitive used as in English

22. The verbs **iubeō**, *command*; **cupiō**, *wish*; **vetō**, *forbid*, and the like are often followed by an infinitive clause as object (§ 367).
23. Verbs of incomplete predication are often followed by an infinitive (§ 369).

SECOND HALF YEAR

Genitive Case

1. A genitive denoting the whole is used with words denoting a part, and is known as the genitive of the whole, or the partitive genitive (§ 541).
2. The adjectives **cupidus**, *desirous*; **perītus**, *skilled*; **imperītus**, *ignorant*, and others of similar character are followed by the objective genitive (§ 554).
3. The genitive or the ablative, with a modifying adjective, is used in expressions of quality or description (§ 562).

Dative Case

4. Some verbs compounded with **ad, ante, con, dē, in, inter, ob, post, prae, prō, sub**, and **super** take the dative of the indirect object (§ 623).
5. The dative is used to denote the purpose or end for which, often with another dative denoting the person or thing affected (§ 686).

Accusative Case

6. The place to which is expressed by **ad** or **in** with the accusative (§ 481).
7. Duration of time and extent of space are expressed by the accusative (§ 547).
8. Verbs of *making, choosing, calling*, and the like may take a predicate accusative along with the direct object. With the passive voice the two accusatives become nominatives (§ 684).

Ablative Case

9. With comparatives and words implying comparison the ablative is used to denote the measure of difference (§ 452).
10. The place from which is expressed by **ā** or **ab, dē, ē** or **ex**, with the ablative (§ 482; cf. § 295).
11. The place at or in which is expressed by the ablative with **in** (§ 483).
12. The time when or within which anything happens is expressed by the ablative without a preposition (§ 493).
13. The ablative is used to denote in what respect something is true (§ 552).

Moods and Tenses of Verbs

14. In a complex sentence a primary tense of the indicative in the principal clause is followed by a primary tense of the subjunctive in the dependent clause, and a secondary by a secondary (§ 595).
15. A clause expressing purpose takes the subjunctive (§ 588).
16. Verbs denoting a purpose or desire that something be done are followed by a subjunctive clause as object, introduced by **ut** or **nē** (§ 602).
17. Clauses of result are introduced by **ut** (negative **ut nōn**) and have the verb in the subjunctive (§ 616).
18. Object clauses of result introduced by **ut** (negative **ut nōn**) are found after verbs of effecting or bringing about (§ 618).
19. **Cum** means *when, since*, or *although*, and takes the subjunctive except in a temporal or descriptive clause of present or future time (§ 643).

Moods and Tenses of Verbs (Continued)

20. When a direct statement becomes indirect, the principal verb is changed to the infinitive and its subject nominative becomes subject accusative of the infinitive (§ 654).

21. A present indicative of a direct statement becomes present infinitive of the indirect, a past indicative becomes perfect infinitive, and a future indicative becomes future infinitive (§ 656).

22. The accusative-with-infinitive construction in indirect statements is found after verbs of *saying, telling, knowing, thinking,* and *perceiving* (§ 657).

23. In an indirect question the verb is in the subjunctive, and its tense is determined by the rule for the sequence of tenses (§ 671).

ROMAN MOSAIC

GRAMMATICAL APPENDIX

DECLENSION OF NOUNS

804. Nouns are inflected in five declensions, distinguished by the termination of the genitive singular.

805.   **FIRST DECLENSION**

aqua (base **aqu-**), *water*

	SINGULAR			PLURAL	
Nom.	aqua	-a		aquae	-ae
Gen.	aquae	-ae		aquārum	-ārum
Dat.	aquae	-ae		aquīs	-īs
Acc.	aquam	-am		aquās	-ās
Abl.	aquā	-ā		aquīs	-īs

a. **Dea** and **filia** have the termination **-ābus** in the dative and ablative plural.

806.   **SECOND DECLENSION**

a. MASCULINES IN **-us**

servus (base **serv-**), *slave*

Nom.	servus	-us		servī	-ī
Gen.	servī	-ī		servōrum	-ōrum
Dat.	servō	-ō		servīs	-īs
Acc.	servum	-um		servōs	-ōs
Abl.	servō	-ō		servīs	-īs

1. Nouns in **-us** of the second declension have the termination **-e** in the vocative singular: as, **serve**.

2. Proper names in **-ius**, and **filius**, end in **-ī** in the vocative singular, and the accent rests on the penult: as, **Vergi'lī, fīlī.**

325

b. Neuters in -um

oppidum (base oppid-), *town*

Nom.	oppidum	-um	oppida	-a
Gen.	oppidī	-ī	oppidōrum	-ōrum
Dat.	oppidō	-ō	oppidīs	-īs
Acc.	oppidum	-um	oppida	-a
Abl.	oppidō	-ō	oppidīs	-īs

1. Masculines in -ius and neuters in -ium end in -ī in the genitive singular, *not* in -iī, and the accent rests on the penult.

c. Masculines in -er and -ir

puer (base puer-), *boy*; ager (base agr-), *field*; vir (base vir-), *man*

Nom.	puer	ager	vir	—
Gen.	puerī	agrī	virī	-ī
Dat.	puerō	agrō	virō	-ō
Acc.	puerum	agrum	virum	-um
Abl.	puerō	agrō	virō	-ō
Nom.	puerī	agrī	virī	-ī
Gen.	puerōrum	agrōrum	virōrum	-ōrum
Dat.	puerīs	agrīs	virīs	-īs
Acc.	puerōs	agrōs	virōs	-ōs
Abl.	puerīs	agrīs	virīs	-īs

THIRD DECLENSION

807. Nouns of the third declension are classified as consonant stems or i-stems.

808.   I. CONSONANT STEMS

a. Masculines and Feminines

cōnsul (base cōnsul-), M., *consul*; legiō (base legiōn-), F., *legion*; pater (base patr-), M., *father*

Nom.	cōnsul	legiō	pater	—
Gen.	cōnsulis	legiōnis	patris	-is
Dat.	cōnsulī	legiōnī	patrī	-ī
Acc.	cōnsulem	legiōnem	patrem	-em
Abl.	cōnsule	legiōne	patre	-e

Nom.	cōnsulēs	legiōnēs	patrēs	-ēs
Gen.	cōnsulum	legiōnum	patrum	-um
Dat.	cōnsulibus	legiōnibus	patribus	-ibus
Acc.	cōnsulēs	legiōnēs	patrēs	-ēs
Abl.	cōnsulibus	legiōnibus	patribus	-ibus

prīnceps (base prīncip-), M., *chief*; mīles (base mīlit-), M., *soldier*;
rēx (base rēg-), M., *king*

Nom.	prīnceps	mīles	rēx	-s
Gen.	prīncipis	mīlitis	rēgis	-is
Dat.	prīncipī	mīlitī	rēgī	-ī
Acc.	prīncipem	mīlitem	rēgem	-em
Abl.	prīncipe	mīlite	rēge	-e

Nom.	prīncipēs	mīlitēs	rēgēs	-ēs
Gen.	prīncipum	mīlitum	rēgum	-um
Dat.	prīncipibus	mīlitibus	rēgibus	-ibus
Acc.	prīncipēs	mīlitēs	rēgēs	-ēs
Abl.	prīncipibus	mīlitibus	rēgibus	-ibus

NOTE. For vowel and consonant changes in the nominative singular
cf. § 405. *a*.

b. NEUTERS

flūmen (base flūmin-), N., *river*; tempus (base tempor-), N., *time*;
caput (base capit-), N., *head*

Nom.	flūmen	tempus	caput	—
Gen.	flūminis	temporis	capitis	-is
Dat.	flūminī	temporī	capitī	-ī
Acc.	flūmen	tempus	caput	—
Abl.	flūmine	tempore	capite	-e

Nom.	flūmina	tempora	capita.	-a
Gen.	flūminum	temporum	capitum	-um
Dat.	flūminibus	temporibus	capitibus	-ibus
Acc.	flūmina	tempora	capita	-a
Abl.	flūminibus	temporibus	capitibus	-ibus

809.　　　　　　　　II. *I*-STEMS

a. MASCULINES AND FEMININES

caedēs (base **caed-**), F., *slaughter*; hostis (base **host-**), M., *enemy*; **urbs**
(base **urb-**), F., *city*; cliēns (base **client-**), M., *retainer*

NOM.	caedēs	hostis	urbs	cliēns	-s, -is, *or* -ēs
GEN.	caedis	hostis	urbis	clientis	-is
DAT.	caedī	hostī	urbī	clientī	-ī
ACC.	caedem	hostem	urbem	clientem	-em (-im)
ABL.	caede	hoste	urbe	cliente	-e (-ī)
NOM.	caedēs	hostēs	urbēs	clientēs	-ēs
GEN.	caedium	hostium	urbium	clientium	-ium
DAT.	caedibus	hostibus	urbibus	clientibus	-ibus
ACC.	caedīs, -ēs	hostīs, -ēs	urbīs, -ēs	clientīs, -ēs	-īs, -ēs
ABL.	caedibus	hostibus	urbibus	clientibus	-ibus

b. NEUTERS

mare (base **mar-**), N., *sea*; animal (base **animāl-**), N., *animal*;
calcar (base **calcār-**), N., *spur*

NOM.	mare	animal	calcar	— *or* -e
GEN.	maris	animālis	calcāris	-is
DAT.	marī	animālī	calcārī	-ī
ACC.	mare	animal	calcar	— *or* -e
ABL.	marī	animālī	calcārī	-ī
NOM.	maria	animālia	calcāria	-ia
GEN.	——	animālium	calcārium	-ium
DAT.	maribus	animālibus	calcāribus	-ibus
ACC.	maria	animālia	calcāria	-ia
ABL.	maribus	animālibus	calcāribus	-ibus

810.　　　　　　FOURTH DECLENSION

adventus (base **advent-**), M., *arrival*; cornū (base **corn-**), N., *horn*

			MASC.	NEUT.
NOM.	adventus	cornū	-us	-ū
GEN.	adventūs	cornūs	-ūs	-ūs
DAT.	adventuī (-ū)	cornū	-uī (-ū)	-ū
ACC.	adventum	cornū	-um	-ū
ABL.	adventū	cornū	-ū	-ū

Nom.	adventūs	cornua	-ūs	-ua
Gen.	adventuum	cornuum	-uum	-uum
Dat.	adventibus	cornibus	-ibus	-ibus
Acc.	adventūs	cornua	-ūs	-ua
Abl.	adventibus	cornibus	-ibus	-ibus

811.   FIFTH DECLENSION

diēs (base di-), M., *day*; rēs (base r-), F., *thing*

Nom.	diēs	rēs	-ēs
Gen.	diēī	reī	-ĕī
Dat.	diēī	reī	-ĕī
Acc.	diem	rem	-em
Abl.	diē	rē	-ē

Nom.	diēs	rēs	-ēs
Gen.	diērum	rērum	-ērum
Dat.	diēbus	rēbus	-ēbus
Acc.	diēs	rēs	-ēs
Abl.	diēbus	rēbus	-ēbus

812.   CONSPECTUS OF THE FIVE DECLENSIONS

	Decl. I	Decl. II	Decl. III	Decl. IV	Decl. V
Nom.	aqua	servus	prīnceps	adventus	diēs
Gen.	aquae	servī	prīncipis	adventūs	diēī
Dat.	aquae	servō	prīncipī	adventuī (-ū)	diēī
Acc.	aquam	servum	prīncipem	adventum	diem
Abl.	aquā	servō	prīncipe	adventū	diē

Nom.	aquae	servī	prīncipēs	adventūs	diēs
Gen.	aquārum	servōrum	principum	adventuum	diērum
Dat.	aquīs	servīs	prīncipibus	adventibus	diēbus
Acc.	aquās	servōs	prīncipēs	adventūs	diēs
Abl.	aquīs	servīs	prīncipibus	adventibus	diēbus

813. **SPECIAL PARADIGMS**

homō, M., *man*; domus, F., *house*; vīs, F., *strength*; iter, N., *way*

Nom.	homō	domus	vīs	iter
Gen.	hominis	domūs (loc. domī)	vīs (rare)	itineris
Dat.	hominī	domuī, -ō	vī (rare)	itinerī
Acc.	hominem	domum	vim	iter
Abl.	homine	domō, -ū	vī	itinere
Nom.	hominēs	domūs	vīrēs	itinera
Gen.	hominum	domuum, -ōrum	vīrium	itinerum
Dat.	hominibus	domibus	vīribus	itineribus
Acc.	hominēs	domōs, -ūs	vīrīs, -ēs	itinera
Abl.	hominibus	domibus	vīribus	itineribus

DECLENSION OF ADJECTIVES

814. **FIRST AND SECOND DECLENSIONS**

bonus (base bon-), *good*

	Masc.	Fem.	Neut.	Masc.	Fem.	Neut.
Nom.	bonus	bona	bonum	bonī	bonae	bona
Gen.	bonī	bonae	bonī	bonōrum	bonārum	bonōrum
Dat.	bonō	bonae	bonō	bonīs	bonīs	bonīs
Acc.	bonum	bonam	bonum	bonōs	bonās	bona
Abl.	bonō	bonā	bonō	bonīs	bonīs	bonīs

liber (base līber-), *free*

Nom.	līber	lībera	līberum	līberī	līberae	lībera
Gen.	līberī	līberae	līberī	līberōrum	līberārum	līberōrum
Dat.	līberō	līberae	līberō	līberīs	līberīs	līberīs
Acc.	līberum	līberam	līberum	līberōs	līberās	lībera
Abl.	līberō	līberā	līberō	līberīs	līberīs	līberīs

pulcher (base pulchr-), *pretty*

Nom.	pulcher	pulchra	pulchrum	pulchrī	pulchrae	pulchra
Gen.	pulchrī	pulchrae	pulchrī	pulchrōrum	pulchrārum	pulchrōrum
Dat.	pulchrō	pulchrae	pulchrō	pulchrīs	pulchrīs	pulchrīs
Acc.	pulchrum	pulchram	pulchrum	pulchrōs	pulchrās	pulchra
Abl.	pulchrō	pulchrā	pulchrō	pulchrīs	pulchrīs	pulchrīs

815.   **IRREGULAR ADJECTIVES**

alius (base ali-), *another*

	MASC.	FEM.	NEUT.	MASC.	FEM.	NEUT.
NOM.	alius	alia	aliud	aliī	aliae	alia
GEN.	alīus	alīus	alīus	aliōrum	aliārum	aliōrum
DAT.	aliī	aliī	aliī	aliīs	aliīs	aliīs
ACC.	alium	aliam	aliud	aliōs	aliās	alia
ABL.	aliō	aliā	aliō	aliīs	aliīs	aliīs

ūnus (base ūn-), *one, only*

	MASC.	FEM.	NEUT.	MASC.	FEM.	NEUT.
NOM.	ūnus	ūna	ūnum	ūnī	ūnae	ūna
GEN.	ūnīus	ūnīus	ūnīus	ūnōrum	unārum	ūnōrum
DAT.	ūnī	ūnī	ūnī	ūnīs	ūnīs	ūnīs
ACC.	ūnum	ūnam	ūnum	ūnōs	ūnās	ūna
ABL.	ūnō	ūnā	ūnō	ūnīs	ūnīs	ūnīs

816. ADJECTIVES OF THE THIRD DECLENSION, *I*-STEMS

ācer, ācris, ācre (base ācr-), *keen, eager*

	MASC.	FEM.	NEUT.	MASC.	FEM.	NEUT.
NOM.	ācer	ācris	ācre	ācrēs	ācrēs	ācria
GEN.	ācris	ācris	ācris	ācrium	ācrium	ācrium
DAT.	ācrī	ācrī	ācrī	ācribus	ācribus	ācribus
ACC.	ācrem	ācrem	ācre	ācrīs, -ēs	ācrīs, -ēs	ācria
ABL.	ācrī	ācrī	ācrī	ācribus	ācribus	ācribus

omnis, omne (base omn-), *every, all*

	MASC. AND FEM.	NEUT.	MASC. AND FEM.	NEUT.
NOM.	omnis	omne	omnēs	omnia
GEN.	omnis	omnis	omnium	omnium
DAT.	omnī	omnī	omnibus	omnibus
ACC.	omnem	omne	omnīs, -ēs	omnia
ABL.	omnī	omnī	omnibus	omnibus

pār (base **par-**), *equal*

Nom.	pār	pār	parēs	paria
Gen.	paris	paris	parium	parium
Dat.	parī	parī	paribus	paribus
Acc.	parem	pār	parīs, -ēs	paria
Abl.	parī	parī	paribus	paribus

817.   PRESENT ACTIVE PARTICIPLES

vocāns (base **vocant-**), *calling*

	Masc. and Fem.	Neut.	Masc. and Fem.	Neut.
Nom.	vocāns	vocāns	vocantēs	vocantia
Gen.	vocantis	vocantis	vocantium	vocantium
Dat.	vocantī	vocantī	vocantibus	vocantibus
Acc.	vocantem	vocāns	vocantīs, -ēs	vocantia
Abl.	vocante, -ī	vocante, -ī	vocantibus	vocantibus

iēns (base **ient-, eunt-**), *going*

Nom.	iēns	iēns	euntēs	euntia
Gen.	euntis	euntis	euntium	euntium
Dat.	euntī	euntī	euntibus	euntibus
Acc.	euntem	iēns	euntīs, -ēs	euntia
Abl.	eunte, -ī	eunte, -ī	euntibus	euntibus

818.   REGULAR COMPARISON OF ADJECTIVES

POSITIVE	COMPARATIVE		SUPERLATIVE		
Masc.	Masc. and Fem.	Neut.	Masc.	Fem.	Neut.
clārus, *clear*	clārior	clārius	clārissimus	-a	-um
brevis, *short*	brevior	brevius	brevissimus	-a	-um
vēlōx, *swift*	vēlōcior	vēlōcius	vēlōcissimus	-a	-um
ācer, *sharp*	ācrior	ācrius	ācerrimus	-a	-um
pulcher, *pretty*	pulchrior	pulchrius	pulcherrimus	-a	-um
līber, *free*	līberior	līberius	līberrimus	-a	-um

819.   DECLENSION OF COMPARATIVES

clārior, *clearer*

	MASC. AND FEM.	NEUT.	MASC. AND FEM.	NEUT.
NOM.	clārior	clārius	clāriōrēs	clāriōra
GEN.	clāriōris	clāriōris	clāriōrum	clāriōrum
DAT.	clāriōrī	clāriōrī	clāriōribus	clāriōribus
ACC.	clāriōrem	clārius	clāriōrēs	clāriōra
ABL.	clāriōre	clāriōre	clāriōribus	clāriōribus

plūs, *more*

NOM.	——	plūs	plūrēs	plūra
GEN.	——	plūris	plūrium	plūrium
DAT.	——	——	plūribus	plūribus
ACC.	——	plūs	plūrīs, -ēs	plūra
ABL.	——	plūre	plūribus	plūribus

820.   IRREGULAR COMPARISON OF ADJECTIVES

POSITIVE	COMPARATIVE	SUPERLATIVE
bonus, -a, -um, *good*	melior, melius, *better*	optimus, -a, -um, *best*
magnus, -a, -um, *great*	maior, maius, *greater*	maximus, -a, -um, *greatest*
malus, -a, -um, *bad*	peior, peius, *worse*	pessimus, -a, -um, *worst*
multus, -a, -um, *much*	——, plūs, *more*	plūrimus, -a, -um, *most*
parvus, -a, -um, *small*	minor, minus, *smaller*	minimus, -a, -um, *smallest*
facilis, -e, *easy*	facilior, *easier*	facillimus, *easiest*
difficilis, -e, *hard*	difficilior, *harder*	difficillimus, *hardest*
similis, -e, *like*	similior, *more like*	simillimus, *most like*
dissimilis, -e, *unlike*	dissimilior, *more unlike*	dissimillimus, *most unlike*
inferus, -a, -um, *below*	īnferior, *lower*	{ infimus / imus } *lowest*
superus, -a, -um, *above*	superior, *higher*	{ suprēmus / summus } *highest*
	prior, *former*	prīmus, *first*
	propior, *nearer*	proximus, *next*
	ulterior, *farther*	ultimus, *farthest*
	interior, *inner*	intimus, *inmost*
	citerior, *hither*	citimus, *hithermost*

821.   REGULAR COMPARISON OF ADVERBS

POSITIVE	COMPARATIVE	SUPERLATIVE
cārē, *dearly*	cārius	cārissimē
pulchrē, *beautifully*	pulchrius	pulcherrimē
līberē, *freely*	līberius	līberrimē
ācriter, *sharply*	ācrius	ācerrimē
similiter, *similarly*	similius	simillimē

822.   IRREGULAR COMPARISON OF ADVERBS

POSITIVE	COMPARATIVE	SUPERLATIVE
bene, *well*	melius, *better*	optimē, *best*
diū, *long, a long time*	diūtius, *longer*	diūtissimē, *longest*
magnopere, *greatly*	magis, *more*	maximē, *most*
parum, *little*	minus, *less*	minimē, *least*
prope, *nearly, near*	propius, *nearer*	proximē, *nearest*
saepe, *often*	saepius, *oftener*	saepissimē, *oftenest*

NUMERAL ADJECTIVES

823. The cardinal numerals are indeclinable, except **ūnus, duo, trēs,** the hundreds above one hundred, and **mīlle** used as. a noun. The ordinals are declined like **bonus, -a, -um.**

CARDINALS (*How many*)		ORDINALS (*In what order*)	
1, ūnus, -a, -um	*one*	prīmus, -a, -um	*first*
2, duo, duae, duo	*two*	secundus (*or* alter)	*second*
3, trēs, tria	*three*	tertius	*third*
4, quattuor	etc.	quārtus	etc.
5, quīnque		quīntus	
6, sex		sextus	
7, septem		septimus	
8, octō		octāvus	
9, novem		nōnus	
10, decem		decimus	
11, ūndecim		ūndecimus	
12, duodecim		duodecimus	
13, tredecim (decem (et) trēs)		tertius decimus	
14, quattuordecim		quārtus decimus	

15, quīndecim	quīntus decimus
16, sēdecim	sextus decimus
17, septendecim	septimus decimus
18, duodēvīgintī	duodēvīcēnsimus
19, ūndēvīgintī	ūndēvīcēnsimus
20, vīgintī	vīcēnsimus *or* vīcēsimus
21, { vīgintī ūnus *or* { ūnus et vīgintī, etc.	{ vīcēnsimus prīmus *or* { ūnus et vīcēnsimus, etc.
30, trīgintā	trīcēnsimus
40, quadrāgintā	quadrāgēnsimus
50, quīnquāgintā	quīnquāgēnsimus
60, sexāgintā	sexāgēnsimus
70, septuāgintā	septuāgēnsimus
80, octōgintā	octōgēnsimus
90, nōnāgintā	nōnāgēnsimus
100, centum	centēnsimus
101, centum (et) ūnus, etc.	centēnsimus (et) prīmus, etc.
200, ducentī, -ae, -a	ducentēnsimus
300, trecentī	trecentēnsimus
400, quadringentī	quadringentēnsimus
500, quīngentī	quīngentēnsimus
600, sescentī	sescentēnsimus
700, septingentī	septingentēnsimus
800, octingentī	octingentēnsimus
900, nōngentī	nōngentēnsimus
1000, mīlle	mīllēnsimus

824. Declension of **duo**, *two*; **trēs**, *three*; and **mille**, *thousand*.

	MASC.	FEM.	NEUT.	M. AND F.	NEUT.	SING.	PLUR.
NOM.	duo	duae	duo	trēs	tria	mīlle	mīlia
GEN.	duōrum	duārum	duōrum	trium	trium	mīlle	mīlium
DAT.	duōbus	duābus	duōbus	tribus	tribus	mīlle	mīlibus
ACC.	duōs *or* duo	duās	duo	trīs *or* trēs	tria	mīlle	mīlia
ABL.	duōbus	duābus	duōbus	tribus	tribus	mīlle	mīlibus

NOTE. **Mīlle** is used in the plural as a noun with a modifying genitive, and is occasionally so used in the nominative and accusative singular. For the declension of **ūnus** cf. § 534.

DECLENSION OF PRONOUNS

825.   **PERSONAL**

	ego, *I*		tū, *you*		suī, *of himself*, etc.	
NOM.	ego	nōs	tū	vōs	——	——
GEN.	meī	nostrum, -trī	tuī	vestrum, -trī	suī	suī
DAT.	mihi	nōbīs	tibi	vōbīs	sibi	sibi
ACC.	mē	nōs	tē	vōs	sē, sēsē	sē, sēsē
ABL.	mē	nōbīs	tē	vōbīs	sē, sēsē	sē, sēsē

826.   **POSSESSIVE**

MASC.	FEM.	NEUT.	
meus	mea	meum	*my, mine*
tuus	tua	tuum	*your, yours*
suus	sua	suum	*his* (own), *her* (own), *its* (own)
noster	nostra	nostrum	*our, ours*
vester	vestra	vestrum	*your, yours*
suus	sua	suum	*their* (own), *theirs*

NOTE. The vocative singular masculine of **meus** is **mī**.

827.   **INTENSIVE**

ipse, *self*

	MASC.	FEM.	NEUT.	MASC.	FEM.	NEUT.
NOM.	ipse	ipsa	ipsum	ipsī	ipsae	ipsa
GEN.	ipsī′us	ipsī′us	ipsī′us	ipsōrum	ipsārum	ipsōrum
DAT.	ipsī	ipsī	ipsī	ipsīs	ipsīs	ipsīs
ACC.	ipsum	ipsam	ipsum	ipsōs	ipsās	ipsa
ABL.	ipsō	ipsā	ipsō	ipsīs	ipsīs	ipsīs

828.   DEMONSTRATIVE

hic, *this* (here), *he*

	MASC.	FEM.	NEUT.	MASC.	FEM.	NEUT.
NOM.	hic	haec	hoc	hī	hae	haec
GEN.	huius	huius	huius	hōrum	hārum	hōrum
DAT.	huic	huic	huic	hīs	hīs	hīs
ACC.	hunc	hanc	hoc	hōs	hās	haec
ABL.	hōc	hāc	hōc	hīs	hīs	hīs

iste, *this, that* (of yours), *he*

NOM.	iste	ista	istud	istī	istae	ista
GEN.	istī′us	istī′us	istī′us	istōrum	istārum	istōrum
DAT.	istī	istī	istī	istīs	istīs	istīs
ACC.	istum	istam	istud	istōs	istās	ista
ABL.	istō	istā	istō	istīs	istīs	istīs

ille, *that* (yonder), *he*

NOM.	ille	illa	illud	illī	illae	illa
GEN.	illī′us	illī′us	illī′us	illōrum	illārum	illōrum
DAT.	illī	illī	illī	illīs	illīs	illīs
ACC.	illum	illam	illud	illōs	illās	illa
ABL.	illō	illā	illō	illīs	illīs	illīs

is, *this, that, he*

NOM.	is	ea	id	iī, eī	eae	ea
GEN.	eius	eius	eius	eōrum	eārum	eōrum
DAT.	eī	eī	eī	iīs, eīs	iīs, eīs	iīs, eīs
ACC.	eum	eam	id	eōs	eās	ea
ABL.	eō	eā	eō	iīs, eīs	iīs, eīs	iīs, eīs

īdem, *the same*

NOM.	īdem	e′adem	idem	{ iī′dem ei′dem	eae′dem	e′adem
GEN.	eius′dem	eius′dem	eius′dem	eōrun′dem	eārun′dem	eōrun′dem
DAT.	eī′dem	eī′dem	eī′dem	{ iīs′dem eīs′dem	iīs′dem eīs′dem	iīs′dem eīs′dem
ACC.	eun′dem	ean′dem	idem	eōs′dem	eās′dem	e′adem
ABL.	eō′dem	eā′dem	eō′dem	{ iīs′dem eīs′dem	iīs′dem eīs′dem	iīs′dem eīs′dem

829.   **RELATIVE**

quī, *who, which, that*

	Masc.	Fem.	Neut.	Masc.	Fem.	Neut.
Nom.	quī	quae	quod	quī	quae	quae
Gen.	cuius	cuius	cuius	quōrum	quārum	quōrum
Dat.	cui	cui	cui	quibus	quibus	quibus
Acc.	quem	quam	quod	quōs	quās	quae
Abl.	quō	quā	quō	quibus	quibus	quibus

830.   **INTERROGATIVE**

quis, substantive, *who, what*

	Masc. and Fem.	Neut.	Masc.	Fem.	Neut.
Nom.	quis	quid	quī	quae	quae
Gen.	cuius	cuius	quōrum	quārum	quōrum
Dat.	cui	cui	quibus	quibus	quibus
Acc.	quem	quid	quōs	quās	quae
Abl.	quō	quō	quibus	quibus	quibus

The interrogative adjective **quī, quae, quod,** is declined like the relative.

INDEFINITE

831. Quis and quī, as declined above,[1] are used also as indefinites (*some, any*). The other indefinites are compounds of quis and quī.

quisque, *each*

	SUBSTANTIVE		ADJECTIVE		
	Masc. and Fem.	Neut.	Masc.	Fem.	Neut.
Nom.	quisque	quidque	quisque	quaeque	quodque
Gen.	cuius'que	cuius'que	cuius'que	cuius'que	cuius'que
Dat.	cuique	cuique	cuique	cuique	cuique
Acc.	quemque	quidque	quemque	quamque	quodque
Abl.	quōque	quōque	quōque	quāque	quōque

[1] **Qua** is generally used instead of **quae** in the feminine nominative singular and in the neuter nominative and accusative plural.

quīdam, *a certain one, a certain*

	MASC.	FEM.	NEUT.
NOM.	quīdam	quaedam	{ quoddam quiddam (*subst.*)
GEN.	cuius′dam	cuius′dam	cuius′dam
DAT.	cuidam	cuidam	cuidam
ACC.	quendam	quandam	{ quoddam quiddam (*subst.*)
ABL.	quōdam	quādam	quōdam
NOM.	quīdam	quaedam	quaedam
GEN.	quōrun′dam	quārun′dam	quōrun′dam
DAT.	quibus′dam	quibus′dam	quibus′dam
ACC.	quōsdam	quāsdam	quaedam
ABL.	quibus′dam	quibus′dam	quibus′dam

aliquis, substantive, *someone, something*; **aliquī,** adjective, *some*

	SUBSTANTIVE		ADJECTIVE		
	MASC. AND FEM.	NEUT.	MASC.	FEM.	NEUT.
NOM.	aliquis	aliquid	aliquī	aliqua	aliquod
GEN.	alicu′ius	alicu′ius	alicu′ius	alicu′ius	alicu′ius
DAT.	alicui	alicui	alicui	alicui	alicui
ACC.	aliquem	aliquid	aliquem	aliquam	aliquod
ABL.	aliquō	aliquō	aliquō	aliquā	aliquō

	MASC.	FEM.	NEUT.
NOM.	aliquī	aliquae	aliqua
GEN.	aliquō′rum	aliquā′rum	aliquō′rum
DAT.	ali′quibus	ali′quibus	ali′quibus
ACC.	aliquōs	aliquās	aliqua
ABL.	ali′quibus	ali′quibus	ali′quibus

CONJUGATION OF REGULAR VERBS

832. FIRST CONJUGATION. Ā-VERBS. *VOCŌ, I CALL*

PRINCIPAL PARTS: **vocō, vocāre, vocāvī, vocātus**

Pres. stem **vocā-**; perf. stem **vocāv-**; part. stem **vocāt-**

ACTIVE		PASSIVE	
	INDICATIVE		
	PRESENT		
I call, am calling, do call, etc.		*I am called*, etc.	
vocō	vocāmus	vocor	vocāmur
vocās	vocātis	vocāris, -re	vocāminī
vocat	vocant	vocātur	vocantur
	PAST		
I called, was calling, did call, etc.		*I was called*, etc.	
vocābam	vocābāmus	vocābar	vocābāmur
vocābās	vocābātis	vocābāris, -re	vocābāminī
vocābat	vocābant	vocābātur	vocābantur
	FUTURE		
I shall call, etc.		*I shall be called*, etc.	
vocābō	vocābimus	vocābor	vocābimur
vocābis	vocābitis	vocāberis, -re	vocābiminī
vocābit	vocābunt	vocābitur	vocābuntur
	PERFECT		
I have called, called, did call, etc.		*I have been (was) called*, etc.	
vocāvī	vocāvimus		
vocāvistī	vocāvistis	vocātus, sum es est	vocātī, sumus estis sunt
vocāvit	vocāvērunt, -re	-a, -um	-ae, -a
	PAST PERFECT		
I had called, etc.		*I had been called*, etc.	
vocāveram	vocāverāmus		
vocāverās	vocāverātis	vocātus, eram erās erat	vocātī, erāmus erātis erant
vocāverat	vocāverant	-a, -um	-ae, -a
	FUTURE PERFECT		
I shall have called, etc.		*I shall have been called*, etc.	
vocāverō	vocāverimus		
vocāveris	vocāveritis	vocātus, erō eris erit	vocātī, erimus eritis erunt
vocāverit	vocāverint	-a, -um	-ae, -a

SUBJUNCTIVE
PRESENT

vocem	vocēmus	vocer	vocēmur
vocēs	vocētis	vocēris, -re	vocēminī
vocet	vocent	vocētur	vocentur

PAST

vocārem	vocārēmus	vocārer	vocārēmur
vocārēs	vocārētis	vocārēris, -re	vocārēminī
vocāret	vocārent	vocārētur	vocārentur

PERFECT

vocāverim	vocāverimus	vocātus, { sim	vocātī, { sīmus
vocāveris	vocāveritis	-a, -um { sīs	-ae, -a { sītis
vocāverit	vocāverint	{ sit	{ sint

PAST PERFECT

vocāvissem	vocāvissēmus	vocātus, { essem	vocātī, { essēmus
vocāvissēs	vocāvissētis	-a, -um { essēs	-ae, -a { essētis
vocāvisset	vocāvissent	{ esset	{ essent

IMPERATIVE
PRESENT

vocā, *call thou*	vocāre, *be thou called*
vocāte, *call ye*	vocāminī, *be ye called*

FUTURE

vocātō, *thou shalt call*	vocātor, *thou shalt be called*
vocātō, *he shall call*	vocātor, *he shall be called*
vocātōte, *you shall call*	———
vocantō, *they shall call*	vocantor, *they shall be called*

INFINITIVE

PRES. vocāre, *to call* — vocārī, *to be called* [*called*
PERF. vocāvisse, *to have called* — vocātus, -a, -um esse, *to have been*
FUT. vocātūrus, -a, -um esse, *to be* — [vocātum īrī, *to be about to be*
about to call — *called*]

PARTICIPLES

PRES. vocāns, -antis, *calling* — PRES. ———
FUT. vocātūrus, -a, -um, *about to* — GERUNDIVE [1] vocandus, -a, -um, *to*
call — *be called*
PERF. ——— — PERF. vocātus, -a, -um, *having been called*

GERUND

NOM. ———
GEN. vocandī, *of calling*
DAT. vocandō, *for calling*
ACC. vocandum, *calling*
ABL. vocandō, *by calling*

SUPINE (ACTIVE VOICE)

ACC. vocātum, *to call*
ABL. vocātū, *to call, in the calling*

[1] Sometimes called the future passive participle.

833. SECOND CONJUGATION. *Ē*-VERBS. *MONEŌ, I ADVISE*

PRINCIPAL PARTS: **moneō, monēre, monuī, monitus**

Pres. stem **monē-**; perf. stem **monu-**; part. stem **monit-**

ACTIVE	PASSIVE

INDICATIVE

PRESENT

I advise, etc.		*I am advised*, etc.	
moneō	monēmus	moneor	monēmur
monēs	monētis	monēris, -re	monēminī
monet	monent	monētur	monentur

PAST

I was advising, etc.		*I was advised*, etc.	
monēbam	monēbāmus	monēbar	monēbāmur
monēbās	monēbātis	monēbāris, -re	monēbāminī
monēbat	monēbant	monēbātur	monēbantur

FUTURE

I shall advise, etc.		*I shall be advised*, etc.	
monēbō	monēbimus	monēbor	monēbimur
monēbis	monēbitis	monēberis, -re	monēbiminī
monēbit	monēbunt	monēbitur	monēbuntur

PERFECT

I have advised, I advised, etc.		*I have been (was) advised*, etc.			
monuī	monuimus	monitus, -a, -um	{ sum / es / est	monitī, -ae, -a	{ sumus / estis / sunt
monuistī	monuistis				
monuit	monuērunt, -re				

PAST PERFECT

I had advised, etc.		*I had been advised*, etc.			
monueram	monuerāmus	monitus, -a, -um	{ eram / erās / erat	monitī, -ae, -a	{ erāmus / erātis / erant
monuerās	monuerātis				
monuerat	monuerant				

FUTURE PERFECT

I shall have advised, etc.		*I shall have been advised*, etc.			
monuerō	monuerimus	monitus, -a, -um	{ erō / eris / erit	monitī, -ae, -a	{ erimus / eritis / erunt
monueris	monueritis				
monuerit	monuerint				

SUBJUNCTIVE

PRESENT

moneam	moneāmus	monear	moneāmur
moneās	moneātis	moneāris, -re	moneāminī
moneat	moneant	moneātur	moneantur

PAST

monērem	monērēmus	monērer	monērēmur
monērēs	monērētis	monērēris, -re	monērēminī
monēret	monērent	monērētur	monērentur

PERFECT

monuerim	monuerimus	monitus, { sim	monitī, { sīmus
monueris	monueritis	-a, -um { sīs	-ae, -a { sītis
monuerit	monuerint	{ sit	{ sint

PAST PERFECT

monuissem	monuissēmus	monitus, { essem	monitī, { essēmus
monuissēs	monuissētis	-a, -um { essēs	-ae, -a { essētis
monuisset	monuissent	{ esset	{ essent

IMPERATIVE

PRESENT

monē, *advise thou*   monēre, *be thou advised*
monēte, *advise ye*   monēminī, *be ye advised*

FUTURE

[monētō, *thou shalt advise*   monētor, *thou shalt be advised*]
[monētō, *he shall advise*   monētor, *he shall be advised*]
[monētōte, *you shall advise*   ———]
[monentō, *they shall advise*   monentor, *they shall be advised*]

INFINITIVE

PRES. monēre, *to advise*   monērī, *to be advised*
PERF. monuisse, *to have advised* monitus, -a, -um esse, *to have been advised*
FUT. monitūrus, -a, -um esse, *to be about to advise*   [monitum īrī, *to be about to be advised*]

PARTICIPLES

PRES. monēns, -entis, *advising*   PRES. ———
FUT. monitūrus, -a, -um, *about to advise*   GER. monendus, -a, -um, *to be advised*
PERF. ———   PERF. monitus, -a, -um, *having been advised, advised*

GERUND

NOM. ———
GEN. monendī, *of advising*
DAT. monendō, *for advising*
ACC. monendum, *advising*
ABL. monendō, *by advising*

[SUPINE (ACTIVE VOICE)]
[ACC. monitum, *to advise*]
[ABL. monitū, *to advise, in the advising*]

834. THIRD CONJUGATION. Ĕ-VERBS. *REGŌ, I RULE*

PRINCIPAL PARTS: regō, regere, rēxī, rēctus

Pres. stem rege-; perf. stem rēx-; part. stem rēct-

ACTIVE		PASSIVE	
		INDICATIVE	

PRESENT

I rule, etc.		*I am ruled*, etc.	
regō	regimus	regor	regimur
regis	regitis	regeris, -re	regiminī
regit	regunt	regitur	reguntur

PAST

I was ruling, etc.		*I was ruled*, etc.	
regēbam	regēbāmus	regēbar	regēbāmur
regēbās	regēbātis	regēbāris, -re	regebāminī
regēbat	regēbant	regēbātur	regēbantur

FUTURE

I shall rule, etc.		*I shall be ruled*, etc.	
regam	regēmus	regar	regēmur
regēs	regētis	regēris, -re	regēminī
reget	regent	regētur	regentur

PERFECT

I have ruled, etc.		*I have been ruled*, etc.	
rēxī	rēximus	rēctus, -a, -um { sum / es / est }	rēctī, -ae, -a { sumus / estis / sunt }
rēxistī	rēxistis		
rēxit	rēxērunt, -re		

PAST PERFECT

I had ruled, etc.		*I had been ruled*, etc.	
rēxeram	rēxerāmus	rēctus, -a, -um { eram / erās / erat }	rēctī, -ae, -a { erāmus / erātis / erant }
rēxerās	rēxerātis		
rēxerat	rēxerant		

FUTURE PERFECT

I shall have ruled, etc.		*I shall have been ruled*, etc.	
rēxerō	rēxerimus	rēctus, -a, -um { erō / eris / erit }	rēctī, -ae, -a { erimus / eritis / erunt }
rēxeris	rēxeritis		
rēxerit	rēxerint		

SUBJUNCTIVE
PRESENT

regam	regāmus	regar	regāmur
regās	regātis	regāris, -re	regāminī
regat	regant	regātur	regantur

PAST

regerem	regerēmus	regerer	regerēmur
regerēs	regerētis	regerēris, -re	regerēminī
regeret	regerent	regerētur	regerentur

PERFECT

rēxerim	rēxerimus	rēctus, -a, -um { sim / sīs / sit }	rēctī, -ae, -a { sīmus / sītis / sint }
rēxeris	rēxeritis		
rēxerit	rēxerint		

PAST PERFECT

rēxissem	rēxissēmus	rēctus, -a, -um { essem / essēs / esset }	rectī, -ae, -a { essēmus / essētis / essent }
rēxissēs	rēxissētis		
rēxisset	rēxissent		

IMPERATIVE
PRESENT

rege, *rule thou*	regere, *be thou ruled*
regite, *rule ye*	regiminī, *be ye ruled*

FUTURE

regitō, *thou shalt rule*	regitor, *thou shalt be ruled*
regitō, *he shall rule*	regitor, *he shall be ruled*
regitōte, *ye shall rule*	———
reguntō, *they shall rule*	reguntor, *they shall be ruled*

INFINITIVE

PRES.	regere, *to rule*	regī, *to be ruled*
PERF.	rēxisse, *to have ruled*	rēctus, -a, -um esse, *to have been ruled*
FUT.	rēctūrus, -a, -um esse, *to be about to rule*	[rēctum īrī, *to be about to be ruled*]

PARTICIPLES

PRES.	regēns, -entis, *ruling*	PRES.	———
FUT.	rēctūrus, -a, -um, *about to rule*	GER.	regendus, -a, -um, *to be ruled*
PERF.	———	PERF.	rēctus, -a, -um, *having been ruled, ruled*

GERUND

NOM.	———
GEN.	regendī, *of ruling*
DAT.	regendō, *for ruling*
ACC.	regendum, *ruling*
ABL.	regendō, *by ruling*

SUPINE (ACTIVE VOICE)

ACC.	rēctum, *to rule*
ABL.	rēctū, *to rule, in the ruling*

835. FOURTH CONJUGATION. *Ī-VERBS. AUDIŌ,* *I HEAR*

PRINCIPAL PARTS : **audiō, audīre, audīvī, audītus**

Pres. stem **audī-** ; perf. stem **audīv-** ; part. stem **audīt-**

ACTIVE   PASSIVE

INDICATIVE

PRESENT

I hear, etc.   *I am heard*, etc.

audiō	audīmus	audior	audīmur
audīs	audītis	audīris, -re	audīminī
audit	audiunt	audītur	audiuntur

PAST

I was hearing, etc.   *I was heard*, etc.

audiēbam	audiēbāmus	audiēbar	audiēbāmur
audiēbās	audiēbātis	audiēbāris, -re	audiēbāminī
audiēbat	audiēbant	audiēbātur	audiēbantur

FUTURE

I shall hear, etc.   *I shall be heard*, etc.

audiam	audiēmus	audiar	audiēmur
audiēs	audiētis	audiēris, -re	audiēminī
audiet	audient	audiētur	audientur

PERFECT

I have heard, etc.   *I have been heard*, etc.

audīvī	audīvimus	audītus, -a, -um ⎰sum / es / est⎱	audītī, -ae, -a ⎰sumus / estis / sunt⎱
audīvistī	audīvistis		
audīvit	audīvērunt, -re		

PAST PERFECT

I had heard, etc.   *I had been heard*, etc.

audīveram	audīverāmus	audītus, -a, -um ⎰eram / erās / erat⎱	audītī, -ae, -a ⎰erāmus / erātis / erant⎱
audīverās	audīverātis		
audīverat	audīverant		

FUTURE PERFECT

I shall have heard, etc.   *I shall have been heard*, etc.

audīverō	audīverimus	audītus, -a, -um ⎰erō / eris / erit⎱	audītī, -ae, -a ⎰erimus / eritis / erunt⎱
audīveris	audīveritis		
audīverit	audīverint		

SUBJUNCTIVE
PRESENT

audiam	audiāmus	audiar	audiāmur
audiās	audiātis	audiāris, -re	audiāminī
audiat	audiant	audiātur	audiantur

PAST

audīrem	audīrēmus	audīrer	audīrēmur
audīrēs	audīrētis	audīrēris, -re	audīrēminī
audīret	audīrent	audīrētur	audīrentur

PERFECT

audīverim	audīverimus	audītus, -a, -um { sim, sīs, sit	audītī, -ae, -a { sīmus, sītis, sint
audīveris	audīveritis		
audīverit	audīverint		

PAST PERFECT

audīvissem	audīvissēmus	audītus, -a, -um { essem, essēs, esset	audītī, -ae, -a { essēmus, essētis, essent
audīvissēs	audīvissētis		
audīvisset	audīvissent		

IMPERATIVE
PRESENT

audī, *hear thou*   audīre, *be thou heard*
audīte, *hear ye*   audīminī, *be ye heard*

FUTURE

⌈ audītō, *thou shalt hear*   audītor, *thou shalt be heard* ⌉
| audītō, *he shall hear*   audītor, *he shall be heard* |
| audītōte, *ye shall hear*   ————— |
⌊ audiuntō, *they shall hear*   audiuntor, *they shall be heard* ⌋

INFINITIVE

PRES. audīre, *to hear*   audīrī, *to be heard*
PERF. audīvisse, *to have heard*   audītus, -a, -um esse, *to have been heard*

FUT. audītūrus, -a, -um esse, *to be about to hear*   [audītum īrī, *to be about to be heard*]

PARTICIPLES

PRES. audiēns, -entis, *hearing*   PRES. —————
FUT. audītūrus, -a, -um, *about to hear*   GER. audiendus, -a, -um, *to be heard*
PERF. —————   PERF. audītus, -a, -um, *having been heard, heard*

GERUND

NOM. —————
GEN. audiendī, *of hearing*
DAT. audiendō, *for hearing*
ACC. audiendum, *hearing*
ABL. audiendō, *by hearing*

⌈ SUPINE (ACTIVE VOICE) ⌉
| ACC. audītum, *to hear* |
⌊ ABL. audītū, *to hear, in the hearing* ⌋

836. THIRD CONJUGATION. VERBS IN –_ĪŌ_. _CAPĪŌ, I TAKE_

PRINCIPAL PARTS: capiō, capere, cēpī, captus

Pres. stem cape–; perf. stem cēp–; part. stem capt–

ACTIVE		PASSIVE	

INDICATIVE

PRESENT

capiō	capimus	capior	capimur
capis	capitis	caperis, -re	capiminī
capit	capiunt	capitur	capiuntur

PAST

capiēbam	capiēbāmus	capiēbar	capiēbāmur
capiēbās	capiēbātis	capiēbāris, -re	capiēbāminī
capiēbat	capiēbant	capiēbātur	capiēbantur

FUTURE

capiam	capiēmus	capiar	capiēmur
capiēs	capiētis	capiēris, -re	capiēminī
capiet	capient	capiētur	capientur

PERFECT

cēpī	cēpimus	captus,	sum	captī,	sumus
cēpistī	cēpistis	-a, -um	es	-ae, -a	estis
cēpit	cēpērunt, -re		est		sunt

PAST PERFECT

cēperam	cēperāmus	captus,	eram	captī,	erāmus
cēperās	cēperātis	-a, -um	erās	-ae, -a	erātis
cēperat	cēperant		erat		erant

FUTURE PERFECT

cēperō	cēperimus	captus,	erō	captī,	erimus
cēperis	cēperitis	-a, -um	eris	-ae, -a	eritis
cēperit	cēperint		erit		erunt

SUBJUNCTIVE

PRESENT

capiam	capiāmus	capiar	capiāmur
capiās	capiātis	capiāris, -re	capiāminī
capiat	capiant	capiātur	capiantur

PAST

caperem	caperēmus	caperer	caperēmur
caperēs	caperētis	caperēris, -re	caperēminī
caperet	caperent	caperētur	caperentur

PERFECT

cēperim	cēperimus	captus, -a, -um $\begin{cases} sim \\ sīs \\ sit \end{cases}$	captī, -ae, -a $\begin{cases} sīmus \\ sītis \\ sint \end{cases}$
cēperis	cēperitis		
cēperit	cēperint		

PAST PERFECT

cēpissem	cēpissēmus	captus, -a, -um $\begin{cases} essem \\ essēs \\ esset \end{cases}$	captī, -ae, -a $\begin{cases} essēmus \\ essētis \\ essent \end{cases}$
cēpissēs	cēpissētis		
cēpisset	cēpissent		

IMPERATIVE

PRESENT

2D PERS.	cape	capite	capere	capiminī

FUTURE

2D PERS.	capitō	capitōte	capitor	———
3D PERS.	capitō	capiuntō	capitor	capiuntor

INFINITIVE

PRES.	capere	capī
PERF.	cēpisse	captus, -a, -um esse
FUT.	captūrus, -a, -um esse	[captum īrī]

PARTICIPLES

PRES.	capiēns, -entis		PRES.	———
FUT.	captūrus, -a, -um		GER.	capiendus, -a, -um
PERF.	———		PERF.	captus, -a, -um

GERUND

NOM.	———
GEN.	capiendī
DAT.	capiendō
ACC.	capiendum
ABL.	capiendō

SUPINE (ACTIVE VOICE)

ACC.	captum
ABL.	captū

837.   **DEPONENT VERBS**

PRINCIPAL
PARTS

I. hortor, hortārī, hortātus sum, *urge*
II. vereor, verērī, veritus sum, *fear*
III. { sequor, sequī, secūtus sum, *follow*
      { patior, patī, passus sum (-iō verb), *suffer*
IV. partior, partīrī, partītus sum, *share, divide*

NOTE. In addition to the passive conjugation, deponent verbs use certain forms from the active. These are marked with a star.

INDICATIVE

PRES.	hortor	vereor	sequor	patior	partior
	hortāris, -re	verēris, -re	sequeris, -re	pateris, -re	partīris, -re
	hortātur	verētur	sequitur	patitur	partītur
	hortāmur	verēmur	sequimur	patimur	partīmur
	hortāminī	verēminī	sequiminī	patiminī	partīminī
	hortantur	verentur	sequuntur	patiuntur	partiuntur
PAST	hortābar	verēbar	sequēbar	patiēbar	partiēbar
FUT.	hortābor	verēbor	sequar	patiar	partiar
PERF.	hortātus	veritus	secūtus	passus	partītus
	sum	sum	sum	sum	sum
P. PERF.	hortātus	veritus	secūtus	passus	partītus
	eram	eram	eram	eram	eram
F. PERF.	hortātus erō	veritus erō	secūtus erō	passus erō	partītus erō

SUBJUNCTIVE

PRES.	horter	verear	sequar	patiar	partiar
PAST	hortārer	verērer	sequerer	paterer	partīrer
PERF.	hortātus sim	veritus sim	secūtus sim	passus sim	partītus sim
P. PERF.	hortātus	veritus	secūtus	passus	partītus
	essem	essem	essem	essem	essem

IMPERATIVE

PRES.	hortāre	verēre	sequere	patere	partīre
[FUT.	hortātor	verētor	sequitor	patitor	partītor]

INFINITIVE

PRES.	hortārī	verērī	sequī	patī	partīrī
PERF.	hortātus	veritus	secūtus	passus esse	partītus
	esse	esse	esse		esse
FUT.	*hortātūrus	*veritūrus	*secūtūrus	*passūrus	*partītūrus
	esse	esse	esse	esse	esse

PARTICIPLES

PRES.	*hortāns	*verēns	*sequēns	*patiēns	*partiēns
FUT.	*hortātūrus	*veritūrus	*secūtūrus	*passūrus	*partītūrus
PERF.	hortātus	veritus	secūtus	passus	partītus
GER.	hortandus	verendus	sequendus	patiendus	partiendus

GERUND

*hortandī	*verendī	*sequendī	*patiendī	*partiendī
etc.	etc.	etc.	etc.	etc.

SUPINE

[*hortātum	*veritum	*secūtum	*passum	*partītum]
[*hortātū	*veritū	*secūtū	*passū	*partītū]

CONJUGATION OF IRREGULAR VERBS

838. **sum,** *am,* *be*

PRINCIPAL PARTS: **sum, esse, fuī, futūrus**

Pres. stem **es-**; perf. stem **fu-**; part. stem **fut-**

INDICATIVE

PRESENT

sum, *I am*	sumus, *we are*
es, *thou art*	estis, *you are*
est, *he (she, it) is*	sunt, *they are*

PAST

eram, *I was*	erāmus, *we were*
erās, *thou wast*	erātis, *you were*
erat, *he was*	erant, *they were*

FUTURE

erō, *I shall be*	erimus, *we shall be*
eris, *thou wilt be*	eritis, *you will be*
erit, *he will be*	erunt, *they will be*

PERFECT

fuī, *I have been, was*	fuimus, *we have been, were*
fuistī, *thou hast been, wast*	fuistis, *you have been, were*
fuit, *he has been, was*	fuērunt fuēre } *they have been, were*

PAST PERFECT

fueram, *I had been*	fuerāmus, *we had been*
fuerās, *thou hadst been*	fuerātis, *you had been*
fuerat, *he had been*	fuerant, *they had been*

FUTURE PERFECT

fuerō, *I shall have been*	fuerimus, *we shall have been*
fueris, *thou wilt have been*	fueritis, *you will have been*
fuerit, *he will have been*	fuerint, *they will have been*

SUBJUNCTIVE

PRESENT

sim	sīmus
sīs	sītis
sit	sint

PAST

essem	essēmus
essēs	essētis
esset	essent

PERFECT

fuerim	fuerimus
fueris	fueritis
fuerit	fuerint

PAST PERFECT

fuissem	fuissēmus
fuissēs	fuissētis
fuisset	fuissent

IMPERATIVE

PRESENT

2D PERS. SING. es, *be thou*
2D PERS. PLUR. este, *be ye*

FUTURE

⎡2D PERS. SING. estō, *thou shalt be*⎤
| 3D PERS. SING. estō, *he shall be* |
| 2D PERS. PLUR. estōte, *ye shall be* |
⎣3D PERS. PLUR. suntō, *they shall be*⎦

INFINITIVE

PRES. esse, *to be*
PERF. fuisse, *to have been*
FUT. futūrus, -a, -um esse or fore,
 to be about to be

PARTICIPLE

futūrus, -a, -um, *about to be*

839. **possum,** *be able,* *can*

PRINCIPAL PARTS : **possum, posse, potui,** ——

INDICATIVE		SUBJUNCTIVE	
PRES.	possum pos'sumus	possim póssĭ'mus
	potes potes'tis	possīs possĭ'tis
	potest possunt	possit possint
PAST	poteram poterāmus	possem possē'mus
FUT.	poterō poterimus	—— ——
PERF.	potuī potuimus	potuerim potuerimus
P. PERF.	potueram potuerāmus	potuissem potuissēmus
F. PERF.	potuerō potuerimus	—— ——

INFINITIVE

PRES.· pcsse PERF. potuisse

PARTICIPLE

PRES. potēns, -entis (adjective), *powerful*

840. PRINCIPAL PARTS

{ **volō, velle, voluī,** ——, *be willing, will, wish*
  nōlō, nōlle, nōluī, ——, *be unwilling, will not*
  mālō, mālle, māluī, ——, *be more willing, prefer* }

Nōlō and **mālō** are compounds of **volō**. **Nōlō** is for **ne** (*not*) + **volō**, and **mālō** for **mā** (from **magis,** *more*) + **volō**.

INDICATIVE

PRES.	volō	nōlō	mālō
	vīs	nōn vīs	māvīs
	vult	nōn vult	māvult
	volumus	nōlumus	mālumus
	vultis	nōn vultis	māvul'tis
	volunt	nōlunt	mālunt
PAST	volēbam	nōlēbam	mālēbam
FUT.	volam, volēs, etc.	nōlam, nōlēs, etc.	mālam, mālēs, etc.
PERF.	voluī	nōluī	māluī
P. PERF.	volueram	nōlueram	mālueram
F. PERF.	voluerō	nōluerō	māluerō

SUBJUNCTIVE

PRES.	velim	nōlim	mālim
	velīs	nōlīs	mālīs
	velit	nōlit	mālit
	velī′mus	nōlī′mus	mālī′mus
	velī′tis	nōlī′tis	mālī′tis
	velint	nōlint	mālint
PAST	vellem	nōllem	māllem
PERF.	voluerim	nōluerim	māluerim
P. PERF.	voluissem	nōluissem	māluissem

IMPERATIVE

PRES.	——	2D PERS. SING.	nōlī	——
		2D PERS. PLUR.	nōlīte	——
[FUT.	——	2D PERS. SING.	nōlītō, etc.	——]

INFINITIVE

PRES.	velle	nōlle	mālle
PERF.	voluisse	nōluisse	māluisse

PARTICIPLE

PRES.	volēns, -entis	nōlēns, -entis

841.   **ferō,** *bear, carry,* **endure**

PRINCIPAL PARTS : **ferō, ferre, tulī, lātus**

Pres. stem **fer-** ; perf. stem **tul-** ; part. stem **lāt-**

INDICATIVE

	ACTIVE		PASSIVE	
PRES.	ferō	ferimus	feror	ferimur
	fers	fertis	ferris, -re	feriminī
	fert	ferunt	fertur	feruntur
PAST	ferēbam		ferēbar	
FUT.	feram, ferēs, etc.		ferar, ferēris, etc.	
PERF.	tulī		lātus, -a, -um sum	
P. PERF.	tuleram		lātus, -a, -um eram	
F. PERF.	tulerō		lātus, -a, -um erō	

SUBJUNCTIVE

PRES.	feram, ferās, etc.		ferar, ferāris, etc.
PAST	ferrem		ferrer
PERF.	tulerim		lātus, -a, -um sim
P. PERF.	tulissem		lātus, -a, -um essem

IMPERATIVE

PRES. 2D PERS.	fer	ferte	ferre	feriminī
⌈ FUT. 2D PERS.	fertō	fertōte	fertor	——— ⌉
⌊ 3D PERS.	fertō	feruntō	fertor	feruntor ⌋

INFINITIVE

PRES.	ferre		ferrī
PERF.	tulisse		lātus, -a, -um esse
FUT.	lātūrus, -a, -um esse		[lātum īrī]

PARTICIPLES

PRES.	ferēns, -entis		PRES.	———
FUT.	lātūrus, -a, -um		GER.	ferendus, -a, -um
PERF.	———		PERF.	lātus, -a, -um

GERUND				⌈SUPINE (ACTIVE VOICE)⌉
GEN.	ferendī	ACC.	ferendum	ACC. lātum
DAT.	ferendō	ABL.	ferendō	ABL. lātū

842. **eō**, *go*

PRINCIPAL PARTS : **eō, īre, iī (īvī), ītūrus** (fut. part.)

Pres. stem **ī-**; perf. stem **ī-** or **īv-**; part. stem **it-**

	INDICATIVE		SUBJUNCTIVE	IMPERATIVE		
PRES.	eō	īmus	eam	2D PERS. ī	īte
	īs	ītis			
	it	eunt			
PAST	ībam		īrem		
FUT.	ībō		———	⌈2D PERS. ītō	ītōte ⌉
				⌊3D PERS. ītō	euntō ⌋
PERF.	iī (īvī)		ierim (īverim)		
P. PERF.	ieram (īveram)		īssem (īvissem)		
F. PERF.	ierō (īverō)		———		

INFINITIVE			PARTICIPLES	
PRES.	īre		PRES.	iēns, euntis (§ 817)
PERF.	īsse (īvisse)		FUT.	itūrus, -a, -um
FUT.	itūrus, -a, -um esse		GER.	eundum

GERUND				SUPINE	
GEN.	eundī	ACC.	eundum	ACC.	itum
DAT.	eundō	ABL.	eundō	ABL.	itū

a. The verb **eō** is used impersonally in the third person singular of the passive : as, **ītur, itum est,** etc.

b. In the perfect system the forms with **v** are rare.

843. fīō (passive of **faciō**), *be made, become, happen*

PRINCIPAL PARTS : **fīō, fierī, factus sum**

INDICATIVE			SUBJUNCTIVE	IMPERATIVE		
PRES.	fīō	———	fīam	2D PERS.	fī	fīte
	fīs	———				
	fit	fīunt				
PAST	fīēbam		fierem			
FUT.	fīam		———			
PERF.	factus, -a, -um sum		factus, -a, -um sim			
P. PERF.	factus, -a, -um eram		factus, -a, -um essem			
F. PERF.	factus, -a, -um erō		———			

INFINITIVE		PARTICIPLES	
PRES.	fierī	PERF.	factus, -a, -um
PERF.	factus, -a, -um esse	GER.	faciendus, -a, -um
[FUT.	factum īrī]		

WORD LIST FOR FIRST HALF YEAR

Proper nouns and adjectives are omitted

VERBS

abdūcō	discēdō	iubeō	parō	respondeō
absum	dō	labōrō	pateō	sedeō
agō	dūcō	līberō	persuādeō	servō
amō	ēdūcō	locō	perterreō	spectō
appellō	ēvocō	mittō	petō	studeō
ascendō	expugnō	moneō	portō	sum
audiō	faciō	moveō	possum	superō
capiō	faveō	mūniō	prōcēdō	suscipiō
comparō	fugiō	nārrō	prōdūcō	teneō
cōnfīrmō	gerō	nāvigō	prohibeō	timeō
cōnservō	habeō	noceō	properō	vāstō
convocō	habitō	nūntiō	pugnō	veniō
crēdō	iaciō	obtineō	putō	vetō
cupiō	incipiō	occupō	rapiō	videō
dēfendō	indūcō	oppugnō	regō	vincō
dīcō	interficiō	pācō	remittō	vocō
dīmittō	inveniō	pāreō	resistō	

NOUNS

ager	arma	cōnsilium	fābula	fossa
agricola	auxilium	cōpia	factum	frūmentum
amīcitia	barbarus	dea	fāma	impedīmentum
amīcus	bellum	deus	fīlia	imperium
animus	captīvus	dīligentia	fīlius	iniūria
annus	casa	equus	fīnitimī	inopia
aqua	castrum	exemplum	fortūna	īnsula

357

iūdicium	nāvigium	perīculum	puer	terra
lēgātus	negōtium	poena	rēgīna	vāllum
liber	numerus	poēta	rēgnum	via
locus	officium	populus	sapientia	victōria
memoria	oppidum	praemium	servus	vīlla
mūrus	ōra	praesidium	silva	vir
nātūra	patria	proelium	socius	vīta
nauta	pecūnia	puella	tēlum	

PRONOUNS

is   ea   id   quī   quid   quis

ADJECTIVES

altus	fīnitimus	longus	nōtus	sacer
amīcus	firmus	magnus	novus	suus
amplus	grātus	malus	parvus	tardus
barbarus	inimīcus	medius	paucī	timidus
bonus	inīquus	meus	proximus	tuus
clārus	integer	miser	pūblicus	vērus
crēber	lātus	multus	pulcher	vester
ēgregius	līber	noster	reliquus	

ADVERBS

anteā	diū	longē	numquam	saepe
celeriter	fortiter	magnopere	nunc	semper
certē	iam	minimē	posteā	statim
cūr	ibi	mox	quam	tum
dēnique	ita	nōn	quō	ubi

CONJUNCTIONS

ac *or* atque	et	nam	nec ... nec	sed
cum	itaque	nec *or* neque	que	sī

PREPOSITIONS

ā *or* ab	ante	dē	in	post	sine
ad	cum	ē *or* ex	per	prō	trāns

WORD LIST FOR SECOND HALF YEAR

VERBS

accipiō	conveniō	impediō	pellō	redūcō
addūcō	dēbeō	imperō	perdūcō	relinquō
āmittō	dēiciō	incendō	permaneō	retineō
appropinquō	dēligō	incolō	permoveō	rogō
audeō	dēmōnstrō	īnferō	pertineō	sciō
circummūniō	dēpōnō	īnstruō	perveniō	scrībō
cognōscō	dēsum	intellegō	pōnō	sentiō
cōgō	dīcō	interclūdō	postulō	sequor
committō	doceō	intermittō	praeficiō	spērō
commoveō	eō	iūdicō	praemittō	sūmō
cōnficiō	excēdō	mālō	praesum	sustineō
coniciō	exīstimō	maneō	premō	temptō
cōnscrībō	expellō	negō	prōpōnō	trādūcō
cōnsistō	exspectō	nōlō	prōvideō	vereor
cōnsulō	ferō	oportet	quaerō	volō
contendō	fīō	ostendō	recipiō	vulnerō
contineō	hortor	patior	reddō	

NOUNS

aciēs	causa	difficultās	frāter	iter
adventus	celeritās	dolor	fuga	iūs
aestās	cīvis	domus	genus	laus
altitūdō	cīvitās	dux	grātia	legiō
animal	cohors	eques	hiems	lēx
auctōritās	condiciō	equitātus	homō	lībertās
beneficium	cōnsuētūdō	exercitus	hōra	lingua
caedēs	cōnsul	explōrātor	hostis	lūx
Caesar	cornū	fidēs	ignis	magnitūdō
calcar	corpus	fīnis	imperātor	manus
caput	diēs	flūmen	impetus	mare

359

māter	nāvis	pater	rēs frūmentāria	spatium
mātrimōnium	nēmō	pāx	rēs pūblica	spēs
mēns	nihil	pedes	rēx	tempus
mīles	nōmen	pēs	rūs	timor
modus	nox	pōns	salūs	turris
mōns	ōrātiō	potestās	senātus	urbs
mors	ōrdō	prīnceps	servitūs	virtūs
mulier	pars	ratiō	signum	vīs
multitūdō	passus	rēs	soror	vulnus

PRONOUNS

aliquis	hic	ille	is	quīdam	suī
ego	īdem	ipse	iste	quisque	tū

ADJECTIVES

ācer	dissimilis	levis	prīmus	sinister
aequus	ducentī	mīlitāris	quārtus	summus
brevis	duo	mīlle	quattuor	tālis
celer	duodecim	nōbilis	quīnque	tantus
centum	duodecimus	nōnus	quīntus	tertius
certus	equester	novem	satis	trēs
commūnis	facilis	octāvus	secundus	ūndecim
cupidus	fortis	octō	septem	ūndecimus
decem	frūmentārius	omnis	septimus	ūnus
decimus	gravis	pār	sex	
dexter	idōneus	pedester	sextus	
difficilis	imperītus	perītus	similis	

ADVERBS

bene	molestē
deinde	plūrimum
dīligenter	prīmō
etiam	prīmum
facile	quidem
interim	tam
maximē	vērō

CONJUNCTIONS

aut	nē
aut . . . aut	quam
autem	quod
enim	tamen
et . . . et	ut

PREPOSITIONS

apud
inter
propter

SPECIAL VOCABULARIES

The related English words that are given will often suggest others. Always try to add to them and so increase your English vocabulary. Latin is the key to the mastery of English. If the meaning of any of the related words is unknown to you, consult the English dictionary.

LESSON V, § 63

LATIN WORD	MEANING	RELATED WORDS
dat	he (she, it) gives, is giving	data, dative
est	he (she, it) is	essence, essential
fā′bula	story	fable, fabulous
nār′rat	he (she, it) tells	narrate, narrative
pecū′nia	money	pecuniary
sunt	they are	

LESSON VII, § 81

ā, ab, *prep. with abl.*	from	
ad, *prep. with acc.*	to, *expressing motion*	
a′qua	water	aquarium, aqueduct
cum, *prep. with abl.*	with	
in, *prep. with acc.*	into	
in, *prep. with abl.*	in, on	
nau′ta	sailor	nautical
per, *prep. with acc.*	through	
ter′ra	earth, land	terrace, terrestrial

LESSON VIII, § 94

NOTE. Learn the three essential facts about each Latin noun: its nominative, its genitive, and its gender. When reciting the vocabularies, give all three: as, "**aqua, aquae,** *feminine,* water."

bo′na	good, kind	bonus, bounty
ca′sa, -ae, *f.*	hut, cottage	
et	and	
ha′bitat	he (she, it) lives	habitation, inhabitant
par′va	small, little	
pul′chra	pretty, beautiful	pulchritude

361

LESSON IX, § 100

Latin Word	Meaning	Related Words
ami'cus, -ī, *m.*	friend	amicable, amiable
e'quus, -ī, *m.*	horse	equine
Mār'cus, -ī, *m.*	Marcus	Mark
quō, *interrog. adv. with verbs of motion*	whither	
ser'vus, -ī, *m.*	slave	servant, serf
u'bi, *interrog. adv. with verbs of rest*	where	

LESSON X, § 105

a'ger, a'grī, *m.*	field	acre, agrarian
labō'rat	he (she, it) toils	labor, laboratory
por'tat	he (she, it) carries	porter, portable
pu'er, pu'erī, *m.*	boy	puerile
quid, *interrog. pron.*	what	
quis, *interrog. pron.*	who	
vir, vi'rī, *m.*	man	virile, virtue

LESSON XI, § 113

ar'ma, -ō'rum, *n. plur.*	arms	armament
con'vocat	he (she, it) calls together	convoke, convocation
cūr, *interrog. adv.*	why	
nōn, *neg. adv.*	not	non- *in many compounds*: *as*, nonessential, nonsense
op'pidum, -ī, *n.*	town	
po'pulus, -ī, *m.*	people	population, popular

LESSON XII, § 118

auxi'lium, auxi'lī, *n.*	aid	auxiliary
bel'lum, -ī, *n.*	war	belligerent
fī'lius, fī'lī, *m.*	son	filial, affiliate
frūmen'tum, -ī, *n.*	grain	
mag'nus, -a, -um	great, large	magnitude, magnify
no'vus, -a, -um	new	novel, novelty
pa'rat	he (she, it) prepares	compare, repair
so'cius, so'cī, *m.*	ally, companion	society, associate

LESSON XIII, § 124

fā'ma, -ae, *f.*	rumor, report, reputation	fame, famous
lon'gus, -a, -um	long	longitude, prolong

LATIN WORD	MEANING	RELATED WORDS
mul'tus, -a, -um	much, many	multitude, multiply
nō'tus, -a, -um	known, well-known, famous	noted, notable
sae'pe, *adv.*	often	
tē'lum, -ī, *n.*	weapon, missile, spear	
vi'a, -ae, *f.*	way, road	via (by way of) *in time-tables, on guide-boards, etc.*

LESSON XIV, § 131

al'tus, -a, -um	high, deep, lofty	altitude, exalt
amī'cus, -a, -um	friendly	*See the noun* **amīcus**, Lesson IX
grā'tus, -a, -um	pleasing	grateful
inimī'cus, -a, -um	unfriendly, hostile	inimical, enemy
īn'sula, -ae, *f.*	island	insulate, peninsula
lī'ber, lī'bera, lī'berum	free	liberal, liberate
nā'vigat	he (she, it) sails	navigate, navigation
pro'ximus, -a, -um	nearest, very near	approximate, proximity
sed, *conj.*	but	

LESSON XVI, § 151

Gal'lia, -ae, *f.*	Gaul (modern France)	
Gal'lus, -ī, *m.*	a Gaul	
Germā'nus, -ī, *m.*	a German	
oc'cupat	he (she, it) seizes	occupy, occupation
pug'nat	he (she, it) fights	pugnacious, pugilist
sem'per, *adv.*	ever, always	
tum, *adv.*	then, at that time	
victō'ria, -ae, *f.*	victory	victor

LESSON XIX, § 172

cas'trum, -ī, *n.*	fort; *plur.* camp	*Appears as* -cester, -chester, *or* -caster *in names of English towns founded by the Romans:* Worcester, Winchester, Lancaster, etc.

Latin Word	Meaning	Related Words
cō'pia, -ae, f.	plenty, abundance; *plur.* forces	copious
crē'ber, -bra, -brum	thick, frequent, crowded	
dīligen'tia, -ae, f.	industry	diligence
Germā'nia, -ae, f.	Germany	
mox, *adv.*	soon, presently	
perī'culum, -ī, *n.*	danger	peril, perilous
Rōmā'nus, -a, -um	Roman. *As a noun in the masc. or fem.*, a Roman	

LESSON XX, § 181

amīci'tia, -ae, f.	friendship	amity. *See also* amīcus, Lesson IX
bar'barus, -a, -um	savage, uncivilized. *As a noun in the masc. or fem.*, a savage	barbarous, barbarian
Britan'nī, -ōrum, *m.*	the Britons	
Britan'nia, -ae, f.	Britain, England	
iam, *adv.*	already, immediately, presently, now	
i'taque, *conj.*	and so, therefore	
sil'va, -ae, f.	forest	silvan, Pennsylvania (Penn's Forest)

LESSON XXI, § 185

mi'ser, mi'sera, mi'serum	wretched	miserable, miser
ō'ra, -ae, f.	shore, coast	
prae'mium, prae'mī, *n.*	prize, reward	premium
proe'lium, proe'lī, *n.*	battle	
su'perō, -ā're	overcome, conquer	superable, insuperable

LESSON XXII, § 195

numquam, *adv.*	never	
nunc, *adv.*	now, the present time	
sine, *prep. with abl.*	without	sinecure

LESSON XXIV, § 206

cōnsi'lium, cōnsi'lī, *n.*	plan, advice	counsel
iniūria, -ae, f.	wrong	injury, injustice

SPECIAL VOCABULARIES 365

Latin Word	Meaning	Related Words
nūntiō, -ā're	announce	enunciate, pronunciation
servō, -ā're	save	preserve, conserve
vīta, -ae, *f.*	life	vital, vitality

LESSON XXV, § 210

clārus, -a, -um	clear, bright; famous	Clara
fīnitimī, -ōrum, *m. plur.*	neighbors	
fīnitimus, -a, -um	adjoining, neighboring	
lātus, -a, -um	wide, broad	latitude
mūrus, -ī, *m.*	wall	mural
patria, -ae, *f.*	native land	patriot, patriotism

LESSON XXVI, § 216

dē, *prep. with abl.*	down from, concerning	
dīcō, -ere	say, speak	diction, dictionary
dūcō, -ere	lead	conduct, aqueduct
Italia, -ae, *f.*	Italy	
liber, librī, *m.*	book	library, librarian
pateō, -ē're	lie open, extend, stretch	patent (*adj.*)
regō, -ere	rule	regulate, regal
Rōma, -ae, *f.*	Rome	

LESSON XXVII, § 221

audiō, -ī're	hear	audible, audience
fossa, -ae, *f.*	ditch	fosse, fossil
medius, -a, -um	middle, middle part of	medium, mediocre
mūniō, -ī're	fortify	munition, ammunition
quī, *rel. pron.*	who	
vāllum, -ī, *n.*	palisade, wall (*of a camp*)	
veniō, -ī're	come	advent, convention

LESSON XXIX, § 233

dea, -ae, *f.* (*dat. and abl. plur.* deābus)	goddess	deity, deify
deus, -ī, *m.*	god	
malus, -a, -um	evil, bad	malice, malicious, malefactor
numerus, -ī, *m.*	number	numerous, numerator
poēta, -ae, *m.*	poet	
sapientia, -ae, *f.*	wisdom	sapient

LESSON XXX, § 239

LATIN WORD	MEANING	RELATED WORDS
animus, -ī, *m.*	mind, spirit, heart	animate, unanimous
gerō, -ere	wage, carry on, wear	belligerent
indūcō, -ere	lead in *or* against	induce, inductive
mittō, -ere	send	mission, remit
poena, -ae, *f.*	punishment; **poenam dare,** suffer punishment, pay a penalty	penalty, penalize, subpœna

LESSON XXXI, § 244

capiō, -ere	take, seize	capture
cele′riter, *adv.*	quickly	celerity, accelerate
faciō, -ere	make, do, form; **proelium facere,** fight a battle	fact, affect, defect, effect, infect, perfect
posteā, *adv.*	thereafter, afterwards	
vincō, -ere	conquer	vanquish, invincible

LESSON XXXII, § 254

cum, *conj.*	when	
nāvi′gium, nāvi′gī, *n.*	boat	navigable
petō, -ere	seek, ask, beg, make for	petition, compete
respondeō, -ē′re	reply	respond, responsive

LESSON XXXIII, § 259

dēnique, *adv.*	at last, finally	
diū, *adv.*	a long time	
ēdūcō, -ere	lead out	educe
fortiter, *adv.*	bravely	fortitude
Graecia, -ae, *f.*	Greece	
nec *or* neque, *conj.*	and not, nor; **nec (neque) ... nec (neque),** neither ... nor	

LESSON XXXVI, § 275

captīvus, -ī, *m.*	captive	captivate
firmus, -a, -um	strong, trusty, loyal	firm
ibi, *adv.*	there, in that place	
praesi′dium, praesi′dī, *n.*	garrison, guard	

LESSON XXXVIII, § 283

LATIN WORD	MEANING	RELATED WORDS
certē, *adv.*	certainly, surely	certify
memoria, -ae, *f.*	memory	memorable
sedeō, -ē're	sit	sedentary
spectō, -ā're	look at	spectacle, spectator
tardus, -a, -um	slow, dull, stupid	tardy

LESSON XL, § 292

agō, -ere	drive, lead, do	agitate, act
factum, -ī, *n.*	deed, act	fact
nam, *conj.*	for	
oppugnō, -ā're	attack, assault	
rapiō, -ere	seize	rapture, rapacious

LESSON XLI, § 297

abdūcō, -ere	lead away	abduct
absum, abesse, *irreg. verb*	be away, be off	absent, absence
dīmittō, -ere	send away, let go	dismiss
discēdō, -ere	depart, go away	
līberō, -ā're	set free	liberate
locus, -ī, *m., plur.*	place, spot	local, locality
loca, -ō'rum, *n.*		
longē, *adv.*	far away, distant	
prohibeō, -ē're	hinder, prevent	prohibit

LESSON XLII, § 306

amplus, -a, -um	large, abundant; famous	ample
comparō, -ā're	get together, provide	compare
cōnfirmō, -ā're	strengthen, encourage	confirm
dēfendō, -ere	defend	defensive
locō, -ā're	put, set	locate, locative
quam, *adv.*	how	
timidus, -a, -um	fearful, cowardly	timid

LESSON XLIII, § 309

annus, -ī, *m.*	year	annual, perennial
ēgregius, -a, -um	remarkable, marvelous	egregious, congregate
exemplum, -ī, *n.*	example, specimen	exemplary
offi'cium, offi'cī, *n.*	duty, service	office
pācō, -ā're	subdue, pacify	pacific
vīlla, -ae, *f.*	farm, villa, countryseat	village

LESSON XLIV, § 320

Latin Word	Meaning	Related Words
in'teger, in'tegra, in'-tegrum	whole, fresh, pure	integer, integrity
lēgātus, -ī, *m.*	ambassador, lieutenant	legate
pūblicus, -a, -um	public, official	publicity
vērus, -a, -um	true, genuine	veracious, verity

LESSON XLV, § 324

ante, *prep. with acc.*	before	*In English compounds, as,* anteroom, antebellum
impe'rium, impe'rī, *n.*	command, supreme power, realm	empire, imperial
inveniō, -ī're	find, come upon	invent
minimē, *adv.*	not at all, least of all	minimum
nātūra, -ae, *f.*	nature	natural

LESSON XLIX, § 343

ascendō, -ere, ascendī, ascēnsus	climb	ascend, ascension, descend
expug'nō, -ā're, -ā'vī, -ā'tus	take by storm, capture; *distinguish from* oppugnō, assault	
fu'giō, -ere, fūgī, fugitū'rus	flee, run	fugitive, refuge
ia'ciō, ia'cere, iēcī, iactus	throw, hurl	inject, eject, *and many other compounds*
magno'pere, *adv.*	greatly	
perter'reō, -ē're, -uī, -itus	terrify, alarm	terror, terrible
sacer, sacra, sacrum	sacred	
vāstō,-ā're,-ā'vī,-ā'tus	lay waste	waste, devastate

LESSON LI, § 359

ac (*before cons.*), atque (*before either vowels or cons.*), *conj.*	and, and what is more	
anteā, *adv.*	heretofore, previously, formerly	

LATIN WORD	MEANING	RELATED WORDS
ē′vocō, -ā′re, -ā′vī, -ā′tus	call out, summon	evoke
fortūna, -ae, *f.*	fortune	
inī′quus, -a, -um	uneven, unequal, un-favorable	iniquity
post, *prep. with acc.*	after, behind.	postponᶒ, postscript
prō, *prep. with abl.*	for, in behalf of; *rarely*, in front of	procccd, procure
rēgnum, -ī, *n.*	realm, kingdom; sovereignty	interregnum, reign
Rhēnus, -ī, *m.*	the Rhine	
trāns, *prep. with acc.*	across	transport, transpose

LESSON LII, § 363

inopia, -ae, *f.*	want, need, scarcity	
interfi′ciō, -ere, -fē′cī, -fec′tus	put out of the way, kill	
negō′tium, negō′tī, *n.*	business, affair, matter	negotiate
obti′neō, -ē′re, -uī, -ten′tus	possess, keep, gain	obtain
prōcē′dō, -ere, -ces′sī, -cessū′rus	go forward, advance	proceed
prōdū′cō, -ere, -dū′xī, -duc′tus	lead forward	produce
susci′piō, -ere, -cē′pī, -cep′tus	undertake, assume	

LESSON LIII, § 371

cu′piō, -ere, -ī′vī, -ī′tus	wish, desire	cupidity
inci′piō, -ere, -cē′pī, -cep′tus	begin	incipient, inceptive
iu′beō, -ē′re, iussī, iussus	command	
possum, posse, po′tuī	be able, can	pussible, poᴏᴏᴏ, potent
vetō, -ā′re, -uī, -itus	forbid	veto

LESSON LIV, § 379

appel′lō, -ā′re, -ā′vī, -ā′tus	call, name	appellation, appeal

Latin Word	Meaning	Related Words
cōnser'vō, -ā're, -ā'vī, -ā'tus	preserve, keep safe	conserve, conservation
ita, *adv.*	thus, so	
iūdi'cium, iūdi'cī, *n.*	judgment, trial	judicial
remit'tō, -ere, -mī'sī, -mis'sus	send back	remit, remiss, remission
sī, *conj.*	if	
statim, *adv.*	at once, instantly	

LESSON LV, § 391

impedīmentum, -ī, *n.*	hindrance ; *plur.* baggage	impediment
mo'veō, -ē're, mōvī, mōtus	move	
paucī, -ae, -a	few, only a few	paucity
putō, -ā're, -ā'vī, -ā'tus	think	repute, impute, compute
re'liquus, -a, -um	the rest, remaining, remainder of	relic, relinquish, derelict

LESSON LVII, § 406

cōnsul, -is, *m.*	consul	
le'giō, -ō'nis, *f.*	legion	
mīles, -itis, *m.*	soldier	military, militia
pater, patris, *m.*	father	paternal
pāx, pācis, *f.*	peace	pacify
prīnceps, -ipis, *m.*	chief, leader	prince
rēx, rēgis, *m.*	king	regal, regent

LESSON LVIII, § 409

accipiō, -ere, -cēpī, -ceptus	receive	accept
caput, capitis, *n.*	head, capital	decapitate, chapter
et . . . et, *conj.*	both . . . and	
flūmen, flūminis, *n.*	river	flume
frāter, frātris, *m.*	brother	fraternal
māter, mātris, *f.*	mother	maternal
soror, -ō'ris, *f.*	sister	sorority
tempus, -oris, *n.*	time	temporal

LESSON LIX, § 411

LATIN WORD	MEANING	RELATED WORDS
autem, *conj.,* *never stands first*	however, but, moreover	
dēiciō, -ere, -iē'cī, -iectus (dē + iaciō)	throw down	dejected
nōmen, -inis, *n.*	name	nomenclature, noun
pellō, -ere, pe'pulī, pulsus	drive, banish	repel, compel
pōnō, -ere, posuī, positus	place, set, build; **castra pōnere,** pitch camp	position, positive, propose, expose
reddō, -ere, red'didī, red'ditus	give back, return	render

LESSON LX, § 414

caedēs, -is (-ium), *f.*	slaughter, carnage	-cide *in* suicide, homicide, etc.
cohors, cohortis (-ium), *f.*	cohort, company (consisting of one tenth of a legion, or about 360 men)	
hostis, hostis(-ium), *m.*	enemy (in war)	hostile
mātrimō'nium, -ō'nī, *n.*	marriage; **in mātrimōnium dūcere,** marry	matrimony
mu'lier, muli'eris, *f.*	woman	
signum, -ī, *n.*	sign, signal, standard	signify, design
urbs, urbis (-ium), *f.*	city	urban, suburbs, urbane

LESSON LXI, § 417

animal, animālis (-ium), *n.*	animal	animate, inanimate
calcar, calcāris (-ium), *n.*	spur	
cī'vitās, -ā'tis, *f.*	state	civic
contineō, -ēre, -tinuī, -tentus	hold together, bound, restrain, keep	contain, continent
e'ques, e'quitis, *m.*	horseman	equestrian
lingua, -ae, *f.*	language, tongue	linguist
mare, -is (-ium), *n.*	sea	marine

LESSON LXII, §420

Latin Word	Meaning	Related Words
committō, -ere, -mīsī, -missus	join together; intrust; proelium committere, join battle, begin an engagement	commit, commission
homō, -inis, *m. and f.*	human being, man	homicide, human
iter, itineris, *n.*	journey, march, route; iter dare, give a right of way; iter facere, march	itinerary, itinerant
redūcō, -ere, -dūxī, -ductus	lead back	reduce, reduction
tamen, *conj.*	nevertheless	
virtūs, virtū'tis, *f.*	manliness; courage, valor; worth, virtue	virtuous
vīs, (vīs), *f.*	strength, power, violence	vim, violent

LESSON LXIII, §422

aequus, -a, -um	even, level, equal; fair, just	equal, equation, equator
audeō, -ēre, ausus sum [1]	dare	audacity
etiam, *adv., standing before the emphatic word*	even, also	
mors, mortis (-ium), *f.*	death	mortal
relinquō, -ere, -līquī, -lictus	leave behind, desert	relinquish
salūs, -ū'tis, *f.*	safety	salutary, salvation, save

LESSON LXV, §432

ācer, ācris, ācre	keen, sharp, eager, courageous	acrid, acrimonious
aut, *conj.*	or; aut . . . aut, either . . . or	
celer, celeris, celere	swift	celerity
equester, -tris, -tre	of cavalry	equestrian

[1] **Audeō** is a semi-deponent verb. These verbs will be explained later.

LATIN WORD	MEANING	RELATED WORDS
fuga, -ae, *f.*	flight; **in fugam dare,** put to flight	fugitive
pedester, -tris, -tre	on foot; *with* **cōpiae,** infantry	pedestrian

LESSON LXVI, § 436

certus, -a, -um	sure, certain	ascertain, certify
cōgō, -ere, coē'gī, coāc- tus	collect; compel, force	
commūnis, -e	common	commune, community
gravis, -e	heavy; severe; weighty	grave, gravity
omnis, -e	all, every	omnibus, omnipotent
similis, -e	similar, like	simile, simulate

LESSON LXVII, § 439

benefi'cium, benefi'cī, *n.*	favor, kindness	benefit
corpus, -oris, *n.*	body	corporal, corpse, incor- porate
grātia, -ae, *f.*	favor, thanks; **grātiās agere,** *with dat.,* thank	gratitude, gratis, ingra- tiate
maximē, *adv.*	most of all, especially	maximum
pār	equal	par, peer, parity, pair

LESSON LXVIII, § 447

brevis, -e	short	brief, brevity
difficilis, -e	hard	difficult
facilis, -e	easy	facility
fortis, -e	brave, courageous, strong	fortitude, fort, fortify
ignis, -is (-ium), *m.*	fire	ignite, ignition

LESSON LXIX, § 453

dux, ducis, *m.*	leader, commander	duke
inter, *prep. with acc.*	between, among	interim, intervene
levis, -e	light, trivial, fickle	levity
nihil, *n., indecl.*	nothing. *An abl.* **nihilō,** *from a nom.* **nihilum,** *occurs as an abl. of measure of difference*	nihilist, annihilate

Latin Word	Meaning	Related Words
pēs, pedis, *m.*	foot	pedal, pedestal, pedestrian
spatium, spatī, *n.*	space, distance	spacious, expatiate

LESSON LXX, § 459

auctōritās, -ātis, *f.*	authority	author
dissimilis, -e	unlike, dissimilar	dissimulate, dissemble
lēx, lēgis, *f.*	law	legal, legislate
līber'tās, -ā'tis, *f.*	freedom, liberty	liberal
servitūs, -ūtis, *f.*	slavery	servitude

LESSON LXXI, § 468

addūcō, -ere, -dūxī, -ductus	lead to, bring to, influence	adduce
cognōscō, -ere, -gnōvī, -gnitus	learn, find out; *in perf. tenses,* know	recognize
exspectō, -āre, -āvī, -ātus	await, expect, wait for	expectation
quod, *conj.*	because	
vulnerō, -āre, -āvī, -ātus	wound	vulnerable, invulnerable

LESSON LXXII, § 473

bene, *adv., from* bonus	well	benediction, benefit
deinde, *adv.*	next, then, thereafter	
facile, *adv.*	easily	facile
maneō, -ēre, mānsī, mānsūrus	remain, abide, stay	mansion
plūrimum, *adv.*	very much, most; *with* posse, be most powerful	plural, plurality
prīmō, *adv., referring to time*	at first, *as opposed to* afterwards; in the beginning	prime, primary, primeval
prīmum, *adv., referring to order*	first, in the first place	primitive

LESSON LXXIII, § 478

adventus, -ūs, *m.*	arrival	advent
Caesar, -aris, *m.*	Cæsar	kaiser, czar
celeritās, -ātis, *f.*	speed, swiftness	celerity

LATIN WORD	MEANING	RELATED WORDS
cornū, -ūs, *n.*	horn	cornucopia
dexter, -tra, -trum	right	dexterity, dexterous
equitātus, -ūs, *m.*	cavalry	equine
exercitus, -ūs, *m.*	army	exercise
impetus, -ūs, *m.*	attack; **impetum facere in,** make an attack on	impetus, impetuous
sinister, -tra, -trum	left	sinister

LESSON LXXIV, § 486

contendō,-ere, -dī, -tus	hasten; strive, fight	contend, contention
domus, -ūs, *f.*	home; **domī,** at home	domesticate, domicile
nāvis, -is (-ium), *f.*	ship	navy, naval
pedes, -itis, *m.*	foot soldier; *plur.* infantry	pedestrian
rūs, rūris, *n.*; *plur. only nom. and acc.,* rūra	country; **rūrī,** in the country	rural, rustic

LESSON LXXV, § 494

aestās, -ātis, *f.*	summer	
diēs, diēī, *m.*	day	diary, dial
hiems, hiemis, *f.*	winter	
lūx, lūcis, *f.*	light; **prīma lūx,** daylight	lucid, elucidate
nox, noctis (-ium), *f.*	night	nocturnal, equinox
rēs, reī, *f.*	thing, matter	real, reality

LESSON LXXVIII, § 514

cīvis, -is (-ium), *m. and f.*	citizen	civic, civil
commoveō, -ēre, -mōvī, -mōtus	alarm, excite, move	commotion
ego, meī	I ; *plur.* we	egotism
imperātor, -ōris, *m.*	general	emperor
suī, *gen.*	of himself (herself, itself, themselves); **in fugam sēsē dare,** flee	suicide
timor, -ōris, *m.*	fear	timorous
tū, tuī	thou, you	

LESSON LXXIX, § 519

Latin Word	Meaning	Related Words
dēpōnō, -ere, -posuī, -positus	put down, lay down, lay aside	deponent, deposit
īdem, eadem, idem	same	identity, identical, identify
incolō, -ere, -uī, ——	inhabit, *trans.*; *also intrans.*, dwell	
ipse, ipsa, ipsum	self, himself, herself, itself; very	
manus, -ūs, *f.*	hand; group, force	manual, manufacture, manuscript
pars, partis (-ium), *f.*	part, share; side, direction	party, particle, partner, partial
spēs, speī, *f.*	hope	

LESSON LXXX, § 525

dēbeō, -ēre, -uī, -itus	owe, ought	debt, debit
dēmōnstrō, -āre, -āvī, -ātus	point out, show	demonstrate
fīnis, -is (-ium), *m.*	end, limit; *plur.* territory, country	finish, final, finite, infinite
hic, haec, hoc	this; *as pers. pron.*, he, she, it	
ille, illa, illud	that; *as pers. pron.*, he, she, it	
iste, ista, istud	that; *as pers. pron.*, he, she, it	
modus, -ī, *m.*	measure; manner	mode, model, mood
mōns, montis (-ium), *m.*	mountain	mount, amount

LESSON LXXXI, § 530

aliquis, aliquid	someone, something	
aliquī, aliqua, aliquod	some	
exīstimō, -āre, -āvī, -ātus	think, consider	estimate
quīdam, quaedam, quiddam (quoddam)	a certain one, a certain	
quisque, quidque	each one	

LATIN WORD	MEANING	RELATED WORDS
quisque, quaeque, quodque	each	
retineō, -ēre, -tinuī, -tentus	hold back, retain	retention
sustineō, -ēre, -tinuī, -tentus	hold up, maintain; endure	sustain

LESSON LXXXIII, § 544

causa, -ae, *f.*	cause, reason; **quā dē causā**, for this reason	because
expellō, -ere, -pulī, -pulsus	drive out, expel	expulsion
permaneō,-ēre,-mānsī, -mānsūrus	last, endure, continue	permanent

LESSON LXXXIV, § 549

aciēs, aciēī, *f.*	line of battle	
cōnficiō, -ere, -fēcī, -fectus	do completely, finish	
īnstruō, -ere, -strūxī, -strūctus	draw up, arrange	instruct, instructor
passus, -ūs, *m.*	step, pace; **mīlle passūs**, a thousand paces, a mile	
pōns, pontis (-ium), *m.*	bridge	pontoon
trādūcō, -ere, -dūxī, -ductus	lead across	traduce

LESSON LXXXV, § 555

cupidus, -a, -um	desirous of, eager for, *with gen.*	cupidity
imperītus, -a, -um	unskilled, inexperienced, *with gen.*	
intermittō, -ere, -mīsī, -missus	leave off, suspend, suffer to elapse, leave vacant	intermittent, intermission
laus, laudis, *f.*	praise	laud, laudatory
mīlitāris, -e	military; **rēs mīlitāris**, art of war	militia, militant
perītus, -a, -um	skilled, experienced, *with gen.*	experience

LESSON LXXXVI, § 563

Latin Word	Meaning	Related Words
altitūdō, -inis, *f.*	height, depth	altitude
dolor, -ōris, *m.*	pain, grief	dolorous, doleful
excēdō, -ere, -cessī, -cessūrus	go out, depart	exceed, excessive
hortor, -ārī, hortātus sum, *dep. verb*	urge, encourage	exhort
patior, patī, passus sum, *dep. verb*	suffer, allow, permit	patient, passion
sequor, sequī, secūtus sum, *dep. verb*	follow	sequence, execute
vereor, -ērī, veritus sum, *dep. verb*	fear, respect	reverence

LESSON LXXXVII, § 571

dēligō, -ere, -lēgī, -lēctus	choose, select	
explōrātor, -ōris, *m.*	spy, scout	explorer
hōra, -ae, *f.*	hour	
idōneus, -a, -um	suitable, fitting	
magnitūdō, -inis, *f.*	size, greatness	magnitude
multitūdō, -inis, *f.*	crowd, throng, multitude	
praemittō, -ere, -mīsī, -missus	send ahead, send forward	premise
scrībō, -ere, scrīpsī, scrīptus	write	scribble, scribe, script
sūmō, -ere, sūmpsī, sūmptus	take up, assume; **supplicium sūmere dē,** inflict punishment on	presume, consume

LESSON LXXXVIII, § 575

apud, *prep. with acc.*	among, in the presence of	
doceō, -ēre, -uī, -tus	teach	docile
interim, *adv.*	meanwhile, in the meantime	interim
potestās, -ātis, *f.*	power	potent
vērō, *adv.*	in truth, verily	veracity, verity

LESSON XC, § 590

LATIN WORD	MEANING	RELATED WORDS
āmittō, -ere, -mīsī, -missus	send away, lose	
condiciō, -ōnis, *f.*	terms, agreement	condition
cōnsulō, -ere, -uī, -tus	ask for advice, consult, counsel with, *with acc.*	consultation
quaerō, -ere, quaesīvī, quaesītus	seek for, ask, inquire for	question
ratiō, -ōnis, *f.*	method, arrangement, plan	rational
summus, -a, -um	(*superl. of the adj.* superus, high) highest, supreme	sum, summit

LESSON XCI, § 597

nēmō, *gen.* nūllīus, *dat.* nēminī, *acc.* nēminem, *abl.* nūllō, *m. and f.*	no one	
perdūcō, -ere, -dūxī, -ductus	lead through, bring; construct (a wall)	
permoveō, -ēre, -mōvī, -mōtus	move deeply, arouse, influence	
perveniō, -īre, -vēnī, -ventus	arrive, *with* ad *or* in *and acc.*	
propter, *prep. with acc.*	on account of, because of	
rēs pūblica, reī pūblicae, *f.*	commonwealth, republic, state	republican
vulnus, -eris, *n.*	wound	vulnerable

LESSON XCII, § 604

frūmentārius, -a, -um	of grain; rēs frūmentāria, grain supply	
imperō, -āre, -āvī, -ātus	command, *with dat. and a subjv. clause*	imperative, imperious
postulō, -āre, -āvī, -ātus	demand, require	expostulate
prōvideō, -ēre, -vīdī, -vīsus	look out for, foresee	provide

Latin Word	Meaning	Related Words
rogō, -āre, -āvī, -ātus	ask, request	interrogate
temptō, -āre, -āvī, -ātus	try, attempt	temptation

LESSON XCIII, § 608

appropinquō, -āre, -āvī, -ātus	draw near, approach, *with dat.*	propinquity
cōnscrībō, -ere, -scrīpsī, -scrīptus	enroll	conscript
impediō, -īre, -īvī, -ītus	hinder, obstruct	impede
interclūdō, -ere, -clūsī, -clūsus	cut off, block up	*The root word,* claudō, close, *appears in* include, exclude, etc.
ōrātiō, -ōnis, *f.*	speech, oration; ōrātiōnem habēre, make a speech	oratory
quidem, *adv.,* *never stands first*	indeed, in fact. Nē . . . quidem, not even, *the emphatic word standing between*	

LESSON XCIV, § 613

difficultās, -ātis, *f.*	difficulty	difficult
dīligenter, *adv.*	carefully, industriously, attentively	diligently
nōbilis, -e	well-known, famous, noble	nobility
turris, -is (-ium; *abl.* turrī *or* turre), *f.*	tower	turret

LESSON XCV, § 620

coniciō, -ere, -iēcī, -iectus	hurl	*The root word,* iaciō, throw, *appears in* inject, object, etc.
cōnsistō, -ere, -stitī, -stitus	stand still, take a stand, halt, be at rest	consist, consistent
cōnsuētūdō, -inis, *f.*	custom	
mēns, mentis (-ium), *f.*	mind	mental
premō, -ere, pressī, pressus	press hard	compress, express, impress, oppress
tālis, -e	such	
tantus, -a, -um	so great	

LESSON XCVI, § 624

Latin Word	Meaning	Related Words
conveniō, -īre, -vēnī, -ventus	come together, assemble	convene, convention
dēsum, -esse, -fuī, -futūrus	be lacking, be wanting, *with dat.*	
incendō, -ere, -cendī, -cēnsus	set on fire, burn	incendiary, incense
iūs, iūris, *n.*; *plur. only nom. and acc.,* iūra	law, right	justice, judge
praeficiō, -ere, -fēcī, -fectus	set over, place in command, *with acc. and dat.*	prefect
praesum, -esse, -fuī, ——	be before, be over, be in command	present
prōpōnō, -ere, -posuī, -positus	set forth, offer	propose, proposition
senātus, -ūs, *m.*	senate	senator

LESSON XCVIII, § 636

circummūniō, -īre, -īvī, -ītus	wall around, fortify all about	
enim, *conj., never stands first*	for	
fidēs, fideī, *f.*	good faith, protection	fidelity
genus, -eris, *n.*	race, kind	generic, genus
oportet, -ēre, oportuit	it is fitting, is necessary; *an impers. verb, often used with an infin. and subj. acc.*	
ōrdō, -inis, *m.*	rank, class, order	ordinary
ostendō, -ere, -dī, -tus	show, display	ostensible, ostentation
pertineō, -ēre, -uī, ——	reach, extend, pertain	pertinacity
recipiō, -ere, -cēpī, -ceptus	take back; receive; *with sē,* withdraw	recipient, reception
satis, *indecl. adj.; also used as a neut. noun and as an adv.*	enough, sufficient; sufficiently	satisfy, satisfactory

DERIVATION NOTEBOOK [1]

TYPE I (Without Definitions)

locō, locāre, locāvī, locātus, *place*	locate, location, locative, local, locality, localize, locally, locus, collocate, collocation, dislocate, localization, locomotive, locomotor

TYPE II (With Definitions)

vocō, vocāre, vocāvī, vocātus, *call*	vocation : *a calling, occupation* vocational : *pertaining to a vocation or calling* vocal : *pertaining to voice* evoke : *call out* convoke : *call together* vocative : *case of calling, case of address* revoke : *call back, rescind* invoke : *call upon, ask for* vociferous : *with large calling power, with loud tones* invocation : *a calling upon, a prayer*

TYPE III (With Examples of Use in English)

mittō, mittere, mīsī, missus, *send*	mission : *He was sent on a mission to Europe* missionary : *He was sent as a missionary to China* missive : *The letter was a formidable missive* missile : *Stones were the missiles of early warfare* transmit : *They will transmit the message to us* remission : *He preached the remission of sins* commit : *She was committed to his care* submit : *They submitted to the inevitable* submissive : *The slave was not submissive* omit : *Omit the nonessential*

[1] This is a specimen page based on the Latin syllabus for secondary schools published by the University of the State of New York.

COMMON LATIN ABBREVIATIONS

A.B. *or* B.A. = Artium Baccalaureus, *Bachelor of Arts*
A.D. = annō Dominī, *in the year of our Lord*
ad lib. = ad libitum, *at pleasure*
a.m. = ante merīdiem, *before noon*
A.M. *or* M.A. = Artium Magister, *Master of Arts*
A.U.C. = ab urbe conditā, *from the founding of the city*, that is, of Rome, 753 B.C.
cf. = cōnfer, *compare*
e.g. = exemplī grātiā, *for example*
etc. = et cētera, *and the rest, and so forth*
ib. *or* ibid. = ibīdem, *in the same place*
i.e. = id est, *that is*
I H S = first three letters of the Greek for *Jesus*, but often taken as the abbreviation for the Latin "Iēsus Hominum Salvātor," *Jesus, the Saviour of Men*
I.N.R.I. = Iēsus Nazarēnus, Rēx Iūdaeōrum, *Jesus of Nazareth, King of the Jews*
lb. = lībra, *pound*; lbs. = lībrae, *pounds*
LL.D. = Lēgum Doctor, *Doctor of Laws*
M.D. = Medicīnae Doctor, *Doctor of Medicine*
N.B. = notā bene, *note well, take notice*
no. = numerō (plural nos.), *by number*
Ph.D. = Philosophiae Doctor, *Doctor of Philosophy*
p.m. = post merīdiem, *after noon*
P.S. = post scrīptum, *postscript*
Q.E.D. = quod erat dēmōnstrandum, *which was to be demonstrated*
R. = recipe, *take* (placed before a doctor's prescription)
R.I.P. = requiēscat in pāce, *may he* (or *she*) *rest in peace*
sc. = scīlicet, *namely*
S.P.Q.R. = Senātus Populusque Rōmānus, *the Senate and Roman People*
st. = stet, *let it stand*
s.v. = sub voce, *under the word*
ult. = ultimō, *of last month*
v. *or* vid. = vidē, *see*
viz. = vidēlicet, *namely*
vs. = versus, *against*

SERMONETA

Sermoneta is a characteristic hill town of Italy. The picture gives a good idea of Italian scenery. The country is very mountainous, and south of the valley of the Po there are few large plains. Note the great grove of olive trees covering the slopes below Sermoneta. Olives were as important to ancient as they are to modern Italy; but the Romans of Cæsar's time had neither oranges nor lemons

LATIN–ENGLISH VOCABULARY

ā, ab, *prep. with abl.*, from, by
abdō, -ere, -didī, -ditus, hide; *with*
sē, conceal one's self, hide
abdūcō, -ere, -dūxī, -ductus, lead
  away
absum, abesse, āfuī, āfutūrus, *irreg.*,
  be away, be off, be distant; *with*
  ā *or* **ab** *and abl.* (§ 838)
Abȳdus, -ī, *m.*, Abydus
ac (*before consonants*), **atque** (*before
  either vowels or consonants*),
  conj., and, and what is more;
  simul atque, as soon as
accidō, -cidere, -cidī, happen
accipiō, -ere, -cēpī, -ceptus, receive
accurrō, -ere, accurrī, ——, run to,
  run up
ācer, ācris, ācre, keen, sharp; eager,
  courageous
aciēs, aciēī, *f.*, line of battle; **prīma
  aciēs,** the front line
ācriter, *adv.*, sharply, fiercely
ad, *prep. with acc.*, to, towards,
  near, by; at, on
adamō, -āre, -āvī, -ātus, fall in love
  with
addūcō, -ere, -dūxī, -ductus, lead to,
  bring to, influence
adeō, -īre, -iī, -itus, go to
adferō, -ferre, attulī, adlātus, bring,
  carry to (§ 841)
adhūc, *adv.*, until now, as yet, still

aditus, -ūs, *m.*, privilege of admit-
  tance
admīrātiō, -ōnis, *f.*, wonder, surprise; **tibi admīrātiōnem movēre,**
  cause you surprise
adsīdō, -ere, -ēdī, ——, sit by (*especially a sick person*)
adstō, -āre, astitī *or* **adstitī, ——,**
  stand by, stand near
adsum, -esse, -fuī, -futūrus, be
  present, be at hand, *with dat.*
  (§ 838)
adulēscēns, -entis, *m.*, youth
adveniō, -īre, -vēnī, -ventus, come,
  arrive
adventus, -ūs, *m.*, arrival
adversus, -a, -um, ill, unfavorable;
  opposite
aeger, -gra, -grum, sick
aequus, -a, -um, even, level, equal;
  fair, just
aestās, -ātis, *f.*, summer; **initā aestāte,** at the beginning of summer
aetās, -tātis, *f.*, age
Aethiopia, -ae, *f.*, Ethiopia
ager, agrī, *m.*, field
agmen, agminis, *n.*, an army (*on the
  march*), column; **prīmum agmen,**
  the van; **novissimum agmen,** the
  rear; **agmen claudere,** bring up
  the rear
agō, -ere, ēgī, āctus, drive, lead; do

385

386 LATIN-ENGLISH VOCABULARY

agricola, -ae, *m.*, farmer
agricultūra, -ae, *f.*, agriculture
āla, -ae, *f.*, wing
Albānī, -ōrum, *m.*, the Albans
aliquandō, *adv.*, some day
aliquis (-quī), -qua, -quid (-quod), *indef. pron.*, someone, anyone, some, any (§ 831)
alius, alia, aliud (*gen.* -īus, *dat.* -ī), other, another (*of several*); alius . . . alius, one . . . another; aliī . . . aliī, some . . . others (§ 815)
Allobrogēs, -um, *m.*, the Allob'roges
Alpēs, -ium, *f.*, the Alps
altē, *adv.*, high, on high
alter, -era, -erum (*gen.* -īus, *dat.* -ī), the one, the other (*of two*); alter . . . alter, the one . . . the other; alterī . . . alterī, the one party . . . the other party (§ 502)
altitūdō, -inis, *f.*, height; depth
altus, -a, -um, high, deep, lofty
amanter, *adv.*, lovingly, affectionately
amīcitia, -ae, *f.*, friendship
amīcus, -a, -um, friendly, affectionate
amīcus, -ī, *m.*, friend
āmittō, -ere, -mīsī, -missus, send away; lose
amō, -āre, -āvī, -ātus, love
amor, -ōris, *m.*, love
amplus, -a, -um, large, abundant; famous, distinguished; copious
Amūlius, Amūlī, *m.*, Amulius
Andromeda, -ae, *f.*, Andromeda
angustē, *adv.*, narrowly, closely
angustus, -a, -um, narrow
animal, -ālis (-ium), *n.*, animal

animus, -ī, *m.*, mind, spirit, heart; in animō esse, *with dat.*, intend; animum tenēre, hold attention; *in plur. often* courage
annus, -ī, *m.*, year
anser, -eris, *m.*, goose
ante, *prep. with acc.*, before, in front of; *adv.*, before, previously
anteā, *adv.*, heretofore, previously, formerly
antīquus, -a, -um, ancient
aperiō, -īre, -uī, -pertus, open
apertus, -a, -um, open
appellō, -āre, -āvī, -ātus, call, name
Appius, -a, -um, Appian
appropinquō, -āre, -āvī, -ātus, draw near, approach, *with dat.*
apud, *prep. with acc.*, among, in the presence of
aqua, -ae, *f.*, water
aquilifer, -erī, *m.*, standard-bearer (*of the eagle*)
Aquitānī, -ōrum, *m.*, the Aquitani
arbor, -oris, *f.*, tree
arca, -ae, *f.*, chest
ārdeō, -ēre, ārsī, ārsūrus, be afire, glow, burn
Ariadnē, -ēs, *f.* (*Greek noun*), Ariadne
Ariōn, -onis, *m.*, Arion
Ariovistus, -ī, *m.*, Ariovistus
arma, -ōrum, *n. plur.*, arms
armātus, -a, -um, armed; *as a noun in the masc. plur.*, armed men
armō, -āre, -āvī, -ātus, arm
arō, -āre, -āvī, -ātus, plow
ascendō, -ere, ascendī, ascēnsus, climb
ascrībō, -ere, -īpsī, -īptus, enroll
asper, -era, -erum, rough, wild

Athēnae, -ārum, *f.*, Athens
ātrāmentum, -ī, *n.*, ink
attingō, -ere, -tigī, -tāctus, touch upon, reach
aspiciō, -ere, -ēxī, -ectus, behold, see
auctōritās, -ātis, *f.*, authority
audācia, -ae, *f.*, daring, boldness, presumption
audeō, -ēre, ausus sum, *semi-dep. verb*, dare
audiō, -īre, -īvī, -ītus, hear
auferō, auferre, abstulī, ablātus, remove (§ 841)
aura, -ae, *f.*, air
aureus, -a, -um, golden
aurum, -ī, *n.*, gold
aut, *conj.*, or; aut . . . aut, either . . . or
autem, *conj.* (*never stands first*), however, but, moreover
auxilium, auxilī, *n.*, aid
āvertō, -ere, -tī, -sus, turn away, withdraw

Bacchus, -ī, *m.*, Bacchus
Baculus, -ī, *m.*, Baculus
barbarus, -a, -um, savage, uncivilized; *as a noun in the masc. or fem.*, a savage
Belgae, -ārum, *m.*, the Belgæ
bellō, -āre, -āvī, -ātus, wage war
bellum, -ī, *n.*, war; bellum īnferre, *with dat.*, make war upon
bene, *adv. from* bonus, well
beneficium, beneficī, *n.*, favor, kindness
benīgnē, *adv.*, kindly
benīgnus, -a, -um, kind
Bibracte, -is, *n.*, Bibracte

bonus, -a, -um, good, kind (§ 820)
brevis, -e, short
brevitās, -ātis, *f.*, shortness; brevitās temporis, want of time
breviter, *adv.*, briefly
Britannia, -ae, *f.*, Britain, England
Britannī, -ōrum, *m.*, the Britons
Brūtus, -ī, *m.*, Brutus

Caecilius, -ī, *m.*, Cæcilius
caedēs, -is (ium), *f.*, slaughter, carnage
caelum, -ī, *n.*, sky, heaven
Caesar, -is, *m.*, Cæsar
calamitās, -ātis, *f.*, loss, disaster
calcar, -āris (ium), *n.*, spur
cālō, -ōnis, *m.*, camp follower
Camillus, -ī, *m.*, Camillus
canō, -ere, cecinī, ——, sing
capiō, -ere, cēpī, captus, take, seize
Capitōlium, -tōlī, *n.*, the Capitolium
capra, -ae, *f.*, goat
captīvus, -ī, *m.*, captive
caput, capitis, *n.*, head; capital
careō, -ēre, -uī, -itūrus, go without, be without, *with abl.*
carrus, -ī, *m.*, baggage wagon
cārus, -a, -um, dear
casa, -ae, *f.*, hut, cottage
Cassiopēia, -ae, *f.*, Cassiopeia
castrum, -ī, *n.*, fort; *plur.*, camp; castra movēre, break camp; castra pōnere, pitch camp
causa, -ae, *f.*, cause, reason; quā dē causā, for this reason; causam dīcere, plead a case; causā, *with preceding genitive*, for the sake of, in order to
celer, celeris, celere, swift

celeritās, -ātis, *f.*, speed, swiftness

celeriter, *adv.*, quickly

cēlō, -āre, -āvī, -ātus, conceal

Celtae, -ārum, *m.*, the Celts

cēna, -ae, *f.*, dinner

centum, *indecl. num. adj.*, one hundred

centuriō, -ōnis, *m.*, centurion

Cēpheus, -ī, *m.*, Cepheus

Cerēs, -eris, *f.* (*Greek noun*), Ceres

certāmen, -inis, *n.*, contest

certē, *adv.*, certainly, surely

certus, -a, -um, sure, certain; true; certiōrem facere, inform; certior fierī, be informed

cibus, -ī, *m.*, food

Cicerō, -ōnis, *m.*, Cicero

Cincinnātus, -ī, *m.*, Cincinnatus

circummūniō, -īre, -īvī, -ītus, wall around, fortify all about

circumsistō, -ere, -stetī, ——, surround

circumveniō, -īre, -vēnī, -ventus, surround

cīvis, -is (-ium), *m. and f.*, citizen

cīvitās, -ātis, *f.*, state

clāmō, -āre, -āvī, -ātus, cry out, shout

clāmor, -ōris, *m.*, shout, cry

clārus, -a, -um, clear, bright; famous

claudō, -ere, -sī, -sus, close, end; agmen claudere, bring up the rear

cognōscō, -ere, -gnōvī, -gnitus, find out, learn; *in perf. tenses*, know

cōgō, -ere, coēgī, coāctus, collect; compel, force

cohors, cohortis (-ium), *f.*, cohort, company (*consisting of one tenth of a legion, or about 360 men*)

collis, collis (-ium), *m.*, hill; summus collis, the top of the hill

colō, -ere, coluī, cultus, till; cherish, foster

commendō, -āre, -āvī, -ātus, intrust, commit

commīlitō, -ōnis, *m.*, fellow soldier, comrade

committō, -ere, -mīsī, -missus, commit, intrust; proelium committere, join battle

commoveō, -ēre, -mōvī, -mōtus, excite, alarm, move

commūnis, -e, common

commūtātiō, -ōnis, *f.*, change

comparō, -āre, -āvī, -ātus, get together, provide

comportō, -āre, -āvī, -ātus, collect

cōnātus, -ūs, *m.*, undertaking, attempt

concidō, -ere, -cidī, ——, fall down, fall

condiciō, -ōnis, *f.*, terms, agreement, condition

cōnfectus, -a, -um, exhausted

cōnferō, -ferre, -tulī, -lātus, bring together, collect (§ 841)

cōnfertus, -a, -um, dense, closely crowded

cōnficiō, -ere, -fēcī, -fectus, do completely, finish; subdue, overcome, exhaust

cōnfirmō, -āre, -āvī, -ātus, encourage, strengthen

coniciō, -ere, -iēcī, -iectus (con + iaciō), hurl

coniūnx, -iugis, *m. and f.*, husband, wife

coniūrō, -āre, -āvī, -ātus, conspire, plot

conlocō, -āre, -āvī, -ātus, place

cōnor, -ārī, -ātus sum, *dep. verb,* attempt, try

cōnsequor, -sequī, -secūtus sum, *dep. verb,* follow, overtake

cōnservō, -āre, -āvī, -ātus, preserve, keep safe

cōnscrībō, -ere, -scrīpsī, -scrīptus, enroll

cōnsilium, cōnsilī, *n.,* plan, advice, resource; cōnsilium capere, form a plan ; cōnsilium omittere, leave a plan untried

cōnsistō, -ere, -stitī, ——, stand still, take a stand ; halt, be at rest

cōnspectus, -ūs, *m.,* sight

cōnspiciō, -ere, -spēxī, -spectus, get sight of, see

cōnstituō, -ere, -uī, -ūtus, appoint; determine, decide ; station

cōnsuētūdō, -inis, *f.,* custom, habit

cōnsul, -is, *m.,* consul

cōnsulō, -ere, -uī, -tus, ask for advice, consult, counsel with, *with acc.*

contendō, -ere, -dī, -tus, hasten; strive, fight

continenter, *adv.,* continuously

contineō, -ēre, -tinuī, -tentus, hold together, bound; restrain, keep ; hem in

contrā, *prep. with acc.,* against; opposite to

conveniō, -īre, -vēnī, -ventus, come together, assemble

convocō, -āre, -āvī, -ātus, call together

coörior, -īrī, -ortus sum, *dep. verb,* rise

cōpia, -ae, *f.,* plenty, abundance; *plur.,* forces ; cōpiam facere, give an opportunity

cōpiōsus, -a, -um, wealthy, well supplied

cornū, -ūs, *n.,* horn ; wing (*of an army*); ā dextrō cornū, on the right wing

corpus, -oris, *n.,* body

corripiō, -ere, -ripuī, -reptus, seize

cotīdiānus, -a, -um, daily

cotīdiē, *adv.,* daily, everyday

crēber, -bra, -brum, thick, frequent, crowded

crēdō, -ere, -didī, -ditus, believe, trust

cremō, -āre, -āvī, -ātus, burn, consume

creō, -āre, -āvī, -ātus, make

crēscō, -ere, crēvī, crētus, increase

Crēta, -ae, *f.,* Crete

culpa, -ae, *f.,* fault

cum, *prep. with abl.,* with

cum, *conj.,* when, since, although

cupidus, -a, -um, desirous of, eager for, *with gen.*

cupiō, -ere, -īvī, -ītus, wish, desire

cūr, *interrog. adv.,* why

Curiātius, Curiātī, *m.,* Curiatius

Curius, Curī, *m.,* Curius

cūrō, -āre, -āvī, -ātus, care for, take care of ; cure

currus, -ūs, *m.,* chariot

cursus, -ūs, *m.,* course; march, journey

dē, *prep. with abl.,* down from ; concerning, about

dea, -ae, *f.* (*dat. and abl. plur.* deābus), goddess

dēbeō, -ēre, -uī, -itus, owe, ought

dēbitor, -ōris, *m.*, debtor

dēbitum, -ī, *n.*, debt

decem, *indecl. num. adj.*, ten

December, -bris, -bre, of December

decimus, -a, -um, *num. adj.*, tenth

dēditiō, -ōnis, *f.*, surrender; in dēditiōnem accipere, receive in surrender

dēdō, -ere, -didī, -ditus, surrender; *with* sē, surrender one's self

dēdūcō, -ere, -dūxī, -ductus, lead down *or* from; escort

dēfendō, -ere, -dī, -fēnsus, defend

dēfēnsor, -ōris, *m.*, defender

dēfessus, -a, -um, tired out, weary

dēficiō, -ere, -fēcī, -fectus, fail, be wanting

dēiciō, -ere, -iēcī, -iectus (dē + iaciō), throw down

deinde, *adv.*, next, then, thereafter

dēligō, -ere, -lēgī, -lēctus, choose, select

delphīnus, -ī, *m.*, dolphin

dēmōnstrō, -āre, -āvī, -ātus, point out, show

dēnique, *adv.*, at last, finally

Dentātus, -ī, *m.*, Dentatus

dēpōnō, -ere, -posuī, -positus, put down, lay down, lay aside; memoriam dēpōnere, forget

dēscendō, -ere, -dī, -scēnsus, climb down, descend

dēsīderō, -āre, -āvī, -ātus, long for

dēsiliō, -īre, -siluī, -sultus, leap down

dēsistō, -ere, -stitī, -stitūrus, desist from

dēspērō, -āre, -āvī, -ātus, despair of

dēstringō, -ere, -strīnxī, -strictus, draw

dēsum, -esse, -fuī, -futūrus, be lacking, be wanting, *with dat.* (§ 838)

dētrahō, -ere, -trāxī, -tractus, snatch, *with acc. and dat.*

dētrīmentum, -ī, *n.*, loss; disaster

deus, -ī, *m.*, god

dēvorō, -āre, -āvī, -ātus, devour, consume

dexter, -tra, -trum, right

dextra, -ae, *f.*, right hand

Diāna, -ae, *f.*, Diana

dīcō, -ere, dīxī, dictus, say, speak, tell

dictātor, -ōris, *m.*, dictator

diēs, -ēī, *m.*, day; in diēs, every day

differō, -ferre, distulī, dīlātus, *irreg.*, be different, differ (§ 841)

difficilis, -e, hard, difficult (§ 820)

difficultās, -ātis, *f.*, difficulty

dīiūdicō, -āre, -āvī, -ātus, decide

dīligenter, *adv.*, carefully, industriously, attentively

dīligentia, -ae, *f.*, industry

dīmittō, -ere, -mīsī, -missus, send away; let go

discēdō, -ere, -cessī, -cessūrus, depart from, leave, withdraw, go away

discipulus, -ī, *m.*, pupil

discrīmen, -inis, *n.*, turning point; discrīmen rērum, crisis

dispōnō, -ere, -posuī, -positus, station

dissimilis, -e, unlike, dissimilar (§ 820)

diū, *adv.* (*compared* diūtius, diūtissimē), for a long time, long (§ 822)

diurnus, -a, -um, of the day, daily; nocturnō diurnōque (itinere), by night and day

dīversus, -a, -um, different

dīvidō, -ere, -vīsī, -vīsus, divide
dō, dare, dedī, datus, give
doceō, -ēre, -uī, -tus, teach
dolor, -ōris, *m.*, pain, grief
domus, -ūs, *f.*, house, home; domī,
  at home (§ 813)
dōnum, -ī, *n.*, gift
dubius, -a, -um, doubtful, uncertain;
  sine dubiō, certainly
ducentī, -ae, -a, two hundred
dūcō, -ere, dūxī, ductus, lead
dulcis, -e, sweet
duo, duae, duo, *num. adj.*, two
  (§ 824)
duodecim, *indecl. num. adj.*, twelve
duodecimus, -a, -um, *num. adj.*,
  twelfth
dux, ducis, *m.*, leader, commander

ē *or* ex, *prep. with abl.*, out of, from,
  off, of
ecce, *adv.*, lo! see! behold! look!
edō, -ere, ēdī, ēsus, eat
Eburōnēs, -um, *m. plur.*, the Ebu-
  ro'nes
ēdūcō, -ere, -dūxī, -ductus, lead out
effugiō, -ere, -fūgī, -fugitūrus, escape
ego, meī, *per. pron.*, I; *in plur.*, we
ēgredior, -ī, -gressus sum, *dep. verb*,
  go out, march out; *with* nāve,
  disembark
ēgregius, -a, -um, remarkable, marvelous, distinguished
ēmittō, -ere, -mīsī, -missus, send
  out, send forth
enim, *conj.*, for, *never stands first*
eō, īre, iī (īvī), itūrus, go (§ 842)
epistula, -ae, *f.*, letter

eques, equitis, *m.*, horseman
equester, -tris, -tre, of cavalry
equitātus, -ūs, *m.*, cavalry
equus, -ī, *m.*, horse
ergō, *adv.*, therefore
ēripiō, -ere, -ripuī, -reptus, snatch
  away, rescue
ēruptiō, -ōnis, *f.*, sally
et, *conj.*, and; et ... et, both ... and
ērumpō, -ere, -rūpī, -ruptus, burst
  out, make a sally
etiam, *adv., standing before the
  emphatic word* even, also
Etrūscī, -ōrum, *m. plur.*, the Etruscans
Eurydicē, -ēs, *f. (Greek noun)*,
  Eurydice
ēvocō, -āre, -āvī, -ātus, call out, summon
excēdō, -ere, -cessī, -cessūrus, go
  out, depart
excitō, -āre, -āvī, -ātus, arouse
exemplum, -ī, *n.*, example, specimen
exeō, -īre, -iī, -itūrus, go forth (§ 842)
exerceō, -ēre, -uī, -itus, train
exercitus, -ūs, *m.*, army
exīstimō, -āre, -āvī, -ātus, think,
  consider
expellō, -ere, -pulī, -pulsus, drive
  out, expel
expiō, -āre, -āvī, -ātus, atone for
explōrātor, -ōris, *m.*, spy, scout
expūgnō, -āre, -āvī, -ātus, take by
  storm, capture; *distinguish from*
  oppūgnō, assault
exspectātus, -a, -um, expected, appointed
exspectō, -āre, -āvī, -ātus, await, expect, wait for

fābula, -ae, *f.,* story

faciēs, faciēī, *f.,* beauty

facile, *adv.,* easily

facilis, -e, easy (§ 820)

faciō, -ere, fēcī, factus, make, do, form, cause; **proelium facere,** fight a battle; **aliquem certiōrem facere,** inform someone; **cōpiam facere,** give an opportunity

factum, -ī, *n.,* deed, act

fāma, -ae, *f.,* rumor, report, reputation

famēs, -is (-ium), *f.,* hunger

faveō, -ēre, fāvī, fautūrus, be favorable to, favor, *with dat.*

Februārius, -a, -um, of February

ferē, *adv.,* nearly, almost, about

ferō, ferre, tulī, lātus, bear, carry; **graviter** *or* **molestē ferre,** *with acc. and inf.,* be annoyed; **subsidium ferre,** go to the rescue (§ 841)

fidēs, fideī, *f.,* good faith, protection; **fidēs pūblica,** the promise given by the state

fīlia, -ae, *f. (dat. and abl. plur.* **fīliābus),** daughter

fīlius, fīlī, *m.,* son (§ 806.2)

fīlum, -ī, *n.,* string

fīnis, -is (-ium), *m.,* end, limit; *in the plur.,* territory, country

fīnitimī, -ōrum, *m. plur.,* neighbors

fīnitimus, -a, -um, adjoining, neighboring

fīō, fierī, factus sum, *used as the passive of* **faciō,** be done, be made, happen; **certior fierī,** be informed (§ 843)

fīrmus, -a, -um, strong, trusty, loyal

flagrō, -āre, -āvī, -ātūrus, burn, be on fire; glow, be stirred

Flāminius, -a, -um, Flaminian

flūmen, flūminis, *n.,* river

fluō, -ere, fluxī, fluxūrus, flow

fortasse, perhaps, possibly

fortis, -e, brave, courageous, strong

fortiter, *adv.,* bravely

fortūna, -ae, *f.,* fortune, circumstances

fossa, -ae, *f.,* ditch

frāter, frātris, *m.,* brother

frūmentārius, -a, -um, of grain; **rēs frūmentāria,** grain supply

frūmentor, -ārī, -ātus sum, *dep. verb,* gather grain

frūmentum, -ī, *n.,* grain

frūstrā, *adv.,* in vain

fuga, -ae, *f.,* flight; **in fugam dare,** put to flight; **in fugam sēsē dare,** flee

fugiō, -ere, fūgī, fugitūrus, flee, run

Galba, -ae, *m.,* Galba

Gallia, -ae, *f.,* Gaul (modern France)

Gallicus, -a, -um, Gallic

Gallus, -ī, *m.,* Gaul

Garumna, -ae, *m.,* the Garonne

gaudeō, -ēre, gāvīsus sum, *semi-dep. verb,* rejoice

gaudium, gaudī, *n.,* joy, gladness

gemitus, -ūs, *m.,* groan

Genāva, -ae, *f.,* Geneva

generōsus, -a, -um, honorable, noble

gēns, gentis (-ium), *f.,* tribe, nation

genus, -eris, *n.,* race, tribe; kind, method

Germānia, -ae, *f.,* Germany

Germānus, -ī, *m.,* a German

gerō, -ere, gessī, gestus, wage, carry on, wear, have; bear, wear; rēs gestae, exploits

glōria, -ae, *f.*, glory, praise, thirst for glory

Graecia, -ae, *f.*, Greece

Graecus, -a, -um, Greek; Graecus, -ī, *m.*, a Greek

grātia, -ae, *f.*, influence, favor, thanks; grātiās agere, *with dat.*, thank

grātus, -a, -um, pleasing

gravis, -e, heavy; severe; weighty, serious

graviter, *adv.*, heavily; graviter ferre, bear ill, take ill

habeō, -ēre, -uī, -itus, have

habitō, -āre, -āvī, -ātus, live

hāctenus, *adv.*, thus far

Haeduī, -ōrum, *m.*, the Haeduī

harēna, -ae, *f.*, sand

Hellēspontus, -ī, *m.*, the Hellespont

Helvetiī, -ōrum, *m. plur.*, the Helvetii

hercle, *interj.*, by Hercules, assuredly, indeed

Hērō, -ūs, *f.* (*Greek noun*), Hero

hērōs, -ōis, *m.* (*Greek noun*), hero

heu! *interj. of grief or pain*, oh! ah! alas! *followed by the acc. of exclamation*

hiberna, -ōrum, *m. plur.*, winter quarters

hic, haec, hoc, *demon. adj. and pron.*, this; *as per. pron.*, he, she, it (§ 828)

hiemō, -āre, -āvī, -ātus, pass the winter

hiems, hiemis, *f.*, winter

hodiē, *adv.*, today

homō, -inis, *m. and f.*, human being, man (§ 813)

Horātius, Horātī, *m.*, Horatius

hōra, -ae, *f.*, hour

hortor, -ārī, - hortātus sum, *dep. verb*, urge, encourage

hospes, -itis, *m.*, stranger

hostis, hostis (-ium), *m.*, enemy (*in war*)

humerus, -ī, *m.*, shoulder

iaciō, iacere, iēcī, iactus, throw, hurl

iam, *adv.*, already, immediately; presently, soon, now

Iānuārius, -a, -um, of January

ibi, *adv.*, there, in that place

īdem, eadem, idem, *demon. adj. and pron.*, same (§ 828)

idōneus, -a, -um, suitable, fitting

ignis, -is (-ium), *m.*, fire

ille, illa, illud, *demon. adj. and pron.*, that; *as per. pron.*, he, she, it (§ 828)

immineō, -ēre, ——, ——, threaten; be at hand

impedīmentum, -ī, *n.*, hindrance; *plur.* baggage; magnum numerum impedīmentōrum, a very long baggage train

impediō, -īre, -īvī, -ītus, hinder, obstruct, prevent

imperātor, -ōris, *m.*, general

imperītus, -a, -um, unskilled, inexperienced, *with gen.*

imperium, imperī, *n.*, command, supreme power, realm

imperō, -āre, -āvī, -ātus, command, *with dat. and a subj. clause* impetus, -ūs, *m.*, attack; **facere impetum in**, make an attack upon

improbus, -a, -um, evil

imprōvīsō, *adv.*, unexpectedly

imprōvīsus, -a, -um, unforeseen, unexpected

in, *prep. with acc.*, into, against, to; **in**, *prep. with abl.*, in, on ; among

incendō, -ere, -cendī, -cēnsus, set on fire, burn

incipiō, -ere, -cēpī, -ceptus, begin

incitō,-āre,-āvī,-ātus, hasten, hurry, arouse

incognitus, -a, -um, unknown

incolō, -ere, -uī, ——, *trans. with acc.*, inhabit; *also intrans.*, dwell

incolumis, -e, unharmed, safe

incrēdibilis, -e, incredible, extraordinary

incūsō, -āre, -āvī, -ātus, rebuke, chide

indūcō, -ere, -dūxī, -ductus, lead in *or* against

induō, -ere, -uī, -ūtus, put on

industrius, -a, -um, diligent

ineō, -īre, -īvī *or* **-iī, -itus,** enter upon ; **initā aestate**, at the beginning of summer (§ 842)

īnfēlix, -īcis, unfortunate, ill-fated

īnferī, -ōrum, *m. plur.*, shades, lower world

īnferior, -ius, inferior (§ 820)

īnferō, -ferre, -tulī, -lātus, bring in, inflict; **spem īnferre**, *with dat.*, inspire hope (§ 841)

ingēns, -entis, huge

ingredior, ingredī, ingressus sum, *dep. verb*, proceed, advance, march ; enter

iniciō, -ere, -iēcī, -iectus (in + iaciō), thrust

inimīcus,-a,-um, unfriendly, hostile

inīquus, -a, -um, uneven, unequal ; unfavorable, hostile; steep, dangerous

iniūria, -ae, *f.*, wrong, injury; **iniūriās alicuī īnferre**, inflict injuries on someone

inopia, -ae, *f.*, want, need, scarcity

inquit, said he, said she ; **inquiunt**, said they. *Inserted in a direct quotation*

īnstitūtum, -ī, *n.*, custom

īnstruō, -ere, -strūxī, -strūctus, draw up, arrange

īnsula, -ae, *f.*, island

integer, integra, integrum, whole, fresh, pure

intellegō, intellegere, intellēxī, intellēctus, understand

intentus, -a, -um, attentive, eager

inter, *prep. with acc.*, between, among

intercēdō, -ere, -cessī, -cessūrus, come between, intervene

interclūdō, -ere, -clūdī, -clūsus, cut off, block up

interdiū, *adv.*, during the day, by day

interficiō, -ere, -fēcī, -fectus, put out of the way, kill

interfluō, -ere, ——, ——, flow between

interim, *adv.*, meanwhile, in the meanwhile

intermittō,-ere,-mīsī,-missus,leave off, discontinue, stop, cease

interpōnō, -ere, -posuī, -positus, put between, interpose intersum, -esse, -fuī, -futūrus, be between (§ 838)

intrā, *prep. with acc.*, within, in, into

intrō, -āre, -āvī, -ātus, enter

intus, *adv.*, within

inūsitātus, -a, -um, .unusual, extraordinary

inveniō, -īre, -vēnī, -ventus, find, come upon

invidia, -ae, *f.*, envy, jealousy

invītō, -āre, -āvī, -ātus, invite

invītus, -a, -um, against the will; sē invītō, against his will

iō, *interj. (expressing joy)*, hurra! *common in the phrase* iō triumphe

ipse, ipsa, ipsum, *intens. adj. and pron.*, self, himself, herself, itself; very (§ 827)

is, ea, id, *dem. adj. and pron.*, this, that; he, she, it (§ 828)

iste, ista, istud, *dem. adj. and pron.*, that; he, she, it (§ 828)

ita, *adv.*, thus, so

Italia, -ae, *f.*, Italy

itaque, *conj.*, and so, therefore

iter, itineris, *n.*, journey, march, route; iter dare, give a right of way; iter facere, march; iter magnum, forced march; itinere prohibēre, keep from passing; itinere conversō, changing their course (§ 813)

iubeō, -ēre, iussī, iussus, command, order, *with acc. and infin.*

iūdicium, iūdicī, *n.*, judgment, trial

iūdicō, -āre, -āvī, -ātus, judge, decide

Iūnō, -ōnis, *f.*, Juno

Iuppiter, Iovis, *m.*, Jupiter

iūs, iūris, *n. (plur. only nom. and acc.* iūra), law, right

iuvenis, -is, young; *as subst.*, iuvenis, -is (-ium), *m. or f.*, youth

labor, -ōris, *m.*, labor, toil

labōrō, -āre, -āvī, -ātus, toil; suffer

labyrinthus, -ī, *m.*, labyrinth

lacessō, -ere, -īvī, -ītus, attack, assail,

lacrima, -ae, *f.*, tear

laetus, -a, -um, glad

lātus, -a, -um, wide, broad

laudō, -āre, -āvī, -ātus, praise

laus, laudis, *f.*, praise

lavō, -ere, lāvī, lautus *or* lōtus, wash

Lēander, -drī, *m.*, Leander

lēgātus, -ī, *m.*, ambassador; lieutenant

legiō, -ōnis, *f.*, legion

legō, -ere, lēgī, lēctus, read

leō, -ōnis, *m.*, lion

Lesbia, -ae, *f.*, Lesbia

levis, -e, light, trivial, fickle

lēx, lēgis, *f.*, law

libenter, *adv.*, willingly, gladly

liber, librī, *m.*, book

līber, lībera, līberum, free

līberī, līberōrum, *m. plur.*, children

līberō, -āre, -āvī, -ātus, set free

lībertās, -ātis, *f.*, freedom, liberty

līctor, līctōris, *m.*, lictor

līgneus, -a, -um, wooden

ligō, -āre, -āvī, -ātus, bind

lingua, -ae, *f.*, language, tongue

litterae, -ārum, *f. plur.*, letter

lītus, -oris, *n.*, shore, beach

Līvia, -ae, *f.*, Livia

locō, -āre, -āvī, -ātus, put, set

locus, -ī, *m. (plur.* loca, -ōrum, *n.*), place, spot

longē, *adv.*, far away, distant
longus, -a, -um, long
lucerna, -ae, *f.*, lamp
lūdus, -ī, *m.*, elementary school
lupa, -ae, *f.*, wolf
lūx, lūcis, *f.*, light; **prīma lūx**, day-light
lūxuria, -ae, *f.*, luxury

magis, *adv.* (*in comp. degree*), more (§ 822)
magister, -trī, *m.*, teacher
magnitūdō, -inis, *f.*, size, greatness
magnoperē, *adv.*, greatly (§ 822)
magnus, -a, -um, great, large (§ 820)
maior, maius (*gen.* -ōris), *adj.* (*comp. of* magnus, *compared* magnus, maior, maximus), greater, larger (§ 820)
mālō, mālle, māluī, ——, *irreg. verb*, prefer (§ 840)
malus, -a, -um, evil, bad (§ 820)
maneō, -ēre, mānsī, mānsūrus, remain, abide, stay
Mānlius, Mānlī, *m.*, Manlius
manus, -ūs, *f.*, hand; group, force; **manūs cōnserere**, join in a hand to hand struggle
Mārcus, -ī, *m.*, Marcus
mare, -is (-**ium**), *n.*, sea
Marius, Marī, *m.*, Marius
Mārs, Mārtis, *m.*, Mars
Mārtius, -a, -um, of March
māter, mātris, *f.*, mother
mātrimōnium, -ōnī, *n.*, marriage; **in mātrimōnium dūcere**, marry; **in mātrimōnium dare**, give in marriage
Mātrona, -ae, *m.*, the Marne

mātūrō, -āre, -āvī, -ātus, hasten
maximē, *adv.* (*in superl. degree, compared* magnoperē, magis, maximē), most of all, especially (§ 822)
maximus, -a, -um (*superl. of* magnus, *compared* magnus, maior, maximus), greatest, extreme (§ 820)
medius, -a, -um, middle, middle part of
melior, -ius (*gen.* -ōris), *adj.* (*comp. of* bonus, *compared* bonus, melior, optimus), better (§ 820)
melius, *adv.* (*in comp. degree, compared* bene, melius, optimē), better (§ 822)
memorābilis, -e, noteworthy, memorable
memoria, -ae, *f.*, memory; **habēre in memoriā**, remember; **memoriā tenēre**, remember; **memoriam dēponere**, forget
mēns, mentis (-**ium**), *f.*, mind
mēnsa, -ae, *f.*, table
mēnsis, -is (-**ium**), *m.*, month
Metellus, -ī, *m.*, Metellus
meus, -a, -um, *poss. adj. and pron.*, my, mine
Midās, -ae, *m.* (*Greek noun*), Midas
mīles, mīlitis, *m.*, soldier
mīlitāris, -e, military; **rēs mīlitāris**, art of war; **aetās mīlitāris**, age of military service
mīlitō, -āre, -āvī, -ātus, serve as a soldier
mīlle (*plur.* **mīlia, -ium**), *num. adj. and subst.*, thousand (§ 820)
Minerva, -ae, *f.*, Minerva
minimē, *adv.*, not at all, least of all (§ 822)

minimus, -a, -um (*superl. of* parvus, *compared* parvus, minor, minimus), least, smallest (§ 820)

minor, minus (*gen.* -ōris) (*comp. of* parvus, *compared* parvus, minor, minimus), smaller, less (§ 820)

Mīnōs, -ōis, *m.* (*Greek noun*), Minos

Mīnōtaurus, -ī, *m.*, the Minotaur

miser, misera, miserum, wretched

mittō, -ere, mīsī, missus, send

modus, -ī, *m.*, measure; manner

molestē, *adv.*, ill, with trouble; molestē ferre, bear ill, be vexed

moneō, -ēre, -uī, -itus, advise; warn

mōns, montis (-ium), *m.*, mountain

mōnstrum, -ī, *n.*, monster

mora, -ae, *f.*, delay

morior, morī, mortuus sum, *dep. verb*, die

mors, mortis (-ium), *f.*, death

moveō, -ēre, mōvī, mōtus, move

mox, *adv.*, soon, presently

Mūcius, Mūcī, *m.*, Mucius

mulier, mulieris, *f.*, woman

multitūdō, -inis, *f.*, crowd, throng, multitude

multus, -a, -um, much, many; multā nocte, late at night (§ 820).

mūniō, -īre, -īvī *or* -iī, -ītus, fortify

mūnītiō, -ōnis, *f.*, fortification

mūrus, -ī, *m.*, wall

mūtō, -āre, -āvī, -ātus, change

nancīscor, nancīscī, nactus sum, *dep. verb*, find, light upon

nam, *conj.*, for

nārrō, -āre, -āvī, -ātus, tell

nāscor, nāscī, nātus sum, *dep. verb*, be born; rise

nātūra, -ae, *f.*, nature

nauta, -ae, *m.*, sailor

nāvigium, nāvigī, *n.*, boat

nāvigō, -āre, -āvī, -ātus, sail

nāvis, -is (-ium), *f.*, ship

nē, *conj. and adv.*, in order that not, lest; not; nē ... quidem, not even

-ne, *interrog. adv.*, *enclitic*

nec *or* neque, *conj.*, and not, nor; nec (neque) ... nec (neque), neither ... nor

neglegō, -legere, -lēxī, -lēctus, disregard, neglect

negō, -āre, -āvī, -ātus, deny, say not

negōtium, negōtī, *n.*, business, affair, matter; negōtium dare, give a commission, employ

nēmō (*gen.* nūllīus, *dat.* nēminī, *acc.* nēminem, *abl.* nūllō), *m. and f.*, no one

Neptūnus, -ī, *m.*, Neptune

Nerviī, -iōrum, *m. plur.*, the Nervii

neuter, -tra, -trum (*gen.* -īus, *dat.* -ī), neither (*of two*) (§ 502)

nihil, *n. indecl.*, nothing. *An abl.* nihilō, *from a nom.* nihilum, *occurs as an abl. of degree of difference*; nihil posse, have no power

nisi, *conj.*, if not, unless

nōbilis, -e, well known, famous, noble

noceō, -ēre, -uī, -itūrus, injure, *with dat.*

noctū, *adv.*, at night, by night

nocturnus, -a, -um, of the night, nightly, by night

nōlō, nōlle, nōluī, ——, *irreg. verb*, be unwilling (§ 840)

nōmen, -inis, *n.*, name; nōmen dare, enlist

nōn, *neg. adv.*, not

nōndum, *adv.*, not yet

nōn-ne, *interrog. adv. (suggesting an affirmative answer)*, not?

nōnus, -a, -um, *num. adj.*, ninth

nōs, *per. pron.*, we (*see* ego)

nōscō, -ere, nōvī, nōtus, come to know ; *in perf. tenses*, know

noster, -tra, -trum, *poss. adj. and pron.*, our, ours. *Plur.* nostrī, -ōrum, *m.*, our men [famous

nōtus, -a, -um, known, well known,

novem, *indecl. num. adj.*, nine

November, -bris, -bre, of November

novus, -a, -um, new, fresh

nox, noctis (-ium), *f.*, night ; prīmā nocte, at nightfall ; multā nccte, late at night

nūllus, -a, -um (*gen.* -īus, *dat.* -ī), none, no (§ 503)

num, *interrog. adv., suggesting a negative answer*; *in indirect questions*, whether

numerus, -ī, *m.*, number ; numerus impedīmentōrum, quantity of baggage, long baggage train

Numitor, -ōris, *m.*, Numitor

numquam, *adv.*, never

nunc, *adv.*, now, the present time

nūntiō, -āre, -āvī, -ātus, announce

nympha, -ae, *f.*, nymph

Ō, *interj.*, O ! ah !

obsecrō, -āre, -āvī, -ātus, I pray, I beseech you ; *as exclamation*, in heaven's name

obses, -idis, *m. and f.*, hostage

obtineō, -ēre, -uī, -tentus, possess, keep, gain

occāsus, -ūs, *m.*, going down, setting ; sub occāsum sōlis, just at sunset, just before sunset

occīdō, -ere, -cīdī, -cīsus, kill

occupō, -āre, -āvī, -ātus, seize ; in opere occupārī, be engaged *or* employed on the works *or* fortifications

octāvus, -a, -um, *num. adj.*, eighth

octō, *indecl. num. adj.*, eight

Octōber, -bris, -bre, of October

Octōdūrus, -ī, *m.*, Octodurus

oculus, -ī, *m.*, eye

officium, officī, *n.*, duty, service

ōlim, *adv.*, once upon a time

omittō, -ere, -mīsī, -missus, let go by ; cōnsilium omittere, leave a plan untried

omnīnō, *adv.*, in all, altogether ; but, just

omnis, -e, all, every

opera, -ae, *f.*, labor, work ; operam dare, give attention

opīniō, -ōnis, *f.*, supposition, opinion

oportet, -ēre, oportuit, it is fitting, is necessary ; *an impers. verb, often used with an infin. and subj. acc.*

oppidum, -ī, *n.*, town

oppūgnō, -āre, -āvī, -ātus, attack, assault

optimē, *adv. (in superl. degree, compared* bene, melius, optimē), best; well done (§ 822)

optimus, -a, -um (*superl. of* bonus, *compared* bonus, melior, optimus), best, most excellent (§ 820)

optiō, optiōnis, *m.*, aide-de-camp

opus, operis, *n.*, work; fortifications, works

ōra, -ae, *f.*, shore, coast
ōrāculum, -ī, *n.*, oracle
ōrātiō, -ōnis, *f.*, speech, oration;
ōrātiōnem habēre, make a speech
ōrdō, -inis, *m.*, rank; class, order
Orpheus, -ī, *m.*, Orpheus
ostendō, -ere, -dī, -tus, show, display
ōstium, ōstī, *n.*, door
ovis, -is, *f.*, sleep

pācō, -āre, -āvī, -ātus, subdue, pacify
paene, *adv.*, nearly, almost
pallidus, -a, -um, pale
pār, pāris, equal
parcō, -ere, pepercī, parsus, spare,
  with dat.
pāreō, -ēre, -uī, ——, obey, *with dat.*
parō, -āre, -āvī, -ātus, prepare
pars, partis (-ium), *f.*, part, share;
  side, direction; ex omnibus partī-
  bus, on all sides
partior, partīrī, partītus sum, *dep.
  verb*, share
parvus, -a, -um (*compared* parvus,
  minor, minimus), small, little (§ 820)
passus, -ūs, *m.*, step, pace; mille
  passūs, a thousand paces, a mile
pāstor, -ōris, *m.*, shepherd
pateō, -ēre, patuī, ——, lie open,
  extend, stretch
pater, patris, *m.*, father
patior, patī, passus sum, *dep. verb*,
  suffer, allow, permit
patria, -ae, *f.*, native land
paucī, -ae, -a, few, only a few
paulisper, *adv.*, a little while
paulō, *adv.*, by a little, little
paulum, *adv.*, a little, somewhat
pāx, pācis, *f.*, peace

pectus, -oris, *n.*, heart
pecūnia, -ae, *f.*, money
pecus, pecoris, *n.*, cattle
pedes, -itis, *m.*, foot soldier; peditēs,
  infantry
pedester, -tris, -tre, on foot; *with*
  cōpiae, infantry
peior, peius (*gen.* -ōris), *adj.* (*in
  comp. degree, compared* malus,
  peior, pessimus), worse (§ 820)
pellō, -ere, pepulī, pulsus, drive,
  banish; defeat
per, *prep. with acc.*, through, by
perditiō, -ōnis, *f.*, destruction
perdūcō, -ere, -dūxī, -ductus, lead
  through, bring; construct
pereō, -īre, -īvī *or* -iī, -itūrus, be
  lost, perish
perficiō, -ere, -fēcī, -fectus, finish
perfringō, -ere, -frēgī, -frāctus,
  break through
perīculum, -ī, *n.*, danger
perītus, -a, -um, skilled, experi-
  enced, *with gen.*
permaneō, -ēre, -mānsī, -mānsūrus,
  last, endure, continue
permoveō, -ēre, -mōvī, -mōtus, move
  deeply, arouse, influence
peropportunē, *adv.*, most opportunely
perrumpō, -ere, -rūpī, -ruptus, force
  a way through, break in
Perseus, -ī, *m.*, Perseus
perspiciō, -ere, -spēxī, -spectus, observe, learn, discover
persuādeō, -ēre, -suāsī, -suāsus, persuade, *with dat.*
perterreō, -ēre, -uī, -itus, terrify,
  alarm

pertineō, -ēre, -uī, ——, reach, extend, pertain

perveniō, -īre, -vēnī, -ventus, arrive, *with* ad *or* in *and acc.*

pēs, pedis, *m.*, foot

pessimus, -a, -um, *adj.* (*in superl. degree, compared* malus, peior, pessimus), worst (§ 820)

petō, -ere, -īvī *or* -iī, -ītus, seek, ask, beg; make for, attack

pictūra, -ae, *f.*, picture

pīlus, -ī, *m.*, company of veteran reserves; prīmus pīlus, chief centurion of a legion

plānus, -a, -um, flat, level, even

plēnus, -a, -um, full

plūrimum, *adv.* (*in superl. degree, compared* multum, plūs, plūrimum), very much, most; *with* posse, be most powerful

plūrimus, -a, -um (*superl. of* multus, *compared* multus, plūs, plūrimus), most, very many (§ 820)

plūs (*gen.* plūris), *adj.* (*in comp. degree, compared* multus, plūs, plūrimus); *sing. n. as subst.*, more; *plur.*, more, many, several (§§ 819, 820)

Plūtō, -ōnis, *m.*, Pluto

poena, -ae, *f.*, punishment; poenam dare, suffer punishment, pay a penalty

poēta, -ae, *m.*, poet

pōnō, -ere, posuī, positus, place, set, build; castra pōnere, pitch camp; positus, -a, -um, *past part.*, situated

pōns, pontis (-ium), *m.*, bridge

populus, -ī, *m.*, people

porrigō, -ere, -rēxī, -rectus, extend

Porsenna, -ae, *m.*, Porsenna

porta, -ae, *f.*, gate

portō, -āre, -āvī, -ātus, carry

possum, posse, potuī, ——, be able, can; nihil posse, have no power (§ 839)

post, *prep. with acc.*, after, behind

posteā, *adv.*, thereafter, afterwards, hereafter, after this

postulō, -āre, -āvī, -ātus, demand, require

potentia, -ae, *f.*, power

potestās, -ātis, *f.*, power

praebeō, -ēre, -uī, -itus, offer, present

praecēdō, -ere, -cessī, -cessus, surpass

praeceptum, -ī, *n.*, instruction, order

praeda, -ae, *f.*, booty, plunder

praeficiō, -ere, -fēcī, -fectus, set over, place in command, *with acc. and dat.*

praemittō, -ere, -mīsī, -missus, send ahead, send forward

praemium, praemī, *n.*, prize, reward

praesertim, *adv.*, especially

praesidium, praesidī, *n.*, garrison, guard; praesidiō cīvitātī esse, be a defense to the state

praesum, -esse, -fuī, -futūrus, be before, be over, be in command, *with dat.* (§ 838)

praeter, *prep. with acc.*, except

praetereā, *adv.*, furthermore, besides

praetōrium, praetōrī, *n.*, general's tent

premō, -ere, pressī, pressus, press hard; harass

prīmō, *adv.*, at first (*as opposed to afterwards*); in the beginning (*referring to time*) prīmum, *adv.*, first, in the first place (*referring to order*)

prīmus, -a, -um, *adj.* (*in superl. degree*), first (§ 820)

prīnceps, -ipis, *m.*, chief, leader

prō, *prep. with abl.*, for, in behalf of; *rarely* in front of

prōcēdō, -ere, -cessī, -cessūrus, go forward, advance

prōcōnsul, -is, *m.*, proconsul, governor (*of a province*)

prōcōnsulātus, -ūs, *m.*, proconsulship, governorship

prōcurrō, -ere, -currī, -cursūrus, run forward, charge

prōdō, -dere, -didī, -ditus, go forth; betray [forward

prōdūcō, -ere, -dūxī, -ductus, lead

proelium, proelī, *n.*, battle; proelium facere, engage in battle; proelium committere, join battle

profectiō, -ōnis, *f.*, departure

prōficīscor, -ī, -fectus sum, *dep. verb*, set out

prohibeō, -ēre, -uī, -itus, hinder, prevent, keep away from

prōiciō, -ere, -iēcī, -iectus (prō + iaciō), throw forward; sē prōicere, leap

prope, *prep. with acc.*, near; *adv.*, near; *comp.* propius, *superl.* proximē (§ 822)

properō, -āre, -āvī, -ātus, hasten

prophēta, -ae, *m.*, prophet

prōpōnō, -ere, -posuī, -positus, set forth, offer; *with* vēxillum, hang out, display

propter, *prep. with acc.*, on account of; because of; near, next to, close to

Prōserpina, -ae, *f.*, Proserpina

prōvideō, -ēre, -vīdī, -vīsus, look out for, foresee

prōvincia, -ae, *f.*, province

prōvolō, -āre, -āvī, -ātūrus, fly forth; rush forth

proximus, -a, -um, *adj.* (*in superl. degree*), nearest, very near, next; last (§ 820)

pūblicus, -a, -um, public, official

puella, -ae, *f.*, girl

puer, puerī, *m.*, boy; ā puerīs, from boyhood

pūgnō, -āre, -āvī, -ātus, fight

pulcher, -chra, -chrum, pretty, beautiful

pulsō, -āre, -āvī, -ātus, knock

putō, -āre, -āvī, -ātus, think, reckon

Q., *abbreviation for* Quīntus

quaerō, -ere, quaesīvī, quaesītus, seek for, ask, inquire for

quam, *adv.*, how; *conj. after a comp.*, than; *with a superl.*, as . . . as possible

quandō, *interrog. adv.*, when?

quārtus, -a, -um, *num. adj.*, fourth

quattuor, *indecl. num. adj.*, four

-que, *conj.*, enclitic, and

quia, *conj.*, because

quī, quae, quod, *rel. pron. and adj.*, who, which, what, that (§ 829)

quīcumque, quaecumque, quodcumque, *adj.*, *pron.*, whoever, whatever, whosoever, whatsoever

quīdam, quiddam, *indef. pron.*, a certain one (§ 831)

quīdam, quaedam, quoddam, *indef. adj.*, a certain (§ 831)

quidem, *adv.*, indeed, in fact; *never stands first*; **nē . . . quidem**, not even (*the emphatic word standing between*)

quīndecim, *indecl. num. adj.*, fifteen

quīnque, *indecl. num. adj.*, five

Quīntus, -ī, *m.*, Quintus

quīntus, -a, -um, *num. adj.*, fifth

quis (quī), quae, quid (quod), *interrog. pron. and adj.*, who? what? which?·(§ 830)

quis (quī), qua (quae), quid (quod), *indef. pron. and adj. used after* **sī, nisi, nē, num**, anyone, anything, someone, something, any, some (§ 831)

quisque, quidque, *indef. pron.*, each one (§ 831)

quisque, quaeque, quodque, *indef. adj.*, each (§ 831)

quō, *interrog. adv. with verbs of motion*, whither

quod, *conj.*, because; that

quō modo, *adv.*, how

quotannīs, *adv.*, every year, yearly

rapiō, -ere, -uī, -tus, seize

rāpulum, -ī, *n.*, young turnip

ratiō, -ōnis, *f.*, method, arrangement, plan

recipiō, -ere, -cēpī, -ceptus, take back, receive; *with* **sē**, withdraw, retreat

recūsō, -āre, -āvī, -ātus, refuse, reject

reddō, -ere, reddidī, redditus, give back, return

redūcō, -ere, -dūxī, -ductus, lead back

referō, -ferre, -ttulī, -lātus, bring back, return; **pedem referre**, retreat (§ 841)

rēgīna, -ae, *f.*, queen

rēgnum, -ī, *n.*, realm, kingdom; sovereignty

regō, -ere, rēxī, rēctus, rule, guide

relanguēscō, -ere, -languī, ——, be weakened, be relaxed

relinquō, -ere, -līquī, -lictus, leave, leave behind, desert

reliquus, -a, -um, the rest, remaining, remainder of, the other, other

remittō, -ere, -mīsī, -missus, send back; pardon, forgive

remōtus, -a, -um, far away, distant

Remus, -ī, *m.*, Remus

repellō, -ere, -ppulī, -pulsus, repulse, repel

repentīnus, -a, -um, sudden

rēs, reī, *f.*, thing, matter, affair; **rēs frūmentāria**, grain supplies; **rēs gestae**, exploits; **rēs mīlitāris**, art of war; **rēs pūblica**, commonwealth, republic, state; **novīs rēbus studēre**, be eager for a revolution; **rēs est in perīculō**, the situation is critical

resistō, -ere, -stitī, ——, resist, *with dat.*

respondeō, -ēre, -spondī, -spōnsus, reply

retineō, -ēre, -tinuī, -tentus, hold back, retain

revertō, -ere, -vertī, ——, *or deponent*, **revertor, -ī, -versus sum**, turn back, return

revocō, -āre, -āvī, -ātus, call back, recall

rēx, rēgis, *m.*, king

Rhea, -ae, *f.,* Rhea
Rhēnus, -ī, *m.,* the Rhine
Rhodanus, -ī, *m.,* the Rhone
rīdeō, -ēre, rīsī, rīsus, laugh
rīpa, -ae, *f.,* bank
rogō, -āre, -āvī, -ātus, ask, request
Rōma, -ae, *f.,* Rome
Rōmānus, -a, -um, Roman; *as a noun in the masc. or fem.,* a Roman
Rōmulus, -ī, *m.,* Romulus
rudīmentum, -ī, *n.,* beginning, commencement; **prīma castrōrum rudīmenta,** first principles of military service
rūrsus, *adv.,* again
rūs, rūris, *n.* (*plur. only nom. and acc.,* **rūra**), country; **rūrī,** in the country
rūsticus, -a, -um, of the country, rustic

Sabīnī, -ōrum, *m.,* the Sabines
sacer, sacra, sacrum, sacred
sacerdōs, -ōtis, *m. and f.,* priest *or* priestess
saeculum, -ī, *n.,* age; **in saecula,** forever
saepe, *adv.,* often
saevus, -a, -um, fierce, savage, cruel
salūs, -ūtis, *f.,* safety; **salūtem dīcere,** send greeting
salvē, *imper.,* hail, greetings
Samnītēs, -ium, *m. plur.,* the Samnites
sānctificō, -āre, -āvī, -ātus, hallow
sapientia, -ae, *f.,* wisdom
satis, *indecl. adj.; also used as a neut. n. and as an adv.,* enough, sufficient; sufficiently

saxum, -ī, *n.,* rock
Scaevola, -ae, *m.,* Scaevola
sciō, scīre, scīvī, scītus, know
scrībō, -ere, scrīpsī, scrīptus, write
scūtum, -ī, *n.,* shield
secundus, -a, -um, following, next, second
sed, *conj.,* but
sedeō, -ēre, sēdī, sessūrus, sit; be settled, be established
semper, *adv.,* ever, always
senātus, -ūs, *m.,* senate
sentiō, sentīre, sēnsī, sēnsus, feel, perceive
sēparō, -āre, -āvī, -ātus, separate
septem, *indecl. num. adj.,* seven
September, -bris, -bre, of September
septimus, -a, -um, *num. adj.,* seventh
Sēquana, -ae, *f.,* the Seine
Sēquanī, -ōrum, *m.,* the Sequani
sequor, sequī, secūtus sum, *dep. verb,* follow
servātor, -ōris, *m.,* deliverer, preserver, savior
servitūs, servitūtis, *f.,* slavery
servō, -āre, -āvī, -ātus, save
servus, -ī, *m.,* slave
Sēstus, -ī, *f.,* Sestos
sex, *indecl. num. adj.,* six
Sextus, -ī, *m.,* Sextus
sextus, -a, -um, *num. adj.,* sixth
sī, *conj.,* if
sīc, *adv.,* thus, in this way, so
Sicilia, -ae, *f.,* Sicily
sīcut, just as
signum, -ī, *n.,* sign, signal; standard, ensign
silentium, silentī, *n.,* silence

silva, -ae, *f.*, forest

Silvia, -ae, *f.*, Silvia

similis, -e, similar, like (§ 820)

simul, *adv.*, at the same time; simul atque, *conj.*, as soon as

simulō, -āre, -āvī, -ātus, pretend.

sine, *prep. with abl.*, without

singulī, -ae, -a, *distributive num. adj.*, one at a time; inter singulās legiōnēs, between every two legions

sinister, -tra, -trum, left

societās, -ātis, *f.*, association, alliance

socius, socī, *m.*, ally, companion

sōl, sōlis, *m.*, the sun

solidus, -a, -um, solid

sollicitūdō, -inis, *f.*, care, anxiety

sōlum, *adv.*, only; nōn sōlum . . . sed etiam, not only . . . but also

sōlus, -a, -um (*gen.* -īus, *dat.* -ī), alone (§ 502)

solvō, -ere, solvī, solūtus, loose; (*of navigation*) set sail

somnus, -ī, *m.*, sleep

sonitus, -ūs, *m.*, noise, sound

soror, -ōris, *f.*, sister

spatiōsus, -a, -um, broad

spatium, spatī, *n.*, space, distance, interval

speciēs, -iēī, *f.*, appearance

spectāculum, -ī, *n.*, spectacle, game

spectō, -āre, -āvī, -ātus, look at

spērō, -āre, -āvī, -ātus, hope

spēs, speī, *f.*, hope; spem īnferre, inspire hope, *with dat.*

statim, *adv.*, at once, instantly, immediately

statiō, -ōnis, *f.*, a post, a picket; in statiōne, on guard

stō, -āre, stetī, statūrus, stand

studeō, -ēre, -uī, ——, be eager; study, *with dat.*; novīs rēbus studēre, to be eager for a revolution

stultus, -a, -um, foolish

sub, *prep. with acc. and abl.*, under beneath, underneath

subitō, *adv.*, suddenly

subsellium, -sellī, *n.*, bench

subsidium, -sidī, *n.*, assistance, reenforcement; subsidium ferre, go to the rescue

succēdō, -cēdere, -cessī, -cessūrus, come up, advance

suī, *gen.*, of (himself, herself, itself, themselves); in fugam sēsē dare, flee; inter sē, to each other *or* from each other

sum, esse, fuī, futūrus, be, am (§ 838)

summus, -a, -um (*superl. of* superus, *compared* superus, superior, suprēmus *or* summus), highest, supreme, greatest, most violent; summus mōns, the top of the mountain; summus collis, the top of the hill (§ 820)

sūmō, -ere, sūmpsī, sūmptus, take up, assume; sūmere supplicium dē, inflict punishment on

superbia, -ae, *f.*, pride

superior, -ius (*gen.* -ōris), *comp. of* superus (§ 820)

superō, -āre, -āvī, -ātus, overcome, conquer; go over, ascend

superus, -a, -um, higher, upper (§ 820)

supplicium, supplicī, *n.*, punishment, torture; supplicium sūmere dē, inflict punishment on; supplicium dare, suffer punishment surgō, -ere, surrēxī, surrēctus, rise, get up

suscipiō, -ere, -cēpī, -ceptus, undertake, assume

suscitō, -āre, -āvī, -ātus, arouse, awaken

sustineō, -ēre, -tinuī, -tentus, hold up, maintain ; endure, withstand ; sē sustinēre, stand up

suus, -a, -um, *reflex. poss. adj. and pron.*, his, her, hers, its, their, theirs

tabella, -ae, *f.*, writing tablet

tabernāculum, -ī, *n.*, tent

tabula, -ae, *f.*, map

taceō, -ēre, -cuī, -citus, be silent

tālis, -e, such

tam, *adv.*, so, such

tamen, *conj.*, nevertheless

tandem, *adv.*, pray, pray now, now

tangō, -ere, tetigī, tāctus, touch

tantum, *adv.*, only

tantus, -a, -um, so great

tardō, -āre, -āvī, -ātus, check

tardus, -a, -um, slow, dull, stupid ; backward, reluctant

tēlum, -ī, *n.*, weapon, missile, spear

tempestās, -ātis, *f.*, storm; weather

templum, -ī, *n.*, temple

temptō, -āre, -āvī, -ātus, try, attempt

tempus, -oris, *n.*, time, season; in reliquum tempus, for the future

teneō, -ēre, tenuī, ——, hold, keep, retain; vestīgia tenēre, keep footing

tentātiō, -ōnis, *f.*, temptation, trial

tergum, -ī, *n.*, back

terra, -ae, *f.*, earth, land

terribilis, -e, dreadful, terrible

terreō, -ēre, -uī, -itus, frighten, terrify

tertius, -a, -um, *num. adj.*, third

Thēseus, -ī, *m.*, Theseus

Tiberis, -eris, *m.*, the Tiber

timeō, -ēre, -uī, ——, fear

timidus, -a, -um, fearful, cowardly

timor, -ōris, *m.*, fear

toga, -ae, *f.*, toga

tolerō, -āre, -āvī, -ātus, bear, endure

tot, *indecl. adj.*, so many

tōtus, -a, -um (*gen.* -īus, *dat.* -ī), all, whole, entire (§ 502)

trādō, -ere, -didī, -ditus, give over, surrender ; pass along

trādūcō, -ere, -dūxī, -ductus, lead across

trānō, -āre, -āvī, ——, swim across

trāns, *prep. with acc.*, across

trānseō, -īre, -iī, -itus, go across, cross

trānsgredior, -gredī, -gressus sum, *dep. verb*, cross

trēs, tria, *num. adj.*, three (§ 820)

tribūnus, -ī, *m.*, tribune

trigeminus, -a, -um, triplet

tū, tuī, *per. pron.*, thou, you

tuba, -ae, *f.*, trumpet

tum, *adv.*, then, at that time

tunicātus, -a, -um, dressed in a tunic

turbidus, -a, -um, stormy

turris, -is (-ium; *abl.* turrī *or* turre), *f.*, tower

tuus, -a, -um, *poss. adj. and pron.*, your, yours

ubi, *interrog. adv. with verbs of rest*, where (§ 502)

ūllus, -a, -um (*gen.* -īus, *dat.* -ī), any

umquam, *adv.*, ever

unde, *adv.*, whence

ūndecim, *indecl. num. adj.*, eleven

ūndecimus, -a, -um, *num. adj.*, eleventh

undique, *adv.*, on all sides

ūniversus, -a, -um, all together, all

ūnus, -a, -um (*gen.* ius, *dat.* -ī), *num. adj.*, one; alone (§ 815)

urbs, urbis (-ium), *f.*, city [hard

urgeō, -ēre, ursī, ——, press, press

ūsque, *adv.*, even, even till

ut, *conj. with subjv.*, that, in order that, so that, to; *with indic.*, as

uter, utra, utrum (*gen.* -ius, *dat.* -ī), which? (*of two*) (§ 502)

utrimque, *adv.*, on both sides, from each side

vadum, -ī, *n.*, shallow place, ford

vagor, -ārī, -ātus sum, *dep. verb*, roam, wander

valē, *imper.*, good-by

valeō, -ēre, -uī, -itūrus, be well, be in health, be powerful

valētūdō, -inis, *f.*, state of health, health [*camp*)

vāllum, -ī, *n.*, rampart, wall (*of a*

vāstō, -āre, -āvī, -ātus, lay waste, devastate, destroy

vātēs, -is (-ium), *m. and f.*, bard, inspired singer [much

vehementer, *adv.*, strongly, very

vehō, -ere, vexī, vectus, carry

venia, -ae, *f.*, favor

veniō, -īre, vēnī, ventus, come

Venus, -eris, *f.*, Venus

verbum, -ī, *n.*, word

vereor, -ērī, veritus sum, *dep. verb*, fear, respect

vērō, *adv.*, in truth, verily

vertō, -ere, vertī, versus, turn

vērus, -a, -um, true, genuine; vērum dīcere, tell the truth

vesper, -erī, *m.*, evening

vester, -tra, -trum, *poss. adj. and pron.*, your, yours

vestīgium, vestīgī, *n.*, step; vestīgia tenēre, keep footing

vetō, -āre, -uī, -itus, forbid

vēxillum, -ī, *n.*, flag

via, -ae, *f.*, way, road

victōria, -ae, *f.*, victory

videō, -ēre, vīdī, vīsus, see

vigilia, -ae, *f.*, watching; watch (*of the night*)

vīgintī, *indecl. num. adj.*, twenty

vīlla, -ae, farm, villa, country seat, farmhouse

vincō, -ere, vīcī, victus, conquer

vinculum, -ī, *n.*, rope, cord, fetter

vindicō, -āre, -āvī, -ātus, claim

vīnum, -ī, *n.*, wine

vir, virī, *m.*, man

virga, -ae, *f.*, rod

virgō, -inis, *f.*, maiden

virtūs, virtūtis, *f.*, manliness; courage, valor; worth, virtue (§ 813)

vīs, (vīs), *f.*, strength, power, violence

vīta, -ae, *f.*, life

vix, *adv.*, with difficulty, scarcely

vocō, -āre, -āvī, -ātus, call

volō, velle, voluī, ——, *irreg. verb*, wish (§ 840)

volūmen, -inis, *n.*, roll

voluntās, -ātis, *f.*, will

vōx, vōcis, *f.*, voice; word; magna vōx, a loud voice

vulnerō, -āre, -āvī, -ātus, wound

vulnus, -eris, *n.*, wound

vultus, -ūs, *m.*, looks, expression; face

ENGLISH–LATIN VOCABULARY

a, an, *commonly not translated*
abandon, relinquō, 3
able (be), possum, posse, potuī, —— (§ 839)
about, *prep.*, dē, *with abl.*
about to, *expressed by fut. act. part.*
absent (be), absum, -esse, āfuī, āfuturus (§ 838)
abundance, cōpia, -ae, *f.*
abundant, amplus, -a, -um
accept, accipiō, 3
according to, *expressed by abl.*
across, trāns, *with acc.*
advance, prōcēdō, 3
advise, moneō, 2
after, *prep.*, post, *with acc.*
after, *conj.*, postquam; *often expressed by past part.*
afterwards, posteā
against, in, *with acc.*
aid, auxilium, auxi'lī, *n.*
alarm, commoveō, 2
alarmed, commōtus, -a, -um
all, omnis, -e; tōtus, -a, -um (§ 502)
ally, socius, socī, *m.*
alone, ūnus, -a, -um; sōlus, -a, -um (§502)
already, iam
always, semper
ambassador, lēgātus, -ī, *m.*
among, apud, *with acc.*
ample, amplus, -a, -um
and, et, atque (ac), -que

and so, itaque
Andromeda, Andromeda, -ae, *f.*
animal, animal, -ālis, *n.*
announce, nūntiō, 1
annoy, molestē ferō
another, alius, -a, -ud (§ 502)
any, ūllus, -a, -um (§ 502)
approach, appropinquo, 1, *with dat.*
approach, *n.*, adventus, -ūs, *m.*
are, *used as auxiliary, not translated; as copula,* sum (§ 838)
are of, sum, *with pred. gen.* (*cf.* belong to)
arms, arma, -ōrum, *n. plur.*
army, exercitus, -ūs, *m.*
arrival, adventus, -ūs, *m.*
arrive, perveniō, 4
art of war, rēs mīlitaris
ask, petō, 3; quaerō, 3; rogō, 1
assault, oppugnō, 1
assemble, conveniō, 4
assistance, auxilium, auxi'lī, *n.*
at, in, *with acc. or abl.*; *with names of towns, locative case or abl. without a preposition* (§ 484); *time when or within which, abl.*
at once, statim
Athens, Athēnae, -ārum, *f.*
attack, *v.*, oppugnō, 1
attack, *n.*, impetus, -ūs, *m.*; make an attack upon, impetum faciō in, *with acc.*

407

attempt, temptō, 1
attentively, dīligenter
authority, auctōritās, -ātis, *f.*
away (be), absum, -esse, āfuī, āfutūrus (§ 838)

bad, malus, -a, -um (§ 456)
baggage, impedīmenta, -ōrum, *n.
plur.*
barbarians, barbarī, -ōrum, *m. plur.*
battle, proelium, proelī, *n.*
be, sum, esse, fuī, futūrus (§ 838)
be absent, be far, absum, -esse, āfuī,
āfutūrus (§ 838)
be afraid, timeō, 2 ; vereor, 2
be away, absum, -esse, āfuī, āfutūrus (§ 838)
be in command of, praesum, -esse,
-fuī, -futūrus, *with dat.* (§ 623)
be informed, certior fīō (§ 843)
be off, be distant, absum, -esse, āfuī,
āfutūrus (§ 838)
bear, ferō, ferre,. tulī, lātus (§ 841)
beautiful, pulcher, -chra, -chrum
because, quod, *conj.*; because (of),
abl. of cause or propter *with
acc.*
become, fīō, fierī, factus sum (§ 843)
been, *expressed in verb form*
before, heretofore, *adv.*, anteā
before, *prep.*, ante, *with acc.*
beg, beg for, petō, 3
begin, incipiō, 3
believe, crēdō, 3, *with dat.* (§ 224)
belong to, *see* are of
benefit, beneficium, benefi'cī, *n.*
best, optimus, *superl. of* bonus
better, melior, *comp. of* bonus
between, inter, *with acc.*

boat, nāvigium, nāvi'gī, *n.*; nāvis,
-is, *f.*
body, corpus, -oris, *n.*
book, liber, librī, *m.*
both . . . and, et . . . et
bound, contineō, 2
boy, puer, -erī, *m.*
brave, fortis, -e
bravely, fortiter
bridge, pōns, pontis, *m.*
bring, bring to, addūcō, 3
bring upon, īnferō, -ferre, -tulī,
-lātus, *with acc. and dat.* (§ 841)
Britain, Britannia, -ae, *f.*
Britons, Britannī, -ōrum, *m.*
brother, frāter, -tris, *m.*
Brutus, Brūtus, -ī, *m.*
build, pōnō, 3 ; faciō, 3
burn, incendō, 3
business, negōtium, negō'tī, *n.*
but, however, autem, sed
by, ā, ab, *with abl.*; *denoting
means, abl. alone*; *sometimes
implied in a participle*

Cæsar, Caesar, -aris, *m.*
call, vocō, 1 ; appellō, 1
call out, ēvocō, 1
call together, convocō, 1
camp, castra, -ōrum, *n. plur.*
can, could, possum, posse, potuī,
—— (§ 839)
capital, caput, capitis, *n.*
Capitolium, Capitōlium, Capitō'lī, *n.*
captive, captīvus, -ī, *m.*
capture, capiō, 3 ; occupō, 1
carry, ferō, ferre, tulī, lātus (§ 841);
portō, 1
carry on, gerō, 3

cause, *v.*, *expressed by* faciō *followed by* ut *and subjv.* *clause of result*

cause, *n.*, causa, -ae, *f.*

cavalry, equitātus, -ūs, *m.*; (of) cavalry, equester, -tris, -tre

certain (a), quīdam, quaedam, quoddam (quiddam) (§ 831)

certain, sure, certus, -a, -um

certainly, certē

chief, prīnceps, -ipis, *m.*

children, līberī, -ōrum, *m. plur.*

choose, dēligō, 3

choose, elect, creō, 1

citizen, cīvis, -is, *m.* and *f.* (§ 412. *a*)

city, urbs, urbis, *f.*

claim attention, animum teneō

climb, ascendō, 3

cohort, cohors, -rtis, *f.*

collect, cōgō, 3

come, veniō, 4

command, imperō, 1, *with dat.* (§ 224); iubeō, 2; praesum, -esse, -fuī, -futūrus, *with dat.* (§ 623)

commander, dux, ducis, *m.*; imperātor, -ōris, *m.*

common, commūnis, -e

commonwealth, rēs pūblica, reī pūblicae

compel, cōgo, 3

concerning, dē, *with abl.*

condition, condiciō, -ōnis, *f.*

conquer, superō, 1; vincō, 3

consider, exīstimō, 1

construct (a ditch), perdūcō, 3; dūcō, 3

consul, cōnsul, cōnsulis, *m.*

consult, cōnsulō, 3

Cornelius, Cornēlius, Cornē′lī, *m.*

cottage, casa, -ae, *f.*

could, *see* can

country, *as distinguished from the city*, rūs, rūris, *n.*; *as territory*, fīnēs, -ium, *m. plur.*

country, fatherland, patria, -ae, *f.*

country house, country seat, farm, vīlla, -ae, *f.*

courage, virtūs, -ūtis, *f.*

courageous, fortis, -e

cowardly, timidus, -a, -um

cross, trānseō, -īre, -īvī (-iī), -itus, 4 (§ 842)

crowd, multitūdō, -inis, *f.*

crowded, crēber, -bra, -brum

custom, cōnsuētūdō, -inis, *f.*

cut off, interclūdō, 3

danger, perīculum, -ī, *n.*

dare, audeō, audēre, ausus sum

daughter, fīlia, -ae, *f.* (§ 70. *a*)

day, diēs, -ēī, *m.*

daybreak, daylight, prīma lūx

death, mors, mortis, *f.*

deed, rēs, reī, *f.*; factum, -ī, *n.*

deep, altus, -a, -um

defend, dēfendō, 3

defense, praesidium, praesi′dī, *n.*

demand, postulō, 1

Dentatus, Dentātus, -ī, *m.*

deny, negō, 1

depart, depart from, discēdō, 3; exeō, -īre, -īvī (-iī), -itūrus (§ 842); excēdō, 3

desert, relinquō, 3

desire, cupiō, 3

desirous of, cupidus, -a, -um, *with gen.* (§ 554)

different, dissimilis, -e

difficult, difficilis, -e (§ 457)
difficulty, difficultās, -ātis, *f.*
diligence, dīligentia, -ae, *f.*
diligently, dīligenter
display, ostendō, 3
distance, spatium, spatī, *n.*
distant (be), absum, -esse, āfuī, āfutūrus (§ 838)
ditch, fossa, -ae, *f.*
do, agō, 3 ; faciō, 3 ; *when used as auxiliary, not translated*
do completely, cōnficiō, 3
do harm to, noceō, 2, *with dat.* (§ 224)
down from, dē, *with abl.*
draw up, īnstruō, 3
drive, agō, 3
drive out, pellō, 3 ; expellō, 3
due the state, pūblicus, -a, -um
dull, slow, tardus, -a, -um
duty, officium, offi′cī, *n.*
dwell, habitō, 1 ; incolō, 3

each, quisque, quaeque, quidque (quodque) (§ 831)
each other, inter *with acc. of a reflex. pron.*
eager, ācer, ācris, ācre
eager (be) for, studeō, 2, *with dat.* (§ 224)
easily, facile
easy, facilis, -e
either . . . or, aut . . . aut
elapse (suffer to *or* let), intermittō, 3
encourage, cōnfīrmō, 1
enemy, hostis, -is, *m. and f.*; inimīcus, -ī, *m.*
enough, satis, *indecl.*
enroll, cōnscrībō, 3

entire, tōtus, -a, -um (§ 502)
equal, aequus, -a, -um
even, etiam ; **not even**, nē . . . quidem
evil, malus, -a, -um (§ 456)
example, exemplum, -ī, *n.*
expect, exspectō, 1
expose, committō, 3
extend, pateō, 2 ; pertineō, 2

fact, rēs, reī, *f.*
faith, fidēs, fideī, *f.*
fame, fāma, -ae, *f.*
famous, clārus, -a, -um
far, far away, far distant, longē
farm, vīlla, -ae, *f.*
farmer, agricola, -ae, *m.*
farther, *adj.*, ulterior, -ius ; *adv.*, longius
father, pater, patris, *m.*
fatherland, patria, -ae, *f.*
favor, faveō, 2, *with dat.* (§ 224)
favor, gratia, -ae, *f.*
favorable, idōneus, -a, -um
fear, timor, -ōris, *m.*
fear, be afraid, timeō, 2 ; vereor, 2
few, paucī, -ae, -a
field, ager, agrī, *m.*
fifth, quīntus, -a, -um
fight, contendō, 3 ; pugnō, 1 ; **fight a battle**, proelium faciō
finally, dēnique
find, inveniō, 4
finish, cōnficiō, 3
fire, ignis, -is, *m.* (§ 412. *a*)
first, *adj.*, prīmus, -a, -um
first, *adv.*, *referring to order*, prīmum ; *referring to time*, prīmō
fitting (be), oportet, 3

five, quīnque
flee, fugiō, 3
flight, fuga, -ae, *f.*
follow, sequor, 3
foot, pēs, pedis, *m.*
foot soldier, pedes, -itis, *m.*
for, *prep.*, *sign of dat.* ; dē, prō (*in behalf of*), *with abl.* ; *to express purpose*, ad, *with gerundive* ; *in expressions of time or space* per *may be used, but usually it is implied in acc. of time and of extent of space*
for, *conj.*, enim (*postpositive*), nam
for a long time, diū
for the future, in reliquum tempus
forbid, vetō, 1
force, vīs, (vīs), *f.* (§ 813)
forces, cōpiae, -ārum, *f. plur.*
foresee, prōvideō, 2
forest, silva, -ae, *f.*
formerly, anteā
fort, castrum, -ī, *n.*
fortify, mūniō, 4
fortify (all) about, circummūniō, 4
fortune, fortūna, -ae, *f.*
four, quattuor
fourth, quārtus, -a, -um
free, līber, -era, -erum
free, liberate, līberō, 1
frequent, crēber, -bra, -brum
fresh, integer, -gra, -grum
friend, amīcus, -ī, *m.*
friendly, amīcus, -a, -um
friendship, amīcitia, -ae, *f.*
frighten, perterreō, 2
from, ā *or* ab, dē, ē, ex, *with abl.* *Often expressed by the abl. of separation without a prep.*

Galba, Galba, -ae, *m.*
garrison, praesidium, praesi′dī, *n.*
gate, porta, -ae, *f.*
Gaul, Gallia, -ae, *f.*
Gaul (a), Gallus, -ī, *m.*
general, imperātor, -ōris, *m.*
Germans (the), Germānī, -ōrum, *m. plur.*
Germany, Germānia, -ae, *f.*
girl, puella, -ae, *f.*
give, dō, dare, dedī, datus (§ 161. N.)
give back, reddō, 3
give a right of way, iter dō
go, eō, īre, iī (īvī), itūrus (§ 842)
go out, excēdō, 3
god, deus, -ī, *m.*
goddess, dea, -ae, *f.* (§ 70. *a*)
gold, aurum, -ī, *n.*
good, bonus, -a, -um (§ 456)
grain, frūmentum, -ī, *n.*
grain supply, rēs frūmentāria
great, magnus, -a, -um (§ 456)
greatest, maximus, -a, -um ; summus, -a, -um
greatly, magnopere
greatness, magnitūdō, -inis, *f.*
Greece, Graecia, -ae, *f.*
grief, dolor, -ōris, *m.*
guard, praesidium, praesi′dī, *n.*

had, *as auxiliary, expressed in verb form*
hand, manus, -ūs, *f.*
harm, noceō, 2, *with dat.* (§ 224)
has, *as auxiliary, expressed in verb form*
hasten, contendō, 3 ; properō, 1
have, habeō, 2 ; *when auxiliary of perfect, not expressed*

he, is, hic, ille, *or not expressed*
head, caput, -itis, *n.*
hear, audiō, 4
heart, animus, -ī, *m.*
heavy, gravis, -e
height, altitūdō, -inis, *f.*
Helvetii (the), Helvētiī, -ōrum, *m. plur.*
hem in, contineō, 2
her, eius, huius, istīus, illīus; *reflex.*, suus, -a, -um (§ 135)
heretofore, anteā
herself, suī. *See* self
high, altus, -a, -um
highest, summus, -a, -um
him, *see* he
himself, suī. *See* self
hinder, prohibeō, 2; impediō, 4
hindrance, impedīmentum, -ī, *n.*
his, eius, huius, istīus, illīus; *reflex.*, suus, -a, -um (§ 135)
hold, teneō, 2; obtineō, 2
hold back, retineō, 2
home, domus, -ūs, *f.* (§ 813); at home, domī (§ 485)
hope, *v.*, spērō, 1
hope, *n.*, spēs, speī, *f.*
horn, cornū, -ūs, *n.*
horse, equus, -ī, *m.*
horseman, eques, -itis, *m.*
hostile, inimīcus, -a, -um
hour, hōra, -ae, *f.*
how, quam; how far, quam longē; how long, quam diū
hurl, iaciō, 3; coniciō, 3

I, ego (§ 825), *or not expressed*
if, sī; if not, nisi
immediately, statim

in, *of place*, in, *with abl.*; *of time or of respect*, abl. *without prep.*
in command of (be), praesum, -esse, -fuī, -futūrus, *with dat.* (§ 623)
in order that, ut, *with subjv.*; in order that not, lest, nē, *with subjv.*
in the presence of, apud, *prep. with acc.*
in truth, vērō
in vain, frūstrā
industry, dīligentia, -ae, *f.*
infantry, pedes, -itis, *m.*
infantry (of), pedester, -tris, -tre
inflict punishment upon, supplicium sūmō dē, *with abl.*
influence, addūcō, 3
inform someone, aliquem certiōrem faciō
injure, noceō, 2, *with dat.* (§ 224)
injury, iniūria, -ae, *f.*
inquire, quaerō, 3
intend, in animō esse, *with dat.*
into, in, *with acc.*
intrust, committō, 3
is, *used as auxiliary, not translated*; *as copula*, sum, esse, fuī, futūrus (§ 838)
island, īnsula, -ae, *f.*
it, is, hic, iste, *or not expressed*
Italy, Italia, -ae, *f.*
its, eius, huius, istīus, illīus; *reflex.*, suus, -a, -um (§ 135)
itself, suī. *See* self

join together, committō, 3
journey, iter, itineris, *n.* (§ 813)
judgment, iūdicium, iūdi'cī, *n.*
justice, iūs, iūris, *n.*

keep (in), restrain, contineō, 2
keep (out *or* from), prohibeō, 2
kill, interficiō, 3 ; necō, 1
kind, genus, -eris, *n.*
king, rēx, rēgis, *m.*
kingdom, rēgnum, -ī, *n.*
know, cognōscō, 3, *in perf. tenses*;
    sciō, 4
known, nōtus, -a, -um

labor, *v.*, labōrō, 1
labor, *n.*, labor, -ōris, *m.*; opera,
    -ae, *f.*
lack, *v.*, dēsum, deesse, dēfuī, dē
    futūrus, *with dat.* (§ 623)
lack, *n.*, inopia, -ae, *f.*
lacking (be), dēsum, deesse, dēfuī,
    dēfutūrus, *with dat.* (§ 623)
lamp, lūcerna, -ae, *f.*
land, terra, -ae, *f.*
language, lingua, -ae, *f.*
large, magnus, -a, -um
law, lēx, lēgis, *f.*
lay down, lay aside, dēpōnō, 3
lay waste, vāstō, 1
lead, dūcō, 3
lead across, trādūcō, 3
lead away, abdūcō, 3
lead back, redūcō, 3
lead forward, prōdūcō, 3
lead in, conduct, indūcō, 3
lead out, lead forth, ēdūcō, 3
lead through, perdūcō, 3
lead to, addūcō, 3
Leander, Lēander, -drī, *m.*
learn, know (*in perf. tenses*), cog-
    nōscō, 3
leave, depart from, discēdō, 3
leave behind, abandon, relinquō, 3

leave off, intermittō, 3
left, sinister, -tra, -trum
legion, legiō, -ōnis, *f.*
length, longitūdō, -inis, *f.*
Lesbia, Lesbia, -ae, *f.*
lest, nē, *with subjv.*
liberty, lībertās, -ātis, *f.*
lieutenant, lēgātus, -ī, *m.*
life, vīta, -ae, *f.*
light, levis, -e
light, lūx, lūcis, *f.*
lightly, leviter
like, *adj.*, similis, -e (§ 457)
like, love, amō, 1
line of battle, aciēs, aciēī, *f.*
listen, audiō, 4
little, parvus, -a, -um (§ 456)
little, by a little, paulō
live, habitō, 1 ; incolō, 3
lofty, altus, -a, -um
long, longus, -a, -um
long, for a long time, diū
look at, spectō, 1
look for, quaerō, 3
look out for, prōvideō, 2
lose, āmittō, 3
love, amō, 1
loyal, fīrmus, -a, -um

make, faciō, 3 (§ 843)
make a speech, ōrātiōnem habeō
make war upon, bellum īnferō, *with*
    dat. (§ 623)
man, homō, -inis, *m. and f.* (§ 813);
    vir, virī, *m.*
manner, modus, -ī, *m.*
many, multī, -ae, -a
march, iter, itineris, *n.* (§ 813)
march (to), iter faciō

Marcus, Mārcus, -ī, *m.*
Mark, Mārcus, -ī, *m.*
marry, in mātrimōnium dūcō
matter, nęgōtium, negō'tī, *n.*; rēs, reī, *f.*
me, *see* I
means, by means of, *expressed by the abl.*
meanwhile, in the meantime, interim
memory, memoria, -ae, *f.*
method, ratiō, -ōnis, *f.*
midst of, medius, -a, -um
mile, mīlle passūs (§ 536); *plur.*, mīlia passuum
military, mīlitāris, -e
mind, animus, -ī, *m.*; mēns, mentis, *f.*
mine, meus, -a, -um
Minerva, Minerva, -ae, *f.*
Minotaur, Mīnōtaurus, -ī, *m.*
money, pecūnia, -ae, *f.*
month, mēnsis, -is, *m.*
more, *adj.*, plūs, plūris (§ 458), *or expressed by a comparative*; *adv.*, magis
most, *adj.*, plūrimus, -a, -um, *or expressed by a superl.*; *adv.*, maximē, plūrimum
mother, māter, mātris, *f.*
mountain, mōns, montis, *m.*
move, moveō, 2
move deeply, commoveō, 2; permoveō, 2
moved, commōtus, -a, -um; permōtus, -a, -um
much (by), multō
Mucius, Mūcius, Mūcī, *m.*
multitude, multitūdō, -inis, *f.*
my, meus, -a, -um

name, nōmen, -inis, *n.*
native land, patria, -ae, *f.*
nature, nātūra, -ae, *f.*
near, propinquus, -a, -um
nearest, proximus, -a, -um
necessary (be), oportet, 3
neighbor, fīnitimus, -ī, *m.*
neighboring, fīnitimus, -a, -um
neither (*of two*), neuter, neutra, neutrum (§ 502)
neither, neque *or* nec; neither . . . nor, neque (nec) . . . neque (nec)
never, numquam
nevertheless, tamen
new, novus, -a, -um
next, proximus, -a, -um
night, nox, noctis, *f.*
nine, novem
no, minimē, *or repeat verb with a negative* (§ 110)
no, none, nūllus, -a, -um (§ 503)
no one, nēmō, nųllīus
noble, nōbĭlis, -e
nor, neque *or* nec
not, nōn
not at all, minimē
not even, nē . . . quidem
nothing, nihil *or* nihilum, -ī, *n.*
now, nunc, iam
number, numerus, -ī, *m.*

O, *usually expressed by a vocative, occasionally by the interj.* Ō
obey, pāreō, 2, *with dat.* (§ 224)
observe, spectō, 1
of, *sign of gen.*; dē, *with abl.*; out of, ē *or* ex, *with abl.*
offer, prōpōnō, 3
often, saepe

on, *of place*, in, *with abl.*; *of time*,
     abl. without prep.
on account of, propter, *with acc.*;
     abl. of cause
once (upon a time), ōlim
one, ūnus, -a, -um (§ 815)
one ... another, *of several*, alius ...
     alius; the one ... the other, *of*
     two, alter ... alter (§ 504)
only, sōlum, tantum
only a few, paucī, -ae, -a
onto, *see* on
or, aut
oration, ōrātiō, -ōnis, *f.*
order, imperō, 1; iubeō, 2
other, alius, -a, -ud (§ 503); the one
     ... the other, *of two*, alter ...
     alter (§ 504)
others (the), reliquī, -ōrum, *m. plur.*
ought, dēbeō, 2
our, noster, -tra, -trum
out from, outside of, ē *or* ex *with*
     abl
overcome, superō, 1; vincō, 3
owe, dēbeō, 2
own (his, her, its, their), suus, -a, -um

pace, passus, -ūs, *m.*
pain, dolor, -ōris, *m.*
part, pars, partis, *f.*
peace, pāx, pācis, *f.*
penalty, poena, -ae, *f.*; supplicium,
     suppli'cī, *n.*
people, populus, -ī, *m.*
perceive, sentiō, 4
peril, perīculum, -ī, *n.*
Perseus, Perseus, -ī, *m.*
persuade, persuādeō, 2, *with dat.*
     (§ 224)

pertain, pertineō, 2
place, *n.*, locus, -ī, *m.*; *plur.*, loca,
     -ōrum, *n.*
place, put, pōnō, 3; locō, 1
place in command of, praeficiō, 3,
     with acc. and dat. (§ 623)
plan (a), cōnsilium, cōnsi'lī, *n.*; ratiō,
     -ōnis, *f.*
plead, dīcō, 3
please, placeō, 2, *with dat.* (§ 224)
pleasing, grātus, -a, -um
plenty, cōpia, -ae, *f.*
poet, poēta, -ae, *m.*
poor, miser, misera, miserum
possess, obtineō, 2
power, imperium, impe'rī, *n.*; po
     testās, -ātis, *f.*
powerful, be most powerful, plūri-
     mum possum
praise, laudō, 1
praise, laus, laudis, *f.*
prefer, mālō, mālle, māluī, ——
     (§ 840)
prepare, prepare for, parō, 1, *with*
     acc.
preserve, servō, 1; cōnservō, 1
press hard, premō, 3
pretty, pulcher, -chra, -chrum
prize, praemium, praemī, *n.*
protection, fidēs, fideī, *f.*
provide, comparō, 1
public, pūblicus, -a, -um
punishment, poena, -ae, *f.*; suppli-
     cium, suppli'cī, *n.*
purpose, for the purpose of, ut *or*
     quī,▪ *with subjv.*; ad, *with ger-*
     und or gerundive; causā, *follow-*
     ing the genitive of a gerund or
     gerundive

put, pōnō, 3
put down, dēpōnō, 3
put to death, in mortem dō
put to flight, in fugam dō

queen, rēgīna, -ae, *f.*
quickly, celeriter
Quintus, Quīntus, -ī, *m.*

rampart, vāllum, -ī, *n.*
rank, ōrdō, -inis, *m.*
rather, *see* wish rather
reach, pertineō, 2 ; pateō, 2
realm, rēgnum, -ī, *n.*
reason, causa, -ae, *f.*
receive, accipiō, 3
remain, maneō, 2 ; permaneō, 2
remainder (the), reliquī, -ōrum, *m.*
  plur.
remaining, reliquus, -a, -um
remarkable, ēgregius, -a, -um
remember, memoriā teneō
reply, respondeō, 2
report, fāma, -ae, *f.*
republic, rēs pūblica
reputation, fāma, -ae, *f.*
resist, resistō, 3, *with dat.* (§ 224)
respect, vereor, 2
rest (the), reliquī, -ōrum, *m. plur.*
restrain, contineō, 2
retain, retineō, 2
return, give back, reddō, 3
revolution, rēs novae, *f. plur.*
reward, praemium, praemī, *n.*
Rhine, Rhēnus, -ī, *m.*
right, *adj.*, dexter, -tra, -trum
right, *n.*, iūs, iūris, *n.*; give a right
  of way, iter faciō
river, flūmen, -inis, *n.*

road, via, viae, *f.*
Roman, Rōmānus, -a, -um ; *often
  used as a noun*
Rome, Rōma, -ae, *f.*
Romulus, Rōmulus, -ī, *m.*
route, iter, itineris, *n.*
rule, regō, 3
rumor, fāma, -ae, *f.*

sacred, sacer, -cra, -crum
safety, salūs, -ūtis, *f.*
sail, nāvigō, 1
sailor, nauta, -ae, *m.*
same, īdem, eadem, idem (§ 518)
satisfaction (give), satis faciō, 3,
  with dat.
satisfactory, satis, *indecl.*
savage, barbarus, -a, -um
savages, barbarī, -ōrum, *m. plur.*
save, servō, 1
say, dīcō, 3 ; say not, negō, 1
scarcity, inopia, -ae, *f.*
school, lūdus, -ī, *m.*
science of war, rēs mīlitaris, *f.*
scout, explōrātor, -ōris, *m.*
sea, mare, -is, *n.*
second, secundus, -a, -um
see, videō, 2
seek, petō, 3 ; quaerō, 3
seem, videor, 2, *pass. of* videō
seize, rapiō, 3 ; occupō, 1
self, ipse, -a, -um (§ 517); suī (§ 512)
senate, senātus, -ūs, *m.*
send, mittō, 3
send ahead *or* forward, praemittō, 3
send away, dīmittō, 3 ; āmittō, 3
send back, remittō, 3
serious, gravis, -e
set fire to, incendō, 3

set forth, prōpōnō, 3
settle, sedeō, 2
seven, septem
seventh, septimus, -a, -um
several, plūres, plūra
severe, gravis, -e
severely, graviter
Sextus, Sextus, -ī, *m.*
shall, *expressed by future tense*
sharp, ācer, ācris, ācre [*expressed*
she, ea, haec, ista, illa (§ 205), *or not*
ship, nāvis, -is, *f.* (§ 412. *a*)
shore, ōra, -ae, *f.*
short, brevis, -e
show, dēmōnstrō, 1 ; ostendō, 3
signal, signum, -ī, *n.*
similar, similis, -e
since, cum (§ 642)
sister, soror, -ōris, *f.*
sit, sedeō, 2
size, magnitūdō, -inis, *f.*
six, sex
sixth, sextus, -a, -um
skillful, skilled, perītus, -a, -um
slaughter, caedēs, -is, *f.*
slave, servus, -ī, *m.*
slavery, servitūs, -ūtis, *f.*
slow, tardus, -a, -um
slowly, tardē
small, parvus, -a, -um
smallest, minimus, -a, -um
so, ita, sīc, tam
so great, tantus, -a, -um
so that, ut ; so that not, ut nōn
soldier, mīles, -itis, *m.*
some, *often not expressed*; aliquī,
    aliqua, aliquod (§ 831)
some . . . others, aliī . . . aliī (§ 504)
someone, aliquis (§ 831)

something, aliquid (§ 831)
son, fīlius, fīlī, *m.*
soon, mox
sovereignty, rēgnum, -ī, *n.*
space, spatium, spatī, *n.*
speak, dīcō, 3
spear, tēlum, -ī. *n.*
speech, ōrātiō, -ōnis, *f.*
spirit, animus, -ī, *m.*
spur, calcar, -āris, *n.*
spy, explōrātor, -ōris, *m.*
stand still, take a stand, cōnsistō, 3
state, cīvitās, -ātis, *f.*
stay, permaneō, 2
steadfast, fīrmus, -a, -um
storm, oppugnō, 1 ; take by storm,
    expugnō, 1
story, fābula, -ae, *f.*
strange, nōvus, -a, -um
street, via, -ae, *f.*
strength, vīs, (vīs), *f.*
strong, fortis, -e ; fīrmus, -a, -um
stupid, tardus, -a, -um
subdue, pācō, 1
such, tālis, -e
suffer, patior, 3 ; labōrō, 1
suffer punishment, poenam *or* sup-
    plicium dō
sufficient, satis, *indecl.*
suitable, idōneus, -a, -um
summer, aestās, -ātis, *f.*
summon, vocō, 1
supply, cōpia, -ae, *f.*
supreme, summus, -a, -um
sure, certus, -a, -um
suspend, intermittō, 3
swift, celer, -eris, -ere
swiftly, celeriter
swiftness, celeritās, -ātis, *f.*

take, sūmō, 3
take, capture, take up, capiō, 3
take back, recipiō, 3
take by storm, expugnō, 1
tall, altus, -a, -um
teach, doceō, 2
tell, dīcō, 3 ; nārrō, 1
ten, decem
tenth, decimus, -a, -um
terrified, perterritus, -a, -um
terrify, perterreō, 2
territory, fīnēs, -ium, *m. plur.*
than, quam
thank, grātiās agō, *with dat.*
that, *demon. pron.*, is (§ 203), iste, ille
  (§ 524); *rel. pron.*, quī, quae, quod
that, in order that, *in purpose
  clauses*, ut
that not, lest, *in purpose clauses*, nē
the, *not expressed*
the one, the other (*of two*), alter,
  altera, alterum
their, *gen. plur. of* is ; *reflex.*, suus,
  -a, -um (§ 135)
their own, suus, -a, -um (§ 135)
them, *see* they
then, at that time, tum
then, in the next place, deinde
there, *as expletive, not expressed*
there, in that place, ibi
therefore, itaque
these, *see* this
Theseus, Thēseus, -ī, *m.*
they, iī, hī, istī, illī, *or not expressed*
  (§ 205)
thick, crēber, -bra, -brum
thing, rēs, reī, *f.*
think, arbitror, 1 ; exīstimō, 1 ;
  putō, 1

third, tertius, -a, -um
this, hic, haec, hoc (§ 523); is, ea, id
  (§ 203)
those, *see* that, *dem. pron.*
though, cum
thousand, mīlle (§ 536)
three, trēs, tria (§ 824)
three hundred, trecentī, -ae, -a
through, per, *with acc.*
throw, iaciō, 3
throw down, dēiciō, 3
time, tempus, -oris, *n.*
timid, timidus, -a, -um
to, *sign of dat.*; ad, in, *with acc.*;
  expressing purpose, ut, quī, *with
  subjv.* ; ad, *with gerund or gerundive*
to each other, inter *with acc. of a
  reflex. pron.*
toil, labōrō, 1
top of, summus, -a, -um
tower, turris, -is, *f.*
town, oppidum, -ī, *n.*
troops, cōpiae, -ārum, *f. plur.*
true, vērus, -a, -um
try, temptō, 1
twelfth, duodecimus, -a, -um
twelve, duodecim
two, duo, duae, duo (§ 824)
two hundred, ducentī, -ae, -a

undertake, suscipiō, 3
unfavorable, inīquus, -a, -um
unskilled, imperītus, -a, -um
unwilling (be), not willing, nōlō,
  nōlle, nōluī, ———— (§ 840)
uphold, sustineō, 2
urge, hortor, 1
us, nōs, *acc. plur. of* ego (§ 509)

valor, virtūs, -ūtis, *f.*
very, *superl. degree*, maximē; *intensive*, ipse, -a, -um (§ 517)
victory, victōria, -ae, *f.*
villa, vīlla, -ae, *f.*
violence, vīs, (vīs), *f.* (§ 419)

wage, gerō, 3
wait, wait for, exspectō, 1
wall, mūrus, -ī, *m.*; vāllum, -ī, *n.*
want, inopia, -ae, *f.*
war, bellum, -ī, *n.*
warn, moneō, 2
was, *see* be
water, aqua, -ae, *f.*
way, manner, modus, -ī, *m.*; ratiō, -ōnis, *f.*
we, nōs, *plur. of* ego (§ 509); *or not expressed*
wear, gerō, 3
well, bene
well-known, nōtus, -a, -um
were, *see* be
what, quis (quī), quae, quid (quod) (§§ 394, 395)
when, ubi, cum (§ 641); *often expressed by a participle*
whether, *introducing an indirect question*, num
where, ubi
which, quī, quae, quod (§ 387); **which of two**, uter, utra, utrum (§ 503)
whither, quō
who, *rel.*, quī, quae (§ 387); *interrog.*, quis (§ 394)
whose, cuius *or* quōrum, quārum, quōrum, *gen. of* quī, quae, quod, *rel.* (§ 387), *or of* quis, quid, *interrog.* (§ 394)

why, cūr
wicked, malus, -a, -um
wide, lātus, -a, -um
will, *expressed by future tense*
willing (be), volō, velle, voluī, ——— (§ 840)
wind, ventus, -ī, *m.*
wing, cornū, -ūs, *n.*
winter, hiems, -emis, *f.*
wisdom, sapientia, -ae, *f.*
wish, cupiō, 3; volō, velle, voluī, ——— (§ 840)
wish not, nōlō, nōlle, nōluī, ——— (§ 840)
wish rather, mālō, mālle, māluī, ——— (§ 840)
with, cum, *with abl.*; *sometimes abl. alone*
withdraw, mē recipiō
without, sine, *with abl.*
woman, mulier, -eris, *f.*
work, labōrō, 1
worst, pessimus, -a, -um, *superl. of* malus
wound, *verb*, vulnerō, 1
wound, *n.*, vulnus, -eris, *n.*
wretched, miser, -era, -erum
write, scrībō, 3
wrong, iniūria, -ae, *f.*

year, annus, -ī, *m.*
yes, certē, ita, vērō, *or, more usually, repeat the verb* (§ 110)
yet, tamen
you, *sing.*, tū; *plur.*, vōs (§ 509); *or not expressed*
your, *sing.*, tuus, -a, -um; *plur.*, vester, -tra, -trum (§ 133)
yourself, tū

INDEX

The numbers, unless pages are specified, refer to sections

421